BACK FROM THE BRINK

SAVING SOME OF THE WORLD'S RAREST ANIMALS

MALCOLM SMITH

Whittles Publishing

For all those people who are attempting to make this planet of ours a richer place and especially for those who risk their lives in doing so

Published by
Whittles Publishing,
Dunbeath,
Caithness KW6 6EG,
Scotland, UK

www.whittlespublishing.com

© 2015 Malcolm Smith

ISBN 978-184995-147-0

Printed by
Latimer Trend & Company Ltd., Plymouth

CONTENTS

'If you have men who will exclude any of God's creatures from the shelter of compassion and pity, you will have men who will deal likewise with their fellow men.' *St Francis of Assisi (1181–1226), Italian Catholic friar and preacher*

'The greatness of a nation and its moral progress can be judged by the way its animals are treated.' *Mahatma Gandhi (1869–1948), inspirational and pre-eminent leader of Indian nationalism in British-ruled India*

'For if one link in nature's chain might be lost, another might be lost, until the whole of things will vanish piecemeal.' *Thomas Jefferson (1743–1826), American Founding Father and the third President of the US*

'The beauty and genius of a work of art may be re-conceived though its first material expression be destroyed; a vanished harmony may yet again inspire the composer; but when the last individual of a race of living beings breathes no more, another heaven and another earth must pass before such a one can be again.' *William Beebe (1877–1962), American naturalist, explorer and author*

ACKNOWLEDGEMENTS

This book would not exist without an enormous amount of help and information I have received from a large number of experts both in writing and in giving up their time in the field to accompany me. They have responded patiently to many of my (I'm sure frequently irritating) questions. I have tried to be assiduous in keeping a record of everyone's name but to anyone I have inadvertently missed, please accept my apologies.

I am particularly grateful to Mark Rose, CEO of Fauna & Flora International (FFI) who has written the Foreword and supported this project since its inception. Mark's Executive Assistants, Esperanza Fernandez and Hannah Becker, have had to endure many requests from me over the last year and have been unfailingly patient and helpful when I know they have had much else to do.

Many FFI staff have given me invaluable advice and information along the way. I thank:

Dr Rob Brett, Regional Director, Africa; Ally Catterick, Deputy Director of Communications; Dr Jenny Daltry, Senior Conservation Biologist; Dr Abigail Entwistle, FFI Director of Science; Dr Chloe Hodgkinson, Programme Manager, Conservation Capacity and Leadership; Paul Hotham, Regional Director, Eurasia; Dr Matthew Linkie, Regional Conservation & Development Adviser/Aceh Programme Manager, FFI Singapore; Dr Arthur Mugisha, FFI Uganda; Stuart Paterson, Programme Manager, Conservation Partnerships; Dr Benjamin Rawson, Manager Indo-Burma Primate Conservation Programme; and Sue Sargent, Conservation Partnerships Manager, FFI Australia.

I want to thank:

Don Airton, Chairman, Zululand Rhino Reserve in KwaZulu Natal, South Africa; François Arcangeli, Conseiller Régional de Midi-Pyrénées and Président de L'association Pays de l'Ours –Adet, Haute-Garonne, France; Regina Asmutis-Silvia, Executive Director, North America, Whale and Dolphin Conservation; Mohammed Saleh Hasan Al Baidani, Director General, International Fund for Houbara Conservation, Abu Dhabi, UAE; Dr Robert Baldwin, Director of Conservation, Five Oceans Environmental Services, Oman; Eric Bedin, formerly with the Saudi Wildlife Commission, Taif, Saudi Arabia.

Mark Bidwell, Species at Risk Biologist and Canadian Whooping Crane Recovery Coordinator, Canadian Wildlife Service, Environment Canada, Saskatoon, Canada; Chris

Bowden, SAVE (Saving Asia's Vultures from Extinction) Programme Manager and International Species Recovery Officer at the UK's RSPB, Bedfordshire, UK; Dr Urs Breitenmoser, Institut für Veterinär-Virologie der Universität Bern and IUCN/SSC Cat Specialist Group, Bern, Switzerland; Chris Butler-Stroud, CEO and Danny Groves, Communications Manager, Whale and Dolphin Conservation, Chippenham, Wiltshire, UK.

Dr Ramana Callan, Assistant Professor of Environmental and Natural Resources Conservation, SUNY-ESF Ranger School, Wanakena, New York, USA; Scott Calleson, Biological Scientist, Florida Fish and Wildlife Conservation Commission, Tallahassee, Florida, USA; Dr Luis M. Carrascal, Department of Biogeography & Global Change, Museo Nacional de Ciencias Naturales, Madrid, Spain; Dr Samantha Cartwright, Research Ecologist, Reading University, UK; Robin Clegg, Media Relations Manager, WWF-UK, Woking, Surrey, UK; Nadia Coelho, Divisão da Conservação da Natureza Serviço do Parque Natural da Madeira, Portugal.

Dr Rochelle Constantine, Director, Joint Graduate School in Coastal and Marine Science, University of Auckland, New Zealand; Alina Corcoran, Research Scientist, Harmful Algal Bloom Program, Florida Fish and Wildlife Conservation Commission, Tallahassee, Florida, USA; Dr Peter Corkeron, National Oceanic and Atmospheric Administration, Woods Hole, Massachusetts, USA; Nuno Curado, Field Technician, LIFE Habitat Lince Abutre (LPN), Liga para a Protecção da Natureza, Moura, Portugal; Dr Katarzyna Daleszczyk, Białowieża National Park Research Unit, Białowieża, Poland; Delphine Delire, International Fund for Houbara Conservation, Abu Dhabi, UAE; George Edgar, HM Ambassador, British Embassy, Tashkent, Uzbekistan.

Pontious Ezuma, Chief Warden, Bwindi National Park, Uganda; Carol Fan, Deputy Company Secretary, SOCO International, London, UK; Dr Jacques Flamand, Project Leader, the Black Rhino Range Expansion Project, WWF, Cape Town, South Africa; Trish & Wally Franklin, The Oceania Project, Byron Bay, New South Wales, Australia; Jeff Gaisford, formerly with Ezemvelo KwaZulu-Natal Wildlife, Pietermaritzburg, South Africa; Paul Goriup, Managing Director, Fieldfare International Ecological Development plc, Newbury, UK; Dr Boris Gubin, International Fund for Houbara Conservation, Kazakhstan; Dr Brahim Haddane, wildlife management consultant and IUCN/SSC Vice Chair for North Africa, Rabat, Morocco; Wade Harrell, US Fish & Wildlife Service, Aransas State Wildfowl Refuge, Texas, USA.

Wayne Hartley, Manatee Specialist, Save the Manatee Club, Maitland, Florida, USA; Dr Barry K. Hartup, Director of Veterinary Services, International Crane Foundation, Baraboo, Wisconsin, USA; Dick Hornby, Founding Partner, Nautica Environmental Associates, Abu Dhabi; Tom Hughes, Wildlife Biologist & Assistant Vice President for Conservation Programs, National Wild Turkey Federation, South Carolina, USA; Dr Zafar-ul Islam, Research Coordinator & Manager Reintroduction programs, National Wildlife Research Centre, Taif, Saudi Arabia. Dr Christine Kreuder Johnson and Dr Terra Kelly, Wildlife Health Center, School of Veterinary Medicine, University of California-Davis.

Professor Carl G Jones, International Conservation Fellow, Durrell Wildlife Conservation Trust and Scientific Director, Mauritian Wildlife Foundation, Mauritius; Simon Jones, Head of Major Projects, Scottish Wildlife Trust UK; Jacky Judas, Emirates Wildlife Society/ WWF, United Arab Emirates; Sandy Jumper, Director of Tourism and Events, Rockport/Fulton Chamber of Commerce, Rockport, Texas, USA; Caroline Kelly, Conservation Officer, Butterfly Conservation, Wareham, Dorset; Dr Michael H Knight, Chairman, IUCN/SSC African Rhino Specialist Group, South African National Parks, Port Elizabeth, South Africa.

Dr hab. Rafał Kowalczyk, Director, Mammal Research Institute, Polish Academy of Sciences, Białowieża, Poland; Professor Malgorzata Krasinska, Mammal Research Institute, Polish Academy of Sciences, Białowieża, Poland; Dr Frédéric Launay, Assistant Secretary General for Science & Research, Environmental Research & Wildlife Development Agency and Chairman, IUCN/SSC Houbara Bustard Working Group, Abu Dhabi, UAE; Lee Ann Linam, formerly Wildlife Biologist for Texas Parks and Wildlife, Austin, Texas, USA.

Juan Antonio Lorenzo, Coordinador de proyectos Delegación Territorial de Canarias SEO/ BirdLife and formerly Marcial Armas and Elena Betancor, La Laguna, Tenerife, Spain; Laurie Macdonald, Florida Director, Defenders of Wildlife, St. Petersburg, Florida, USA; Dr Mark Madison, US Fish and Wildlife Service Historian, Shepherdstown, West Virginia, USA; Dale Miquelle, Director of the WCS Russia Programme, Sikhote-Alin, Siberia, Russian Federation; Ming Zeng and Quanhua Shi, WWF China, Beijing, People's Republic of China; Ron Nelsen of Providence Forge, Virginia, USA; Dr Michael Noad, Associate Professor, School of Veterinary Science, University of Queensland, Australia.

Gary Norman, Wild Turkey Project Leader, Virginia Department of Game and Inland Fisheries, Richmond, Virginia, USA; Susie Offord, Deputy Director, Save the Rhino International, London; Dr Wanda Olech-Piasecka, Dept of Genetics and Animal Breeding, Warsaw University of Life Sciences, Warsaw, Poland; Dr Stéphane Ostrowski, formerly at the Saudi National Wildlife Research Centre, Taif, Saudi Arabia; Dr Debbie Pain, Director of Conservation, Wildfowl and Wetlands Trust, UK and formerly at RSPB, UK; Jemima Parry-Jones, Director, International Centre for Birds of Prey, Newent, Gloucestershire, UK; Jessica Pernell, Outreach Coordination Office and Ron Mezich, Biological Administrator, FWC Fish and Wildlife Research Institute, Florida Wildlife Commission, Tallahassee, Florida, USA.

Dr Vibhu Prakash, Principal Scientist, Bombay Natural History Society, Mumbai, India; Jenny van Rijn, Sr adviseur Communicatie, Zuid-Kennemerland National Park, The Netherlands; Dr Alejandro Rodríguez, Department of Conservation Biology,Estación Biológica de Doñana, Sevilla, Spain; Dr Patrick M. Rose, Executive Director, Save the Manatee Club, Maitland, Florida, USA; Dr Sonia Cabezas Ruiz, University of Saskatchewan, Canada; Eduardo Santos, Coordinator, LIFE Habitat Lince Abutre (LPN), Liga para a Protecção da Natureza, Lisboa, Portugal; Catherine Sayer, Junior Professional Associate, Red List Unit, IUCN-UK, Mold, Flintshire, UK.

Sam Sealie, Conservation Manager, Zululand Rhino Reserve, KwaZulu Natal, South Africa; Philip Seddon, Associate Professor of Zoology and Chair of the Bird Section of IUCN's Reintroduction Specialist Group, University of Otago, New Zealand; Rodrigo Cunha Serra, Director, Centro Nacional de Reprodução de Lince Ibérico, São Bartolomeu de Messines, Portugal; Pamela Sherriffs, Black Rhino Range Expansion Project, WWF, Cape Town, South

Africa; David Simcox, Large Blue Butterfly reintroduction Programme Manager, Dorset, UK; Miguel Ángel Simón, Director, Programme for the reintroduction of Lynx, Andalusia, Spain.

Dr Andrew Spalton, Office of the Adviser for Conservation of the Environment in the Omani government, Muscat, Oman; Dr Debbie Steel, Marine Mammal Institute and Department of Fisheries and Wildlife, Oregon State University, USA; Maartin Strauss, formerly with the Saudi Wildlife Commission, Taif, Saudi Arabia; Dr Simon N. Stuart, Chair, IUCN Species Survival Commission, Bath, UK; Chris van Swaay, Dutch Butterfly Conservation, Wageningen, The Netherlands; Andy Symes, Global Species Officer (Red List Coordination), BirdLife International, Cambridge, UK; Dr Vikash Tatayah, Conservation Director, Mauritian Wildlife Foundation, Mauritius; Dr Andrew Terry, Durrell Wildlife Conservation Trust, Trinity, Jersey, UK.

Professor Jeremy A Thomas, President, Royal Entomological Society and Professor of Ecology, Department of Zoology, University of Oxford, UK; Lucy Vigne and Esmond Martin, Independent Consultants working on the illegal animal trade worldwide, South Africa; Richard Vigne, CEO, Ol Pejeta Conservancy, Nanyuki, Kenya; Dr Martin Warren, CEO, Butterfly Conservation, Wareham, Dorset, UK.

Professor Tomasz Wesolowski, Laboratory of Forest Biology, Wrocław University, Poland; Phil West, formerly of the Virginia Department of Game and Inland Fisheries, Richmond, Virginia, USA; Alana Westwood, Department of Biology, Dalhousie University Halifax, Nova Scotia, Canada; Kate Wilson, International Whaling Commission, Cambridge, UK; Dr Frank Zino, Funchal, Madeira, Portugal.

I also want to thank the following who have been kind enough to supply photographs:

Khalfan Butti Alqubaisi; Rob Brett; Department of Game and Inland Fisheries, Virginia, USA; Trish Franklin; Neil Hulme; Dr Rafal Kowalczyk; Dr David Mallon; Dale Miquelle; Manuel Moral; Juan Pablo Moreiras; Reinier Munguia; Dr Pat Rose; Pamela Sherriffs; Jacques de Spéville; Gustavo Peña Tejero; Ami Vitale; Frank Zino. I am also grateful for the photographic help given by Roger Ingle, Ken Richard and Rebecca Costello at FFI.

I also wanted to record my thanks to Keith Whittles, my publisher, who has been highly supportive of this project and encouraging from its inception and has offered invaluable advice along the way. I'm grateful.

FOREWORD

*C*onservation can be a depressing business. We are all too familiar with stories of rainforests razed to the ground, of oceans fished out and choked with plastic, of wetlands drained, of invasive species running rampant, and of animal populations decimated by the illegal wildlife trade. This surfeit of bad news tends to have a numbing effect on the general public. There are only so many articles that people can read about the latest devastating blow to biodiversity dealt by poaching, pollution and over-population before they start to tune it out like so much white noise. The cumulative effect of all that doom-laden stuff is that we switch off, telling ourselves that we're all going to hell in a handcart whatever we do.

Amid all the negativity, this book is a welcome fillip, and a timely reminder that the direction of travel is not entirely one way. In compiling this representative sample of the preceding half-century's most heart-warming conservation stories, Malcolm Smith has provided us with a fascinating insight into the numerous threats faced by some of our most vulnerable wildlife and the resourcefulness of those who dedicate their lives to protecting it.

As I read through these chapters, I was struck by several recurring themes, foremost among which was the importance of a 'can do' attitude and single-minded pursuit of a conservation goal. The pages of this book are populated with people who have demonstrably gone the extra mile, in some cases literally: Alec Zino and his son abseiling hundreds of feet down the precipitous cliff faces of Madeira to reach the otherwise inaccessible nest burrows of the petrel that bears his name; entomologist Jeremy Thomas dedicating five successive summers to the painstaking minute-by-minute study of a vanishing butterfly's unfathomable life cycle; Major Ian Grimwood, undeterred by a couple of broken ribs sustained during a bumpy ride across the rocky desert, unswerving in his determination to capture some of the last surviving wild Arabian oryx for captive breeding and future re-introduction.

From a personal viewpoint, it is also gratifying to note how many of these stories feature species with whose conservation Fauna & Flora International (FFI) has been intimately associated.

It was FFI, in one of its earlier guises as the Fauna Preservation Society, who kick-started 'Operation Oryx' in the nick of time in 1962, setting in motion the train of events that culminated in the first successful reintroduction of a species declared Extinct in the Wild.

In the following decade, the same organisation launched an appeal to fund the establishment of the Mountain Gorilla Project, which helped pull the greatest of the great apes back from the brink. Precursor of the International Gorilla Conservation Programme, the coalition co-founded by FFI, this earlier initiative was instrumental in protecting Rwanda's dwindling mountain gorilla population from the ravages of poaching and habitat loss, paving the way for the highly successful regional collaboration that today encompasses all three countries where mountain gorillas occur.

These are uplifting tales of hurdles overcome, crises averted and disasters prevented. They demonstrate that wildlife conservation, local community welfare and economic progress, far from being mutually exclusive, are actually inextricably linked. Above all, they send a powerful message to the doom-mongers. We don't have time to be pessimistic. There is too much work to be done.

Mark Rose, Chief Executive Officer, Fauna & Flora International (FFI)

1

INTRODUCTION

*W*riting about animals whose populations are recovering from near extinction is rather like paddling a canoe upstream against the water's flow. It is all too easy to become overwhelmed with the never-ending deluge going the other way. It was to break out from this seemingly continuous flood of bad news that made it all the more important to tell the story, or some of the stories, of the enormous successes that there have been in recovering rapidly declining populations of animals – several on the very verge of extinction – stories that rarely seem to get told. Yet there are many such successes. And those successes need celebrating.

Anyone with a passing interest in what is happening to our wild habitats and wild places can hardly fail to know that Arctic ice is melting at an unprecedented rate; that the horrendous illegal trade in ivory is killing huge numbers of rhino and elephant in Africa; or that forests are being felled and burnt on a massive scale in some parts of the world, Southeast Asia in particular. But there are positive stories not as often heard. Perhaps it's inevitable that the media gets dominated by negative stories: species in decline, habitats being destroyed, wild places urbanised and the inexorable rise of humankind in many parts of the world leaving little room for wildlife. And all that without even factoring in the threatening spectre of climate warming, already seemingly altering our climate and weather patterns for the worse. Dig past the headlines, though, and more positive news emerges.

How well known is it that wolves are gradually recolonising much of western Europe from where they were once hunted out of existence? Has there been much publicity to tell us that there are now around 80,000 Humpback Whales in the world's oceans – each one the weight of 20 family saloon cars – almost as many as had existed before commercial whaling decimated their populations? And while China's burgeoning urbanisation and its resulting pollution grab headlines, does anyone hear about its vast areas of abandoned farmland that are returning to wild habitat? Or the extensive Tigris-Euphrates marshes in Iraq, drained on orders from the then Iraqi government in the 1990s, re-flooded and starting to recover? Who knows that one of Europe's most beautiful butterflies, the Large Blue that fluttered its last in England in 1979, is today such a reintroduction success that its British populations are now larger than in any other country? And, when we in the west celebrate Christmas or Thanksgiving and munch our way through a roast turkey, are we aware that its wild cousin – decimated across North America by early white settlers – is once again thriving in almost every US State?

The Endangered Species Act in the US has been criticised for failing to bring about the recovery of declining and threatened US species. But an independent analysis by the Center for Biological Diversity published in 2012, *On Time, On Target: How the Endangered Species Act Is Saving America's Wildlife* found that 90% of the 110 protected species from all US States are recovering on time to meet the recovery goals set by federal scientists. In the UK, there are persistent reports of many bird species in decline; that's certainly true, particularly some that were once abundant in farmland and some characteristic of broadleaved woodland. The full picture, though, is rather more balanced. According to the vast amount of data collected for *Bird Atlas, 2007–11*, analysed by the authoritative British Trust for Ornithology, in the 40 years between 1968 and 2008 the range of 72 British bird species contracted, the range of 47 remained stable, but 74 species actually increased their range.

Nevertheless, there is bad news and much of it is entirely justifiable. The *Living Planet Report*, published by the World Wide Fund for Nature in 2012, measured the health of more than 2,600 species of fish, amphibians, reptiles, mammals and birds worldwide and found a decline in almost a third of them since 1970. If current warming trends aren't reduced and the polar ice cap continues to shrink, experts believe that polar bears will be vulnerable to extinction within the next century. And three-quarters of the world's coral reefs – home to countless species of fish and other marine life – are in decline, some of them terminally. In the past three decades, populations of amphibians worldwide – frogs, toads, salamanders and newts – have declined so much that a third of species are now threatened with extinction; more than 100 species have become extinct since 1980. And according to a study published in 2014, three quarters of the world's large carnivores – including lions, wolves and bears – are in decline. They have long disappeared from much of the developed world but today they are under increasing pressure elsewhere too. So what's going wrong? Almost anywhere in the world the reasons are pretty much the same: habitat destruction; hunting and poaching; increasingly intensive farming; climate change; pollution; invasive species ousting native ones; disease; and, in some places, collection for the pet trade.

But do these declines matter? Should we be bothered if our planet and, likewise, our own favourite woodland, seashore or meadow is becoming less and less rich in plants and animals? Is our wildlife just something that's nice to look at occasionally, a kind of reassurance that the natural world is still out there, that much of it survives but what's lost and can never be replaced doesn't matter unduly?

The US Congress answered that question in the preamble to the Endangered Species Act back in the 1970s. It remains just as relevant today. It recognised that endangered and threatened species of animals and plants 'are of aesthetic, ecological, educational, historical, recreational, medicinal and scientific value to the Nation and its people'. It's easy to forget, for instance, that we all rely on insects like bees to pollinate our crops. Without them, our food supplies would dwindle. Nearly 300 million people in the world are dependent on coral reefs for food, coastal protection and their livelihoods. Millions more rely on natural coastal defences such as mangroves to soften the impact of increasingly stormy seas that might otherwise wash away their homes and wreak enormous suffering.

❖   ❖   ❖

Finding out how many animal species in the world are under threat is relatively easy. The IUCN's (International Union for the Conservation of Nature) Red List of Threatened Species is widely recognised as the most comprehensive and objective global system for evaluating the conservation status of plant and animal species. It relies on worldwide research to provide new and better information and experts are called upon to update its lists periodically. Of the world's 5,506 mammals, 79 are either extinct (since 1500 AD) or a few remain in zoos but not in the wild. Those considered as threatened total 1,143 (21%), while 3,125 species are categorised by the IUCN as of Least Concern; in other words, their populations are stable and safe, maybe even increasing. Of the 10,065 species of the world's birds, 134 are extinct; 1,308 (13%) are categorised as threatened while 7,675 are of Least Concern. But, although the great majority of mammals and birds worldwide are not under threat, the number of species in both the Critically Endangered and Endangered categories (the two most threatened out of three threatened categories) increased between 1996 and 2013. In other words, they were in decline.

There is, though, no equivalent comprehensive listing of the species that are doing well; those that are increasing naturally or with the help of humankind. There is perhaps institutional bias towards providing information on those that are threatened. Maybe it's easily explained: there are so many species in decline, and so many habitats too, that conservationists are overwhelmed trying both to document what's happening and trying to reverse, or slow, at least some of it. Even when I talk to experts involved directly in the day to day recovery of an animal species that was formerly in decline but whose fortunes have been reversed, they are often more likely to emphasise the problems and threats the creature still faces rather than celebrate their success.

For this book I was determined to focus on success. My choice of animals is subjective, mostly those I have some direct experience of in the field, however limited. I have no doubt that others would have chosen different, but equally relevant, examples. The book is entitled *Back From The Brink* for good reason; it's about animals that had become extinct in the wild (such as the European Bison), or were close to becoming so (like the Mauritius Kestrel), but which have been put on the road to recovery. Some of them – the Wild Turkey is the leading example – have recovered in such numbers that their future is undoubtedly secure. But the inclusion in these chapters of many of the others does not mean that their long-term survival as self-sustaining populations is guaranteed. They have, though, reached at least base camp on their upward trajectory. Some experts will disagree with some of the animals I have included; some will argue, for instance, that the Houbara never faced extinction. I disagree; this attractive ground bird had been hugely depleted across North Africa and the Middle East, it had declined in western Asia and, at one time, its population on the Canary Islands was distinctly insecure too.

Investing the often huge efforts and cash required to restore dwindling individual species like this always begs the question of whether such effort would not be more effectively expended on protecting and increasing wildlife habitat, the loss of much of which is jeopardising the existence of some of these species in the first place. In practice the two are complementary. There is no hope for the survival of the mighty Siberian Tiger unless vast areas of its plant- and animal-rich forests are conserved. Getting the habitat right, and thereby the species that rely on it, has proved equally important for an animal at the other end of the size spectrum, the Large Blue Butterfly. With some exceptions, it's often very much harder to get public attention and money to protect habitats than it is to protect individual species. And it's inevitably easier to attract money if a species of bird or mammal is in trouble rather than a snake or a lizard; that's just human nature, however biased.

In theory it is not usually difficult to stop the decline of an animal and restore its populations as several examples in this book illustrate. In practice it is usually very much more difficult, time consuming, frustrating, sometimes incredibly dangerous and it requires long term commitment. There are certainly no quick fixes. For many imperilled animals, though, the action needed to recover them is often very similar.

Protecting their habitat is essential, maybe formally as a national park, as was done for the forest of the Mountain Gorilla in Central Africa, a step that requires governmental support. Degraded habitat has to be restored, or wildlife corridors need to be created to link existing fragments of habitat, as is being done for the Iberian Lynx in Spain and Portugal. And enough habitat has to be available; species such as the Siberian Tiger need vast areas; Large Blue butterflies need very much less.

Many endangered species – and those extinct in the wild – have to be bred in captivity to boost their populations before any consideration can be given to reintroducing them to suitable habitat; both the European Bison and the Arabian Oryx became extinct in the wild and this was the only way to give them a future. For others such as the Mauritius Kestrel, captive breeding has been used to boost their numbers alongside better protection for wild-breeding birds.

Anti-poaching and hunting bans or restrictions are obviously essential if a species is to stand a chance of recovery; protecting Black Rhinos (along with White Rhinos and elephants) from vicious gangs targeting them for their horns is now one of the most dangerous animal protection jobs in the world and can quite frequently put rangers' lives at risk. Many have died doing it. For others such as the Humpback Whale and the Wild Turkey, their populations recovered when hunting was brought under control. National legislation might be required to protect a species before much progress can be made; Florida Manatees didn't have effective legal protection until well into the 1970s. And trapping predators (often mammals introduced to a location where they don't naturally occur) or preventing them from accessing breeding sites can be essential; for Zino's Petrel on Madeira, preventing feral cats and rats from getting to their nesting burrows has been a major factor in their recovery.

Reducing or eliminating pollution, or banning the use of a particular chemical for agricultural or other purposes, might be essential too. The vultures of the Indian subcontinent couldn't recover until diclofenac was banned as a livestock treatment and several other birds at the apex of food chains – the Peregrine and Bald Eagle for example – might not be with us today if DDT and fellow insecticides had not been banned.

It might sound obvious but it's not feasible to reintroduce a species unless its ecological requirements are understood: its habitat needs; its food requirements; how it interacts with or relies on other species. There is arguably no better example than that of the Large Blue butterfly. Until its highly complex life cycle – its very precise habitat needs and its utter reliance on another invertebrate – was unravelled, it had no chance of survival.

Where the species concerned is to be reintroduced or its faltering numbers boosted, it is equally important to make sure that local human communities are on-side and fully aware of what is about to happen on land that they rely upon and might have occupied for generations. Without local support, recovering an animal's numbers will simply not succeed.

There are plenty of success stories around. In 2013, IUCN published *Global Reintroduction Perspectives*, a set of 52 case studies that included 34 mammals and birds. Sixty percent were assessed as 'successful' or 'highly successful' and another 37% as 'partially successful'. There was just one failure. We need to acknowledge that, although there are most certainly immense challenges facing global wildlife, some conservation achievements of the last half century have been – and continue to be – both extraordinary and inspirational. Many of them form the chapters of this book.

Pessimism can be as infectious as optimism, so not acknowledging what has, and can be, achieved could mean that the prophecies of doom might become self-fulfilling. Giving people – and politicians and policy makers – hope that conservation can, and usually does, succeed is vital. We know what to do. There's enormous experience worldwide of doing it successfully. We know how to turn around the declining fortunes of a huge range of species. What is desperately needed is the support and resources to do much more of it.

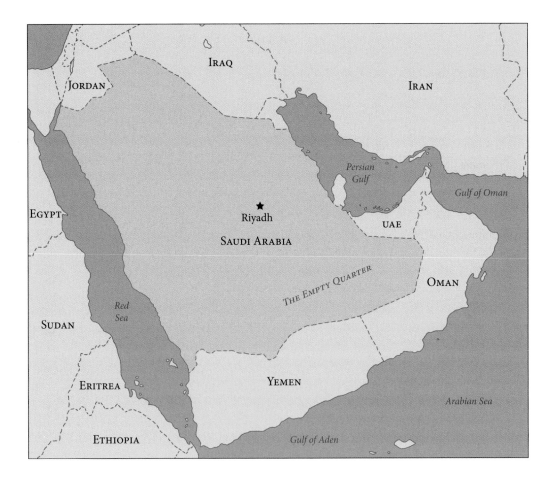

2

BRINGING THE EMPTY
QUARTER BACK TO LIFE

ARABIAN ORYX

Decimated by hunters, by the 1960s the enigmatic antelope of the great Saudi sand deserts was driven to the brink of extinction. Supported by the then Fauna Preservation Society (now FFI), 'Operation Oryx' captured some of the last few wild Arabian Oryx in 1962. Successfully bred in captivity, the first animals were reintroduced in Oman in the 1980s. Initially successful, hunting again depleted their numbers until more reintroductions, this time in the Saudi sector of the Rub' al-Khali, the famed Empty Quarter, proved an eventual success. Today, over 1,000 oryx roam wild once more over these vast, scorching dunes and gravel plains.

It had been bread-oven hot all day and by mid afternoon I had begun to wonder how any animal could possibly exist in such an inhospitable place, let alone thrive, give birth and raise young. I was in the Empty Quarter, the Rub' al-Khali of southern Saudi Arabia – an uninhabited desert the size of France – to see for myself one of the world's most successful reintroductions of an animal once extinct in the wild and now breeding again in the core of its former range. Strikingly beautiful, salt-white Arabian Oryx had roamed these sculpted dunes and shimmering gravel plains until the last one was killed five decades ago. Now, this fabulous animal was back in one of the harshest, most unforgiving places on Earth and the animals were seemingly doing very well.

Scanning ahead with binoculars, it was Maartin Strauss who spotted them. 'Over there, a few kilometres away!' he shouted. Some distant, fuzzy white shapes and a flurry of sand were all that was obvious to me as I searched the vast, heat-shimmering plain. Could these hazy objects possibly be the fabled Arabian Oryx? 'Seven oryx. All adults I think. They're grazing on some bushes. They look pretty settled; I don't think they're going to move on for a while anyway. We'll try and get closer', commented Strauss, a South African mammal expert who, with Eric Bedin, a French biologist, was monitoring oryx for the Saudi Wildlife Commission which has reintroduced them here.

We drove further into the sands to get a closer view of the remote white spots, bumping along in our four-wheel drive Jeep across grey-white gravel plains, the only flat land between the exquisite folds of massive sand dunes stretching as far as I could see. Eventually we got within a kilometre of them; seven oryx watching our every move. The size of large deer, their gorgeous deep, black eyes contrasted with their bleached-white coats while their enormous pairs of parallel, barley-sugar twist horns caught the bright sun like skyward-pointing rapiers.

'Four of them are tagged with collars', whispered Maartin as we sat huddled in the Jeep, binoculars held handcuff-tight, the sweltering heat building by the minute. 'The numbers printed on their tags means that these four are released animals. I can date the releases from the tag numbers when we're back at camp tonight. The other three must have been born here in the wild', he added with obvious pleasure.

We left them there, eloquent testimony to their ability to live out their lives in one of the most arid places imaginable. Here, in the scorching heat of summer where temperatures in the sun can easily reach 50°C, a human can barely survive for eight hours without water.

❖   ❖   ❖

The Arabian Desert is a vast wilderness centred on modern day Saudi Arabia, stretching from Yemen and Oman in the south, north to Iraq and Jordan. At well over 2 million km², it is nearly four times the size of France. At its centre is the virtually uninhabited Rub' al-Khali, The Empty Quarter, the bulk of it within Saudi territory; a smaller portion in Oman. 'A desert within a desert' was how it was described by Wilfred Thesiger (1910–2003), the famous explorer and writer who twice crossed it on foot and camel in the late 1940s with Bedu companions. It is one of the largest continuous bodies of sand in the world, and it is here that the handsome Arabian Oryx has made a comeback, albeit with considerable help.

Information on the probable historic distribution of Arabian Oryx has been compiled by Saudi Arabia's National Wildlife Research Centre (NWRC) using accounts in Arab and western literature – mostly the accounts of 19th and 20th century travellers – and from archaeological findings such as animal remains and rock art. It suggests strongly that they once inhabited almost all of the Arabian Peninsula and beyond into modern day Iraq, Syria and Jordan, maybe Israel too. During the 19th and early 20th centuries, their range became increasingly limited to the more remote parts of Saudi Arabia, especially the Rub' al-Khali, and by 1914 there were only a few survivors outside Saudi Arabia.

The desert-living Bedu had always hunted oryx. After all, oryx provide a much more bountiful supply of meat than a desert hare and add variety to an otherwise torrid diet. Their hides were important too. But, armed only with primitive rifles until perhaps the 1920s, they would probably have been able to kill very few. The reasons for the oryx's range contraction are thought to include the capture of animals to keep in private collections, shooting for food and leather, and some hunting for their magnificent horns to display as trophies. The capture of wild animals is a very old tradition in most Arab cultures and the Arabian Oryx is one animal that is relatively easy to tame and adapts well to captivity. As they became less and less common, the international market for oryx increased, stimulating yet more capture of live animals and the illegal export to overseas collectors prepared to pay to have these attractive animals 'decorating' their property.

How abundant Arabian Oryx were in any part of their original range no one really knows. Thesiger records seeing them in the Rub' al-Khali in the 1940s, but not often, and he was aware that hunting parties were already killing scores of them. In *Crossing The Sands* (1999) he wrote:

> It is sad to think that the Arabian Oryx...are also doomed as soon as cars penetrate into the southern desert. Unfortunately oryx prefer the hard, flat sands and gravel plains to the heavy dunes. It means that yet another kind of animal will soon be extinct.

Thesiger's concern that the Arabian Oryx would become extinct (as it did within another 30 years) failed, though, to overcome his temptation to shoot one, albeit for food:

> On the second day [their second crossing of the Empty Quarter when they were not, yet, short of food], just after we had unloaded, we saw a bull oryx walking straight towards us. As only about three Englishmen have shot an Arabian Oryx, I whispered to bin Ghabaisha to let me shoot, while the oryx came steadily on. Now he was only a quarter of a mile away, now three hundred yards, and still he came on. The size of a small donkey – I could see his long straight horns, two feet or more in length, his pure white body, and the dark markings on his legs and face...Bin Kabina whispered to me to shoot. Slowly I pressed the trigger. The oryx spun round and galloped off. Muhammad muttered disgustedly, 'A clean miss', and bin Kabina said loudly, 'If you had let bin Ghabaisha shoot we should have had meat for supper'; all I could say was 'Damn and blast!'

The demise of the Arabian Oryx became a virtual certainty when Arabian princes and newly oil-rich Arabs in Jeeps and big American cars fitted with sand tyres started making incursions into the Rub' al-Khali in the 1930s and 1940s. Armed with more powerful rifles, oryx hunts grew in size and some were reported to employ as many as 300 vehicles. Unlike the desert-living Bedu, these callous individuals were not killing in order to eat their quarry. They didn't need to. According to the naturalist Guy Mountfort in *Success in Wildlife Conservation: Back from the Brink* (1978):

> Parties of oil-rich sheikhs, armed not only with high powered rifles but with sub-machine guns, scoured even the remotest deserts, slaughtering everything that moved. They were not interested even in trophies but in shooting. Carcasses of oryx, gazelles, hyaenas, wolves, leopards, jackals and foxes were left to litter the desert where they fell.

By the early 1950s, oryx were extinct across much of their former range. They remained only around the southern margins of the Rub' al-Khali from Yemen to Oman. By the early 1960s, they survived only in the very south of this desert within a desert. Estimates put the total Arabian Oryx population at no more than 100. The Bedu were killing them at a rate of about five annually, a level of loss that was probably sustainable assuming reasonably successful breeding. But more and more reports were circulating of mass killings; Mountfort mentions one Saudi killing party that had driven into the Rub' al-Khali and slaughtered 48 oryx. Another raid on this scale and conservationists knew that the animal would be extinct. This magnificent white antelope had succumbed to an increase in so-called sport hunting, the practice of animal-exhausting chases in Jeeps – or even helicopters – the 'hunters' equipped with powerful rifles or sub-machine guns.

❖   ❖   ❖

Arabian Oryx stand about one metre high at the shoulder, females weigh up to 80 kg; males, up to 100 kg. Apart from this slight difference in weight, and the fact that females usually have longer horns than males, the sexes are very similar and it is very difficult to distinguish them in the field. Their coats are an almost luminous white (and effective at reflecting away the sun's heat), their undersides and legs dark brown, and there are black stripes where the head meets the neck, on the forehead, on the nose and going from the horns down the face to the mouth. The animal's hooves are splayed and shovel-like, providing a large surface area that makes it easier for them to walk on sand. Both sexes have impressive, long, straight or slightly back-curved, barley twist horns that are up to 75 cm long.

Their horns, impressive though they are to look at, certainly are not items of decoration. They are lethal weapons – other species of oryx have been known to kill lions with them – but they also make the animals a prized game trophy, one reason why they were so keenly hunted. Their horns are also the reason why this animal is associated with the myth of the unicorn. Mentioned in many Ancient Greek accounts of natural history, the unicorn is a legendary animal that has been described since antiquity as a beast with a large, pointed, spiraling single horn projecting from its forehead. Ideas of its origin range from an extinct species of rhino with an elongated horn or a single-horned goat to the narwhal (an Arctic Sea cetacean) or the oryx. When it is viewed in profile or from a distance, it looks something like a horse with a single horn although, in the oryx, the 'horn' projects backwards not forwards as in the classic unicorn. Nevertheless, early travellers in Arabia could have derived the tale of the unicorn from these animals. The *Peregrinatio in Terram Sanctam* by Bernhard von Breydenbach, published in 1486, was the first printed and illustrated travel book, describing a pilgrimage to Jerusalem, and on to Egypt by way of Mount Sinai. It features many large woodcuts, mostly detailed and accurate views of cities. But the book also contains pictures of animals seen on the journey, including a crocodile, camel and a unicorn – presumably an Arabian Oryx, which they could easily have seen on their route.

Worldwide, there are three other species of oryx. The Arabian Oryx, though, is the smallest. The Scimitar-horned Oryx was once widespread in the Sahara and across much of Africa to its south but they declined as that desert became more arid around 5,000–10,000 years ago and, much more recently, because of hunting for food and their exquisite horns. Off-white in colour with chestnut fronts, Scimitar-horned Oryx hadn't been seen in the wild for maybe 20 years until they were successfully reintroduced from captive-bred populations a decade ago into large, fenced and protected areas of desert in Tunisia, Morocco and Senegal. Ironically, thousands of them are kept in captivity, in zoos, wildlife parks and in private Middle Eastern collections, plenty to supply any more reintroduction attempts. There are two subspecies of another cousin, the East African Oryx, or Beisa. The Common Beisa is found throughout the Horn of Africa while the very similar Fringe-eared Oryx is native to southern Kenya and parts of Tanzania. Both have thin, straight horns. With maybe three Beisa to one Fringe-eared Oryx, there might be a total of nearly 70,000 of them in the wild. Both, though, are declining because of poaching and because the ever increasing expansion of livestock farming is slowly but inexorably reducing their habitat. The final cousin is the Gemsbok, a South African species which is similar to the Beisa except that it has a black tail with more black on its legs and flanks. Eliminated from many areas because of urban development, its numbers are stable at a little under 400,000.

All oryx species are well adapted to desert or near-desert conditions and can survive perfectly easily without water for long periods, getting all they need from the dry-looking plants they graze as well as by licking up any early morning dew or rooting in the ground for juicy rhizomes. It is why the Bedu of Arabia call the Arabian Oryx, *jawazi* – 'he who drinks not'. All oryx are light coloured, partly for camouflage but also to reflect heat away from their bodies. Fast runners, their newborn calves are able to run with the herd almost immediately after birth.

Little was known about the Arabian Oryx's diet before they were captured for captive breeding, except, of course, that they grazed grasses and desert shrubs. Monitoring the reintroduced populations in Oman and Saudi Arabia has, though, provided more detailed information. Research in Oman by Dr Andrew Spalton of the Office of the Advisor for Conservation of the Environment in the Omani government, found that, especially after rain, perennial grasses of the genus *Stipagrostis* – aptly named desert grasses that grow in dense tufts – are primarily eaten. It turned out that, after it rains, these grasses are high in protein and water, and are more digestible. In drought, the oryx graze perennial grasses and shrubs because *Stipagrostis* will then be all but absent. Detecting rain, even a shower, at a distance of tens of kilometres, maybe further, then heading that way for better grazing is a particular ability these amazing mammals possess.

Their young are born, on average, once a year between October and May after an eight-month gestation and they weigh 2–8 kg at birth. They are fully weaned by eight months, sometimes much less. In periods of utter drought, young are born less frequently. Pale brown in colour, they progressively change to the adult's white pellage after about three months when the dark face and leg markings also start appearing.

Oryx hardly communicate orally – just a few snorts, grunts, and moo-like bleats – a good voice is of little practical use in the vast openness of these extensive deserts. They seemingly rely more on visual clues, mostly using body posture in order to communicate.

❖ ❖ ❖

The future of the Arabian Oryx in the wild was looking extremely bleak by the early 1960s by which time maybe a hundred had survived the onslaught of motorised hunting. In 1962, the then Fauna Preservation Society, FPS, with WWF funding, decided that the only way to guarantee their survival was to capture some animals and set up a captive breeding population before the last wild oryx were hunted down. Time was not on their side. The FPS idea was to produce a sustainable breeding population with an eye to reintroducing them at some future time when raiding and poaching had, hopefully, been outlawed or ceased because it was no longer considered an acceptable practice. The alternative of trying to protect oryx in the vast sands of the Empty Quarter against motorised raiding parties was a non-starter.

'Operation Oryx' had begun. A team of people was selected and led by Major Ian Grimwood, a tough man with considerable experience of dealing with large animals. A biologist, he had joined the Frontier Force of the Indian Army in 1935 and been captured by the Japanese, suffering years in forced labour PoW camps before rejoining, then commanding, his regiment for a short time after World War II. In the 1950s he joined the then Rhodesian Game Department as a biologist and, in 1960, became Chief Game Warden for Kenya.

Timed for May 1962 when the oryx were more likely to be at the edges of the Rub' al-Khali rather than in the ferociously hot centre and a little easier to find and catch using the vehicles the team had, reports continued to come in of yet more raids that killed what few animals had survived the previous onslaughts. Added to that was a whole host of difficulties in getting hold of suitable vehicles that could cope with both rocky and sandy terrain and carry large crates holding oryx, finding copious quantities of grass and other plants for them to eat once they were captured, arranging to have a small spotter plane available, obtaining official permissions from Oman and Saudi Arabia and getting enough able people together to mount the expedition. And all this in one of the most inhospitable places on the planet.

On 23 April 1962, the assembled party, including vets and local animal trackers, set off from the Arabian Sea coast of what is now Yemen and headed north across rocky, often mountainous arid terrain, heading into the interminable sands of the Rub' al-Khali. It was days before the first oryx tracks were even sighted and further days again before the first animal – an adult male – was captured. Chased using a sand-adapted vehicle, this male was lassoed, blindfolded, given an anti-shock injection to keep him calm and put in a crate. Within a month, the group had caught a female and two more males, though one male died shortly after capture, probably from stress. The three oryx were eventually flown to the Phoenix Zoo in Arizona, chosen not only because it was one of the world's leading captive conservation centres with a huge amount of experience breeding animals but also because the Arizona climate was not unlike that of the oryx's natural habitat. Here they were joined by Arabian Oryx already held in captivity which were donated to the programme by the Kuwaiti and Saudi Royal families.

By the summer of 1964, the then nine oryx held at the Phoenix Zoo were given the somewhat presumptuous title of 'World Herd'. The oryx took to their new US home much more readily than even the most optimistic conservationists believed they would. Although some of these animals never bred, the herd grew steadily over the next few years. By 1977, there were around 100 individuals, allowing for some to be sent to other zoos and parks around the world to start new herds, a safeguard policy in case something went wrong at one location, disease outbreak for instance. The Arabian Oryx was safe, in captivity at least.

By the early 1970s it was clear that the FPS had been right to act as they did. The last wild oryx had been spotted in Oman in 1972 and they were either killed or captured a few weeks later. There were unconfirmed reports quoted by Dr Stéphane Ostrowski, an expert on the species who worked at the Saudi National Wildlife Research Centre (NWRC), that a pair and a single oryx had been seen in the Rub'al-Khali in 1978 and 1979, but there are no other reports after these. The Arabian Oryx was extinct in the wild, its downfall the direct result of human greed.

In 1972, Ian Grimwood was awarded the gold medal of the WWF for his inspiring leadership and determination in saving the last wild oryx in the only way that was possible. It was followed, in 1977, by the J. Paul Getty Prize for his outstanding contributions to conservation, around the same time that most Arab rulers banned the motorised hunting of wild oryx, too late for the very few left in the wild to ever again form a natural breeding population.

❖ ❖ ❖

The first desert reintroduction of captive oryx – from the San Diego Wildlife Park in California – took place in Oman in 1982. The early releases were overseen by Mark Stanley-Price, a former Kenyan game warden. In *Animal Reintroductions: The Arabian Oryx* (1989) he wrote of that first moment in which Arabian Oryx once again returned to their desert home:

> Released from their boxes one at a time into pens, the oryx, even though crated for ninety hours, sprang out and explored the new quarters at a spirited trot. After the first batch had arrived – restoring this species to Omani soil – the Bedu rangers murmured in agreement that these certainly were the same animals that they knew long ago and were not imposters.

After acclimatising in their release pens, the oryx were let into a kilometre square fenced enclosure in order to establish a cohesive herd. Past experience with other large mammals had shown that simply releasing them into the wild straight away resulted in their scattering and often dying before they were able to form a group structure and get used to fending for themselves. Very quickly the newly released oryx started to graze on clumps of grass and make use of the tall Umbrella Thorn Acacias whose dense canopies create shade from the sun in the hottest part of the day, and the Salam Acacia, a lower, more shrubby species used as a wind-break at night. They were adapting well.

Together with a few more animals from other captive breeding centres, the first ten founder oryx were reintroduced to the Omani desert. It was almost exactly ten years since the species had gone extinct in the wild. Dr Andrew Spalton says, 'A second release followed in 1984 and the population grew slowly through a three year drought that was broken by rain in June 1986.

Further years of good rainfall and more founders being released meant that by 1990 there were over 100 oryx in the wild, they were independent of supplementary feed and water, and they were using a range of over 11,000 km². By 1995, they were up to about 280 animals.'

But then problems surfaced once more. Early in 1996 the old threat of poaching resumed and oryx were illegally captured for sale to be kept as live animals outside the country. Despite this poaching, the population continued to increase and by October that year there were estimated to be just over 400 oryx. But the poaching intensified. By late 1998 it had reduced the wild population to an estimated 138 animals of which just 28 were females. Personal greed apparently knew no bounds when it came to capturing these magnificent animals to decorate the grounds of some rich Middle Eastern or overseas estates. Hunting an animal like an oryx, whether to kill or capture it, doesn't result only in the targeted animal itself being killed or captured. Chases by vehicles can cause the scattering of a herd, threatening the survival of young animals and tiring several to the point where they might die of stress and exhaustion.

One of the criteria established by IUCN for all reintroductions is that the original cause of the species' demise has been removed. The Omani authorities had assumed that hunting and capture of oryx would not again occur, or at least not on a scale to once more threaten the animals' survival. It had proved to be a mistaken assumption. By 1999 there were 85 oryx left and many were re-caught and protected as a captive breeding herd in a 27,000 km² section (still a vast area) of the Omani desert called, optimistically as it turned out, the 'Arabian Oryx Sanctuary'. Illegal hunting even there – difficult to counter over such a huge area of desert – and habitat degradation reduced their numbers further.

In 2007, by which time oryx numbers had dropped to 65 animals, the sanctuary became notorious as the first UNESCO World Heritage site to be removed from its prestigious list – and this after just 13 years. UNESCO's reason was the Omani government's decision to open 90% of the site to oil prospecting and its inability to stop the poaching. It was a sad end to what had been a forward-looking and initially successful scheme to return oryx to the wild.

Thankfully, in the Saudi Arabian part of the Rub' al-Khali, oryx reintroduction has been much more successful. Between 1995 and 2002, a total of 174 animals, in a large number of social groups, were released into a large section of desert at its western end, the Uruq Bani Ma'arid reserve. It has no fence surrounding it so Uruq is open to the bewildering expanses of the arid Rub' al-Khali to the east. It was selected for the reintroduction because it contains greater biological diversity than any other part of the Empty Quarter, with vegetated wadis, gravel plains and inter-dune corridors. And oryx had historically been present here. A trial reintroduction by the Saudis had begun in 1990 further north and it had proved successful.

In the Saudi reintroduction scheme, a mix of captive-bred Arabian Oryx, some from the US and others from within Saudi Arabia, were released in order to create the most genetically-diverse wild herd they could. This encompasses another vital principle enshrined by the IUCN guidance on the reintroduction of breeding animals into their natural home: their gene pool needs to be as diverse as possible. The theory is that the more genetically diverse a population of any animal is, the more likely it is that there will be survivors if some new disease, for instance, spreads through the population. If the animals were genetically very similar because of inbreeding, when such a potential killer struck, there might be few or no survivors.

Released animals were marked with identification tags and fitted with radio collars to enable them to be relocated afterwards. The post-release progress of oryx has been carefully monitored by staff at the NWRC and the information gained from early releases used in planning subsequent attempts. 'Around 200 oryx now roam wild in the west of the Rub' al-Khali and their breeding is increasingly successful', comments Dr Zafar-ul Islam, the current research coordinator and manager of the Saudi reintroduction programme. Now, with wild-living oryx spread over a very large area of desert, it is impossible to either count each one or to know every detail of what is happening to them. So surveys have to be undertaken by driving along fixed routes in four-wheel drive vehicles and by light aircraft in order to estimate their numbers.

But problems remain. A series of particularly dry years over the last two decades – which might be the result of global climate warming – has caused the death of large numbers of oryx because the grazing has been so poor as a result. 'Of the recorded deaths, 65% have been caused by starvation, especially in the four year drought to 2000, 19% by fights between males and 13% due to poaching', according to Ostrowski. In captivity, and in good conditions in the wild, oryx have a life span of up to 20 years, but in periods of drought this can be significantly reduced by malnutrition and dehydration. Other causes of death include snakebites, disease and drowning during sudden floods.

If what are rather euphemistically called 'drought years' in the Arabian Desert become less common – though climate warming threatens otherwise – oryx numbers should increase faster. Retaining the very scattered but essential, shade-giving acacias that occur here is also vital because they provide oryx with sun protection in the acute heat of summer. So community education has been necessary to get the cooperation of the Bedu who sometimes cut them down for much needed livestock fodder. But poaching here has not been eliminated, though it is much reduced. At the beginning of 2010 at least five oryx were killed by poachers, maybe more, emphasising the need for continuing vigilance and supporting the need for the rangers employed at Uruq to remain armed in case of any future encounters.

❖   ❖   ❖

According to IUCN, one of the largest reintroduced populations of Arabian Oryx today is found in the UAE at the Arabian Oryx Reserve in Abu Dhabi where reintroduction began in 2007. It covers a desert area of nearly 9,000 km² and currently has nearly 155 oryx. There are plans to release many more. The sanctuary started with 99 captive-bred oryx which were reintroduced to the area after 40 years of absence. And, as elsewhere, the reserve also helps the survival of other animals such as deer, foxes, desert rats, hares, reptiles and birds. Israel started reintroducing Arabian Oryx at three desert sites in 1997 and there is a small reintroduced population in the Wadi Rum region of southern Jordan where the local Bedu have welcomed them and have vowed to protect them. Abdul Rahman Al Hassneinn, the manager of the Wadi Rum Oryx Project said in 2014 that their numbers had increased to over 70. Together with other small reintroduced populations elsewhere in the Middle East, as of 2011 the total wild population is over 1,000 individuals (the largest number in Saudi Arabia) with 6,000–7,000 held in captivity at various places around the world, but particularly in the Middle East. Many of the captive populations are kept in very large areas of habitat within which they roam freely.

The huge numbers of oryx held in private collections by rich Middle Eastern families – originating from wild-captured animals – is something that was not known at the time Operation Oryx was set up to capture the last remaining wild animals. If it had been, it is arguable that the massive effort expended by Grimwood and his team, and the cost, could have been directed at captive breeding in Arabia itself. Hindsight, though, is always a wonderful attribute.

In 2011, the IUCN downgraded the Red List status of the Arabian Oryx from Extinct in the Wild to Vulnerable, the first time that a species described as Extinct in the Wild has improved in status; it is a considerable achievement by a large number of committed people from several countries.

Their reintroduction has been a costly and time-consuming business. At the NWRC in Taif, captive oryx are still being bred for release and a thorough veterinary check is made for diseases such as tuberculosis (TB) in any animals in the herd. The original captive herd established there, no less than 57 oryx donated by the late Saudi King Khaled from his private collection, succumbed to TB in 1986 before any reintroductions had been carried out and over a quarter of the animals died. Diseases such as this, easily spread from one animal to another, are always a major risk when animals are kept in unnaturally close contact for long periods. It was an early lesson learnt by the vets and biologists.

To eliminate – or at least greatly reduce – the chances of TB again sweeping through a captive herd, much improved sanitary conditions, antibiotic treatment, annual TB tests, and hand-rearing calves has allowed for the successful breeding of TB-free animals for future reintroductions. What is more, these oryx, reared from a mix donated from Saudi, Qatari, Abu Dhabi and World Herd lineages have a much broader genetic base than those released earlier in Oman which were very largely from the World Herd reared in the US.

Before these captive bred oryx can be released, they have to be transported for eight hours overland in communal crates to maintain their social grouping – some tranquilised to keep them calm – from the NWRC breeding centre to Uruq Bani Ma'arid. There they are held in a small outdoor pen for a couple of days to let them acclimatise to their new location. Then they are moved into fenced, pre-release enclosures and provided with feed and water before being released to the wild after a month or so. Supplementary food and water is put out for a further month in case they need it. They rarely do.

Most reintroductions have been carried out in winter when temperatures are lower and there is more chance of some rain reinvigorating the few thorny shrubs that dot the gravel plains and dune slopes here. When it does rain, bleached and tinder dry shrubs quickly green up, putting on some young growth that is too tempting for grazing animals like oryx to ignore. And plants spring up from the sand-covered ground from hidden underground bulbs and rhizomes, quickly flower and set seed until the next shower passes that way, maybe a couple of years later. Arabian Oryx rest during the hottest part of the day, often digging shallow depressions under a shrub or small tree. In Uruq, Maartin Strauss says that individuals can range over a staggering 1,700 km², though much less – around 300 km² – in summer when they spend more time seeking shade from bushes.

Always living in small herds of mixed sex and usually containing up to about 15 animals, though larger herds of up to 100 have been reported in the distant past, Arabian Oryx are generally not particularly aggressive toward one another. A dominance hierarchy involving all females and males above the age of about seven months is created within the herd by posturing displays which avoid the danger of serious injury that their long, sharp horns could potentially inflict on each other. Both males and females, though, will use their horns to defend their sparse territorial resources against interlopers from another herd. Bachelor herds do not occur, and single territorial males are rare. If they become separated from a herd, males will search areas where the herd last visited, settling into a solitary existence until the herd's return.

Other than humans, grey wolves were historically the Arabian Oryx's main predator. But wolves have long been very scarce and hardly pose any threat to oryx today. Golden Jackals, significantly smaller than Grey Wolves, might take a young oryx, but jackals are generally rare and are not often found in the most inhospitable parts of the Arabian Desert, preferring to concentrate nearer human settlements where the chances of obtaining food are better. Like the Grey Wolf, Golden Jackals are rarely tolerated by people if they know they're around.

But oryx do compete with domesticated livestock for grasses and shrubs to graze. In fenced reserves this isn't a problem because all domestic livestock have been excluded. But out in the Rub' al-Khali there are scattered herds of goats and wandering camels. In years when rains encourage plant growth this competition is not usually a problem according to Stéphane Ostrowski, but in drought conditions – especially if climate warming gathers more pace – it certainly might become a significant issue. What is needed is an overhaul of pastoral farming policy, something that is not being tackled by governments in the region who rely on local 'fixes' such as livestock exclusion zones agreed with local communities. Any wider-scale land use policy changes, though, have to take account of the status and complexity of tribal social structures and the continuing way of life of most Bedu who still rely on livestock. A more sustainable balance needs to be struck between domestic livestock numbers, changing climatic patterns and the needs of the wild mammals existing in these desert regions.

❖ ❖ ❖

Oryx share this vast desert landscape with very few human inhabitants. Traditionally the Rub' al-Khali has been home to some nomadic Bedu, but it is an extremely harsh existence for an albeit highly resilient people. When they were totally nomadic, moving their tents and few possessions to take their goats and their precious camels – a source of milk and blood for drinking – to wherever a shower of rain had nurtured a little vegetation to graze, their lives were notoriously tough and precarious. Today, fewer descendents of those Bedu graze goats out here and usually only for part of the year; the obscene heat of summer is usually spent in a distant village home.

T. E. Lawrence, immortalised as 'Lawrence of Arabia', wrote in *Seven Pillars of Wisdom* (1922), an autobiographical account of his experiences of the Bedu as a British soldier during the so-called Arab Revolt against the Ottoman Turks of 1916–1918:

> Bedouin ways were hard even for those brought up in them and for strangers terrible: a death in life. No man can live this life and emerge unchanged. He will carry however faint the imprint of the desert, the brand which marks the nomad: and he will have within him the yearning to return, weak or insistent according to his nature. For this cruel land can cast a spell which no temperate clime can match.

The majestic natural beauty of this massive, arid sand desert, a place seemingly without end when you are alone in a tiny part of it, is overwhelming; its striking orange-ochre dunes that brighten to an oxide red in the setting sun, sculptured by the wind into huge, sensually smooth mounds, one folded into the next and stretching as far as the eye can see to the horizon. In the west of the Rub' al-Khali these dunes aren't higher than perhaps 50 metres. In the east, though, they are on an epic scale, some of them huge, wind-smoothed ridges five times higher, formidable indeed if you need to cross them! It hardly needs to be said that water in the Rub'al-Khali is its most precious commodity. Where it does rain – and that usually occurs as a sudden downpour – it normally totals no more than 4 cm per year.

At first glance, the Rub'al-Khali's white, sun-reflecting gravel plains and curvaceous dunes appear utterly lifeless. What grows here is a scatter of often rather small, shrivelled-looking, spiny bushes and parched grasses devoid of much life-giving greenery. Clumps of saltbush and other woody, spine-covered shrubs. Or small tufts of rough-feeling sedges and oatgrass. Most of these plants eke out a harsh existence on the gravelly plains but some, too, grow on the lower slopes of dunes or in the hollows between them, their long penetrating roots anchored way below in the deep damp sand often tens of metres below its fiery surface.

Oryx aren't the only animals that have, or continue to live their lives here either. There used to be quite a few others; many such as the Striped Hyena, Arabian Ostrich and Honey Badger are today extinct, the result of hunting, overgrazing with sheep and goats, and destruction of their habitats. Sand Cats still survive; small, light coloured, thick-furred, nocturnal hunters that would captivate anyone with their incredible good looks. Both Sand (or Rhim) and Mountain Gazelles occur in reasonable numbers, their formerly depleted populations having been bolstered, like the oryx, by reintroductions. Numerous species of lizard and snake, a scatter of Arabian Grey Wolves and Caracal (a medium sized, long-eared cat) and, more commonly, long-eared Rüppell's Foxes and Cape Hares are all to be found in small numbers.

One dark, cool desert evening when we returned to camp in Uruq, a visitor was already drinking the typical green, aromatic, cardamom-laced coffee brewed by the local rangers employed to protect the animals. I talked to Mohammed, a man in his eighties, a Bedu of the Dawasir tribe he said, and who had driven his ancient pickup to our camp from his distant home. With a Bedu ranger acting as interpreter, Mohammed recalled with fondness seeing oryx in the Rub' al-Khali half a century ago. His eyes became noticeably brighter in his leathered, weatherworn face, and he tapped his stick excitedly on the floor as he told us how the oryx would move deeper into the sands in the cooler, winter months and return to the edges in the fierce heat of summer. Once again, he said, oryx are rediscovering their old ways. He looked genuinely pleased.

The next day we spotted oryx in the cool of the early morning as we scanned with binoculars along some extensive plains. In the distance we could see two adults running like well-trained horses, clipping the stony, white gravel with their hooves and sending up tiny dust clouds in their wake. It was Maartin Strauss again, his eyes well trained, who noticed something different. There was a young oryx too. 'It's a calf!' he shouted. 'It still has its fawn-coloured infant coat and it can't be more than a few weeks old.' And here it was, little more than 30 cm high, keeping metronome-like pace with its parents, hardly visible above the broken, stony gravel as all three of them cantered elegantly along. A tiny Arabian Oryx calf providing the greatest symbol of hope for the survival of these impressive animals.

The upgrade in IUCN status to Vulnerable in itself gives hope for the future of the Arabian Oryx. Even more so is the increasing recognition – while far from universal – by the Arab states that the desert wildlife is a key part of their heritage that has to be respected and nurtured. And quite contrary to some other large mammals that have been captive bred and reintroduced to their former locations, the Arabian Oryx has a massive, almost completely uninterrupted stretch of habitat available to it. What a contrast with, for instance, the European Bison (Chapter 5). Its largest wild population is resettled in the large – by European standards – Białowieża Forest in Poland and Belarus, something over 1,000 km^2 of forest and forest glades. The Rub'al-Khali alone covers 650,000 km^2, the vast bulk of it potentially habitable by the oryx. It is not an animal short of space.

No one person has been responsible for the success of the Arabian Oryx's return to this desert. Indeed, a vast number of people including biologists, vets, game wardens, politicians, statesmen and others have devoted a considerable amount of their time and effort to its amazing recovery. Many still do. And their continuing efforts are vital to reduce poaching as much as humanly possible, to try and reduce the amount of goat grazing by nomadic Bedu and to continually monitor the oryx population numbers and their health. But without the foresight of the FPS to plan a capture of a few of the last oryx in Arabia and breed them in captivity for future release, they would without doubt have been driven to extinction in the wild.

Maybe the biggest unknown is the impact of climate warming on this remarkable animal. If frequent droughts continue, the future of the Arabian Oryx could again be in doubt, especially in the wild. Captive populations, of course, are far more secure because they can be supplied with food and water. If climate warming eases, and there is no upsurge in poaching as there has been in the past, its future looks bright indeed.

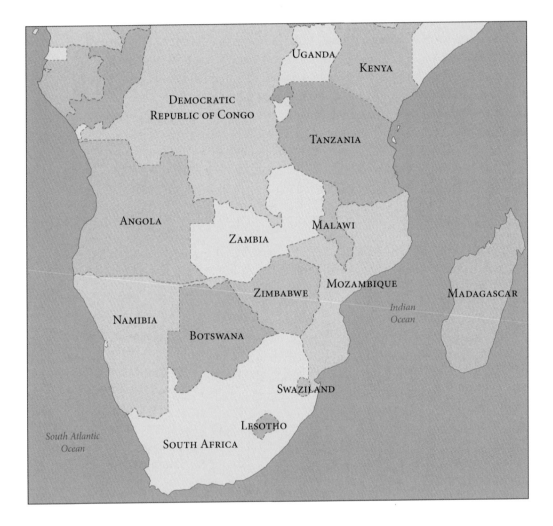

3

OUT OF THE RED AND INTO THE BLACK

BLACK RHINO

Once abundant across much of East and South Africa, Black Rhinos were hunted for sport, shot as vermin, elbowed out as cattle grazing took over more land, and poached for their horns. By the mid 1990s, there were less than 2,500 left. Since then, protection has seen their numbers rise to more than double that, a success story approaching that of their African cousin, the White Rhino. In the last few years, though, poaching has again escalated, this time to satisfy the hedonistic nouveau riche in Vietnam and China with rhino horn bangles, necklaces and après party pick-me-ups in addition to its more traditional – but unproven – medicinal uses. If armed protection and other security measures aren't working, is it now time to contemplate legalising rhino horn sales?

To the safari tourists on the lookout for elephants, wildebeest, rhino and much more in the impressive Hluhluwe-iMfolozi Park in KwaZulu- Natal, we must have looked like a bunch of off-road, four-wheel drive junkies. It certainly felt that way. Crashing through thorny acacia scrub. Hurtling across the bleached savannah grassland. Keeping pace with the two leading Landrovers as they dodged the taller trees and swung wildly through head-high scrub. And after ten minutes of this adrenalin rush, a breathless run from our vehicles to end up cheek by jowl with one of the world's largest, almost prehistoric-looking animals.

Here was a tonne or more of dark grey, leathery-skinned Black Rhino lying sedated on the ground surrounded by a team of vets and conservation workers all busily occupied making sure the felled creature was in good shape. She – this one about eight years old – had been darted by a marksman from the capture team's helicopter that dodged and ducked perilously low over, even seemingly between, the acacia trees that dot the grassland. By the time the powerful sedative had caused her collapse, she had run for about 3 km across the scrubby savannah; hence our need to find her as quickly as possible. When we did, she was lying on a steep grassy slope scattered liberally with thorny acacias and mimosa trees. A cloth was tied over her head and earplugs inserted in her ears as soon as the Zulu team's *nduma* (foreman), Philemon Ndwandwe, got to her. To minimise distress, it's better that the animal can't see and hear. While sedation causes extreme calm, the animal still retains its senses.

But capturing Black Rhino isn't done for an adrenalin-fuelled buzz. Thanks to strict protection and a good breeding record, in state-owned protected reserves like Hluhluwe-iMfolozi – 960 km² of savannah, hill forest and scrub – they have done so well that there are now more Black Rhino than some of these reserves can accommodate. Jeff Gaisford of Ezemvelo KwaZulu-Natal Wildlife, the State Wildlife Authority explains: 'Each bull needs a territory of about 500 ha which it defends against other males. Because the Park is fenced, the population has reached the land's carrying capacity. We have viable young bulls that are failing to nail a territory. So we have been offering spare Black Rhinos to private landowners who have sufficient land that they will guarantee for conservation purposes. It has to be fenced, properly protected and it needs to be around 20,000 ha to be viable.'

This Black Rhino Range Expansion Project is a partnership between Ezemvelo KwaZulu-Natal Wildlife and WWF in collaboration with landowners who can supply the right conditions. The first animals – 21 of them from a number of state-owned reserves – were transferred in 2005 to what was named the Zululand Rhino Reserve, then 17,000 ha of former farmland in 17 different ownerships. Two hundred kilometres of internal fences between the individual farms had been removed a year earlier leaving just the perimeter fence. The following year, the first of many Black Rhino calves was born there. In 2009 the reserve was designated as a nature reserve under South African legislation acknowledging it as a site of biodiversity importance that makes an essential contribution to the conservation of species and habitats. Today, with more landowners having joined and removed their internal fences, it covers 23,000 ha of open savannah, thornveld (savannah with thorny trees), bushveld (bush and shrub-covered grassland) and woodland.

Today the reserve has a thriving Black Rhino population that has grown in numbers considerably. These founder populations of Black Rhino remain the property of Ezemvelo KwaZulu-Natal Wildlife and are looked after on a custodianship basis by the landowners. Any drop in standards of management or care and the state body retains the right to move them elsewhere. 'The aim of the project is to increase the population but also to physically spread them in different locations, thereby reducing the chances of poaching', explains Pamela Sherriffs, WWF South Africa's Communication Manager for the project. 'Today there are roughly 200 Black Rhino in the Hluhluwe-iMfolozi Park although we don't know what its maximum carrying capacity is,' comments Dr Jacques Flamand, the Project's Leader from WWF South Africa. 'We keep the population lower so that we have maximum productivity and a growing population that's not subjected to losses when times are tough, when the habitat suffers because of drought for instance.'

Jacques adds, 'By 2013 on other state-owned land in KwaZulu-Natal we had around 160 Black Rhino and about 120 on private land. Prior to my project there were no Black Rhino on private land here; they were all on state land.' Across the whole of South Africa from 2003 to 2010, the number of private property owners hosting Black Rhino increased from 18 to 43 and they held a total of well over 400 Black Rhinos in 2010. Putting land previously farmed over to wildlife conservation brings in cash by promoting green tourism. It creates jobs, a much sought-after commodity in today's South Africa.

In total, South Africa has 2,044 Black Rhino; that's 40% of the African population, which currently stands at 5,055. Namibia has 1,750 Black Rhino, so between them these two southern African countries hold three quarters of the global population. There are another 200–300 in captivity in zoos and safari parks around the world.

❖ ❖ ❖

For most of the 20th century the Black Rhino was the most numerous of all the rhino species (of which there are five today). Around 1900, there were probably several hundred thousand of them in Africa. But they proved large and easy targets for 19th and 20th century weapons in the hands mostly of British and Dutch colonial settlers and trophy hunters. Their predictable habit of drinking regularly at known water holes increased their vulnerability. As more wild land was converted for farming, cattle ranching especially, their habitat was reduced in area and rhinos were treated as vermin and shot mercilessly. By 1950 or 1960 there were maybe 100,000 left. Through the late 1970s to the mid 1990s, their numbers were decimated; by 1981 they were down to 10,000–15,000. By 1995, only 2,410 Black Rhinos remained, the low point in their chequered existence.

The gains since then have been due largely to substantial breeding successes in South Africa, Namibia and Kenya, all of them in protected reserves or fenced private estates. And none of that would have been remotely possible without the enormous dedication over several decades of thousands of individuals; game wardens and rangers who frequently put their lives at risk to challenge well-armed poachers; vets and landowners; government and NGO employees; and many more besides.The original range of the Black Rhino stretched across much of eastern and central Africa. Today, they have gone from Cameroon, Chad, Mozambique, the Central African Republic, Ethiopia, Somalia and Sudan, probably from Ethiopia and other parts of their range too. They are on the brink of extinction in Angola. But they have been successfully reintroduced to Malawi since 1993 (where they became extinct in 1990), Zambia in 2008 (where they were extinct by 1998) and to Botswana (extinct in 1992, reintroduced in 2003).

Capturing and transferring huge, lumbering Black Rhino to reintroduce them to a new location is fraught with problems. Once an animal has been darted, the noise of the helicopter is used to encourage it to run towards a track or other relatively easy access for the team of vets and operatives who have the difficult task both of ensuring that it stays sedated but suffers as little stress as possible. And they have to be able to get it into a strong, lorry-transported crate to transfer it to its new home. 'Black Rhino have a tendency to run into cover on low ground and hide once they've been darted,' says Dave Cooper, the vet supervising this capture and a veteran of many more. 'Then we might not be able to get it out so we have to administer the antidote to rouse it, then chase it out. That's a dangerous business for the men involved.'

With animals as large as rhino possessing poor eyesight, their first reaction is to get away. Anything – or anyone – in their line of escape simply gets bulldozed. Ironically, much of the frenetic human activity around a sedated rhino is to evaluate its stress levels. Their caring attitude is certainly impressive. 'We take blood samples from their ears to check on stress hormone levels and for a pregnancy test. We monitor their blood pressure and general condition and we take a sample of faeces,' comments Jacques Flamand. 'Dung is also collected from sites where the animals have been released and tested for stress hormones. By knowing more about their stress levels, the team can improve their understanding of what's going on and maybe improve techniques for future captures and reintroductions.'

Having tied large ropes from the transport crate to two of their legs, once the sedative's antidote is injected into the animal it is time to move out of the way as the huge rhino staggers back on to its feet. Then, with some pulling on the ropes by the Zulu team, the great beast is hauled into the crate and its heavy doors locked shut. A sigh of relief goes around; a job well done. And those of us standing behind trees for safety can come out in the open again! Another Black Rhino is taken away to a new home to start a new breeding population.

❖   ❖   ❖

Today's African Black Rhino population of over 5,000 might sound impressive but they are still classified by the IUCN as Critically Endangered meaning that the species 'faces an extremely high risk of extinction in the wild'. That is because, in common with their White Rhino cousins and elephants, they continue to face an enormous threat from poachers. Between the 1970s and 1990s, thousands of rhino – both species – were killed and their horns hacked off to be used as supposed medicines in Southeast Asia or for making dagger handles in Yemen. Coming across a bloody corpse of a poached rhino is a distressing sight and hard to bear for those involved in their protection.

Anyone who has visited Yemen can't fail to notice the *jambiyas* – short curved daggers – carried by adult men on their belts and used almost exclusively today as a status symbol for ceremonial use rather than the effective, close quarter weapon it once was. Virtually every adult male Yemeni wears one, a practice deeply rooted in their culture. *Jambiyas* can have handles made of metal, leather, elephant ivory, even wood or plastic but rhino horn is the 'Rolex' version and highly prized.

The illegal horn trade from Africa to Yemen was fuelled by the oil boom in the 1970s and 1980s when income in the Middle East enabled the rise of a new middle class able to afford luxury products. Back in Africa, so many rhinos were killed to saw off their horn, their population plummeted by 96% between 1970 and 1992. And despite a ban on imports by the Yemeni government in 1982, illegal trade continues in the coveted rhino horn. A basic *jambiya* with perhaps a wooden handle might cost 2,000 Yemeni rials ($9); a top of the range model, 20 million rials ($93,000).

Lucy Vigne and Esmond Martin, two Kenyan-based independent consultants monitoring illegal trade in animal products globally, have been visiting Yemen since the 1980s. Their most recent visit, in 2012, revealed that the political crisis there in recent years had made it easier to smuggle in rhino horn. Writing in the FFI journal *Oryx* in 2013 they observe, 'Ironically, annual imports have perhaps halved since 2008 to about 25 kilos per annum in 2012.' 'Only the rich can afford new rhino horn handles for their daggers; the economic crisis resulted in some Yemenis selling their valuable *jambiyas*… to pay for air passages to leave the country or simply to feed their families.' Vigne and Martin also reported on a rhino horn lookalike material being used for *jambiya* handles made of a hardened gum. Mass produced and cheap, its acceptance is seemingly on the up, offering hope that a harmless alternative will prove universally popular.

❖ ❖ ❖

For decades, much of the poached African rhino horn has been used in the traditional medicine of many Asian countries, from Malaysia, South Korea and Vietnam to India and China, supposedly to cure a variety of ailments. In traditional Chinese medicine, the horn – which is shaved or ground into a powder and dissolved in boiling water – is used to treat fever, rheumatism, gout and other disorders. According to the 16th century Chinese pharmacist Li Shi Chen, it could also cure snakebites, hallucinations, typhoid, headaches, carbuncles, vomiting, food poisoning, and 'devil possession'. Its prescribed use as an aphrodisiac is, however, untrue.

There is no objective evidence to support the plethora of claims about the healing properties of the horns. In 1990, Chinese researchers found that large doses of rhino horn extract could slightly lower fever in rats but the concentration of horn given by a traditional Chinese medicine specialist is many times lower than used in those experiments. Rhino horn is composed of the protein keratin, also the chief component of hair, fingernails and animal hooves, although its precise chemical composition varies depending on a rhino's diet and geographic location. If keratin possessed all these apparent health benefits, anyone chewing on their fingernails would have been extolling its benefits well before now.

Nevertheless, between 2002 and 2007 at least five comprehensive Vietnamese-language traditional medical pharmacopoeias were published that feature sections on rhino horn as medicine. According to a report published by TRAFFIC (the international Wildlife Trade Monitoring Network) in 2012, Vietnamese dealers are even pushing rhino horn as a treatment for life-threatening diseases, including cancers, when there is no shred of objective evidence that it will have any beneficial effect. All the same, its adherents are unlikely to pay much attention to scientific arguments. Commenting on a government-supported publicity drive in Vietnam begun in 2013 to draw attention to the issue, Ha Cong Tuan, Deputy Minister of Agriculture and Rural Development, said at the campaign's launch that, 'Vietnam is committed to implementing in a responsible manner its international conservation commitments.' Time will tell.

A protected species under international wildlife law, the trade in rhino horn is governed by CITES, the Convention on International Trade in Endangered Species, to which Vietnam is a signatory. Since 1977, all rhino species have been listed on Appendix I of CITES which prohibits commercial international trade in rhinos, any parts of rhinos, and their products and derivatives. Seemingly, that makes little or no difference in a country where corruption is rife and criminal syndicates run a ruthless organised trade. The TRAFFIC report goes on to say that in spite of a limited number of rhino horn seizures by Vietnamese authorities:

> Rhino horn trade remains a highly sensitive issue in Vietnam allegedly owing
> to the direct involvement of senior government figures. Anecdotal reports of

government complicity in allowing 'free passage' and 'protection' continue to surface; Vietnamese diplomats in Africa and officials at international airports apparently function as important sources of rhino horn; while certain dealers and users in Vietnam often claim protective immunity from law enforcement actions because of their local connections.

The decimation of Black Rhino (as well as Africa's White Rhino) in the two decades up to the mid 1990s to satisfy such markets stimulated an international outcry. CITES pushed major consuming countries in Southeast Asia and the Middle East to instigate and implement rhino horn trade bans and by the late 1990s, almost all major traditional consuming countries including China, Hong Kong, Japan, South Korea and Taiwan, had bans in place and were beginning to implement them.

Rhino conservationists in Africa were assuming that the tide was turning; the horrendous trade was, at long last, starting to decline. Imagine, then, their concern – in some cases despair – when another surge in poaching began in the last few years, another bloody and highly dangerous odyssey of illegal killing and smuggling.

❖ ❖ ❖

A new, and very different, market has opened up for rhino horn, one that could have very serious consequences for both species of rhino in Africa. Rhino horn products – prayer beads, bracelets, bangles, chopstick sets and more – have become a 'must have' for some of the nouveau riche in Southeast Asia. Vietnam, it seems, is now the world's leading destination and consumer of rhino horn.

In 2013, the campaigning conservationist and wildlife photographer Karl Ammann published an account on his website (www.karlammann.com) of finding that the new status symbols and lifestyle products for those with money in Vietnam are rhino horn jewellery and elephant ivory. He reported on a visit to a rhino horn and elephant ivory workshop near Hanoi:

> We asked where the horn came from and were told Mozambique, the chances being high that it was Kruger [National Park, South Africa] rhino horn via Kenya. This was not very surprising with Mozambique having lost its last rhino…and this trade route being well established.

Workshop horn carvers told him that they used several horns a week and couldn't keep up with the demand for bangles, selling hundreds of them at $10,000 to $15,000 each, mostly to visiting Chinese tourists or to dealers. Horn was priced at around $45,000 per kg making it more expensive by weight than gold, diamonds…or cocaine. Some experts reckon its street value is higher still, maybe $65,000 per kg. He continues:

> Current law enforcement efforts are mostly about lip service and window dressing. None of the people we interacted with seemed to be in any way worried

about any enforcement official putting them in handcuffs. Clearly the buyers of these rhino horn bangles will not want to hide them in a jewellery box. They have to be worn or the status symbol aspect goes out the window.

Another use has appeared in recent years too. Belief in rhino horn's detoxification properties, especially following excessive intake of alcohol, rich food and the 'good life', has given rise to an affluent group of habitual users in Vietnam who routinely mix rhino horn powder with water or alcohol as a general health and hangover-curing tonic. According to Milliken and Shaw:

> Popular websites drive this usage with an endless stream of slick come-on slogans: 'to improve concentration and cure hangovers', 'rhino horn with wine is the alcoholic drink of millionaires', and rhino horn is 'like a luxury car'. Secondary industries supply paraphernalia for self-medication such as special rhino horn grinding bowls that are unique to Vietnam.

Whether any or most of these well-heeled consumers realise that they are buying products that necessitate rare wild animals being killed is anyone's guess. It could be that dealers put about the notion that the horn is removed harmlessly from the animals or that it is only taken from already dead rhino.

What is needed, and urgently, is practical action by the Vietnamese authorities to root out corruption, live up to their international responsibilities and enforce CITES together with a publicity drive to shock the purchasers with gruesome images of the poached rhino so that they understand the reality of what's happening. It needs publicity such as that generated by Prince William, Duke of Cambridge and Hong Kong's action superstar Jackie Chan who, in 2013, publicly supported the Canadian/German film co-production, *Gambling on Extinction*. The documentary investigates the illegal trade of wildlife products, including ivory, rhino horn and tiger parts, with filmmaker Jakob Kneser travelling across Africa and Southeast Asia to jungles and trading hubs to expose the major players feeding and opposing the trade. 'Everyone should dispel the myths that jewellery and carvings are made from tusks and horns that have fallen off the elephant or rhino or from animals that have died of natural causes,' Chan said. 'This is simply not true. They are hunted and killed. The only way to stop the slaughter is to cut the demand. We are all consumers, so we can all make a difference.'

Controversially, because the numbers of White Rhino are high and increasing, a strictly limited number have been hunted legally in South Africa in recent years. The policy had been agreed by CITES but the decision always had its critics. It is a policy that has brought in a sizeable income for conservation with each 'trophy' White Rhino shot costing an average of $30,000. Between 1972 and 2004, an average of 36 were shot annually, though numbers had increased to 100 per year by 2009. The White Rhino population was, of course, growing very much faster so the hunting was easily sustained. And only older, non-breeding animals are shot under supervision.

In the mid 2000s, though, the origin of the hunters was changing. Traditional European and US 'big game' hunters were in steep decline while those from Southeast Asia, Vietnam especially, burgeoned. Trophy prices were soaring and the hunters were, in reality, only after the horns for illegal onward sale. As the South African authorities closed this loophole, thefts of horn from museums and in supposedly secure government stockpiles increased. The stockpiles had been accumulated from horns sawn off sedated rhino whenever they are captured temporarily. The animal feels no pain; it's the equivalent of a haircut for a human, and the horns regrow. Others come from rhino that die naturally.

At the 13th CITES Conference of the Parties in 2004, after an epic verbal battle, the South African and Namibian governments got the go-ahead to each reintroduce hunting of up to five Black Rhino annually. Every one of them had to be an elderly male too old to breed. It was a controversial decision that WWF and others opposed at the time but which most conservation bodies now accept as pragmatic. The South Africans had argued again that such trophy hunting would bring in huge funds that would be channelled into conservation without affecting Black Rhino populations. Nevertheless, there are organisations that remain opposed in principle. In January 2014, the *Corpus Christi Caller Times*, a regional newspaper in Texas, carried the story of a Dallas auction for a permit – auctioned internationally – to shoot one Black Rhino in Namibia (an old, non-breeding male). It sold for $350,000 to an unnamed US buyer. The event, organised by the Dallas Safari Club (a division of Safari Club International whose stated objective is 'protecting hunters' rights and promoting wildlife conservation') attracted an array of critics while the FBI were investigating death threats against members of the Club. 'This auction is telling the world that an American will pay anything to kill an animal. It's making a spectacle of killing an endangered species,' commented Jeffrey Flocken, North American Regional Director of the International Fund for Animal Welfare at the time.

❖   ❖   ❖

Of the world's five species of rhino, two are African – White Rhino and Black– and three are southern Asian – the Indian, Javan and Sumatran Rhinos. The White Rhino, of which there are two subspecies, is by far the most abundant; over 20,000 in Africa, the bulk of them in South Africa followed by Namibia and Kenya. Almost all are the Southern White subspecies. The Northern White subspecies is on the verge of extinction, its best hope for survival being four animals moved in 2009 from Dvur Kralove Zoo in the Czech Republic to the Ol Pejeta Conservancy in eastern Kenya. The hope is that these northern white survivors will breed; up to 2014 they hadn't. In the early 20th century, Dutch and English colonial settlers had shot so many White Rhino for sport and meat that they were on the verge of extinction; the 'best' population, South Africa's, went below 50 individuals. With protection since then their numbers have grown back enormously.

Whites are huge, sometimes weighing three to four tonnes and nearly five metres long. They have two horns on the snout, the front one by far the largest. An adult Black Rhino is smaller than the whites, measuring up to four metres long, and can weigh from one to over one and a half tonnes. Like whites, they have two horns. Depending on whose expertise you rely, there might be anywhere between four and eight subspecies of Black Rhino. Both White and Black Rhino are dark grey and the origin of their names might have arisen from a misunderstanding of their names in Afrikaans.

The Indian Rhino is the same size as the white, but its skin is more silver-brown and forms folds over its body giving it a rather strange, armoured appearance. It has one horn. They used to inhabit a huge area stretching from Pakistan, across India east to Burma, maybe further, but most have been progressively killed off, leaving fewer than 200 earlier in the 20th century. But the recent story of the Indian Rhino is one of success. With strict protection from Indian and Nepalese wildlife authorities, their numbers have recovered to over 3,000. Poaching pressure has, though, remained high in both countries and their recovery is precarious without increased and accelerated support for conservation efforts throughout its range. The IUCN classifies them as Vulnerable.

The Javan Rhino – which looks like a smaller version of its Indian cousin – is down to maybe 40 individuals, all of them now in the Ujung Kulon Conservation area in Java, Indonesia. It was once widespread in lowland forests, most of which have been logged out. Not surprisingly, IUCN classifies it as Critically Endangered.

The last species, the reddish-brown Sumatran Rhino, is the smallest of all, though unlike its Asian cousins, it has two horns. It is found at very high altitudes in Borneo and Sumatra but its numbers have declined enormously because of poaching and habitat loss. By 2012 numbers declined to maybe 200 and local extinctions had occurred. Illegal logging, poaching, human encroachment and degradation of rhino habitat have all taken their toll. No surprise, then, that it too is classed as Critically Endangered.

Rhino ancestry is complex.The family of all modern-day rhinos first appeared around 34 million years ago in some part of Europe or Asia. The earliest members were small and numerous and spread across Europe, Asia and North America until a wave of extinctions about 28 million years ago wiped out most of them. Of those that survived, *Menoceras*, a pig-sized rhinoceros, had two horns side-by-side while the North American *Teleoceras* had short legs, a barrel chest and lived until about five million years ago. The last rhinos in the Americas became extinct three to four million years ago.

Modern rhinos are thought to have begun dispersing from Asia sometime between 10 and 25 million years ago. Two species used to inhabit Europe; one of which was the Woolly Rhinoceros, first arriving in Europe about 600,000 years ago. A huge and numerous animal, it was hunted to extinction by early humans (yes, we were doing it even then!). Of the extant rhino species, the Sumatran Rhino is most closely related to the Woolly Rhinoceros.

All modern-day rhinos are vegetarian, either eating plants by grazing vegetation on the ground or by browsing leafy shrubs and low tree branches. The Black Rhino is a browser, not a grazer, thereby explaining why its head is held higher than that of the white rhino, which feeds by grazing ground vegetation. The square-shaped mouth of the white is an adaptation for grazing, and the 'hooked' lip of the Black Rhinoceros is an adaptation for browsing; hooked lips grab branches more easily. Black Rhinos eat leaves, branches, shoots, thorny bushes and fruit of a huge variety of trees and shrubs. They browse for food in the morning and evening and, in the hottest part of the day, they are mostly inactive, resting, sleeping, and wallowing in mud. Wallowing helps cool down their body temperature and protects them against parasites; if mud is not available then rhinos will take dust baths. Drinking water is most common in the afternoon when they will often congregate at a stream or pool.

All rhinos have skin that is at least a couple of centimetres thick, often more, and it's designed to protect them from thorns and sharp grasses. Their skin is actually a wildlife habitat in its own right; it harbours a plethora of parasites such as mites and ticks which are eaten by small birds called oxpeckers and even by much larger egrets, both of which can often be seen perched and feeding on the back of the moving beast. They have no real natural predators other than humans although youngsters can fall prey to big cats and crocodiles; even to wild dogs and hyenas. Without poachers causing their premature death, they can live for at least 35 years.

Black Rhinos have small brains and poor eyesight, relying more on hearing and smell; their ears possess a relatively wide rotational range to enable them to sense what or who is nearby. They use scent marking to identify themselves to other Black Rhinos, spraying urine on trees and bushes, around water holes and feeding areas. Coming upon these spots, other rhinos will sense who is in the area and add their own marking.

The rhino's horn, that commodity so sought-after for highly dubious uses, is typically about 50 cm long; it is used for defence, intimidation, and for digging up roots and breaking branches during feeding. Rhinos will fight each other, and they have the highest rates of mortal combat recorded for any mammal: it accounts for about 50% of male and 30% of female deaths. Don't ever be fooled by this seemingly cumbersome, often languid beast with very poor eyesight relaxing as it chews at a few shrubs; they can be extremely aggressive and charge readily at a perceived threat, even at tree trunks and termite mounds. But at people too. And they are not as cumbersome as they appear. Running, they can reach speeds of over 50 km per hour. Usain Bolt's fastest is a little less by comparison! If a rhino charges, your only chance of surviving is to get behind – preferably up – a large tree.

Although they are typically solitary animals with the exception of coming together to mate, mothers and calves will sometimes congregate in small groups for short periods. They are not very territorial animals. Males are not as sociable as females, although they will sometimes permit the presence of other rhinos. Home ranges vary depending on season and the availability of food and water; generally they have smaller home ranges and live at a higher density in habitats that have plenty of food and water available.

Sexual maturity takes between five and seven years for females; seven to eight years for males and mating doesn't have a seasonal pattern but births tend to be towards the end of the rainy season in more arid environments. Males will follow females when they are in season and when she defecates he will scrape and spread the dung, making it more difficult for rival adult males to pick up her scent trail. Breeding pairs stay together for two to three days, sometimes even weeks. With seemingly boundless energy, they mate several times a day over this time; each act lasting for half an hour. The gestation period is up to 16 months; the single calf weighs up to 50 kg at birth and it often follows its mother around after just three days.

Weaning occurs at around two years but the mother and calf stay together for two or three years until the next calf is born.

❖   ❖   ❖

Poaching of rhino – both Black and White – remains by far the biggest threat they face and one that has increased very dramatically in the last couple of years, largely to attempt to satisfy the burgeoning Vietnamese market. The IUCN African Rhino Specialist Group, meeting in 2013, was told that the average poaching rate across the continent had almost doubled from 1.17 rhinos per day in 2010 to 2.04 rhinos per day in 2012. Most of these were White Rhino. In 2012, 668 rhinos were poached in South Africa but by 2013 it had increased to 1,004 (966 White and 38 Black Rhino). In the early years of this century, the losses were sometimes less than ten animals per year. It has reached such levels that private landowners are beginning to question the economics of keeping rhino for tourism, both because of their growing investment in protection and because of the risk to their employees and guests from poachers on their land. Every year in Africa, poachers of rhino and elephant kill around 40 wildlife rangers whose families are not only devastated by grief, but also go on to suffer severe financial hardship.

Despite these horrendous losses, Africa's rhino populations continue to increase. Maintaining this growing population is critical to providing the necessary buffer against poaching. Africa-wide, Black Rhinos increased from 4,880 in 2010 to 5,055 in 2012. The worry is, though, that if the currently escalating poaching rate continues, the numbers of rhino killed could outstrip population growth in South Africa by 2015–2016; in Kenya, where there are fewer rhino, even sooner.

Some populations have not been violated by poachers, though the effort required to protect them has increased enormously.'The threat of poaching has increased our costs dramatically. We now spend roughly 2.5 million rand ($250,000) a year on security,' comments Samantha Sealie, the conservation manager for the privately owned, 23,000 ha Zulu Rhineland Reserve. 'It's our biggest expense and we have to make every possible effort to generate the income to cover this cost. But it's well worth the effort for us; the security company we use, Nyati Anti Poaching, is doing an excellent job on the reserve as well as on other reserves in the Zululand area. There's little poaching on the properties they manage and they've been able to make more than ten arrests in the area this year [2013] alone. We haven't had a single White or Black Rhino killed,' she adds.

But poaching is not going to be eliminated – or even reduced to what might be called tolerable levels – by providing more and more armed protection to rhinos in the reserves, sanctuaries and national parks most are located in. 'Unfortunately, there is no one silver single bullet or simple solution that will eliminate poaching. Enhanced and effective protection is needed but there also needs to be long term solutions, including working with local communities where rhinos live and reducing the demand for consuming rhino horn. Only with a combination of activities will we be able to secure the future of rhinos,' says Susie Offord, Deputy Director of Save the Rhino International.

The often huge, and sometimes remote, land areas involved and escalating costs for guards, equipment and fencing makes catching poachers almost impossible. At the same time, the poaching gangs have become more sophisticated; they use high velocity rifles, immobilising darts and there are suggestions of helicopters being used to ferry teams in and out quickly. To reduce the problem, a whole set of supplementary measures are needed, including: better intelligence, using drones for surveillance, a reduction in corruption, more involvement of local communities as eyes and ears, using tracker dogs, better monitoring of rhino populations, micro-chipping of horn, a better understanding of rhino habitat requirements when animals are moved to new quarters, much higher fines and custodial sentences.

In the countries receiving illegal rhino horn a considerable amount of work needs to be undertaken, including: eliminating corruption, particularly in government circles; public education on the source of the horn and getting the message widely understood that rhino are killed to obtain it; and getting governments to act on their international legal responsibilities. Local receivers of illegal horn are sometimes caught but fewer arrests are made further up the chain, that is, the couriers, exporters/importers and the syndicate kingpins controlling these huge money-spinning operations.

Measures to reduce the trade were given a practical boost in July 2013 when US President Obama announced a Presidential Task Force on Wildlife Trafficking that will devise a national strategy aimed at combating the illegal wildlife trade and the poaching of endangered species. His announcement is intended to assert US leadership both in the domestic context – stricter enforcement at its ports, better coordination between federal government agencies – and internationally through bilateral agreements with target countries and using US Government influence and resources in international forums to achieve more impact on the ground. The announcement comes with a much-needed infusion of resources intended to stall the escalating poaching of endangered species. The US State Department will provide $10 million in training and technical assistance to combat poaching in South Africa, Kenya and elsewhere in sub-Saharan Africa. Not all of this is for rhino of course; other species including elephant are at huge risk too.

The Ol Pejeta Conservancy in central Kenya, bought from Lonrho in a deal arranged by FFI, is a good example of where some of these measures are already put into practice. In 2007, the protected 28,000 ha of arid savanna received 27 Black Rhino from another protected area nearby that had a surplus. 'Currently we have 99 Black Rhino [2013] and hope to become East Africa's first "100 Black Rhino" sanctuary later this year,' says Richard Vigne, Ol Pejeta's CEO. 'We have a carrying capacity of about 130 which we intend to achieve in the next four years. Thereafter, we have identified a further 8,000 ha of land adjoining us and we want to secure that as further habitat.' During the translocation, each rhino was fitted with a tiny transmitter buried in its horn to allow for tracking. Combined with effective wildlife protection and constructive working with the local communities in the area, poaching is almost zero. And that's in the context that Kenya as a whole lost considerable numbers of rhino and elephant to poachers in 2012. Ol Pejeta is also working with partners such as Operation Earth China to encourage working visits from Chinese volunteers, thereby helping to promote messages about the implications of the rhino horn trade. Kenya's move in 2013 to toughen up poaching punishments has been welcomed; up to 15 years in jail and/

or a fine of up to 10 million Kenyan shillings (about $114,000). Previously, poachers and traffickers there had been facing derisory penalties of less than $500.

There are lessons to be learnt, too, from the way that Indian Rhino populations have increased in protected areas in West Bengal. Generous funding by federal and state governments there has allowed high staffing levels for protection and habitat management, reflecting acceptance that rhinos are part of the cultural heritage and attract tourists. Villagers in the communities around also benefit from part of the tourist revenue; they receive compensation for damage caused by rhino and other large animals, employment and new cottage industries have been established. Local communities have become part of the protection strategy, acting as 'eyes and ears' locally; consequently poachers rarely penetrate these local barriers.

In southern Africa, poachers are occasionally caught or are sometimes killed by armed rangers. In the eight months to September 2013, 191 poachers had been arrested in South Africa, many of them in the Kruger National Park where hundreds of rhino, mainly whites, are getting killed for their horn. Kruger is huge, about the same size as Wales, and few serviceable roads penetrate large sectors of it. So controlling what happens across its great expanse is well nigh impossible. Add to that the fact that its whole eastern border – all 400 km of it – is open to adjacent Mozambique and the ease with which poachers can get in quickly, kill rhino, saw off the horn and retreat is obvious. In Mozambique, rhino poaching tends to incur a fine rather than imprisonment. Here, the last few surviving rhino were killed by poachers early in 2013, apparently with the collusion of poorly paid government rangers.

The South African government announced in August 2014 that from 2015 it is going to move hundreds of rhino out of Kruger to a number of other state reserves, parks and private land in order to disperse them. The South Africa Environment Ministry said that nearby countries, such as Botswana and Zambia, may also be considered as hosts. Botswana could be an ideal home for the rhinos because it has vast areas of sparsely populated wilderness that are hard to access.

❖ ❖ ❖

One of the hotly debated possible 'solutions' to combating this dreadful trade in rhino horn is to flood the market with legally obtained horns held in secure facilities; some countries, South Africa in particular, have large stockpiles gathered over many years. But several countries have already made their position clear and have destroyed their rhino horn stockpiles. The Philippines and the US did so in 2013. The Obama administration's attitude is one of zero tolerance and would not agree to opening up a legal market, which it claims might increase demand. Duan Biggs of the University of Queensland, Australia, with colleagues, writing in *Science* in 2013, argues that demand could be met into the future even without putting all this stockpiled horn on the market:

> The current speculative estimates of the demand for horn based on the [current] illegal supply could be met by the 5,000 White Rhinos on private conservation

land in South Africa alone. The natural death rate of rhinos of 2.6% would also provide hundreds of horns annually.

This assumes that each of those 5,000 White Rhino is sedated annually – a large and expensive operation – and that the annual sedation and de-horning doesn't affect the animals. It also assumes that each horn can be tracked (for example with a traceable DNA signature) to distinguish it from any illegal horn entering the market, and that some or all of the horn stockpiles could be sold off to start the legal international market.

Biggs and colleagues go on to argue that the huge income from selling the horn on the open market would more than pay the costs of the scheme and bring in considerable funds for conservation into the bargain. They cite the trade in crocodile skin as an example of how a legal market has reduced poaching pressure on wild crocodile populations using a combination of protecting the wild species, commercial breeding at 'crocodile farms' for their skin and the tagging of all legal skins (see Chapter 17). They continue:

> If a legal trade in horn leads to an unexpected and dangerous upsurge in poaching [as many critics assume it will], the legal trade can be restructured or closed down. With these safeguards, a carefully regulated, adaptively managed legal trade is more likely to lead to the successful conservation of Africa's rhino than the current trade ban. Legitimizing the market for horn may be morally repugnant to some, but it is probably the only way to prevent extinction of Africa's remaining rhino.

Critics also argue that marking legal horn will diminish the use of fake horn, often commonplace in Southeast Asia, boosting the demand for yet more genuine horn. They also claim that more supply could re-open markets largely closed down, in Yemen for instance for dagger handles, and in other parts of Southeast Asia, threatening even rarer rhino species there. Clearly, more and more enforcement is hardly keeping pace with the problem in spite of huge resources going into protection and there are those that argue that banning the rhino horn trade has proved as ineffective as many other failed bans such as alcohol prohibition and the war on drugs.

Critics or not, there are influential converts to the free market proposal; Bomo Edna Molewa, South Africa Minister of Environmental Affairs, has stated her acceptance that 'it is the right direction', based on a report released by South Africa's Department of Environmental Affairs in 2013 that recommended legalising and regulating the rhino horn trade while creating a national fund for increased intelligence, security and awareness to combat rhino poaching. This Rhino Issue Management report was compiled by a team led by former South African National Parks CEO Mavuso Msimang after wide consultation.

As a result, the South African government is considering submitting a rhino trade proposal for consideration at the 17th Conference of the Parties of CITES in 2016, as part of a reinvigorated strategy for rhino protection. The strategy will include a serious upgrade of security on the South African border with Mozambique, backed up by agreements to be negotiated with both Mozambique and Zimbabwe that provide for the protection of wildlife in the Kruger National Park where poaching is rife.

Without any doubt, it will be one of the most controversial and hotly debated proposals ever put to CITES if the South Africans go ahead. It is unlikely to succeed because few other governments will support the idea. Whether the proposal to legalise a trade in rhino horn succeeds or not, it is inconceivable that an animal such as the Black Rhino will ever be allowed to decline towards extinction again. There is too much at stake: for the African countries that host it, both in terms of their international standing and their tourism revenues; for the international community through agreements such as CITES; and for countries such as Vietnam and China to risk being labelled as environmental or wildlife pariahs and suffer the inevitable opprobrium if they don't get this illegal trade under control.

Within another decade or so, how many more Black Rhino will there be in Africa? No one will venture a figure but, with over 5,000 now, is it too much to assume that, provided poaching is substantially reduced – one way or another – we might have twice that number roaming the great savannas?

4

WHERE THEY'RE TALKING TURKEY AGAIN

WILD TURKEY

As the early European settlers on the North American continent moved west and grew inexorably in number, not only did they decimate the native Wild Turkey for food but they felled huge areas of its forest habitat too. By the 1930s, the estimated ten million that once roamed most of what had become the US had been reduced to about 30,000 birds. They had been extirpated from 18 states; everywhere they were confined to the most inaccessible locations. Early conservation efforts failed to achieve much success and it was not until the 1950s that new populations were gradually established in most states and numbers began to climb. And while localised habitat destruction remains a check on their numbers, there are maybe seven million Wild Turkeys today across the US and southern Canada. Turkey hunting, now regulated in every state, thrives once more and wild birds can again be savoured at Thanksgiving.

Autumn, and the verdant forests on the other side of the wide river I'm crossing by ferry are tinted in a plethora of orange, rust and olive-green, a sight that has not changed much over the last 400 years. It was here in the late spring of 1607 that the first English settlers disembarked from their three small sailing ships to form a permanent colony in what would eventually become the US. They had sought out a piece of land on the east coast of today's state of Virginia and soon set about constructing a settlement, on the north bank of the river, naming it and their new home in honour of King James I of England. Jamestown on the James River became the first permanent European foothold in the so-called New World. The dense red oak, beech and pine forests that clothed massive swathes of land nurtured a cornucopia of wild food including fruits, nuts, deer and a large ground bird that the early settlers believed was a type of guineafowl (also known as the turkey fowl) that they were familiar with in England. This American version looked similar, though much larger. But the shortened name persisted.

Journals from the time record that Wild Turkeys were abundant and that they were good for eating. And the settlers didn't even need to trap or shoot them. The local Powhatan Indians, initially friendly and who had long occupied this part of the eastern coast, were adept at catching and killing them. Very soon the immigrants were exchanging trinkets for local food. The English colony expanded over the next century in spite of the appalling deprivations they often faced, and by 1790 there were four million settlers. But it wasn't only the Powhatans and other native Indian tribes that became increasingly confined and marginalised. Forest clearance for crop growing and for construction timber depleted the habitat of Wild Turkeys and much other wildlife too. In 1600, US forests covered about 174 million ha; today it's no more than about 8 million ha. With increasing conflict between the settlers and the Powhatans – conflict that would eventually deteriorate into open warfare and the virtual destruction of the Powhatan nation – the settlers were soon shooting turkeys themselves, not only for their own personal consumption but also to sell at market.

Inland from these growing Virginia communities, the remainder of the American continent stretched an incredible 5,000 km west, vast open spaces and extensive forests where no white man had been. And vast space is what this burgeoning population desperately needed. Little over two centuries ago, pioneering Europeans set out west from the towns and villages they had built along the American east coast from Massachusetts in the northeast to the Carolinas in the southeast. And as their horse-pulled wagon trains headed west, trying – not always successfully – to avoid attacks from Native American Indians who had colonised this land aeons before, it wasn't only bison on the great open plains that the settlers hunted in vast numbers. It was Wild Turkeys in the extensive forests too. Difficult though it is to accept today, the settlers were convinced that they were destined, even divinely ordained, to expand across this vast continent and populate it. Native Indians were simply in the way. Bison were there to be hunted for food. And so was the turkey.

'By the turn of the 20th century, the extensive forests of Virginia [in the American east] were gone,' says Gary Norman who leads the Wild Turkey reinstatement project for Virginia's Department of Game and Inland Fisheries (DGIF). 'They had disappeared from two thirds of the state and their populations were probably at their lowest from 1880 to 1910.' According to the National Wild Turkey Federation (NWTF), the birds lived originally in almost all US states (only Alaska and Hawaii were without them) and the Canadian province of Ontario. As the settlers pushed westwards, clearing forests as they established farms and communities en route, turkeys died out. Connecticut lost them by 1813. Vermont held out until 1842. The last birds disappeared from New York state in the mid 1840s. By 1920, Wild Turkeys had been extirpated in 18 states and in Ontario. Elsewhere, few populations survived. Those that did were in the most inaccessible places well away from human habitation. Wild Turkey numbers remained extremely low into the early 1900s and had probably declined to their lowest ebb across the US in the late 1930s. There might have been just 30,000 remaining out of an original population thought to number maybe ten million.

❖ ❖ ❖

Commercial hunters were very effective at killing large numbers; stories of hundreds of turkey carcasses being shipped on trains destined for large cities were commonplace. They sold in the early 1800s for between six and 25 cents each; by 1872, when they were becoming scarce, the price had risen to $1. And one Wild Turkey could feed a family for a week.

For centuries, maybe millennia, Native American tribes had harvested Wild Turkeys. But probably never on a scale that threatened their existence. Although widely consumed by them, some tribes considered these birds stupid and cowardly and didn't eat them for fear of acquiring these characteristics. 'We know much more about the Powhatan uses of turkeys but not much about how they killed them,' says Nancy Egloff, the historian at the Jamestown-Yorktown Foundation at Williamsburg. 'Not only did they eat them but they used their bones and spurs (a male has a sharp claw – a spur – on each leg) for adornment; sometimes they used their spurs for arrow points. The feathers were used to dry hands after washing, especially at ceremonies, while Powhatans of higher status in their society had turkey feather capes. So the turkey was important to them.'

In spite of turkeys being large birds – a male or 'tom' can weigh up to 11 kg and measure well over a metre in length – they are surprisingly difficult to find and to kill in a forest. Yet the Powhatans did it centuries back without guns. Egloff thinks that the Powhatans probably imitated their calls to entice them. Then they perhaps killed them with a spear throw or using their incredibly accurate bows and arrows. There are suggestions that in forests they might have made them fly up to the 'safety' of a tree and then kill them with an arrow. In more open areas where the birds had no trees to fly up into, another suggestion is that young male Native Americans, being physically very fit, might have chased them on foot, maybe with help from dogs or horses, exhausting the birds which they then picked up.

More slender than domesticated turkeys, toms are strikingly colourful with their bronze and blue plumage, though hardly beautiful; the females – known as hens – are duller. Displaying males are a sight to behold; with tails fanned upright, puffed out chests and drooping wings, they strut about on spring mornings to impress the local hens. Walk along almost any sandy or muddy track in a Virginia or North Carolina forest and it's not long before you spot the large, telltale footprints of a turkey. They're here all right. It's just hard to see one. 'It's impossible to find them if you walk off-track into a forest,' comments Phil West, a turkey expert and a former wildlife biologist for DGIF in Virginia I met near the quiet community of Providence Forge about 50 km east of the state capital, Richmond. 'They'll hear you coming way before you see anything. And even though they roost at night high up in a tree, they're real hard to spot in spite of their size. They're much easier to spot in fields where they often feed near the edges of forests. They sure are hard to hunt too. You have to get into a forest you know they're in before first light. Then settle down and, when it's first light, mimic the calls of the hens to attract a tom. If you're lucky, he'll come along looking for her. You don't shoot until they are, say, 30 yards away.'

We met Ron Nelsen from Yorktown, Virginia on a forest track, a lifelong hunter who was packing up after a morning's turkey hunt near Providence Forge. He was only too happy to talk about the patience you need to hunt turkeys. And the unusual equipment many hunters use too. 'I had a jake (a young male) that came pretty close early this morning in the forest but I didn't want to shoot him. He was too young. It's important to have a strong population here. He walked away after a while. I just love being out in the forest with nature. I've been hunting for sixty years and I'm 68 now. I just sit for hours from before dawn, up against a tree maybe, using callers I've gotten to attract a tom,' he commented, dressed in full camouflage gear, shotgun in hand. Nelsen's turkey callers were evidence of a craft in themselves. Little wooden boxes with sliding dowels to make rasping sounds; small wooden 'strikers' to click on a slate; and various other devices that yelp and cluck, some he had made himself, and all to attract an inquiring turkey tom, mimicking its own calls. Ron hadn't shot a turkey that night. He shoots one occasionally. But he obviously revered these magnificent birds and enjoyed his hours in the forest whether he was to eat any turkey or not.

❖　❖　❖

Wild Turkeys aren't the only turkeys in the world, at least not quite. Closely related to guineafowl, and almost as closely to pheasants, grouse and partridges, there are just two living turkey species: the not very romantically named Wild Turkey of the US, southern Canada and northern Mexico and the Ocellated Turkey of Mexico's Yucatan Peninsula and parts of neighbouring Guatemala and Belize.

The Ocellated Turkey is a slightly smaller bird than its North American cousin and it inhabits lowland wet forests and clearings as well as more open, scrubby ground. Often living in groups, they feed on seeds, berries, nuts and insects. More colourful than the Wild Turkey, Ocellated Turkeys have more green and chestnut hues in their plumage; their name derives from eye-like spots on their tail, visible when fanned-out, like a minor version of those found on peacocks. Illegal hunting for food, sport and trade – even sometimes in protected areas – forest clearance and increasing land development for crops all threaten it. It has disappeared from part of its former range and the IUCN classifies it as Near Threatened. While its numbers are hard to gauge, there could be fewer than 50,000.

Wild Turkeys, on the other hand, are not confined these days to the US and southern Canada. They now roam more widely, having been introduced to a diversity of places including Hawaii, parts of Europe, Australia and New Zealand. Across its native range it used to be considered exclusively a forest bird, but that has been revised; they seem equally at home on scrubland, agricultural areas and grasslands though they do need trees to fly up into for roosting.

Wild Turkeys, though, are not simply Wild Turkeys; taxonomists recognise six subspecies, each varying a little in colour, habitat needs, distribution and behaviour from one another. The eastern Wild Turkey is the most abundant and the one encountered by the English settlers at Jamestown; it is distributed, as the name suggests, right across the eastern half of the US and into southern Canada. The Osceola (or Florida) Wild Turkey is found only in that US state. Named after the Seminole native leader, Osceola, it is a smaller and darker subspecies found on more swampy ground where it catches amphibians for food. The Rio Grande Wild Turkey has a south-central and far west US distribution where it inhabits more open prairie grasslands but also scrubby areas next to streams, mesquite (thorny scrub on arid land) and forests. Merriam's Wild Turkey, named after Clinton Hart Merriam (1855–1942), an American zoologist, is another prairie specialist but its range extends into the Rockies and much of the west. Gould's Wild Turkey, always a much rarer subspecies, is an occupant of hotter, drier lands from Mexico up into the south of Arizona. A conservation programme is underway to boost its numbers. The last subspecies, the South Mexican Wild Turkey – which doesn't reach north into the US at all – is the key subspecies that has provided us with the domesticated, farmed turkeys most of us eat today. Although there might have been others that were also domesticated in smaller numbers, it was largely this subspecies that was domesticated on any scale. The Southern Mexican Turkey was probably first domesticated by a number of indigenous peoples in Central America at least 2,000 years ago, and it was certainly bred with great sophistication by the Aztecs who dominated central America from the 14th to the 16th centuries. Turkey meat and eggs were eaten as major sources of protein and their feathers used extensively for decoration. The Aztecs associated the turkey with their trickster god Tezcatlipoca perhaps because of the perceived humorous behaviour of displaying toms.

In the 15th century, Spanish conquistadors brought the first turkeys to Europe, although the 16th century English navigator William Strickland (c.1535–1598) is generally credited with first importing the turkey into England. His family coat of arms – showing a turkey cock as the family crest – is among the earliest known European depictions of a turkey. English poet and farmer Thomas Tusser notes that the turkey was among 'farmer's fare', almost certainly for the well off farmer only, at Christmas in 1573. The majority of people could not possibly afford to buy imported meat.

Although they gradually became common farmyard birds, prior to the late 19th century, turkey remained something of a luxury in Britain with goose or beef a more common Christmas dinner among the working classes. Turkey production in the UK was historically centered in East Anglia using two breeds, the Norfolk Black and the Norfolk Bronze. These would be driven as flocks to markets in London from the 17th century onwards. More recently, the great majority of domesticated turkeys are bred to have white feathers because their pin feathers (the developing feathers on the skin) are less visible when the carcass is prepared for cooking although brown- or bronze-feathered turkey varieties are still also raised. By 1620 it was common enough for the Mayflower's hundred or so English Pilgrim settlers in Massachusetts to bring turkeys with them from England, unaware that it had a larger close relative already occupying the forests where they set up home. Ironically, though, this Mexican subspecies, one of the smallest, is thought to be critically endangered in the wild compared to its domesticated cousins that are today one of the most abundant farmed birds in the world.

❖　❖　❖

Like most game birds such as pheasants and grouse, turkeys aren't much into nest design and adornment; a shallow scrape in a hidden spot on the ground is all that is required for their usually large clutch of eggs, an average of eight to 15. It is not unusual for a turkey nest to contain as many as 30 eggs because more than one female can lay them in the same one! The poults, as the young are called, are ready to leave the nest very soon after hatching; they feed themselves on insects for their first few weeks, staying close to mum. A brood usually remains with its mother for about six months.

Turkeys, much like their close relatives and game birds in general, aren't blessed with much vocal talent; no songs or musical calls, just a range of what are rather euphemistically referred to as 'vocalisations'. 'Gobbles', 'clucks', 'putts', 'purrs', 'yelps', 'whines', 'cackles' and 'kee-kees' are words frequently used to describe them. Ron Nelsen, and other hunters like him, could probably copy most or all of these calls using their turkey callers. And they probably need to. In early spring, male turkeys gobble loudly to announce their presence to females and competing males. The gobble can carry long distances. Males also emit a low-pitched drumming sound produced by the movement of air in the air sac in their chest. In addition they make a sound known as the 'spit' which is a sharp expulsion of air from this very same sac. Hens yelp to let gobblers know their location. Yet more confusingly, gobblers often yelp in the manner of females, and hens can gobble, though they rarely do so. Immature males – the jakes – often yelp too.

Wild Turkeys have evolved into habitat generalists; maybe they were seemingly more confined to forests a few centuries back simply because forests then dominated the land. They prefer hardwood and mixed conifer-hardwood forests but need scattered openings such as pastures, orchards and seasonal marshes – even large fields or other open areas – in which they spend much of their time feeding. In the northeastern US, turkeys are most abundant in hardwood forests of oak and hickory or forests of red oak, beech, cherry and white ash. Nearer the coast and in the eastern US, clearings, farms, and plantations, often along rivers and cypress swamps are generally more favoured.

Omnivorous, turkeys forage on the ground or climb shrubs and small trees to feed. They prefer eating acorns, nuts, and stripping leaves and twigs off various trees including hazel, chestnut, hickory and pinyon pine as well as various seeds, berries such as juniper and bearberry, roots and insects. They also occasionally consume larger insects, amphibians, snails and even small reptiles such as lizards and snakes. Acorns are particularly sought after in forests in the autumn, and in a five-year study in Virginia and West Virginia states quoted by DGIF's Gary Norman, adult survival rates were higher during years with good acorn and other mast crops. In pastures, they will feed on grasses and other plants and sometimes visit bird feeders and scavenge seed left behind when crops are harvested. And while early morning, two to three hours after leaving their roost, and late afternoon – mainly two to three hours before sunset – are their peak times for eating, turkeys can be seen feeding at almost any time, often in groups. This wide-ranging diet, though, does bring them into conflict with farmers and with fruit growers. Most damage is slight but for silage corn, grapes, ginseng, apples, and wheat crops, the damage can occasionally be moderate or heavy.

While man has very obviously been the main predator of these impressive birds by a large margin, some other animals do kill them. Predators of both adults and young include Coyotes, Bobcats, cougars, eagles and (with the exception of adult males) Great Horned Owls, domestic dogs and Red Foxes. A five-year study led by DGIF in Virginia found that the annual mortality rate of hen turkeys averaged 52% but varied between years with a high of 66% during one year. Juvenile hen mortality was even higher. After the brood-rearing season, the leading cause of hen mortality was predation (53% of all mortalities) followed by illegal poaching losses (18%); other losses such as accidents and diseases (17%) while legal hunting accounted for just 12% of all deaths. As with hens, tom annual mortality rates also vary; studies in Virginia have estimated annual mortality of adult males to range from 46% to 69%. Nesting on the ground, it is perhaps not surprising that a larger range of predators will take turkey eggs and nestlings – an equally good feed considering one nest can contain so many eggs – including raccoons, possums, skunks, foxes, birds of prey, marmot-like Groundhogs, even snakes.

When approached by potential predators, turkeys and their poults usually run away and will fly usually only short distances if pressed, often into a tree. But adult turkeys are no walkover. Occasionally if cornered, they will try to fight off predators and large male toms can be especially aggressive in self defence. They can kick with their legs, using the spurs on the back of the legs as weapons, bite with their beak and ram with their relatively large bodies. They are quite capable of deterring predators up to the size of foxes or even larger. Occasionally, too, turkeys may behave aggressively towards humans, especially in areas where natural habitats are scarce, though attacks can usually be avoided by giving the birds a respectful amount of space and keeping outdoor spaces free of anything they might be interested in eating.

The heaviest Wild Turkey ever recorded, according to the NWTF, weighed nearly 17 kg although weights of up to 14 kg, while uncommon, are not rare. After the Trumpeter Swan, the turkey has the second heaviest maximum weight of any North American bird. Despite their weight and bulky appearance, Wild Turkeys, unlike their domestic counterparts, are surprisingly agile fliers. In an ideal habitat of open woodland or wooded grasslands, they can fly perfectly safely beneath the tree canopy and find perches. Their flights are usually short, no more than maybe a few hundred metres at a time. After all, flying must use up a big slice of energy for such heavy birds. Running is more of a speciality; they are estimated to reach 20 km per hour, not bad for such a big bird and approaching the sprint speeds of many human athletes.

Turkeys have a keen sense of vision and they can easily detect movements. With eyes on the sides of their head, they have monocular vision that provides a wide field of view but little depth. To compensate for their lack of depth perception, turkeys frequently move their heads from side to side to get a better look. They also have a remarkable ability to hear and locate sounds but a poor sense of taste and smell.

Male turkeys are notoriously promiscuous, mating with as many hens as they can. Courtship, mainly in March and April, is a pretty spectacular event. The toms display for the smaller, more brown and dark grey hens by puffing out their feathers, fanning out their tails and dragging their wings, a behaviour not surprisingly known as strutting. It is then that their heads and necks become coloured brilliantly with red, blue and white, the colours changing with the turkey's mood, a solid white head and neck indicating maximum excitement. Males often court in groups with the dominant male doing most of the gobbling, spreading his tail feathers, strutting, drumming, booming and spitting.

Life isn't easy for the younger tom turkeys; they might be sexually mature but they have to fight older males to get any chance of establishing themselves in the very hierarchical turkey society. And these fights can be vicious. Contests sometimes last for a couple of hours with the birds hitting each other with their powerful wings and attacking with the sharp spurs on the back of their legs. Rarely is a bird killed, but certainly it does happen. The hens establish a hierarchy too but, in common with females of most species, it is a much gentler affair with no fighting.

❖ ❖ ❖

Not surprisingly – because of their size, their incredible courtship routines and because they were originally abundant – turkeys always played a significant role in the cultures of many Native American tribes. Eastern tribes consumed both the eggs and the meat, sometimes turning the latter into a type of jerky – trimmed of its fat, cut into strips, and dried – to preserve it and make it last through cold winter weather when food was scarce. Some tribes provided turkey-displaying habitat by burning down portions of forest to create artificial meadows which would attract mating birds and thus give a clear arrow shot for hunters. The feathers of turkeys also often made their way into the rituals and headgear of many tribes; leaders such as Catawba chiefs traditionally wore turkey feather headdresses. Significant peoples of several tribes, including the Muscogee Creek and Wampanoag tribes, wore turkey feather cloaks.

The courtship displays of Wild Turkeys inspired the turkey dances of the native Caddo nation, a confederacy of several southeastern Native American tribes who traditionally inhabited much of what is now east Texas, northern Louisiana and parts of southern Arkansas and Oklahoma. Women do the dancing while the men drum and sing the songs which describe events in Caddo history. The dance takes place in the afternoon and finishes by sunset, the time when turkeys return to their roosts. Caddos traditionally founded their villages and camps near turkey roosts because the turkeys served as sentinels, making noises when people approached. The turkey dances are an ancient tradition and there are several stories about their origins. One explanation is that a Caddo man, hunting in the forest, heard singing. The source was a group of turkey hens dancing in a circle around a tom so the hunter carefully observed and memorised the dance to share with his tribe when he returned. The Caddo have continuously maintained the turkey dance; it enjoyed a revival after World War II and still takes place today at the Caddo tribal centre in Binger, Oklahoma.

In another tradition, this one begun by European white settlers, the turkey has become a symbol of Thanksgiving in the US and Canada. Celebrated on the fourth Thursday of November in the US and on the second Monday of October in Canada, Thanksgiving celebrations would be rather bland if the feast did not include a turkey. The Thanksgiving holiday's history in North America is rooted in English traditions dating from the Protestant Reformation. It also has aspects of a harvest festival, even though the harvest in New England occurs well before the late November date on which the modern Thanksgiving holiday is celebrated. It is intended to remind everyone of the four wild fowls eaten at the first Thanksgiving feast in 1621 at Plymouth in present day Massachusetts. This 1621 feast and thanksgiving were prompted by a good harvest that year following on from a devastating winter during which around half of the Mayflower's settlers died. To show their gratitude, they called for a feast where they invited the local Native American tribe leader along with other Native Americans who had helped them sow and harvest their crops. Roasted deer, turkeys and other wild game were eaten amongst other food.

There are, though, plenty of disputes about the origin of Thanksgiving; an alternative to the Plymouth story is that the earliest Thanksgiving service in the Americas was celebrated by the Spanish on 8 September 1565, in what is now Saint Augustine, Florida. And in 1578, the English explorer Martin Frobisher held a ceremony and feast after establishing a settlement in the province now called Newfoundland and Labrador in today's Canada. It was organised to give thanks to God for surviving the long journey from England. Whether they ate turkey, no one knows. In 1777, the first official Thanksgiving Proclamation was issued by the Continental Congress, the governing body of the US during the American Revolution.

The idea that Benjamin Franklin (1706–1790), one of the Founding Fathers of the US, would have preferred the turkey to be the national US bird rather than the Bald Eagle comes from a letter he wrote to his daughter Sarah Bache in 1784 in which he considered the turkey a better choice. He never expressed that view in public, though, and the Bald Eagle was adopted. George Washington, the first President of independent America proclaimed a nationwide Thanksgiving Day on 26 November 1789 'as a day of public thanksgiving and prayer to be observed by acknowledging with grateful hearts the many and signal favours of Almighty God.' From then on, Thanksgiving is marked as a day to have a grand family feast comprising turkey, mashed potatoes, pumpkin pie and other delicacies.

For most Americans, farm-raised, domestic turkeys are the norm at Thanksgiving, as they are throughout much of the world at Christmas and other times. Each year, US turkey growers expect to raise around 270 million turkeys valued as meat at about $8 billion, with one third of all turkey consumption occurring in the Thanksgiving to Christmas season. Intensive farming of turkeys in the US and Europe from the late 1940s dramatically cut the price, making the meat more affordable for the working classes. With the availability of refrigeration, whole turkeys could be shipped frozen to distant markets. Later advances in disease control increased production even more. Advances in shipping, changing consumer preferences and the proliferation of commercial poultry plants has made fresh turkey inexpensive as well as readily available almost worldwide.

But how is it that two birds, the Wild Turkey and the Ocellated Turkey, both confined to the Americas, come to be named after a country in Southeast Europe where turkeys have never existed? It might be because the newly discovered Americas were then believed to be part of Asia and there was a tendency to attribute exotic animals and foods to exotic far-off places such as Turkey. Or maybe it was because the first English settlers were familiar with guineafowl (from West Africa), which they knew as 'turkey coq' because they were imported by Turkish merchants. Spotting their first wild fowl in the woods of the eastern US or in the hands of a Powhatan Indian, the settlers decided to name this new bird they'd never before seen after the African bird, assuming it was just a bigger version. And what is the turkey called in Turkey? It's called 'hindi', one of the main languages of India! It couldn't be more confusing.

❖ ❖ ❖

By the early 1900s, of its original range, Wild Turkeys had gone from 18 states and could rarely be found in the others. According to figures compiled by the National Wild Turkey Federation, centuries of habitat destruction and excessive commercial harvesting had reduced them by the time of the Great Depression (1929–1934) to fewer than 30,000 in the entire US. Before white settlers arrived, the continent had maybe ten million.

But a natural rebound had begun, albeit initially very locally. The agricultural practices of the late 1800s and early 1900s had exhausted the soil's natural fertility and limited crop productivity. Once productivity declined, farmland was abandoned and farmers migrated to cities for industrial jobs. These neglected farmlands developed scrub and trees, slowly developing back into forest which encouraged all wildlife, including turkeys, to reoccupy the regenerating habitats. Game officials made efforts to protect and encourage the breeding of the surviving turkey population, and some trapped birds were relocated to new areas, including some in the western states where the bird was not native. Many populations were relocated to be close to farmland where spilt grain and berry-bearing shrubs seemed to attract them.

But these well meaning efforts were scattered and variably effective. Early laws to help protect dwindling wildlife helped. The Lacey Act, introduced by Iowa Congressman John Lacey in the spring of 1900, for instance, limited trade in wild animals and plants, prohibited the interstate sale of killed wildlife, introduced substantial fines for offences, and authorised the Secretary of Interior to give aid to restoring game and birds in parts of the US where they had become extinct or rare. Federal approval of the Weeks Act in 1911 made it possible to purchase and protect deforested land in Virginia and begin forest restoration on what were later to become National Forest Lands, gradually protecting large forested areas for turkey habitat.

The need for Wild Turkey conservation led to the passage of the 'Robin Bill' in Virginia in 1912 which prohibited the sale on the open market of Wild Turkey and several other species of birds. But effective enforcement of these laws and other legislation restricting hunting methods and bag limits didn't come until 1916 with the creation of Virginia's Game Department. The next milestone in turkey conservation in Virginia came in 1929 when the Virginia Game Commission (the forerunner of the DGIF) began a restocking programme using turkeys captured in the wild and bred in enclosures at game farms. It turned out that turkey breeding was pretty straightforward and a considerable effort was invested in breeding, raising, and releasing game farm turkeys between 1930 and 1955. The Pittman-Robertson Act of 1937 put a tax on the purchase of sporting goods and ammunition. That cash, matched with other money from the issue of hunting licences, provided funding for such recovery programmes for the first time. With these resources, other states started to do much the same and in 1937 the Biological Survey (the forerunner of today's US Fish and Wildlife Service) began coordinating turkey restoration across the country.

In Virginia alone, well over 20,000 game farm turkeys were raised and released. In the final analysis however, very little if any credit can be given to these efforts at re-establishing Wild Turkey populations in any locality in Virginia. Released birds were ill-suited to searching out their own food and ill-equipped to protect themselves from predators. Many had also contracted diseases in confined rearing pens prior to release. Most of the birds died and millions of dollars and two decades of effort had been wasted. 'So, in 1955, a new procedure was developed in which native turkeys were caught in traps baited with grain, or by firing rocket-propelled nets over them, and transferred directly to other areas with suitable habitat. There was no captive breeding. This method proved highly successful and, from then until 1993, nearly 900 Wild Turkeys were trapped and relocated in Virginia,' says Gary Norman of Virginia's DGIF. They proved to be the nuclei of newly established and thriving turkey populations.

In New York State by the early 1900s, farming – which had occupied three quarters of the state's land area a century earlier – began to decline. Old farm fields, beginning with those on the infertile hilltops, gradually reverted to scrub, then woodland. By the late 1940s, much of southern New York State was again capable of supporting turkeys and, around 1948, Wild Turkeys from a small remnant population in northern Pennsylvania decided to cross the border into western New York State. The first birds had taken up residence in the state after an absence of a century. Their return sparked an interest in restoring them to all of New York State. In 1952 and over the next eight years, over 3,000 game farm reared turkeys were released throughout the state. But, as in Virginia, they either died or, if they survived, their breeding proved poor and their populations failed to expand. In the west of the state, though, the turkeys from Pennsylvania had re-established healthy breeding populations and were expanding rapidly; in 1959 a programme began to net-trap wild birds where they were becoming abundant for release elsewhere in New York State where there were none. A typical release consisted of eight to ten females and four to five males. These birds would form the nucleus of a new flock and generally were all that was necessary to re-establish a new breeding population.

Since the first turkeys were trapped, about 1,400 birds have been moved within New York State. Today, their numbers have increased dramatically and the state's turkey population is around 300,000 birds. In addition, New York has sent almost 700 turkeys to seven other northeastern US states as well as to Ontario in Canada, helping to re-establish populations throughout the northeast.

The same good news story has been repeated across the US and southern Canada. By 1973 when the NWTF was founded in Virginia, due to natural recovery augmented with translocations of wild-caught birds, the US population had rebounded to an estimated 1.5 million. Today, the Eastern Wild Turkey, the subspecies with the largest range, numbers well over five million birds and the Rio Grande subspecies well over one million; the Florida (or Osceola) subspecies is up to 100,000 birds; Merriam's numbers are around 350,000; and Gould's is limited to around 800. That means that the North American continent now has an estimated 6.7 million Wild Turkeys. 'Turkey censuses are something of an inexact science, with harvest trends probably being the most reliable index for population monitoring, but that's about as good a guess as we have,' says Tom Hughes, NWTF Wildlife Biologist and Assistant Vice President for Conservation Programs.

The comeback of the Wild Turkey is arguably the greatest conservation success story of a species anywhere. From a low point of about 30,000 and a total absence of birds over a vast proportion of their former territory, today Wild Turkeys occur in every US state except Alaska (although they aren't native to Hawaii, they were introduced there in 1788). In Virginia, as in many US states where lowland forests and farmland predominate, there is little shortage of turkey habitat; only in the more dense urban areas and on intensively managed farmland are the birds absent.

The NWTF, though, still has some concerns. It claims that the US is 'losing' over two million acres of critical wildlife habitat each year, an area equivalent to the Yellowstone National Park. Much of this is land developed for housing, industry and infrastructure; the rest probably lost to more intensive farming. And some local turkey populations have declined in the last few years. For example, according to NWTF, New York State is facing a 20-year low in turkey numbers and Mississippi's turkey populations declined by more than 40% in the five years up to 2009. In Virginia, there is some concern about their numbers having fallen in state-managed forests. DGIF puts this down primarily to a reduction in habitat diversity; with less timber harvesting there are fewer open areas for turkey feeding. Longer term changes, as matured trees are felled or are left to fall naturally, are likely to cause an upsurge again in their numbers as part of the natural cycle of all forests.

'There's a growing sentiment in the turkey world that they are somehow regulated by the density of their populations. Perhaps it's a biological thing where brood survival is best where the brood habitat is better and maybe good brood habitat is being lost. Weather can seriously affect brood survival year on year but the more important question is the long-term trend in turkey densities. There isn't a simple answer,' comments Gary Norman.

'We really don't know for sure what is causing the recent declines,' says the NWTF's Tom Hughes. 'Most likely, like the declines in bobwhite quail in recent decades, there are a number of factors at work. As the population gets more abundant maybe their productivity is declining. Unusually wet springs in recent years certainly could be a major factor as well. These might combine with land development and changing timber management practices, and they may come together as a "perfect storm" affecting turkey populations.'

As Wild Turkey numbers have rebounded, hunting has been legalised in all US states. Hunting under licence is commonplace once more and licences are comparatively cheap. Regulations vary from state to state but several allow a restricted number to be shot per hunter in a short spring season and again in autumn. In Virginia, turkey hunting is second only to deer hunting in popularity. After decades of conservation effort, and failures along the way, the Wild Turkey has been re-instated across its former range. Licensed hunters can, once more, bring a wild turkey rather then a farm-raised bird home for their families at Thanksgiving. No other animal highlighted in this book has made a comeback in such huge numbers.

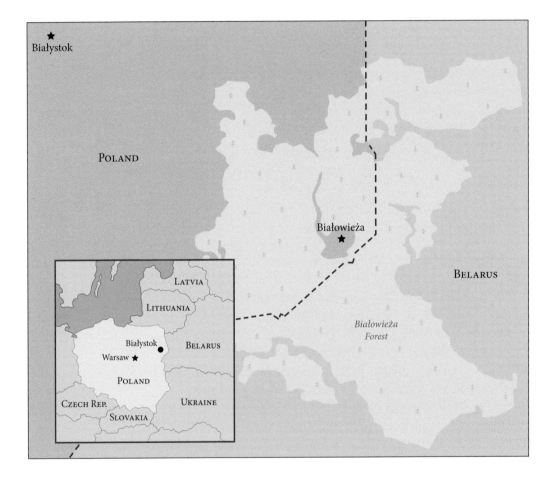

5

THE FOREST EMPEROR RETURNS

EUROPEAN BISON

Hunted for millennia, only two populations of Europe's largest living land mammal, the European Bison – in eastern Poland and southern Russia – survived into the 20th century. By the 1920s they were gone too; the mammal was extinct in the wild. Fewer than 50 survived in zoos and from these a herd was slowly rebuilt and eventually reintroduced to Europe's last great natural forest, Białowieża in eastern Poland. Bringing this giant back from the brink is a story of determination. Today, 1,000 European Bison roam in Białowieża's stunning forest and there are another 3,600 living wild in other populations across Europe or held in captivity.

After two hours of searching from our Jeep, peering across little meadows in the post-dawn mist and driving along narrow forest tracks squeezed between dense-growing oaks, hornbeams and spruce, we had almost given up hope. 'I think the mist this morning is causing us difficulties to see any. But this is nature; sometimes we see several, other times none,' says Michal Krzysiak rather philosophically. Michal is the Białowieża National Park's vet who is guiding me in our search. With around 500 European Bison roaming the Polish side of this forest, animals weighing up to a ton and the size of a large cow, it is all too easy to assume that they are straightforward to find. But this is the largest remaining primaeval forest in Europe, well over 600 km² of it in Poland and much the same on the Belarus side of the border. A few hundred bison suddenly seem rather like the veritable needle in a haystack.

But our luck changes – and rather dramatically. Bumping slowly along another spruce and oak-shaded track, we suddenly lurch to a standstill. It's Michal who spots it first and can't hide his pleasure. 'Look, just there, a three or four year old bull bison!' And what a magnificent sight, Europe's largest land animal 30 metres away, his massive, horned head turned towards us. Watching us watching him. And he doesn't move for what seems like a couple of minutes, giving us a superb, close-up view. Slowly, he walks away, nonchalantly looking back to check us out as we creep a little further along the track to try not to lose sight of him. Then, almost as suddenly as he appeared, he's gone, faded into the shadows of the larger trees, his dark chocolate brown body hidden now by the shrubby saplings that will some day become this forest's giants. A little under a century ago, it would not have been possible to find any bison in this huge forest; they had all been shot. European Bison were extinct in the wild.

Historically, the range of this bison – less well known, maybe, than its cousin, the American bison (or buffalo), courtesy of old, black and white 'cowboy and Indian' films – covered most of lowland Europe from the French Massif Central as far east as western and southern Russia, maybe further east still. Its range decreased as human populations expanded and farmed larger and larger areas of land, confining bison to what forests remained and to more remote regions. By the 8th century they were largely gone from France, the Low Countries and the western part of today's Germany, except for some isolated populations in less inhabited regions such as the Vosges in the east of France, where they lasted maybe until the 15th century. In the 11th century they became extinct in Sweden and the last European Bison in what is now Romania died in 1790.

In Poland, however, bison in the Białowieża Forest were the property of the Polish kings, at least until 1795 when Poland was unceremoniously wiped off the map by its neighbouring countries. 'By the 14th century, Białowieża was set aside as a royal forest and by the 16th century 300 royal wardens were employed to keep it free of intruders, of illegal logging and to stop any animal poaching,' says Professor Tomasz Wesołowski of Wrocław University who has studied the place for 30 years. 'Core areas reserved only for monarchs were designated too. Despite numerous dramatic historical twists, this management system was in operation for nearly 500 years and allowed a large area of natural lowland forest to persist until the beginning of the 20th century.'

Draconian measures were introduced to protect it. In 1538, King Sigismund II Augustus instituted the death penalty for poaching a European Bison here. And in the early 19th century when the forest was part of Russia, its zars also retained old Polish laws protecting them. Nevertheless, habitat degradation and fragmentation due to agricultural development, forest logging and illegal hunting were the probable reasons for a steady decline in bison numbers through the 19th century. A burgeoning deer population probably didn't help either; there's a finite amount of ground vegetation and shrubs to graze even in a forest as large as this.

Only the Białowieża population – numbering maybe 700 – and one population in the Caucasus (today part of the Russian Federation) survived into the 20th century after which the 1917 Russian Revolution and World War I finished them off, albeit indirectly. Occupying German troops killed 600 bison in the Białowieża Forest for sport and for their meat, hides and horns while, at the end of the war, retreating German soldiers shot all but nine animals. The last wild European Bison in Poland was killed in 1919 and the last one in the world was killed by poachers in 1927 in the western Caucasus. By that year fewer than 50 remained, all of them in zoos and private collections.

❖ ❖ ❖

The 'fightback' started in 1923 when the International Society for the Protection of the European Bison was founded with no less than 16 countries participating. A breeding programme with captive bison was started but without genetic knowledge the animal breeders could only check the pedigree of an animal to prove it was a pure European bison and not a hybrid with American bison. They had no ability to determine how genetically diverse the breeding population was. As breeding progressed, the details of every bison in the programme were registered with details of its age, sex and parentage where known: a studbook. Today a studbook is essential for any breeding programme that will eventually lead to reintroduction of a species into the wild. Without it, it is impossible to know to what extent the animals are related and therefore how much genetic diversity exists in the population. It's a core part of IUCN's advice on all such reintroductions. The theory is that the more genetically diverse (derived today from DNA analysis) reintroduced animals are – the less they are related to one another – the more likely it is that some will survive if a new disease strikes or environmental conditions change.

But compiling the register for bison proved to be a somewhat daunting task. There were just 54 of them in the world and most of those were past breeding age. Furthermore, these 29 males and 25 females originated from just 12 wild ancestors. And only seven of these – four bulls and three cows – were guaranteed pure bred animals of the type found in Białowieża, considered then to be physically slightly different from those that used to inhabit the Russian Caucasus (today the Caucasian and Bialowieza populations are known to be different subspecies). Genetic variety was not exactly available in bucket-loads to help the European Bison. A reintroduced herd would have to be bred from just seven animals; they were the founders of the revived population. All the same, by 1929, bison were again in the Białowieża forest, albeit in a small, confined reserve where they were kept for breeding. By 1939, the herd had grown to 16 animals.

Others, though, had different ideas about how to breed them. An attempt to 'increase' the production of European Bison by crossing them with European and American Bison hybrids was promoted by Nazi officials of the Third Reich, seemingly quite contrary to their normal obsession with racial purity. These hybrids were killed during the final phase of World War II in1945. But there was a larger, more predictable setback over the years of World War II, a time of enormous social turmoil in Eastern Europe. Bison suffered a steep decline, the population dropping from 160 animals in 1943 to 93 in 1946 because of hunting and accidental killing.

'Over the years since, the stud or pedigree book has proved invaluable. It is still published annually and is kept up to date by the Białowieża National Park Authority here in Poland,' comments Dr Katarzyna Daleszczyk, a bison expert at the national park. With some exceptions, the stud book continues to list individually most animals kept in enclosed breeding centres wherever they are but only the size (sometimes divided by sex) of free-ranging herds. Every individually registered animal has a pedigree number, name, details of parentage and the name of its breeder or actual owner. It is the only source of information about the genealogy of the species' global population from the beginning of its restitution in the 1920s to the present day.

By the early 1970s, successful breeding and more releases had brought the population in Białowieża up to 200. By 2013, 500 bison were roaming the Polish part of the great forest with another 450 in the Belarus half; since the early 1980s, the border between Poland and Belarus within the forest (a length of more than 50 km) has been fenced, making mixing of the two populations impossible, a situation that will only change if there is substantial political revision. Poland is an EU member state while Belarus, formerly part of the USSR, is today a Member of the Commonwealth of Independent States. Poland's border here at Białowieża marks the eastern extremity of the EU. On both sides of the border, sections of the forest are designated as national parks. And while much of the forest within these National Parks is managed commercially – highly controversial and the subject of a great deal of criticism from conservationists – forestry interests claim that it is managed sympathetically with wildlife a priority. There is no evidence that any forestry practices here are causing bison a problem.

Since the end of World War II, nearly 500 bison have been captured in the Białowieża Forest and moved to form the basis of new populations reintroduced elsewhere in Europe within their original range. Today, as a result of such reintroductions, European Bison occur in free-ranging and semi-free herds in Lithuania, the Russian Federation, Ukraine, Germany, Denmark, the Netherlands, Romania, Slovakia and some of the smaller Commonwealth of Independent States countries. And captive populations are distributed in at least 30 countries worldwide, mostly in zoos and safari parks. The latest reintroduction took place in early 2014 when 17 bison from several different populations across Europe were released in forested mountains in western Romania. 'Europe-wide today there are approximately 4,663 bison, about 40% of them in zoos and other breeding centres, the rest wild, though some are within large confined areas of land,' says Katarzyna Daleszczyk. That compares with about 15,000 wild American Bison within their natural range in North America, though there are many more in captive commercial populations and on several thousand privately owned ranches.

Frans Schepers, managing director of Rewilding Europe, the Netherlands-based charity behind the release said: 'It has a big symbolic value, bringing back animals. Releasing animals, giving them space, is a sign of hope, it shows that if we choose, we can help wildlife come back.'

❖   ❖   ❖

How is it that there are two very similar looking species of bison widely separated from each other on two continents; the American Bison, or Buffalo, in North America and the European Bison in Europe? The answer is that the two almost certainly had a common ancestor – a very long time ago – and the two species, because of their lengthy separation, have evolved slightly differently into what we recognise as two different species.

Their story begins in southern Asia during the Pliocene, two million to five million years ago. From fossil remains we know that from the late Pliocene a type of bison was widespread throughout the temperate zones of Asia and Europe, crossing the Bering Strait to North America. Different forms started to develop depending on geography.

The American, or Plains, Bison evolved on the treeless grasslands in the northern US but was hunted mercilessly by white settlers akin to their hunting of Wild Turkeys (see Chapter 4); the 40 million at the dawn of the 19th century decreased, incredibly, to 800 by 1895. Maybe 15 thousand remain wild today. Wood Bison, closely related to the American Bison, occupying colder lands further north – mainly in Canada – were also massacred but their population has also recovered somewhat. There maybe 10,000 wild today though the two often inter-breed.

The European Bison, meanwhile, became divided into the lowland subspecies (the one in Białowieża) and the Caucasian Bison, which became extinct in 1927. Due to some crossbreeding in captivity between the last surviving Caucasian female and males of the lowland subspecies, there are Caucasian genes in some European Bison today. But these are confined to small numbers at a few locations, mainly in parts of the Caucasus.

The European Bison is the heaviest surviving wild land animal in Europe, an adult male weighing up to 840 kg (with occasional big bulls weighing a little over a 1,000 kg), the females much less. A typical adult is up to 3.5 metres in body length and up to two metres tall. On average, it is slightly lighter in body mass and yet taller at the shoulder than the American Bison with shorter hair on the neck, head and forequarters, but with a longer tail and horns. Both have dark grey-brown body hair.

But never imagine that their size implies an awkward lumbering beast. They might walk slowly but European Bison are surprisingly agile and can clear three metre wide streams or two metre high fences from a standing start. Much more unpredictable in behaviour, European Bison are less easily tamed than their American cousins.

Herd animals, larger groups are led usually by an older cow and consist of adult females, calves, young aged two to three years and young adult bulls. The herd size is dependent on environmental factors and averages 13, though it can range from eight animals up to 20. European Bison herds are not family units; they are never permanent because different herds frequently interact, combine and split after exchanging individuals; and they don't defend their territories either. Older bulls live a solitary life for the bulk of the year; occasionally two bulls will live together.

It is only with recent advances in telemetry that radio collaring has been feasible to allow researchers to find out how far herds move, their composition and how much of the Białowieża forest they use. From this research it seems that a herd has a home range (outside winter when they stray less) of about 100 km²; young bulls range over maybe 40 km² while older bulls cover territory twice this size. In total, Białowieża's bison occupy up to 70% of the forest area, more or less all of the habitat attractive to them, which usually has to include meadows for grazing and water sources.

Cows can breed when they are between four and 20 years old; the males between six and 12 years. The rutting season when they mate is from August through to October and during that time younger bulls, though sexually mature, are often prevented from mating by the older bulls. Gestation lasts about nine months and typically the cows give birth from May to July, producing one calf; male calves weigh around 27 kg at birth, females less, and both are reddish brown in colour. They are licked intensively by the mother, can stand up within half an hour, suckle within an hour or so, and stay with the mother – and its herd – well into its second year before becoming independent.

Like domestic cattle, bison are ruminants, so they are adapted to eat a wide variety of plant food; predominantly grasses, flowering plants and leafy shrubs on the forest floor although they will also browse on shoots and leaves, while bark off trees is no more than a minor addition. Oak acorns are a particular favourite in years when there's a good crop. Bark stripping is usually worse as winter gives way to spring and the forest ground vegetation still hasn't appeared. But they also take bark in midwinter if they don't have access to hay, concentrating their efforts mainly on hornbeam, hazel, birch and willows. In the summer, an adult male can consume over 30 kg of food in a day. They need to drink daily and in winter they often break ice with their heavy hooves to get access to it. Bison have a particular liking for open glades and cut hay meadows, where they will frequently graze at night and in the early morning. They will also take a substantial interest in crops grown outside the forest too, older males in particular being difficult to shift if they've found a tasty area of rapeseed or cereals.

For bison, eating takes up much of their lives. In the summer, they spend about 60% of their time feeding, the remainder resting and roaming. The situation is reversed in winter (when the Białowieża animals are fed with hay) and they spend about 30% of their day feeding. They feed intensively before sunrise to fill up their massive, four-chambered stomachs after a night-time rest. Then they sit down, chewing the cud (the food regurgitated from their stomachs) all over again. This feed, rest, chew, re-feed regime they repeat throughout the day.

Feeding herds are usually led by experienced females and never stay long in one place. So their local impact on the forest plants is slight. For such huge heavy animals, bison have a light touch; it's often very difficult to spot the route a herd has taken by looking for trails on the ground.

Living for up to 30 years in captivity, their lifespan in the wild is shorter, maybe 15–25 years. That's not the result of predation; no other animal can attack and successfully kill an adult bison. Brown bears might be able to kill a calf but there are no bears left in Białowieża. According to recent research, most bison die because of trauma injuries, injuries caused by other bison, disease and poaching.

❖　❖　❖

So what is so unique about the Białowieża forest that makes it home to the world's largest European Bison herd? In short, Białowieża is the best-preserved lowland natural forest in Europe with an exceptionally rich range of plants and animals that has changed little over the centuries. One large part of it is left completely natural with no forest management. Here, any old-age trees that fall, any storm damage or other changes that take place naturally are allowed to happen without interference. It is one of the very few areas of forest in Europe left to its own devices. The bulk of the forest is managed commercially, though with sensitivity to wildlife as a primary objective and has numerous wildlife reserves designated within it ensuring limited or no forestry operations.

The forest boasts well over 1,000 different plant species, over 4,000 different fungi, and over 700 lichens, mosses, liverworts and slime moulds. Many of the fungi are rare or extinct in other managed forests because they are utterly dependent on dead timber which is usually cleared away, altering their natural appearance and limiting their biodiversity. In Białowieża however, decomposing timber, the richest habitat in any forest, often abounds; as a result, a cornucopia of fungi and vast numbers of wood-boring beetles and other invertebrates burgeon. Split-open tree stumps and fallen tree trunks might look like battlefield corpses but are the basis for much of the forest's wildlife. Around 10,000 different species of invertebrate live here, maybe more. No one has checked them all out. Seemingly, though, that total does include well over 20 different mosquito species, all of them keen to alight on an unsuspecting bare arm for a feed.

In places, the towering tree canopy of oaks, limes, ash and spruce soars to 40 or 50 metres and some of the largest trees are thought to be well over 500 years old. There are nearly 30 different tree species, from poplar and hornbeam to alder and hazel. Streamside marshes, open pools, sedge beds, glades and small meadows add to the diversity, leaving little doubt that this is one of the wildlife wonders of Eastern Europe. In spring the forest is alive with the harsh calls and drumming of woodpeckers – virtually all of Europe's woodpeckers abound here – the songs of warblers and the evocative flutes of shy Golden Orioles. Like the orioles, they are not frequently seen but Białowieża is also home to Elk, Red and Roe Deer, Wild Boar, Lynx, wolf, Stone and Pine Martens, Otters, beavers and numerous bats – as well as to bison. The whole of northeastern Europe was originally covered by ancient woodland similar to this.

Until about the 14th century, travel here was limited to river routes; roads and bridges appeared much later. Limited hunting rights were granted throughout the forest in the 14th century and in the 15th century it became the property of King Vladislaus II. It was declared a hunting reserve in 1541 to protect bison. In 1639, King Vladislaus IV issued the Białowieża royal forest decree which freed all peasants living there in exchange for their service as royal foresters. Until the late 17th century, when several small villages were established for the development of local iron-ore deposits and tar production, the place was largely uninhabited. From then on until after World War II, the forest and its inhabitants endured periods of huge upheaval and change, the forest being at times exploited for timber and its range of meaty animals including the bison, boar and prolific numbers of deer; at other times it was protected for its inherent wildlife value.

Tsar Alexander II visited in 1860 and locals, following his orders, killed all predators – wolves, bears and lynx – but protected bison, deer and other animals. Bears never returned, though wolves and lynx rebounded. Between 1888 and 1917, the Russian Tsars owned all the forest and had it kept as a royal hunting reserve. They sent bison as gifts to various European capitals, while at the same time populating the forest with deer, moose, and other animals imported from around their empire. The last major tsarist hunt took place here in 1912. During World War I the German occupiers felled substantial numbers of trees – the timber being processed at newly built timber mills – hunted the bison to extinction and depleted the numbers of many other animals. In 1941 the forest was occupied again by German forces. Hermann Göring planned to create the largest hunting reserve in the world here. But, as with several of his grandiose ideas, they came to nothing. After July 1941 the forest became a refuge for both Polish and Soviet partisans, and German forces carried out many mass executions. In July 1944 the area was liberated by the Red Army and, after the war, the forest was divided between Poland and the Belarusian SSR of the then Soviet Union. The Soviet part was put under public administration while Poland reopened the Białowieża National Park in 1947.

Today, Białowieża forest (both the Polish and Belarus sides) is a World Heritage Site, a Biosphere Reserve and the Polish half is a Special Area of Conservation designated by the EU Habitats Directive. Up to 150,000 tourists visit the Polish part of the forest annually. All of it is in state ownership, both in Poland and in Belarus, but in Poland only one sixth of it is designated as a national park, Poland's strictest level of protection. And therein lies a major conflict.

Conservationists are pressing the case to have the whole of the Polish forest designated a national park and all commercial logging stopped (with the exception of small, local supplies for villagers). But forest management is an ancient tradition here and state forestry interests want to continue extracting timber and allow natural tree regeneration. Because of forest management, the number of old age – the largest – trees has fallen drastically; trees are harvested before maturity and this might explain the decline of some woodpecker species. The amount of dead timber left lying on the forest floor has diminished too. And the structure of parts of the forest has altered; there are more young and medium age trees than before.

Many local people still rely on supplies of timber for heating and construction; many have been schooled over generations in managing the forest to obtain timber but, as they see it, protecting the place as a timber repository for future generations too. Several have worked as foresters or still do. And they have a visceral reaction against proposals to extend the national park to cover all of the forest, or even most of it. 'In Poland conservationists are uncommon beings,' comments Adam Wajrak, nature correspondent for Poland's biggest daily paper, *Gazeta Wyborcza* and a Białowieża village resident. 'Polish people are very different to those in the west. They don't save energy. But they are very connected to nature. Most of us have grandparents in the countryside – some farmers, some foresters – and spend holidays there. I am surprised how much emotion comes out. If they tried to cull wolves here, as they did in Sweden, there would be demonstrations in the street.'

'The Białowieża forest is public property; it belongs to all citizens of Poland and not to local communities and foresters,' says Tomasz Wesołowski, an expert on Białowieża's ecology at Wroclaw University. 'The conflict is not between conservationists and foresters as foresters love to frame it, but between stakeholders at large [70% of Poles want the Białowieża forest to be protected] and a small group of people with vested interests in timber exploitation, mainly local foresters and loggers. We propose to protect the whole area as a national park and we see no place for commercial timber production or exploitation there.' He adds, 'The creation of a national park doesn't mean that no exploitation would be allowed. No one proposes to make the whole forest a strictly protected area. There would be some "no enter" zones but otherwise the forest would be open for low impact use (collection of fungi and berries, tourism and research). We also propose to allow limited fuel wood extraction to cover the needs of local communities.'

So far, the Polish government, harangued by foresters and local interests on one side and by conservationists and academics, including international pressure, on the other, is seemingly doing nothing about extending the national park. Wesolowski is far from optimistic. 'It is impossible to enlarge the park in our current legal system in which local community councils have a veto right. They can block establishment or enlargement of the park forever, without giving any reason. It takes only eight people, the majority of the Białowieża commune council, to block enlargement of the park against the will of the rest of society. This is democracy Polish way. We are trying to change this stupid law in the parliament, but so far without success.'

There are other changes afoot, however, whether natural or manmade. Signs of climate warming that could threaten the forest have become more evident. The average annual temperature has risen by 0.8°C over the past 50 years. There is less rain in the summer; winters are milder and end sooner, prompting vegetation to start growing earlier. National park officials say that the level of ground water has fallen in the past three decades causing shallow-rooted spruce to run out of water; spruce numbers are declining.

Wesołowski likes to compare the forest with the Hubble space telescope. 'Hubble revolutionised astronomy by allowing scientists to peer back in time with unprecedented clarity but there's a key difference with Białowieża,' he says. 'If Hubble gets damaged, it can be replaced. This primaeval forest cannot be bought or reconstructed.' And Adam Wajrak has another reason why the forest must be protected: 'We are a country destroyed by wars and here there is not much heritage left apart from nature. This is the one unique thing we can give to the world.'

❖   ❖   ❖

With nearly 1,000 European Bison once again inhabiting the Białowieża forest and over 4,600 of them across Europe, 60% of them living wild, you might well think that there is no reason to be concerned for the future of this huge animal. Unfortunately, that's not quite true. This beast has come a long way since the 1920s when forward looking conservationists across Eastern Europe started putting plans together to bring it back from extinction in the wild. But IUCN regards the European Bison as Vulnerable, a classification that infers the species still faces some risk of extinction.

That's largely because less than one third of all bison are mature animals capable of breeding, a proportion that is increasing. Another consideration is that their whole population is very restricted genetically, having all descended from just seven animals. More worryingly, 80% of existing bison genes come from just two of those founders. So the reintroduced European Bison are even more inbred than previously thought. The question is whether that matters. And opinions differ.

A report compiled in 2011 by Yannick Exalto for Europe's Large Herbivore Network based on the views of 15 bison experts from different countries found that: 'Of the participating experts a majority expressed the view that loss of genetic diversity will be the most urgent future threat for the survival of wild bison herds across Europe.' They concluded that if a more contiguous range for the bison is not created in the future and the populations remain isolated from each other, the loss of the genetic diversity will continue as a result of the increasing degree of inbreeding within those isolated populations. 'It could make them more susceptible to diseases like tuberculosis or foot and mouth disease, maybe caught from cattle; or parasitic diseases from deer perhaps. Because they are so genetically similar, they could all succumb to a disease. If the population was more genetically diverse, there is more chance of survivors,' says Katarzyna Daleszczyk. 'In the 1950s many bison died of foot and mouth disease. And blue tongue disease [an insect-borne, non-contagious viral disease] might also kill them too. Over time our bison will become more genetically diverse and having populations spread in different parts of Europe is also a safeguard because they are less likely to pick up the same disease in very different places.'

But not everyone is pessimistic. Dr Rafał Kowalczyk, Director of the Mammal Research Institute, Poland, is not so worried by their genetic make-up: 'The bison reproduce well and have no abnormalities; I'm not so sure that their restricted genetic mix makes them more susceptible to diseases. There's no scientific evidence to show they are more vulnerable. Some males develop a urinary disease [the cause of which is poorly understood] and these animals can be identified and humanely culled from herds.' After all, Iberian Lynx (Chapter 13) are genetically very restricted too and, in their case, the evidence shows clearly that they always were. When mitochondrial DNA from lynx fossils spanning the last 50,000 years was examined, hardly any genetic variation between the ancient specimens and today's animals was found.

Since the 19th century, maybe earlier, Białowieża's bison have been fed with hay in winter. The practice continues today and is controversial because it means that their winter survival is likely to be artificially high. The herd is not, therefore, truly wild. It also brings animals together in larger numbers and for longer periods than they might do naturally, increasing the possibility of disease spread. 'The winter feeding with hay cut from meadows is now done in more places,' comments Rafał. 'That's better than before when it was done in very few fixed places which meant that up to 100 bison would congregate in one spot. That was too many; it put a social strain on them because natural herds are much smaller and made them more vulnerable to contagious diseases and parasites.' Professor Dr Wanda Olech-Piasecka of Warsaw University of Life Sciences and Chair of IUCN's European Bison Specialist Group comments, 'We monitor the level of parasites and the situation is normal for wild animals. The feeding is not intended to increase their survival but to decrease problems in local agriculture because the bison will feed on crops outside the forest.'

Between 2006 and 2010, an EU-funded project helped to restore nearly 50 ha of forest meadow in Białowieża on which 19 feeding sites designed for winter hay storage and 14 watering sites were created. As a result, the Białowieża population spread out to utilise an additional 200 km² of forest, often extending their range for part of their time outside the forest. Now the groups of bison in winter are much smaller; 50 individuals in a group is often the largest and most are smaller, but Rafał would still like to see more cutting of open glades, meadows and streamsides so that bison have natural places to get food in winter. 'I think we should let the bison look after themselves with no winter feeding,' he says. 'Then the population would be self sustaining and there would be less chance of disease spread because they wouldn't gather into larger than normal groups. Any animals too old or too weak to survive would die naturally.'

But Katarzyna takes a very practical stance. 'Bison are fed here because, if they were not, much more damage would be done to agricultural areas around the forest and to the forest itself causing conflict with both farmers and foresters. Farmers and private forest owners can gain compensation for the damages to their crops and trees,' she argues. 'In Knyszynska Forest [north of Białowieża] there is now a population of about 100 bison but that forest is mainly conifer, so is not too rich in food for them,' she comments. 'Bison are fed there only occasionally and so they often feed in fields adjoining the forest and the number of applications for compensation from farmers is increasing very fast. Between 2004 and 2009 there were 46 applications for compensation but in 2011 alone, 87 applications. Also the total amount of compensation grew drastically, she adds. 'Even with compensation, damage done by bison gives them a bad reputation with landowners and it's harder to reintroduce bison to new areas because they are less accepted. Here in Białowieża we involve local people in winter feeding such as by contracting meadows from farmers in places where bison do damage most often. We have about 40 local farmers in such a scheme; they are paid to prepare hay and leave it for bison in haystacks on the meadows.'

Research published by Emilia Hofman-Kaminska and Rafał Kowalczyk in 2012 found that damage to crops occurred very close to the forest edge; 69% of cases of damage were closer than 500 metres from the forest at Białowieża and 80% in Knyszynska Forest. The majority of the crops damaged by bison were cereals, particularly rye but also hay and oilseed rape.

The lesson from all this is neatly summed up by Katarzyna: 'If you want to have such a huge bison population in a place inhabited also by people [and in our densely populated world it is more and more difficult to find a place big enough and with few people], you have to deal with potential damage. Here the Białowieża National Park's solution is to feed bison to prevent damage.' She adds, 'Hay is left in feeding sites in the forest in special haystacks; it's accessible for bison [and other mammals] so they decide when they start to use it. Not all bison make use of supplementary feeding sites – if the winter is mild and it's a year with lots of acorns, bison prefer to feed on natural food and join feeding sites late. Some spend the whole winter roaming and searching for food by themselves.'

Nevertheless, over several years, the Białowieża bison population has been invaded massively by a blood-sucking nematode carried by deer. Recent research has found that these infections are more severe wherever winter bison herds are largest. The infection causes pathological changes such as fluid build-up in body tissues, excessive blood in vital organs and damage to part of the animal's stomach and duodenum. These effects are most obvious in highly infected calves and they can lead to chronic diarrhoea, deterioration and death of the young animals.

Naturally, bison would graze more in clearings, hay meadows and on croplands in winter, shifting the snow with their feet and heads to get at the vegetation. The forest floor in winter is almost bereft of vegetation and most of the lower shrubs are leafless so there's little for them to eat. As a result of such winter food shortages, the weaker animals and the older animals would die naturally. Because of winter hay feeding, natural mortality is low and several animals are regularly culled in winter to make up for this. 'In Poland, our government gives permission for killing a small number of bison some winters, about 5% of the herd, and we choose old animals, mostly males. In Belarus, hunting is permitted under licence only for male bison older than 12 years and females older than 15 years. It is acceptable when animals not needed for the population are killed and hunters will pay so this is income to cover the cost of management,' comments Wanda Olech-Piasecka.

But it isn't only the limited genetic diversity of wild bison and their disease susceptibility that worries conservationists. In some countries, the reintroduced populations are declining for other reasons. In the Ukraine, peak numbers of bison were reached in the 1990s; 650–700 animals across ten main populations in different parts of the country, mainly in the west. But their protection has been shoddy. Poaching by local people, habitat degradation, foresters aiding hunters from other countries to shoot them and poor selection of animals in state organised culling programmes has sent them into serious decline. Currently about 200 survive. Ukrainian ecologists are calling for responsible government action without which, they say, bison could become extinct a second time round.

❖　❖　❖

Europe today is nothing like the Europe of several thousand years ago when bison and other mammals could roam almost at will over vast areas of forest and marsh. Few areas were put over exclusively to farming. Today's Europe is dominated by farmed land and most forests form islands, albeit sometimes large ones, within it. But islands nevertheless. Poland has several large, wild-living bison populations. In recent years, an EU-funded project has examined, amongst other things, the potential to link up some of these and enhance the chances of more genetic mixing. The Białowieża population in Poland cannot be connected east because of the high fence with Belarus; to the west, intensively managed farmland mitigates against it. But connecting to the north towards the protected Knyszynska Forest where there is a sizeable bison population and to the south to the Mielnik Forest seems feasible. Further studies – and full consultation with local interests – will be needed before this becomes a reality. It would require the cooperation of large numbers of farmers.

There might however be opportunities to reintroduce bison to more mixed habitats that are thinly inhabited. In parts of Eastern Europe abandonment of farms after the collapse of many of the former Communist governments is widespread and in some regions may exceed a fifth of the area of farmland used in socialist times. These abandoned farmlands typically offer a mix of grassland, scrub and woodland. Russia, in particular, has large land areas with only a scattered human population and a considerable amount of abandoned farmland that could offer a huge opportunity for bison reintroduction. Historically, European Bison have been thought of as forest dwellers. But is forest their natural habitat or are they naturally animals of more open land like their American cousins?

The structure of their jaws and teeth suggests that bison are grazers of open ground, akin to domestic cattle, and not such browsers of leafy shrubs like deer. Grasses and other flowering plants make up at least 70% of their diet, obtained mostly on open ground within forests or on its edges; bark and shrub leaves make up only a very small part of their food. And newborn bison, as soon as they can walk after birth, follow the herd – behaviour typical of open land mammals – rather than being hidden for a few days as most forest dwellers do with their offspring. So it's likely that bison were originally animals of more open areas but gradually retreated into forests as land was developed for farming and their lives came under increasing threat from hunting for their meat and skins. Where better to take refuge than a forest? Today, European Bison are managed as forest animals because it is difficult to allow them to stray far on to farmland. Those that do, and cannot be corralled back into the security of the forest, are often humanely shot.

Almost all the reintroductions of bison in different parts of Europe have been in forests or on land largely dominated by forest. But three bison were introduced in 2007 (and another three the following year) to the Zuid-Kennemerland National Park on the Netherland's west coast. They graze a large area of sand dune grassland, scrub and scattered woodland without winter supplementary feeding. 'In 2009 the first calves were born, four in total that year; since then we have had calves every year, in 2013, six calves! So they do very well in the dunes. This year we also introduced three bulls from France and in total the herd now consists of 24 animals,' says Jenny van Rijn of the national park.

So European Bison are very flexible in their habitat needs. And it is worth remembering that far-sighted and tenacious conservationists have, in less than a century, brought the European Bison back from extinction in the wild to well over 4,000 animals today. And while arguments will continue about how they should be managed, whether and where extensive land areas within and outside forests are available for them, and whether their poor genetic mix will make them more vulnerable to disease and environmental change, the story of Europe's largest land animal is a hugely positive one. King Sigismund II Augustus, the 16th century King of Poland and Grand Duke of Lithuania – and the first person to introduce protection for Poland's bison – would have been very pleased indeed.

6

THE MERMAID THAT'S NO LONGER A MYTH

FLORIDA MANATEE

Hunted and killed over centuries for their meat, hides and oil, by the 1950s perhaps only 600 Florida Manatees remained. Now fully protected and with a huge public following, these gentle, plant-eating giants of the inshore coastal waters of Florida attract thousands of people who come to watch them in the warm river waters they seek out in winter. Boats kill or injure many; others die from cold stress or are poisoned by red algal tides at sea. Nevertheless, their numbers have slowly increased and today there are more than 5,000 in and around the state. Further population growth is by no means guaranteed as these endearing animals still face several problems. But they are back from the brink and the people of Florida are not going to allow their manatees to slip away.

Canoeing slowly along the tree-shaded Blue Spring, it was the sound of frequent nose-blowing on the water's surface that made the experience particularly surreal. These loud exhalations and intakes of air were a reminder that the aquatic creatures lolling away their winter months on the bed of this naturally warm, spring-fed waterway were mammals – and they needed occasional gulps of air to keep body and soul together. The stream, no more than a metre or two deep, was full of grey-brown, leathery skinned Florida Manatees, the adults three metres long, their youngsters smaller.

I was with Wayne Hartley – a Florida Manatee expert with the NGO, Save the Manatee Club – canoeing the 600 metres of Blue Spring stream from its confluence with the wide, slowly meandering St John's River to its underground source. And in this short stretch of naturally warmed water Hartley counted no less than 102 manatees basking in its warmth. Sometimes he counts over 300; that wouldn't leave much space here even for a small canoe! Blue Spring is one of Florida's manatee public viewing sites and attracts tens of thousands of people each winter who come to admire these remarkable and endearing animals. The manatees share the crystal clear water with a motley collection of fish – Tarpon, spotted Florida Gar and Pinocchio-like Long-nosed Gar – as well as with the occasional American Alligator.

Blue Spring is one of four warm-water springs discharging into the St John's, a river that begins its slow-flow life over an almost pancake-flat landscape in a huge, unnavigable marsh and enters the sea on Florida's northeast coast. A vital communication route for thousands of years in a part of the US in which much of the dense forest and swamp was impenetrable, today 3.5 million people live within its catchment. Manatees have used it in winter for even longer. To Blue Spring from the St John's River estuary, it's a 240 km manatee swim each way, a swim that, in the past, would have made them vulnerable to hunters. Avidly sought after for their meat, hides and bones, they were easy to catch and kill, especially in these shallow rivers during winter. By the 1950s or 1960s, they had been reduced to maybe 600. A concerted effort to protect and nurture their population since then brought their numbers up to around 3,300 by 2001 and to over 5,000 by 2014.

The Florida Manatee looks something like a grey-coloured, chubby dolphin with a flattened, wide tail that it uses for propulsion. Manatees lack the blubber layer that allows whales to tolerate cold; in water below 16°C they weaken and die. Through the summer they are found all round the Florida coast in waters close to shore, in winter; when sea temperatures drop, they congregate inland at natural springs and other sources of warm water, including that discharged at electricity generating power stations around the coast. Florida-wide, there are ten significant natural warm water springs manatees can retreat to in winter plus around 13 warm water discharges from power stations, although they regularly use just six of these.

Before we start canoeing along Blue Spring, Wayne Hartley measures its temperature. 'The spring temperature never varies,' he comments. 'Every time it's a constant 22.5°C. That's how it is.' And that's the way the manatees like it, many of the adult females with a youngster at their side and most of them just lounging away the winter months in these clear warm waters; the adults spending a good proportion of their time sleeping while smaller youngsters occasionally suckle.

As Hartley paddles us upstream, not only is he counting the numbers of adult manatees and their calves we pass alongside as they surface for air – or those we glide silently over as they sleep beneath us on the stream bed – incredibly he is also able to almost instantly identify each adult. His database of these animals is the longest running on any group of manatees in the world; over three decades of study. 'Jacques Cousteau [film-maker and conservationist] heard about the Blue Spring manatees and came to film them in 1970. He filmed 11 animals, the only ones here then; six we kept track of and two, Merlin and Brutus, are alive today,' says Hartley. 'Judith came in to Blue Spring in 1998. She had calves over the years; they were Julie, Easter, Jip, Jim, Jemal, Jinx and an unnamed calf. Judith died in 2008 of unknown but natural causes. Julie, Easter and Jim are still with us. Julie had calves over several years; they're Jolly, Mon, Jake, Jerry, Josh, Jaco and two unnamed ones.' He points to those he spots by name as we pootle this way and that in the canoe to check them out.

But how is it that Hartley can possibly differentiate individual manatees? Ironically, this system of recognition relies on one of the major threats to the animals themselves: boats. Collisions between manatees and boat hulls or boat propellers – if they don't kill the hapless animal outright or inflict an injury that causes a lingering death – leave large scars on their backs or chop pieces of flesh out of a manatee's fluke-shaped tail. Often these scars heal slowly over time; more often than not they leave permanent disfigurations in their skin, each pattern unique, thereby allowing an individual to be identified. In an assessment done from 1974 to 2011, the Florida Fish and Wildlife Conservation Commission (FWC) found that over a quarter of manatee deaths were due to boat collisions compared with 17% attributed to natural causes.

'When I first came to Blue Spring in the 1970s I told people that though summer was our busy season we often had 400 visitors coming to see manatees on a weekday in the winter and as many as 600 on a weekend day. That's a joke now! With the publicity generated by the Save the Manatee Club, Blue Spring [a protected state park since 1972] gets 3,000 on a weekday and sometimes 5,000 on a winter weekend day!' comments Hartley.

❖　❖　❖

Often called sea cows, there are just four living manatee species worldwide: the Amazonian Manatee, the West Indian Manatee (divided into the Florida and Antillean subspecies), the West African Manatee and the closely related Dugong of coastal waters in Southeast Asia and northern Australia. They are believed to have evolved from four-legged land mammals like primitive elephants over 60 million years ago. While the general flow of evolution was for land animals to have evolved from aquatic creatures, some land animals later went the other way. And while today's elephants and manatees have obviously very different lifestyles, they do have features in common. Both are largely vegetarian and, while the elephant uses its long trunk to feed, manatees use a snout with a large, flexible upper lip to gather plants from the sea or riverbed. Manatees' flippers retain three or four small claws at their tips; they look rather like the nails on elephants' feet. They have similar tooth structures too.

West Indian Manatees – both subspecies – were traditionally hunted by indigenous Caribbean people. When Christopher Columbus arrived in the region in the late 15th century, hunting was well established. The primary hunting method was for the hunter to approach the manatee in a dugout canoe and stun it with a blow near its head from an oar-like pole. From manatee leather hides, Native Americans made war shields, canoes and shoes, though meat was the main product. It was good and plentiful eating. Later, they were hunted for their bones, which were used to make supposedly curative potions.

The US came late to protecting its manatees. Although their hunting and killing was prohibited in 1893, until the Federal Marine Mammal Protection Act of 1972, the Endangered Species Act of 1973 and the Florida Manatee Sanctuary Act of 1978, there were no effective laws to protect them. The Sanctuary Act allowed for the establishment and enforcement of boating restrictions in important manatee habitats to reduce collisions and injury. The responsibility for administering these laws today lies with the FWC. In 1979 the first warm water wintering sites were given proper protection and, in the 1980s, the first comprehensive manatee protection plans began to be written. Today it is illegal in the US to hunt, feed, harass, harm, pursue, shoot, wound, kill, annoy or molest manatees.

In summer, Florida Manatees are very largely confined to the state's coastal waters, although vagrants have been known to reach the Bahamas around 300 km southeast of southern

Florida. Some migrate to the coastal waters of neighbouring states, particularly southeastern Georgia, while a few have been recorded as far north as Massachusetts and west to Texas. Telemetry studies have demonstrated that they are highly mobile, some migrating season-ally along several hundred kilometres of coastline, seemingly in response to fluctuating water temperatures but also to exploit plant food resources on the shallow seabeds they feed from. Others, though, are more sedentary, year-round residents in a local area, although most return to the same stretch of inland, warm water each winter, whether that is a natural warm spring or an artificial power station warm water discharge.

The average West Indian Manatee of either subspecies grows up to 3.5 metres long – though the Florida Manatee is commonly reported as being larger than the Antillean Manatee – and weighs 200–600 kg, with females generally larger than males. The Florida subspecies is the largest of all living sea cows and also the most northerly-inhabiting (albeit still within the sub-tropics) so it is the species that is most vulnerable to drops in water temperature. The other species have no such problems because their range is virtually entirely within tropical waters where temperatures fluctuate little.

All manatees have thick, wrinkled, leather-look skin on which there is often a growth of greenish algae. Their small front flippers help them steer, or sometimes crawl on the river or seabed, while their powerful, flat tail propels them through the water. Despite their small eyes and lack of outer ears, manatees are thought to see and hear quite well. All of them are herbivores, with a diet consisting mostly of sea grasses and freshwater vegetation. They graze on the seabed, though they will reach out of the water to grasp bankside vegetation too. They feed for between six and eight hours daily, consuming nearly a tenth of their body weight in wet vegetation. Their feeding habits do not require them to have a range of different teeth; just molars to grind their grassy food. Because food is inevitably mixed with abrasive sand, their teeth wear down quickly and fall out at the front of the mouth to be replaced regularly with new ones.

Manatees have to come up to the water's surface at intervals of maybe four minutes to exhale, take in a breath and then sink down a few metres to the seabed to feed. Sleeping on the bed of a warm-water spring in winter, they can sometimes last as long as 20 minutes between breaths. It is these essential surface forays that make them so vulnerable to boat collisions.

After reaching sexual maturity at between four and seven years, female manatees give birth to an average of one calf every two or three years. Born at any season after a gestation of around a year, calves weigh up to 30 kg and measure a metre or so in length. The mother – with one nipple on either side behind each front flipper – nurses and suckles its calf underwater and the pair stay together for up to two or three years. The most thoroughly studied of the sea cows, Florida Manatees have been known to live for more than 50 years in captivity; but in the wild their longevity depends very much whether or not they avoid boat collisions and other threats.

Lounging about in the warm winter waters of Blue Spring, they give every impression of being rather lazy individuals. But they are not. Tracking studies have shown that they swim up to 80 km in a day at speeds of up to 25 km per hour for short bursts.

The other subspecies of the West Indian Manatee, the Antillean Manatee, is sparsely distributed throughout the Caribbean along the northern coast of Central America and the north coast of South America including much of the coast of Brazil. Historically, they were hunted by local natives and sold to European explorers for food; and is the major reason why they are today not found in some former parts of their range, such as Barbados, Dominica and Grenada.

Angel Nuñez, a long time resident of San Pedro, a small fishing town on the island of Ambergris Caye on the east coast of Belize, describes how he and fellow fishermen would kill Antillean Manatees in the 1960s (*ambergriscaye.com/25years/huntingformanatees*):

> Once you got to the manatee area in the sea…you circled the grassy area hoping to see a muddy trail. If you followed the mud trail and it got denser, you knew you were following the animal. The manatee was first spotted when it surfaced to breathe.
>
> When you got your boat close enough, you flung the harpoon hoping to strike it at its head or back. Once injured, the manatee will put on a good fight. It would fling its large tail and pull out all the rope from your harpoon line. It would then start dragging your boat for several minutes until it got tired. Once it got tired, it would rise to the surface and remain floating. Once you got it near your boat you proceeded to kill the animal with the large club.
>
> If the manatee was small, three men could pull it on board. If very large, you then dragged it to some shallow area to begin processing for the meat. First you cut a straight line along the back from the head to its tail. Then the skin was peeled and large chunks of meat were obtained from the back, the belly and even the tail. The meat would be cut into fillet strips and sold for ten cents a pound.
>
> People said that manatee meat resembled the beef meat as there was the dark meat from the back of the animal. There was also a clear meat that looked like pork. On the belly side of the animal there was a fat on the meat that resembles much like the pork. Now for some delicious cooking! Just a little salt and black pepper and you could fry it.

Today, almost throughout their range – in spite of having legal protection in most countries – the Antillean Manatee is threatened by loss of habitat, poaching, entanglement with fishing gear and boat strikes. Its populations are patchy and fragmented and there is almost no population monitoring. The largest numbers seem to occur on the coasts of Mexico and Belize but almost everywhere they are probably in decline; a guesstimate of their total population attempted by IUCN in 2008 put it at around 4,000 animals. In Honduras, there are plans to enlarge the Cuero y Salado Wildlife Refuge, a haven for the Antillean Manatee, from its current 5,000 ha to six times that.

The West Indian Manatee is classified overall as Vulnerable by IUCN, while each of its subspecies – the Florida and the Antillean Manatees – are considered Endangered. Their status, though, has not been reassessed since 2007; consequently the assessment does not consider the increased numbers of Florida Manatees over the last decade.

The Amazonian Manatee is the only sea cow that is exclusive to freshwater, living in the enormous river systems of the Amazon basin; it is also classified by IUCN as Vulnerable. Unlike the Florida Manatee, it can accommodate colder water because it has subcutaneous fat to insulate it and can deflect blood flow away from the outer part of its body. Much like its manatee cousins in appearance, it is smaller and can be distinguished by its distinct white breast patch. Spending its life in muddy waters, they are difficult to see and are distinctly secretive (maybe a response to centuries of hunting); there is no accurate estimate of its population. It is almost certainly in steady decline due, as IUCN says, 'primarily to ongoing levels of hunting, sometimes involving new and sophisticated techniques, coupled with increasing calf mortality, climate change, habitat loss and degradation.' Amazonian Manatee meat and other products are readily available in many markets and fairs throughout their range; it is illegal to kill and sell it but enforcement is what might optimistically be termed patchy. Calves (wounded or not) caught in fishing nets are sometimes sold as pets, kept in pools or areas close to water bodies until they get to adult size for slaughter; some are even sold or given to politicians, authorities and other influential people. None of this provides much hope for its future.

The West African Manatee inhabits much of the west of Africa, both its coast and the major rivers, lakes and estuaries of the Niger, Gambia, Congo and many other rivers, usually far upstream until either they become too shallow or because dams and waterfalls block further travel.

Just like their Amazonian counterparts, West African Manatees are exploited for their meat, skin, bones and oil nearly everywhere that they are found. In Mali, Senegal and Chad, manatee oil is more prized than the meat and is used for its reputed medicinal properties to cure rheumatism, to condition the skin and hair, and to treat ear infections. In Mali, parts of the penis are used to cure impotency in men and the skin can be made into whips. In Sierra Leone, villagers consume all parts of the manatee except the heavy ribs; the meat is shared among villagers and any remains are sold by the trapper; the bones are used to make handles for walking sticks or for spinning-tops used in a local game. Protected in theory in most countries, there is no enforcement and West African Manatee meat is freely available in markets across the region.

They are trapped in nets, weirs and in other ways; some are an incidental catch in fishing nets. And increasing boat traffic, wetland drainage, riverside forest felling, pollution and land development all add to a depressing picture. A few initiatives in a few countries are arresting local declines and reducing the amount of hunting and trapping but, over the bulk of the West African Manatee's range, its long-term prospects look bleak.

Jennifer Welsh, staff writer for *Live Science* (www.livescience.com) wrote in January 2012 that the US Wildlife Conservation Society and Okapi Wildlife Associates (a Canadian wildlife consultancy), in a comprehensive study of fishery records, found that since 1990, people in at least 114 countries had consumed one or more of at least 87 marine mammal species. The list included three species of manatee.

Which brings us, a little more optimistically, to the last of the sea cows: the Dugong of Southeast Asia and Australian tropical waters, named from the Malay, *duyung*, meaning 'lady of the sea'. Found along a total coastline of maybe 140,000 km across nearly 50 countries, the biggest population is in the northern waters of Australia. Unlike the manatees, the Dugong spends its life entirely in saltwater. Many of its populations are today separated physically, several are in decline and some are close to extinction. They have disappeared from the waters of Hong Kong, Mauritius and Taiwan as well as parts of Cambodia, Japan, the Philippines and Vietnam. Further disappearances are likely.

Legally protected in many countries, the main causes of the population declines are illegal hunting, habitat degradation and fishing-related kills. With its slow rate of reproduction, the Dugong is especially vulnerable. Dugongs in southern Asia and Australia have also historically provided easy targets for hunters. Dugong meat and oil have traditionally been some of the most valuable foods of Australian Aborigines and Torres Strait Islanders while the meat is highly prized today in some Asian countries.

The Dugong's closest recent relative, the much larger Steller's Sea Cow, used to occur in coastal areas of the North Pacific Ocean and south as far as Japan and California. It was unusually tame and trusting, a slow swimmer and seemingly poor at submerging; not a combination of factors supporting a long and pleasant life. It was hunted for its meat, skin and its fat. By 1768 it was extinct, a salutary lesson for manatee conservation.

The Dugong's largest populations – many tens of thousands – are found along the Australian coast while the Persian Gulf retains sizeable numbers too. Nevertheless, the IUCN categorises it as declining or extinct in at least a third of its range, of unknown status in about half its range and possibly stable in the remainder; it is classed as Vulnerable. Even so, along with the Florida Manatee, the Dugong stands a good chance of holding its own – or increasing long term – across a significant part of its former range. They will almost certainly be the only two sea cows that will be with us a few decades from now.

❖   ❖   ❖

For centuries, millennia even, the myth of mermaids has been an intrinsic part of many cultures worldwide. But what has this half fish, half human form to do with manatees? The answer to that is that manatees and dugongs are most likely to have been the origin of some, even many, of their reported sightings, most of them by sailors long at sea.

The first known mermaid stories appeared in Assyria about 1000 BC. The goddess Atargatis loved a mortal (a shepherd) and unintentionally killed him. Ashamed, she jumped into a lake and took the form of a fish, but the waters would not conceal her divine beauty. Thereafter, she took the form of a mermaid — human above the waist, fish below. A popular Greek legend turned Alexander the Great's dead sister, Thessalonike, into a mermaid that lived in the Aegean. She would ask the sailors on any ship she would encounter only one question: 'Is King Alexander alive?' to which the correct answer was: 'He lives and reigns and conquers the world.' This answer would please her, and she would accordingly calm the waters and bid the ship farewell. Any other answer would enrage her, and she would stir up a terrible storm, dooming the ship and every sailor on board.

In British folklore, mermaids have been described as able to swim up rivers to freshwater lakes (what mammal does that remind you of?). In one story, the Laird of Lorntie went to aid a woman he thought was drowning in a lake near his house; a servant of his pulled him back, warning that it was a mermaid, and the mermaid screamed at them that she would have killed him if it were not for his servant. Not all mermaids were so nasty. Mermaids from the Isle of Man in the UK are considered more favourable toward humans than those of other regions; there are various accounts of assistance, gifts and rewards. One story tells of a fishing family that made regular gifts of apples to a mermaid and was rewarded with prosperity. Just like manatees, mermaids are vegetarian!

In 1493, sailing off the coast of Hispaniola, Columbus reported seeing three 'female forms', which 'rose high out of the sea, but were not as beautiful as they are represented'. The logbook of Blackbeard, an English pirate, records that he instructed his crew on several voyages to steer away from waters he called 'enchanted' for fear of merfolk or mermaids which Blackbeard himself and members of his crew reported seeing. These sightings were often recounted and shared by sailors and pirates who believed that mermaids brought bad luck and would bewitch them into giving up their gold and dragging them to the bottom of the sea. Of course, most of them had been at sea for months or even years starved of female company and more; any apparition they encountered might have taken on a female form!

There have been contemporary reports too. In August 2009, after dozens of people reported seeing a mermaid leaping out of the water and doing aerial tricks, the Israeli coastal town of Kiryat Yam offered a $1 million award for proof of its existence. Not surprisingly, there are plenty of hoaxes – old and modern – such as that of the American showman P.T. Barnum and his 'Fiji mermaid' (actually part monkey, part fish) displayed in his museum in the 1840s or that of the US television channel *Animal Planet* showing in 2013 a so-called docu-fiction entitled *Mermaids: The New Evidence* with film of an underwater humanoid creature. It was an actor!

So what is the basis for linking manatees and dugongs with mermaids? The manatee's vaguely human-like face is sometimes described as one only a mother could love. Indeed, it is difficult to understand how sailors ever mistook a manatee for a beautiful woman. But how would a sailor view the manatee from hundreds of yards away on a moving ship? When a manatee feeds, it will sometimes bob on the surface, using its flippers and claws to grasp the vegetation off rocks and bring it toward its mouth. When startled in such a position, a manatee will dive head-first, its large, paddle-shaped tail breaking the surface as it does so. With a vivid imagination and embellishment in the story telling, the creature does indeed seem to incorporate some semblance of a woman's head and the tail of a fish. The mermaid myth was born.

❖ ❖ ❖

Although Florida Manatees don't have to fear predators – a few calves might be taken by alligators in rivers or by sharks at sea – they live in a part of the world where severe storms and hurricanes can cause mortality and destroy important seagrass feeding habitat on the sea bed. With the frequency of such catastrophic events already increasing – and climate change models predicting further increases – this could become a significant concern for the future.

Water temperature is a bigger issue. Florida Manatees are unable to tolerate prolonged water temperatures below16°C and in some years, particularly if sea temperatures fall suddenly, large numbers of them can die before they can seek a warmer refuge. In 2010 at least 300 died from cold-related causes, an unsustainable level of deaths if it was to be repeated year on year.

Since the 1950s, artificial warm-water outfalls from coal-fired power stations and other industrial facilities on the Florida coast have probably contributed to their population growth by providing them with access to more habitat during winter, thereby reducing cold-related mortality. Two thirds of wintering manatees use power station warm water discharges. Presumably, before these facilities were built, many manatees in the more northern coastal areas of Florida migrated for the winter to the very south of the state or into the warmer waters of the Caribbean. While many manatees already swim 100–200 km to inland warm water refuges in winter, the sea distance from the furthest point north on Florida's east coast to the southern tip of the state is 600 km, a great deal further. Recent concern that many power stations will be closed has receded temporarily because they have been converted (or will convert) to burning gas and are likely to continue to discharge warmed cooling water for some years. Eventually, though, some at least are likely to close and fewer discharges will be available. No one knows whether the manatees will revert to moving south in the autumn. It will be a survival test.

'The current Power Plant Manatee Protection Plans [which are mandatory] require all power plants to coordinate with FWC if their operations change unexpectedly due to mechanical or other operational issues, or if the plant requires emergency maintenance during the winter,' says Ron Mezich, Biological Administrator at FWC . 'The plans prohibit routine maintenance that may disturb manatees using their warm-water effluent. All of them are also required to inform FWC of plans to retire an individual plant. At all times in winter they are required to operate when the outside water temperature drops to a critical level.' He adds, 'Manatees have proven to be adaptable over the long term. They discover new habitats and modify their behaviour to adapt to changes in their foraging areas and warm-water sites. In the short term, though, some individual manatees may struggle to adapt.'

There are, though, other warm water springs that were once accessible to manatees but development and other changes have rendered them inaccessible. Pat Rose, Executive Director of Save the Manatee Club, is not optimistic. 'There is sufficient room at our natural springs to accommodate a multiple of our current population but we can't necessarily count on those springs flowing due to all the pumping and water diversions for development and human population growth here in the future,' he says. 'There were also more springs in the past than we have today so manatees had more choices historically, while others did move south along the Florida coast. On occasion, when just the right circumstances occurred historically, substantial numbers of manatees likely were literally caught out in the cold every so often.'

'Assuming all springs are maintained, and maybe physical access to them increased, there will be room for growing numbers of manatees. That assumes that the state of Florida does a better job of protecting the springs and the underlying aquifers than they are doing presently because most springs are in decline. There is virtually no hope for restoring lost spring flows and we will be fortunate to hold on to what we have,' he argues. FWC is in the process of evaluating individual springs throughout Florida to determine their potential as manatee warm-water habitat and within the last few years five spring systems have had restoration work completed that will improve manatee access.

FWC is also considering some pretty avant-garde ideas to try and get manatees to adapt if existing power plants shut down at some future time. One idea is to create alternative warm waters, for instance by pumping up saline ground water that is naturally warmer than surface water or using solar energy to create warm-water habitat. These and other options are at no more than the concept stage but whether they are financially possible, dependable or feasible is uncertain.

As with European Bison and Iberian Lynx, Florida Manatees have a low level of genetic diversity compared to other manatee populations, possibly resulting from a time when the population decreased to a small number of individuals. Whether or not this has implications for their adaptability is another unknown.

Manatees on Florida's west coast are frequently exposed to a neurotoxin produced by a tiny marine creature called *Karenia brevis* when these proliferate in vast numbers. When they do, they are so abundant that the sea turns a pink or red colour – a 'red tide'. Although it is a seemingly natural event, no one is yet sure whether it is exacerbated in some way by pollution. Red tides have been recorded since the Spanish explorers came this way in the 15th century but evidence suggests that they have become more abundant in recent years. Each year some manatees die by ingesting the toxin as they feed; the worst recorded episode to date being in 2013 when 276 manatees were confirmed, or suspected to have been, killed by it.

'In contrast to the many red tide species elsewhere that are fuelled by nutrient pollution associated with urban or agricultural runoff into the sea, there is no direct link between pollution and the frequency or severity of red tides caused by *K. brevis*,' says Dr Alina Corcoran, Research Scientist on FWC's Harmful Algal Bloom programme. 'Florida red tides develop up to 60 km offshore, and away from man-made nutrient sources. Red tides occurred in Florida long before human settlement, and severe red tides were observed in the mid 1900s before the state's coastlines were heavily developed. However, once red tides get moved inshore by tidal currents, they are capable of using man-made nutrients for their growth,' she says.

❖ ❖ ❖

Human disturbance has long been an issue for manatees, especially so in this US state with a large and frequently affluent resident population, lots of holidaymakers and a high proportion of people with easy access to the coast and to some of their well-known wintering locations. 'Until 2008, people could swim and canoe in winter in Blue Spring while the manatees were there but they were supposed to avoid them. You can imagine how that worked!' says Wayne Hartley. 'Most people swam and canoed quietly not to cause them disturbance. But others were trying to ride them, put ropes around them or even hit them with canoe paddles to move them. Trying to stop it all got difficult, so swimming and canoeing is banned now all winter. And better viewing platforms anyway give people close-ups right over the waterside. In the last few years, more and more manatees come to Blue Spring each winter; far more than we ever saw before the ban.'

There is, though, one place where people can still swim, dive, snorkel and canoe with them; at Crystal River in King's Bay on the west coast of the state, a reputed 150,000 tourists swim annually with manatees. While the Save the Manatee Club (SMC) is not opposed to people swimming with manatees in principle, they are committed to stopping manatee harassment, which they say is increasing dramatically and must be eliminated through law enforcement and prosecution of violators. Harassment, according to the SMC, can lead to the separation of pups from mothers, to manatees leaving the warm water refuge and to alteration of their behaviour. Calls for limiting these activities have, though, caused an outcry with the large number of diving, snorkelling and boating companies providing services in the area where the local economic gain is at least $20 million annually and, this being the US, sparked off heated exchanges about curtailment of freedoms – for people, not manatees.

Nevertheless, the US Fish and Wildlife Service (USFWS) announced in January 2014 emergency steps to restrict access there between November and March each year by declaring it a manatee refuge. 'By declaring the whole bay a refuge, our staff who notice a problem can quickly move in and post "no-entry" areas. This isn't a blanket ban; it's designed to give federal officials some flexibility in providing greater protection for the manatees while at the same time allowing Crystal River's famous tour boats to continue operating,' said Chuck Underwood, an USFWS spokesman. The announcement also lists specific behaviour that will be prohibited including chasing, cornering, riding, poking or standing on manatees. Violators will face prosecution; SMC and environmental groups locally have welcomed the move as overdue.

For many years all around Florida, boat collisions have been a major cause of death and injury to manatees. With increasing numbers of boats being registered – the vast majority small pleasure craft – and the attractive nature of much of the state's coast, this is not a problem likely to disappear. 'About 60% of these are hits by the hull of the boat; the other 40% are cut by the propeller,' says Pat Rose. In response, FWC started introducing restrictions many years ago. 'By 2014, state-wide there were about 370 ha of waterway and inshore coastal waters where boats are excluded all year and 67 ha where they are excluded seasonally. In addition, boats are restricted to idle speed all year in nearly 3,000 ha of water and to slow speed in nearly 84,000 ha,' comments Scott Calleson, a Biological Scientist at FWC. Cutting speed allows the boat operator more chance of spotting and avoiding a manatee while the manatee gets more chance to get out of the way. Slower speeds also result in lesser injuries if collision does occur.

Research is underway to better understand how manatees behave around boats, whether they can hear them coming, whether they are getting better at taking evasive action and whether boaters should be excluded from more places or particular habitats. Fitting guards around propellers is effective at slow speed but not when boats are travelling at higher speed because impact with the hull then overrides propeller damage. Making it compulsory for all new boats to be powered by water jets rather than propellers would not get political support in a country where personal freedoms are closely protected. Setting a standard, the *MV Freedom Star* and *MV Liberty Star*, ships used by NASA to tow space shuttle rocket boosters back to the Kennedy Space Centre on Florida's east coast, are propelled by water jets in order to protect manatees in the Banana River where the ships are based.

In the decade to 2010, 345 manatee deaths were recorded on average each year, 83 of which were due to boat collisions; that is around a quarter of all deaths, a figure that hasn't altered much since the 1970s. There are well over a million registered boats using Florida's inshore coast and waterways, a doubling since 1980. And that doesn't include boats coming in from other states. Manatee numbers have increased enormously since the 1970s so more collisions should be inevitable. But boat kills are not increasing. That might well be due to the restrictions imposed on boat speeds, the huge amount of publicity about the boat threat to manatees and a general increase in public appreciation of the need to help these popular animals. 'In general I agree that the measures being put in place to deal with boat strikes are working, but it remains a serious threat to their long-term survival', comments Pat Rose. IUCN identifies it as 'Endangered'.

According to FWC statistics, between 2006 and 2013, 129 manatees were rescued and released from being tangled up in discarded monofilament fishing line or in discarded crab pot lines, a problem that equally affects a range of other aquatic animals including dolphins, sea turtles and fish. That is almost as many as in the previous 14 years, indicating either that little attention is being paid by fishermen to campaigns not to discard fishing line or that there is more reporting of stricken manatees. Discarded line can wrap around a manatee's flippers and constrict them, often causing them to swell and preventing a calf access to the mother's teats for nursing. And although deaths are uncommon, these entanglements can result in disfiguring injuries that may hamper an animal's ability to survive and reproduce in the wild.

❖   ❖   ❖

Florida's human population continues to grow; it was close to 20 million by 2014, three quarters of them living within 16 km of the coast. A century ago there were less than one million people living in the state. Urban development on Florida's coast has had indirect effects on manatees. Seagrass beds – essential grazing for the mammals – have declined in many estuaries because of dredging, dumping of spoil, pollution, and boat propeller damage. In Tampa Bay on the west coast, for example, an estimated 80% of the seagrass present in the early 1900s was lost by 1980. The decline is slowly being reversed by reducing pollution carried into the sea by rivers in the area and, hopefully, by better control over developments on the coast.

This continued population increase has major implications for wildlife, wildlife habitats and for individual species. Manatees are no exception. Urbanisation along parts of the coast, changes to the natural flows of rivers, effluent disposal into waterways or the sea and extraction of water for urban communities all have an impact. Water extraction is a thorny issue in Florida where the competing pressures of water supply for the increasing human population is often difficult to reconcile without affecting river water flows, the natural patterns of water dispersal in the state's extensive swamps and lakes (it has 7,700 lakes over four hectares in size) and without depleting underground aquifers. Nevertheless, Florida's population is substantially less than that of England and Wales (57 million) a similar land area. And, though it might seem unimaginable to the millions who visit attractions such as Disney World each year, huge areas of Florida remain wild with extensive swamps and forest without human settlement.

The natural warm water springs that provide essential refuges in winter for manatees are at risk because human demands for water combined with less rain recharging the underground aquifers due to urban development have already resulted in diminished spring flows and declining water quality. Florida's warm water springs provide a rare habitat not solely for wintering manatees but for a wide range of animals and plants. State law requires Florida's five Water Management Districts (WMDs) to establish and maintain minimum flows that cause no significant ecological harm and the state is requiring WMDs to ensure that some spring flows are enhanced. 'Protecting the quantity and the quality of our water systems is priority number one,' argues Pat Rose. 'Water quality is often forgotten about. We're pressing the state's WMDs to impose higher standards. Our second priority is to retain the manatee protection we have; keep the boat speed zones for instance.' In a state with an average rainfall of 130–150 cm, it should be quite possible to provide a sustainable domestic water supply without significantly affecting natural habitats, provided that the state introduces sensible codes to restrict unnecessary use, admittedly not a vote-winning message in a somewhat hedonistic society.

❖   ❖   ❖

It wasn't until the 1970s that the state authorities in Florida started to take the wellbeing of its manatees very seriously. By that time there might have been 600 left; no one can be sure because no one did any systematic monitoring to find out. Since then, substantial resources from local, state, and federal government agencies, as well as from the private sector, have been directed towards research and towards their protection. They are now considered one of the most well-studied of all marine mammals worldwide.

In the last four decades, the state's manatees have become a Florida icon and they engender a national and international level of public support. Founded in 1981, by 2014 the Florida-based Save the Manatee Club had about 30,000 members. There are few residents of Florida who have not heard of their manatees. The current Florida Manatee Management Plan published by FWC on behalf of the state government has as its goal: 'to remove the species from the list of federally endangered and threatened species…and to manage the population in perpetuity throughout Florida by securing its habitat and minimising threats.' The huge conservation effort mounted over the last few decades has resulted in an increase from a low point of maybe 600 to over 5,000 Florida Manatees today. Much of that effort has been invested in protecting their wintering warm water refuges, in reducing human-caused manatee deaths from boat collisions; in creating sanctuary areas where boats are banned or speed restricted; in getting fishermen to act responsibly to reduce manatee entanglement in fishing lines; in reducing disturbance and harassment by people; and in trying to understand the causes of toxic red tides that seem to becoming more of an issue for this sensitive marine mammal.

There are predictable problems ahead for this gentle giant of a mammal, not the least of which is its ability to cope if a reduction in local warm water refuges in winter necessitates migrating south to warmer sea waters. But enormous public support, considerable investment in its conservation by Florida state and by NGOs such as the Save the Manatee Club, plus a public and citizen-led commitment to conserving what is best of Florida's natural heritage, should stand the Florida Manatee in good stead.

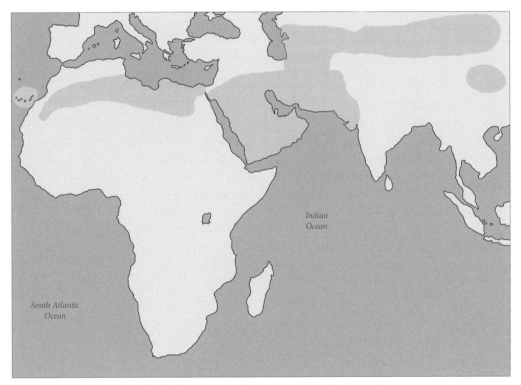

Shaded zone: Houbara/MacQueen's Bustard

7

A DISPLAY OF EXTRAVAGANCE.

HOUBARA

Excessive hunting and falconry, combined with degradation of its arid habitats caused by overgrazing with goats and other livestock, has decimated the Houbara across North Africa. Only on the Canary Islands of Lanzarote and Fuerteventura have these unusual birds, with one of the world's most extravagant courtship displays, recovered naturally. Elsewhere across their extensive range, factory-sized breeding centres are now releasing many tens of thousands of young birds each year. While the majority are seemingly killed in falconry or die naturally of starvation or predation, small numbers are re-establishing in the wild and the future for this ground bird looks secure.

*I*n the bright morning sunshine, it was a sight to add even more cheer to the warming spring day. A couple of hundred metres away, standing on a shrubby bank behind some fields of gritty, black soil, a male Houbara, sandy brown-coloured and the size of a pheasant, was in full courtship display. Running jauntily in seemingly aimless circles, his long white breast feathers turned inside out and fluffed up over his head to show off a frill of brilliant foamy white, this normally slow-stepping ground bird had come to life in style.

Here off the northwest African coast on the volcanic island of Lanzarote, along with its neighbouring island Fuerteventura, the most arid, Houbara are doing better than anywhere else. And yet, just three to four decades ago, there were thought to be no more than 100 Houbara altogether on these two Canary Islands and there were fears that they would become rarer still, or even extinct. In 2012, when the latest survey was organised, there were 193 on Fuerteventura, 926 on Lanzarote and a handful on La Graciosa, the small island off the north coast of Lanzarote. The population on Lanzarote, an average of more than one Houbara per square kilometre of land, is now reckoned to be the highest density of these birds in the world.

I was with Marcial Armas and Elena Betancor of Sociedad Española de Ornitología (SEO), Spain's leading bird conservation charity. 'The males display between December and March,' says Betancor. 'And breeding is usually from March to May. The Houbara spend most time in the semi-desert habitat here but in summer when it is very dry they sometimes go into the vegetable crops farmers grow. Mostly they are feeding off insects in the crops, not the crops themselves. They are very useful for the farmers, eating up a lot of pests.'

The range of this unusual ground bird takes in all of North and Northwest Africa north of the Sahara and east as far as the River Nile in Egypt. How common Houbara once were here, no one is sure. Hunted with falcons, shot for sport or for food, especially from vehicles, and deprived of their habitat as goats and camels ravaged most of the vegetation supporting the insects, seeds and other food they depend upon, Houbaras have been in steep decline across their whole range. By the early decades of the 20th century they had become an unusual sight and in some parts of this huge swathe of desert and semi-desert, they were extinct. Based on information from the 1970s, the authoritative *Handbook of the Birds of Europe, the Middle East and North Africa* (OUP, 1980) concludes that they 'may now be rare or extinct in most of the west Palearctic [the geographical area covered by the book].' According to information compiled by Paul Goriup, an international bustard expert and Managing Director of Fieldfare International Ecological Development plc, by the mid 1990s there were less than 10,000 left. Ten thousand scattered over a vast land area of about 10 million km² (one in every 1,000 km²) is not many Houbara. IUCN classifies the species as Vulnerable largely because of the alarming declines it has suffered.

The Houbara on the Canary Islands, long separated from those on the African mainland, is slightly smaller, less sandy coloured and a little darker; it's considered a different subspecies. The slightly larger and paler coloured populations, found from the River Nile, through the Middle East and on via Pakistan to China, used to be classified as a third Houbara subspecies but are now considered a separate species by most experts (but certainly not all). It is named the MacQueen's Bustard after General Thomas MacQueen (1792–1840), a British army officer in the then 45th Bengal Native Infantry regiment in India who – rather predictably for the times – shot one, presented it to the British Museum in London and had it named after him! Those MacQueen's breeding in the more northerly parts of their Asian range migrate south and southwest for winter to spend it in the warmer Middle East or parts of southern Asia such as Pakistan. The more southerly Asian breeders and those in the Middle East stay put year round.

In recent decades, MacQueen's Bustard is also thought to have declined; substantially in some parts of the region but less in others, the result yet again, of hunting, overgrazing and falconry. According to research by Christophe Tourenq of Abu Dhabi's National Avian Research Centre, and colleagues, between 1998 and 2002 MacQueen's declined by 63% in China, 60% in Kazakhstan and by 50% in Oman, astonishing declines over a short period. They concluded, 'The current levels of hunting and poaching are not sustainable and without immediate conservation measures, the Asian Houbara [now usually referred to as MacQueen's] may face extinction in the wild in the foreseeable future.'

Substantial declines have also occurred throughout the Middle East. In Saudi Arabia, the numbers of both migrant MacQueen's (from further north in Asia coming south for the winter) and resident breeding birds were drastically reduced by the 1980s. In his book, *The Arab of the Desert* (Allen & Unwin, 1949), Lieutenant Colonel Harold Richard Patrick

Dickson, a British colonial administrator and author, comments on the winter abundance of Houbara (now MacQueen's Bustards) in the Gulf States:

> From Kuwait and further south as far as Qatar, the birds are very plentiful throughout the winter and many thousands of birds are each season killed for food by local Arabs. In Kuwait the Shaikh generally bags about two thousand birds every cold weather, and the combined members of the Al Sa'ud [The Saud family that rule Saudi Arabia] get about the same number...as also do the Shaikhs of Bahrain, both on their own islands as well as on the mainland where they regularly hunt.

Between then and the late 1980s, the situation had changed drastically. Take, for instance, the comments made by artist and film-maker Michael McKinnon when he wrote his *Arabia: Sand Sea Sky* (Guild Publishing, 1990):

> Houbara Bustards [McQueen's] do still breed and visit Arabia, albeit in greatly reduced numbers. In earlier times they spread right across the [Arabian] Peninsula and were seen all along….the western coast as well as in the centre and down the east side. Apart from the impact of hunting, they have suffered greatly as a result of habitat deterioration due to goat and sheep grazing in areas previously used as feeding grounds.

The reasons for this drastic decline were clear: excessive hunting for sport and food and for falconry; habitat destruction by ploughing up natural grassland to grow crops; overgrazing of their desert habitat by herds of livestock, goats especially; egg collecting for food and disturbance by farmers, livestock and tourists especially joy-riding off-roaders.

❖ ❖ ❖

In various rather inconspicuous shades of brown, black and white, well camouflaged to suit their often arid surroundings and reluctant to fly if disturbed, bustards – of which there are 26 species worldwide – don't sound a very exciting lot. But to anyone who has witnessed the amazing courtship displays of the males, some of the most incredible for any birds in the world, bustards are very far from boring. The display of the male Houbara is not the most extravagant of the bunch. But what looks so odd about it is that the long white breast feathers it ruffs up over its head render it blind as it cavorts in circles on trotting feet. Displaying male Houbara sometimes bump into bushes or rocks in their headlong sprints. All the same, what appears to us as a rather amateurish and amusing bit of natural theatre is enough to impress the watching females, enough to encourage them to mate with those males that are the best show-offs.

The Great Bustard of the open grasslands of Spain and the Russian steppes – reputedly the heaviest flying bird in the world – has a more extravagant display which is visible from at least a couple of kilometres away. The males, which can weigh up to 19 kg, blow up their chests to the size of a football and invert their tails and wings up and over their bodies, converting themselves in seconds from a sandy chestnut colour to a shimmering white bundle as they shake their feathers and turn this way and that to show off to females in all directions. But that is rather tame compared with the display of the gymnastic Red-crested bustard, an African species. Uttering a series of tongue clicks and whistles, the male suddenly launches into the air, flies almost vertically up to maybe thirty metres or so, closes his wings, somersaults backwards with his legs uppermost and falls back to the ground like a stone, pulling out of the fall a split-second before hitting land and gliding nonchalantly on to the ground.

All this theatrical courtship, though, is seemingly enough work for a male bustard for a whole year. After mating, the males play no role whatsoever in incubating the eggs – typically two to four – in the scrape in the ground that passes muster for a bustard nest. Once the chicks hatch, they are up and feeding within a few hours, following their mother around for several weeks before they become independent. There is far more risk from predators if they hang around the nest site.

Twenty of the bustard species worldwide are found in sub-Saharan Africa. Two species from southern Asia are called floricans (the Bengal Florican and the Lesser Florican) while in southern Africa, where eleven species occur, many are called korhaans (crowing hens) be-cause of their croaking, clattering calls, the only ones with a bit of a voice. Most bustards are notably low on any musicality prowess; grunts and booms are typical, though some hardly call at all. Smaller species, such as the attractive Little Bustard of Western Europe, get by with a persistent, distinctly unmusical but deceptively far-carrying wheezing call, a kind of 'wet raspberry' click. But a good voice is not much use on the large, open and frequently windswept plains they live on. The sound of the wind would drown it out and no other bustard would hear it. The only way to attract a mate is to be seen…and bustards have become masters of the catwalk, modelling some of the most eye-catching bird fashions in the world. The message seems to be: if you've got it, then flaunt it.

Most bustards are beneficial for farmers, eating up huge numbers of locusts, termites, beetles and other insect pests of open pasture and more arid lands. Catholic in their tastes; seeds, flowers, berries and roots are on the menu alongside lizards, mice, and even the eggs and young of other smaller ground-nesting birds. Most species don't seem to need access to open water to drink; they appear to get enough from the insects and vegetation they consume even in arid environments.

Mostly rather slow, ponderous-seeming walkers as they comb across their grasslands and arid lands searching for food, cranes are their closest relatives. Already well camouflaged, if danger approaches these often large birds will lie flat on the ground, maybe on bare soil, exploiting their cryptic sandy brown and dark plumage to good effect. Youngsters do the same. Even the largest such as the Great or Kori Bustards can be frustratingly difficult to spot unless they are walking about. Smaller species, including the Houbara, can be more difficult still. Unless, that is, it is springtime and courtship is in their thoughts.

Several species are in decline, with two species classified as Critically Endangered by IUCN: the Great Indian Bustard, that is down to maybe a couple of hundred birds scattered on small areas of dry grassland in western India and Pakistan; and the Bengal Florican, numbering a few hundred in India and Southeast Asia. Two others are classified as Endangered: Ludwig's Bustard in southern Africa, which, although numbering probably tens of thousands, has been declining extremely quickly, seemingly because of collisions with power lines; and the Lesser Florican, formerly more widespread than it is now in central and western India where its populations are scattered and reduced to maybe 2,000. The Houbara, along with the Great Bustard, is considered Vulnerable. Ploughing up of pastureland, heavy grazing by sheep and cattle, hunting for food, land development for human settlement, and – for smaller species such as the Houbara – falconry have all played roles in their declines.

All bustards are susceptible to disturbance; greater mechanisation of farming on the extensive open areas of dry pasture many favour is causing declines although several species tolerate some crop growing provided these are not intensively cultivated with large doses of fertiliser and pesticides which kill off most of the insects bustards feed partly on.

❖   ❖   ❖

On Lanzarote and Fuerteventura, Houbara hunting and killing is illegal and there is no falconry. As part of Spain, the islands have to adhere to EU laws and the Houbara is a protected species. Several of the best areas for breeding Houbara are protected too; large areas of desert-like, sparse vegetation with a scatter of spiny and succulent shrubs and a number of other uncommon birds such as the elegant little cream-coloured courser, another sandy-coloured bird of arid lands.

Not that Houbara are immune from problems here. Habitat fragmentation remains a threat, mainly because of continued developments around coastal resorts encroaching further inland into the extensive desert-like plains. Disturbance from off-road motorbikes and four-wheel drive joy-riders is an equally important issue that needs to be tackled, by getting local companies that hire such vehicles to take a more responsible attitude and to agree restrictions on where they can be used. Roaming dogs can cause substantial disturbance too.

Surveys on the islands by SEO have confirmed what had been noticed anecdotally for some time: that large numbers of Houbara (and many other birds) are killed by colliding with electricity and phone lines they fail to see in flight. These collisions account for about 17% of Houbara deaths on Fuerteventura. Heavy birds that run on the ground rather than fly, when Houbara do take to the air they fly low and can't always avoid the wires strung between posts. 'Endesa, the electricity company [the largest electric utility company in Spain] is working with us and is placing diverters on those power lines that most often cause bird mortality,' says Juan Antonio Lorenzo, Projects Coordinator for SEO in the Canary Islands. The diverters reflect sulight and flash in the sun; they are also visible in dim light. And they reduce Houbara collisions. 'The worst companies, who do not want to do anything to prevent bird deaths are Red Eléctrica [a part state and part public Spanish corporation which operates the national electricity grid in Spain], and the phone company Movistar [a major Spanish mobile phone operator owned by Telefónica]. They don't want to bother to adapt their lines to reduce bird deaths. It is a very sad situation for us', he adds. Red Eléctrica responds to these criticisms by stating that it has fixed diverters to well over 2,000 km of power line – though seemingly not on Lanzarote in spite of being aware of Houbara kills – a length that it claims is increasing year on year in identified high risk locations. Dr Luis Carrascal of the Museo Nacional de Ciencias Naturales in Madrid and a Houbara expert says, 'Collisions with wires followed by urban sprawl are the two most important threats on Lanzarote. On Fuerteventura, it's urban sprawl and off-road vehicles followed by goats grazing the vegetation and overhead wire collisions.'

On Fuerteventura, Houbara had apparently been fairly numerous in the late 19th century but had declined substantially by 1930 and there were very few records at all in the 1960s. On Lanzarote, though, historic records suggest it was never common and that it had been reduced even further by the 1920s. There were suggestions that numbers had recovered a little in the late 1960s but declined again until the 1990s before reaching the peak of nearly 1,000 in 2012. What caused the depletions in their populations is not clear but a combination of intensive goat grazing, egg collecting by shepherds for food and local hunting of the birds themselves for food, together with more disturbance by farmers and their livestock might all have contributed. By the 1980s, there were thought to be no more than 100 Houbara on Lanzarote and Fuerteventua in total but by the mid 1990s, their population had rocketed to 527 birds in total, with 268 on Lanzarote, 241 on Fuerteventura and 18 on La Graciosa. Over the last six or seven years their numbers have stayed roughly steady on Fuerteventura but have shot up even further on Lanzarote to nearly 1,000 adults.

Why such a recent increase? Formal protection under EU law has helped, while improved living standards (with the increase in tourism) on the islands since the 1980s have almost eliminated any killing or egg taking. But there's another intriguing reason for their increase too. 'Nearly all the tourism development has been on the coast,' says Paul Goriup. 'That's caused a lot of rural depopulation inland on the islands because people went to work in the coastal resorts. So they are spending less time in the heartlands of the bustards' living quarters.' That would also suggest that many farmers have given up farming to take more lucrative service sector jobs. And a drop in goat numbers might be expected. But that is not the case. Ironically, goat numbers today are many times higher on both islands than they were in the 1970s. In spite of concern that goats and Houbara don't mix because goats graze away any vegetation, thereby reducing the invertebrates and seeds the birds eat, the number of goats has risen dramatically at a time when Houbara numbers have increased dramatically too.

Luis Carrascal has compiled figures from various sources to try to put a figure on the numbers of goats on these two islands in recent times. 'The number of goats has increased six fold on Fuerteventura and five fold on Lanzarote between 1978 and 2012,' says Carrascal. 'Fuerteventura is two times larger than Lanzarote so, even though it's a much larger island, its goat density is still twice that of Lanzarote. But many goats on Lanzarote, I believe, are kept more contained on farms rather than grazing over large open areas of land.' If that is the case, goats might be having a much larger impact on Houbara on Fuerteventura because there are many more of them and they are encouraged to graze more widely.

Together with more urban sprawl on Fuerteventura, more golf course development, and more uncontrolled off-road recreation, it could explain its lower number and lack of increase in Houbara. And there's another unusual factor that Luis Carrascal believes could be an issue – the chipmunk-lookalike Barbary Ground Squirrel. Native to North Africa, they were introduced to Fuerteventura in the 1960s as pets but many escaped or were released so that they are now widespread. Some experts estimate that there could be a million on the island. Their eradication is seen as impractical and efforts are concentrated on preventing their spread to Gran Canaria and Lanzarote where they are absent. While these little rodents feed mainly off vegetation, seeds and fruits, they are known to take the eggs and nestlings of small ground-nesting birds. Whether that includes Houbara eggs and nestlings no one knows, although Juan Antonio Lorenzo is not sure that they do; he thinks other introduced mammals such as feral cats, rats and hedgehogs could be culprits instead.

❖   ❖   ❖

Ironically, hunting with falcons – one of the major causes of decline – has stimulated a huge programme of rehabilitation across the vast bulk of the Houbara's once widespread North African homeland, and that of its MacQueen's cousin from the Middle East into Asia. In factory-sized breeding centres, tens of thousands of Houbara and MacQueen's Bustards are today being hatched, raised and then released into the wild. It sounds like just what is needed to rehabilitate their much depleted populations. But whether many of these mass-raised and released birds are equipped to survive in the wild, able to feed adequately and avoid predators is not at all certain. The raison d'être of most of these breeding centres has the appearance of being to assuage the seemingly insatiable demands of Middle Eastern falconers. What is more, with the exception of some fenced areas or tracts of desert where livestock grazing is reduced in intensity, little is being done to improve the habitat these ground feeding birds need, contrary to the basic tenets of the IUCN reintroduction guidance.

The earliest captive breeding and release programme started in the late 1980s in Saudi Arabia. It was designed to try to create sustainable breeding populations and was not set up to produce birds for falconry. Managed on behalf of the Saudi government by the then National Commission for Wildlife Conservation and Development (now the Saudi Wildlife Authority), MacQueen's Bustards were captive bred in large enclosures. Eggs had been collected in 1986 in Pakistan and the first breeding success was achieved in Saudi three years later. This donor population was chosen because the birds in southwest Pakistan are resident all year; a situation that needed to be replicated in Saudi where MacQueen's are naturally resident too.

The first captive-reared MacQueen's were reintroduced into the Mahazat-as-Sayd Protected Area in the southern Saudi desert, but they were quickly killed by predators, mostly foxes. Mahazat as-Sayd is 220,000 hectares of desert, all of it surrounded by chain-linked fencing to prevent any grazing animals entering. Standing on the vegetation-devoid desert outside and looking into it gives a distinct impression of an Eden-like garden; the fencing has allowed a spectacular recovery of native shrubs and grassland speckled with flowers, a reminder of what most of the Arabian peninsula might have looked like before goats and camels began their ravages. Several other long-absent animals have been reintroduced here too: Arabian Oryx (Chapter 2), Rhim Gazelle and Red-necked Ostrich for instance.

After the initial failure with MacQueen's, more attempts were made in the early 1990s. Broods of chicks between 15 and 30 days old were released with their mothers and over a third of these survived. Releasing birds two to four months old proved yet more successful; nearly half of the 90 or so released survived (a better survival rate than with many bird reintroductions) and by the end of 1994, 35 introduced MacQueen's Bustards were living wild in Mahazat and seemingly did not appear to be seriously threatened by predators. They had learnt to outwit them. In 1995, the first wild-living offspring hatched in the reserve. MacQueen's Bustard was back.

In the decade to 2010, about 900 MacQueen's were released in Mahazat and nearly 300 in another protected area further north in the Saudi Desert. Here, there is more predation and, because this reserve is unfenced, much of the area is grazed by Bedouin goats – around 50 MacQueen's remain. It is unlikely that a population of this size will be self-sustaining. However, by 2011, Dr Zafar-ul Islam of the Saudi Wildlife Commission estimated that the population at Mahazat was self-sustaining, numbering maybe 300 adults. More reintroduction areas are planned in Saudi in order to locate birds in geographically different parts of the country, thereby reducing risks such as disease spread. 'I have done field surveys in the north-east of Saudi bordering Iraq and we are planning to reintroduce bustards there either in 2014 or 2015. The place is being fenced and a ranger's camp being built there,' comments Islam.

Since the Saudi initiative got underway, several other breeding centres have been set up elsewhere. The UAE-headquartered International Fund for Houbara Conservation (IFHC), an arm of the UAE government, has set itself the goal of 'utilising the resources at its disposal to save Houbara/MacQueen's Bustard populations by replenishment and reinforcement' and attempts to achieve this are certainly not restricted by funding. IFHC has contracted Reneco, a private company, to run huge breeding centres in Morocco, UAE and Kazakhstan. In Morocco it operates two centres; at Missour it has been breeding Houbara in a huge number of enclosed aviaries since 1995. A second facility nearby was opened in 2006. According to the IFHC's 2012 annual report, these two centres have a combined target to produce and release 15,000 Houbara each year. Since the operation started in Morocco, over 90,000 chicks have been produced of which around 54,000 have been released, most in Morocco but some in Algeria.

Although the survival rates of released birds were relatively low – from one third to one half surviving after just two months – a survey by IFHC in the spring of 2012 in eastern Morocco found over 1,200 Houbara nests with over 3,000 eggs laid. 'The birds are released in the wild but only in areas set aside for hunting and falconry,' comments Dr Brahim Haddane, a wildlife consultant who has studied Houbara in Morocco for 30 years. 'In 2013 they released about 15,000 bustards; I guess up to 80% of the released birds die or are killed.' The IFHC disputes these figures. 'Our post-release monitoring of birds indicates survival rates that are much higher,' comments Mohammed al Baidani, Director General of IFHC. 'The rate of survival after one year is 67% in North Africa and 53% in UAE. By comparison, our studies of the Houbara in the wild indicate a natural survival rate of just 19%.'

Critics are clear, though, that these figures are not comparable. The rate of survival of released birds is a post-release survival rate; it doesn't take into account all the losses from eggs and nestlings up to the release, which accounts for much of the 19% survival in the wild population. Critics also claim that the egg hatching rate in captivity is much lower than in the wild and the loss between hatching and release has been increasing because of factors such as over-crowded cages, too many birds for the number of bird keepers, less care and more disease.

Clearly, though, Houbara populations are increasing in northwest Africa. 'During the last 50 years, Houbara numbers in the wild in Morocco have increased, I estimate by perhaps 60%. But released birds are not well adapted to survive and hunting with falcons has increased, most falconers coming from the Gulf States,' says Haddane. 'Others get killed by feral dogs and wild predators like eagles and foxes; they find released Houbara easy prey although I think the breeding centres have contributed to reduce the impact of falconry on the wild population.'

IFHC's Sheikh Khalifa Breeding Centre in Abu Dhabi in the UAE produced more than 13,000 MacQueen's Bustard chicks in 2012; of these less than 10% were reintroduced 'in the wild'. Most were released purely for falconry, according to the centre's records. Also in the UAE, its National Avian Research Centre had produced its first captive-bred chicks by 1996. Releases began in 2004 and have continued each year at various locations within the UAE. The first chicks hatched in the wild from released females were recorded in 2007. In 2013, 1,450 birds were released in designated protected areas in Kuwait, Qatar and Yemen in addition to over 4,400 in the UAE.

But conditions in the UAE are not very conducive for MacQueen's to breed in any significant numbers. They are more common on migration through the Gulf States and breeding is likely only if there has been rain and it is cooler in early spring to encourage them. 'The climate in Abu Dhabi is too hot and dry for them to be a regular breeder and the conditions are now even less suitable because most of the desert is desperately overgrazed by camels and goats,' comments Dick Hornby, founding partner of an Abu Dhabi based ecological consultancy, Nautica Environmental Associates. 'So I suspect that the great majority of the released Houbara don't live long and are unlikely to establish a permanent breeding population. Climate warming is likely to make things even worse!' Other experts have commented that in the UAE's protected areas where MacQueen's are being reintroduced, and where the habitat is artificially managed to increase food supply, their breeding success stays very low, with few females attempting to breed, poor hatching success, and a nearly nil fledging success, chicks being either very weak or killed by predators. So a sustainable breeding population there seems unlikely.

There are also anonymous claims that many released bustards stay in large groups which they would not do naturally and even some falconers complain that the birds are so tame they have no fear of falcons. There is also the potential issue that some released birds might be carrying diseases; if they are, that could pose a threat to the small numbers of wild bustards they might encounter.

❖　❖　❖

Falconry is an ancient and highly skilful sport. It appears to have been practised in China by 2000 BC, in Japan by 600 BC or earlier, and probably at an equally early date in India, Arabia, Persia and Syria, in all of which it is still practised today. There are claims that it might be much older still, maybe practised as early as 4000–6000 BC in Mongolia for example. Marco Polo, the famous Italian trader and explorer, wrote about Kublai Khan, the great leader of the huge Mongol empire in Asia in the 13th century, who on journeys in his kingdom took with him 10,000 falconers split up into small groups to hunt with Gyrfalcons, Peregrine and Saker Falcons and vultures too. How they ever found enough to hunt is hard to imagine. Through Arab influence, falconry spread across the Islamic World, eastwards into the great Islamic Empires of Central Asia and westwards across North Africa, producing differing styles of falconry in different regions. The Holy Koran itself includes a falconry-related verse that permits falconry as a hunting method. Falconry is considered a symbol of this region's civilisation and culture; half of the world's falconers are in the Middle East. Today, it is practised in 60–70 countries but controls over how it is practised, when and by whom, and what prey they are allowed to hunt, are often absent. When prey such as Houbara/ MacQueen's were abundant, falconry possibly didn't deplete their populations. But as part of the lethal mix of habitat destruction, shooting, egg collecting and disturbance, falconry can be the final straw for an already vulnerable bird.

Today, much of the falconry across North Africa is practised by rich Arabs who have often so drastically reduced the numbers of MacQueen's Bustard in parts of the Middle East that they travel further afield. With no restriction on their spending power and with vehicles that can travel virtually anywhere, it's likely that they have hunted Houbara to the verge of extinction locally, even in places that were formerly too remote to reach.

The United Arab Emirates (UAE) reportedly spends over $27 million annually on the protection and conservation of falcons and has set up several state-of-the-art falcon hospitals in Dubai and Abu Dhabi. In some places, the falcons have almost certainly become more abundant than the quarry they are intended to hunt. Large Saker and Gyrfalcons plus smaller Peregrines are all popular, most of them reared in captivity rather than stolen from nests as they were in the more distant past. The most prized hunting falcons can fetch up to $1 million at auction. Dick Hornby says that falconry is as popular as ever in the Gulf states, in the UAE, Qatar, Saudi Arabia and Kuwait especially. 'According to figures I saw from the Abu Dhabi Hunting and Equestrian Exhibition in 2013 [an annual event], since passports for falcons were introduced in the UAE in 2001 more than 28,000 have been issued! And these are only the falcons that people want to import or export from the UAE. Many more are resident in the country,' he says.

Khalfan Butti Alqubaisi, a keen falconer from Abu Dhabi in the UAE, doesn't agree that there's a problem. 'We hunt mainly with Gyrfalcons or gyrs crossed with Peregrines and they kill Macqueen's Bustards, Stone Curlews [long legged, sandy-coloured, ground birds larger than Lapwings] and rabbits. But we have plenty of bustards because there are rearing farms that release them into the desert,' he says. In the UAE it is supposedly illegal to hunt MacQueen's unless it is by members of the ruling families! 'The UAE sheikhs used to have huge hunting operations in Pakistan, Iraq and even Afghanistan, but these have moved further north to Turkmenistan, Kazakhstan and Uzbekistan. My guess is that the great majority of the wild MacQueen's passing through Qatar and Kuwait are killed by falconers. Possibly also in Bahrain though I'm not too sure about that; anyway, the state of the species in the wild is certainly not healthy,' said an anonymous source.

❖   ❖   ❖

In Asia, the IFHC's Sheikh Khalifa Houbara Breeding Centre in Kazakhstan has been breeding MacQueen's Bustards since 2008. The production target for this facility is 10,000 chicks per year but it isn't yet operating at full capacity. A second Kazakh centre is also under construction and is expected to be operational in 2014; this centre's target is another 5,000–10,000 MacQueen's annually. 'Every year we release thousands of birds in Kazakhstan. I think this is very promising,' says Dr Boris Gubin from the centre who is an expert on these birds. 'Although falconry is still very commonplace and most bustards are killed by falcons, many survive and live wild. They will produce offspring in ever larger quantities.'

Many of the MacQueen's bred in the Kazakh facility are derived from founders of mixed Kazakh and Pakistani origin to diversify their genetic base. Released, they have migrated varying distances in autumn but they all followed the traditional migration routes used by wild MacQueen's heading southwest to western Iran and Iraq for the winter, returning in spring to breed in the wild. Their migration route takes many through Pakistan and that makes them particularly vulnerable to falconers because, controversially, although MacQueen's is fully protected in Pakistan, its government issues permits to Middle Eastern royals and other dignitaries to kill them.

Hunting bustards in Pakistan is only by special permit; a permit allows a maximum total bag of 100 birds; but bans any hunting in reserves. Nevertheless, according to *Dawn*, Pakistan's oldest English language newspaper, Prince Fahd bin Sultan bin Abdul Aziz al Saud, a senior member of the Saudi ruling family, and his entourage killed 2,100 MacQueen's bustards in Balochistan, Pakistan, in January 2014, hunting extensively in reserved areas. In recent years, permits have been given to at least three Middle Eastern rulers, many crown princes and other members of royal families. They included named leaders from the UAE, Bahrain, Qatar, Dubai and Saudi Arabia and included Sheikh Sultan bin Zayed Al-Nahyan, Chairman of the IFHC. In spite of heated debates about the practice in Pakistan's Sindh Regional Parliament and international concern, such permits are still being issued. In November 2013, Sindh Wildlife Department Parliamentary Secretary, Gayan Chan MPA, even said that such hunting was a policy of Pakistan's federal government. 'It is a token of respect for Arab families to develop better ties with them. We have no authority to interfere but facilitate the hunters. The hunting of bustard is protected under national and international law but permits are given only to Arab Sheikhs in order to develop good relations,' said Chan. In March 2014, the UK's *Financial*

Times reported that Saudi Arabia had given $1.5 billion to Pakistan to bolster the country's falling foreign currency reserves and help cement security ties between the two countries. In November 2014 the Balochistan High Court ordered a stop to further hunts. Time will tell whether this ban is upheld.

Yet another breeding centre in Asia, operated by the Emirates Centre for Wildlife Propagation, is located in Uzbekistan and was visited in 2013 by the UK Ambassador to Uzbekistan, George Edgar. 'It's a project funded by the UAE in collaboration with the Uzbek government to breed bustards for hunting by falcons, by hunters from the UAE rather than Uzbekistan. But the project also aims to establish and maintain a viable wild population of bustards in the area rather than purely breeding birds in captivity to be released and hunted,' says Edgar. 'The conservation aspect of the project involves experts from the University of East Anglia and BirdLife International. They are studying the behaviour of the birds, monitoring their breeding and migration patterns, and working with local people to establish how conservation can work alongside use of the land for grazing sheep. I was very impressed by what I saw of the project which offers a real prospect of supporting the continued existence in the wild of this magnificent bird,' he adds.

Since the IFHC centres started up in the mid 1990s they had produced a total in excess of 120,000 bustard chicks by 2013. It doesn't take a mathematical genius to work out that if most of those were successfully reintroduced in the wild across their native range, the Houbara and MacQueen's would come off the conservation Red List in a flash. But the main purpose of these centres seems to be to produce large numbers of birds for falconry; others die of starvation or get killed by predators. Probably only a small proportion survive in the wild because they are ill equipped to do so and because the habitat remains degraded.

IFHC's Director General, Mohammed Al Baidani, rejects these criticisms. 'Far from being mere "production facilities for killing", the four centres managed by IFHC have advanced the techniques for captive breeding and, in particular, are helping to ensure genetic diversity in our release programme. Sites for the release of birds are also studied to ensure there is the required habitat for them. We would also dispute that falconry is the main reason for the bird's decline in the past.'

'One aim of our programme from the beginning has been to breed sufficient numbers of birds to provide to falconers for training without being detrimental to our conservation objectives. We have now reached a level (our annual production rate in 2013 passed 40,000 birds) where we can put this plan into action,' he adds. 'By doing this we hope that the black market demand for illegal birds will be diminished and that wild populations will no longer be subjected to this criminal activity.'

Commenting on observations that many released bustards appear tame and unable to cope in the wild, al Baidani says: 'Of released birds, only a small minority prove to be too tame but our monitoring helps to identify any such individuals which are usually returned to one of our breeding centres.'

The IFHC's releases hardly conform to the reintroduction guidance issued by IUCN, guidance that is adhered to by almost all other similar projects worldwide. Critics doubt that there

is much genetic diversity amongst released birds or that release sites are assessed fully to gauge how many birds they might support. There is seemingly little recognition of the IUCN's statement that, for reintroductions, 'a release should meet all of the species' requirements and that appropriate habitat for the life stage released, and all life stages of the species, should be present.'

Dr Frédéric Launay, Assistant Secretary General for Science and Research at the Environmental Research and Wildlife Development Agency in Abu Dhabi comments that all the projects are conducted by and through government agencies in the UAE, Morocco and Kazakhstan so all the plans are approved by them. Many of those governments, though, have falconers in decision-making positions. And with many of the released birds used as prey in falconry, a major factor responsible for the huge decline in wild Houbara/MacQueen's Bustards is not only not being addressed, it is being positively encouraged.

Contrast this approach with that underpinning the rehabilitation of the Large Blue Butterfly (Chapter 15) where huge care is taken in breeding and in reintroducing them to sites that are examined carefully to ensure that they are suitable for supporting the insect. Or the enormous amount of work done in Spain and Portugal to get support from hunters, improve habitats and reduce non-natural mortality as vital parts of the reintroduction programme for Iberian Lynx (Chapter 13). It is not criticism that IUCN accepts. 'IUCN generally tries to encourage and support best practice, and continual improvements in conservation programmes rather than acting as a certification agency that passes judgement on who does and does not come up to scratch in relation to our guidelines. And where we do intervene to propose improvements, we generally do this out of the limelight through direct communications with project implementers,' comments Dr Simon Stuart, Chair of the IUCN Species Survival Commission.

❖   ❖   ❖

Much of the success in raising Houbara numbers on Lanzarote has been due to a project led by SEO between 2003 and 2007 and funded by the EU with contributions from the Canary Islands government, the councils of Lanzarote and Fuerteventura, the UK's RSPB and Swarovski, the luxury glass fashion products and optical glass company. Half the 1.5 million EUR budget was spent buying 200 ha of prime Houbara habitat on Fuerteventura, a reserve now named Cercado del Jarde, which is being managed for the birds and other wildlife. There is every reason to believe that Houbara numbers will increase there.

On SEO advice, the Canary Islands government has given protection to almost all of the most important Houbara breeding areas on the two islands. They are designated under the EU Habitats Directive. And SEO has erected nearly 300 signs in Houbara breeding zones to encourage local people and tourists to stay on main roads, thereby reducing disturbance. 'Some of the inland areas on the islands that in the past were quiet and uninhabited, and where birds such as the Houbara were living in peace, now there is much disturbance. Importantly, we are not against tourism. We advocate a tourism that should be respectful to the environment and does not cause as much damage as in recent decades,' comments the SEO's Lorenzo.

And they have encouraged farmers to plant up small areas of land with crops that will benefit both them and Houbara – lucerne, chickpeas, beans, lentils, peas, barley and sweet potato – all of which had long declined. They will need government subsidies to help achieve it. 'Vegetation cover is important for Houbara; we found there are fewer birds on the most open sandy areas especially near roads,' comments Luis Carrascal who has studied Houbara on both islands. 'It's probable that arthropods and other invertebrates are less abundant where there's little vegetation. And if these areas are near roads there's more disturbance from off-road vehicles too.'

It is easy to forget that as recently as the 1980s, there were thought to be no more than 100 Houbara on the Canary Islands but, by 2012, they had increased nearly ten fold to well over 1,000 birds. While their population, maybe for a variety of different reasons, is still relatively low on Fuerteventura, their recovery in the Canary Islands has been a notable success. There is every reason for it to continue. Numbers of Houbara are increasing, too, in northwest Africa where large-scale releases are contributing to a revival of the population. In northeast Africa, Houbara probably languish still. In the Middle East and Asia, a small proportion of the huge numbers of the captive bred and released MacQueen's Bustards – many of which are killed in falconry or dying premature deaths – are nevertheless bolstering the depleted numbers of bustards there too.

If considerably more effort was expended addressing the urgent need to reduce the wide-scale problem of overgrazing across their North Africa to Asia range, then the fortunes of these unusual birds – and other desert species too – would be brighter still.

8

A BREACH IN TIME FOR THE OCEAN GIANT

HUMPBACK WHALE

Whaling, arguably one of the most barbaric animal killing sprees ever embarked upon by humans, has taken many species of whale to near extinction. By the mid 1960s, numbers of Humpback Whales had been reduced to 5,000 or less from a pre-whaling population of maybe 125,000. This impressive and huge mammal, known for its tremendous leaps out of the sea before arching over and crashing back in, was heading rapidly towards extinction. Commercial whaling was banned in 1986 and most Humpback populations worldwide have shown a remarkable, and entirely natural, recovery. Today, at least 80,000 Humpbacks grace our oceans once more and numbers are still increasing.

Heading out from Bar Harbor in Maine past a myriad of tiny islands on the US east coast, the *Atlanticat* makes fast progress into the ocean. The catamaran slows once we are about 40 or 50 km from the coast and we keep a watch all around. It might be midsummer but there's a chill in the air, not that it will bother the huge sea mammals I've come to see. This is prime Humpback Whale territory. Each summer, maybe 800, perhaps more, swim from the Arctic through the Gulf of Maine and feed. They attract boat-fulls of whale watchers while they're here. Now, they'll be feasting in waters rich in sand eels, copepods, plankton and fish. Come October, they'll head on south for the winter to warmer subtropical waters in the Caribbean where they'll mate and give birth.

The first whales we see are relatively small Minkes, each a mere six or seven metres in length, swimming quite close to our catamaran. Then there's a shout and – a few hundred metres away – a huge splash as a massive, fluked tail disappears below the waves in a spray of white water. There is no doubt that it's a Humpback, a full grown adult maybe 15 metres long. A few minutes later and there's a magnificent sight: a Humpback, maybe a different one, breaches up and out of the water, turning itself slightly as it does so, before crashing back down out of sight, its whole dark body visible for just a few seconds.

No one is sure why they do these leaps. It is easy to assume that it's show-off time knowing that there's an audience watching them but there is likely a rather more prosaic reason: a need to loosen skin parasites, to show who's dominant to other humpbacks nearby or as a warning of danger maybe. That doesn't, though, rule out play; whales are intelligent and seemingly playful creatures.

In 2014, there were at least 80,000 humpbacks in the world's oceans. That's down from a pre-whaling population thought by some authorities to have been around 125,000 though the International Whaling Commission (IWC) puts the number today between 75,000 and 100,000. Humpbacks are categorised by IUCN as being of Least Concern (upgraded from its Vulnerable status in the late 1990s) because of their numbers and their vast geographical spread. Most of their populations are increasing, with annual increase rates of up to 10% being recorded in a number of areas including off Australia, Southern Africa and South America according to the IWC. Their relative abundance today is a far cry from their low point in the 1960s; whaling on an industrial scale had reduced their numbers worldwide to around 5,000, maybe fewer. A few more years of horrendous killing and this magnificent animal would very likely have been driven to extinction.

❖　❖　❖

Whales, dolphins and porpoises are together classed as cetaceans; of the 86 species, all are marine except for four species of freshwater dolphins. They range in size from the gorgeous black and white Commerson's Dolphin, which is smaller than a human, to the Blue Whale weighing in at 170 tonnes (that's 24 African Elephants' worth), the largest animal ever known to have lived. All are descendants of land-living mammals that returned to the sea about 50 million years ago, and became fully aquatic maybe ten million years after that; they are the water-loving hippopotamus's closest living relatives. In relatively recent times, there have been two whale extinctions; that of the Gray Whale's Atlantic population in the 18th century and, in all probability, that of the Chinese River Dolphin which hasn't been spotted for more than a decade.

Cetaceans are divided into two major groups; the 'toothed whales' – they use their teeth in hunting – include the dolphins and porpoises, the Sperm, Killer and Beluga Whales. The 'baleen whales' are filter feeders that strain seawater through a large, comb-like mouth structure; the water gets expelled through the small gaps in the baleen plates while the retained crustaceans, small fish and other sea life is swallowed. The baleen whales include the Blue, Humpback, Bowhead and Minke. Humpbacks are members of a family within the baleens called rorquals, as is its closest relative, the Fin Whale.

Like all mammals, whales breathe air, are warm-blooded, nurse their young with milk from mammary glands and have body hair. Beneath the skin lies a layer of fat – blubber – which stores energy and insulates the body. All are long-lived; Humpbacks live for nearly 80 years, Bowheads for a century. They breathe via blowholes; baleen whales have two and toothed whales have one. These are located on the top of the head, allowing the animal to remain almost completely submerged while breathing.

Males are called 'bulls'; females, 'cows'; and newborns, 'calves' but most species do not maintain fixed partnerships and females have several mates each season. They are an object lesson in promiscuity. A cow usually delivers a single calf which is birthed tail-first to minimise the risk of it drowning. The mother nurses the bulky youngster, often for more than a year, by actively squirting milk into its mouth; the milk is pink in colour and so rich in fat that it has

the consistency of toothpaste. Intelligent creatures, known to teach, learn and cooperate, there are suggestions that their nervous system is advanced enough to permit feelings of emotion and aspects of judgement. And they most certainly feel pain.

Unlike most animals, whales are conscious breathers. All mammals sleep but whales cannot afford to become unconscious for long because they could drown. While knowledge of sleep in wild cetaceans is limited, toothed cetaceans in captivity have been recorded sleeping with one side of their brain at a time, ostensibly so that they may swim, breathe consciously and maintain social contact during their period of rest.

A review of all cetaceans by IUCN in 2008 found deterioration in the status of many. Overall, nearly a quarter of them are considered threatened, and of those, at least nine species are listed as Endangered or Critically Endangered. The real situation could be much worse because in more than half of the cetacean species (44 species) there isn't enough information on which to base an assessment. The Blue, Fin and Sei Whales all remain listed as Endangered pending more evidence of recovery. The Vaquita, a rare small porpoise found only in the Gulf of California, will most likely be the next cetacean to go extinct. Critically Endangered, an estimated 15% of its dwindling population is killed in gillnets every year, leaving only about 150 alive in the wild.

With less whale hunting over the last few decades, accidental killing in fishing gear has become the main threat to cetaceans. Besides the Vaquita, the Black Sea Harbour Porpoise, the North Atlantic Right Whale and the Western Grey Whale are among the cetaceans most at risk. Finding effective and workable ways of keeping small cetaceans out of fishing nets, disentangling them once trapped, closing critical areas of the sea to certain types of fishing and reducing the amount of noise from underwater sonar, seismic surveys and shipping would all help.

Climate change is also starting to affect whales. The distribution of many species is altering with the potential for a cascade of effects such as exposure to new diseases, inter-species competition and changes in prey populations. Some of the largest whales in our oceans depend on krill (an ocean mix of small crustaceans) for food; as water temperatures rise, krill populations are likely to decline, reducing the chances of recovery of some of these giants of the living world.

❖   ❖   ❖

First identified by Mathurin Jacques Brisson, a French zoologist, in 1756, it was in 1781 that Georg Heinrich Borowski, a German zoologist, described the Humpback Whale more fully. Brisson gave it the name, *baleine de la Nouvelle Angleterre* presumably because, as now, they were often spotted off the coast of New England. It was later named 'humpback' because it curved its back when it dived. Genetic research has shown that there are three major groupings of Humpbacks: the North Atlantic, North Pacific and the Southern Hemisphere populations. They don't mix. These major populations are subdivided into smaller ones; in the North Pacific, for instance, there are at least three discrete subpopulations.

Humpbacks are well known for their long 'pectoral' fins which can reach almost five metres in length; their scientific name, *Megaptera novaeangliae*, means 'big-winged New Englander' because the New England population was the one best known to Europeans. These long fins give them increased manoeuvrability; they can be used for slowing down or even to go backwards. With a primarily dark grey body, some individuals have a variable amount of white on their pectoral fins and belly. This variation is so distinctive that the pigmentation pattern on the undersides of their 'flukes' – the whale tail – is used to identify individuals just like human fingerprinting. An acrobatic animal known for breaching – leaping out of the water then falling back in head first – and slapping the water with its tail and pectoral fins, this species is particularly popular with whale watchers off several of the world's coasts.

Similar to all baleen whales, adult female Humpbacks, at 15–16 metres, are two or three metres larger than adult males, and weigh around 30 tonnes, the weight of about 18 family cars. Females reach sexual maturity at the age of five, achieving full adult size a little later, while males are sexually mature at about seven. Humpbacks can live up to 50 years so there is usually plenty of opportunity for courtship rituals which can include breaching, tail-slapping, fin-slapping, charging at each other and much else. Competition for mating is usually fierce; males gather into competitive groups and fight for females; group size ebbs and flows as unsuccessful males retreat and others arrive to try their luck.

Cows typically give birth every two or three years after a gestation period of almost a year; some individuals, though, have been known to breed in two consecutive years. Newborn Humpback calves are roughly the length of their mother's head and weigh about 900 kg; they nurse for approximately six months, then mix nursing and independent feeding possibly for six months more before becoming fully independent.

Humpbacks make the longest migration of any mammal on land or at sea. Annual migrations of thousands of kilometres are typical; the record is 8,300 km from Costa Rica to Antarctica and was completed by seven animals, including a calf. One of the more closely studied routes is between Alaska and Hawaii where they have been observed making the 4,830 km trip in as few as 36 days. Not all humpback populations migrate; those in the Arabian Sea stay in their subtropical waters year-round.

During the summer months, they spend the majority of their time feeding and building up fat stores (blubber) that they will live off during the winter fast and they can consume well over 1,000 kg of food per day. This is eating on a truly momentous scale. In the North Atlantic, in addition to large quantities of krill, Humpbacks take herring, capelin, sand eels; less often mackerel, pollock and haddock. An adult has up to 400 baleen plates within each side of its mouth to filter the food out of the seawater it gulps; each measures around 40 cm in the front of its mouth but nearly one metre at the rear.

Humpbacks, too, probably have the most diverse repertoire of methods for catching prey of any of the baleen whales. Several of their hunting methods involve using air bubbles to herd, corral or disorient and concentrate krill and fish. One highly complex variant, called 'bubble netting', is unique to Humpbacks. This technique is often performed cooperatively in groups with individuals having defined roles for distracting, scaring and herding before they lunge at prey corralled near the sea surface. It is a sign of these whales' intelligence that they can cooperate so effectively to achieve a joint goal. But Humpbacks also herd, and possibly disable, their prey by manoeuvring, flicking or pounding the water with their tail flukes and flippers. They sometimes also feed in formation and appear to use sounds produced by several whales at once to synchronise feeding lunges in the water.

They might be good at feeding cooperation but they are not particularly social creatures. Typically, individuals live alone or in small, transient groups that disband after a few hours although they might stay together a little longer in summer to forage and feed. And although their range overlaps considerably with other whale and dolphin species – for instance with the Minke Whale – Humpbacks rarely interact socially with them.

Some whales, including the Humpback, communicate using melodic sounds known unpretentiously as whale song. These can be extremely loud, depending on the species. Both male and female Humpbacks make a range of social sounds to communicate: 'grunts', 'groans', 'snorts' and 'barks'. But only males produce the long, loud, complex 'songs' for which the species is famous. Each song consists of several sounds in a low register, varying in amplitude and frequency and typically lasting from 10 to 20 minutes. They sometimes sing continuously for more than 24 hours. Cetaceans have no vocal cords so they generate their songs by forcing air through their massive nasal cavities. Humpbacks within a large sea area all sing the same song. So all North Atlantic Humpbacks have one song sheet while all those in the North Pacific have a different one. Each population's song changes slowly over a period of years, but without repeating itself. Scientists are unsure of the purpose of these songs; with only males singing it suggests that they might be designed to attract females. But many of the whales observed to approach a singer are other males, often resulting in conflict. Singing may, therefore, be a challenge to other males or, as some scientists have suggested, it might serve an echolocation function so they know where each other is. Whatever, Humpback songs remain something of an enigma.

❖   ❖   ❖

Since prehistoric times humans have killed whales. And it has always been an incredibly bloody and barbaric affair. It was never easy or quick to kill such large creatures. The oldest known method of catching them was simply to drive them ashore by placing a number of small boats between them and the open sea, frightening them with noise and activity and herding them towards the shore in an attempt to beach them. Typically, this was used for small species such as Pilot Whales. The next step was to use something that would partly float in sea water; a wooden drum or an inflated sealskin tied to an arrow or a harpoon. Once the arrow or harpoon had been thrown into a whale's body, the idea was that the buoyancy and drag from the float would eventually tire the whale, allowing it to be approached and killed.

Several cultures around the world practiced this primitive whaling: the Ainu (indigenous people of Japan and Siberia), Inuit (inhabiting the Arctic regions of Greenland, Canada and the US), Native Americans and the Basque people of northern Spain and southwest France. The earliest whale-killing rock carvings – in South Korea – suggest that people were using these methods to kill Sperm, Right and Humpback Whales as early as 6000 BC. By the 9th century, whaling had begun in Norway, France and Spain; a little later in England and Denmark.

The Right Whale was particularly sought after for its meat, its blubber and its baleen. It was the most easily hunted: it comes close to shore; it's slow moving; it can be killed from small boats and it had a high fat content and desirable, long baleen plates. So it was given its name – Right Whale – because whalers considered it the 'right' one to catch! The blubber was boiled to produce whale oil for lamps and to make soap and margarine while the baleen was used wherever strength and flexibility were needed: for fishing rods, parasol ribs, collar stiffeners, chair seats and corset stays. Sperm Whales were sought for ambergris, a solid, waxy substance, dull grey or black in colour, and produced in its digestive system. Freshly produced ambergris has a very unpleasant faecal odour but, as it ages it acquires a sweet, earthy scent. It was valued by perfumers as a fixative (allowing the scent to last much longer); it has since been replaced by synthetic chemicals.

By the 19th century, so many nations were sending so many ships whaling that, even though all the harpooning was done by hand throwing, some whale species were already severely depleted. At its peak in 1846, the American whaling industry employed more than 70,000 people and over 700 ships. Through the 20th century, more than two million whales were killed. In 1870, a Norwegian whaling and shipping magnate, Svend Foyn, together with a Norwegian sea captain, Erik Eriksen, patented and pioneered the exploding whaling harpoon and a cannon to fire it. Foyn's basic design is still in use today. The barbed harpoon included a grenade tip that exploded inside the whale, inflicting a mortal wound. The whale was retrieved by a winch and, once alongside the whaling vessel, it was pumped full of air to keep it afloat for it to be towed to a shore-based processing factory.

Faster, steam or diesel-powered whaling ships with a harpoon gun mounted on the bow soon took over from slower sailing ships and ushered in the modern age of commercial whaling. Whalers were now equipped to hunt faster and more powerful species such as the rorquals (Humpback and Minke Whales for example). And because rorquals sank when they died, later versions of the exploding harpoon injected air into the carcass to keep them afloat. Factory ships – to which the whaling boats brought their catches – became the norm, processing the whales on board before the mammals decomposed; they could do so far from shore and exploit tens of thousands of whales in a year. Onshore whaling bases became superfluous.

But the market for whale products was in decline. By the end of the 19th century when natural oil reserves were discovered, kerosene started replacing whale oil in lamps. And by the 1920s and 1930s, electric lighting had completely destroyed the whale oil market. Fibreglass and plastics started coming into mass production in the 1940s and 1950s, cheaper replacements for baleen products. And, as livestock farming became increasingly intensive, many countries had no need to eat whale meat. It was all in the nick of time. By 1930, 80% of the large whale species were on the verge of extinction.

❖ ❖ ❖

While modern whaling kills whales more quickly, the hunting methods have always been cruel. Dr Peter Corkeron, a whale expert at the National Oceanic and Atmospheric Administration (NOAA) at Woods Hole, US, relates a comment by a biologist who argued that if people killed elephants by spearing them from a tank, and then have the elephant drag the tank around until the creature died, people would be horrified. Whales, like all mammals, feel pain. Before explosive harpoons were in common use, death often resulted only when the hapless animal had been hauled back to the ship and a rifle shot to the whale's brain. 'The original harpoon grenades worked like an old-fashioned hand grenade; the harpoon would go inside the whale, explode and throw metal fragments through the whale's body. Those fragments would cut something important (likely a major blood vessel) which caused death,' comments Corkeron. 'In the 1980s, the Norwegians developed a different harpoon grenade, the "penthrite" grenade. It uses a modern explosive charge, and provided it hits accurately, when it goes off it sends a shock wave through the whale's body, causing brain death or at least unconsciousness prior to death.' According to research published in 1995, the use of the penthrite grenade with Minke Whales in Norwegian whaling showed that nearly half died instantaneously. Even so, many of the others suffered for up to several minutes.

In 1925, the League of Nations raised concerns about the over-exploitation of whale stocks and called for conservation measures. This eventually led to the Geneva Convention for the Regulation of Whaling in 1935, but which was ignored by Japan, Russia and Germany. It restricted the kills of some baleen whales including immature and suckling whales. It also introduced the need for whaling vessels to require permits and make regular reports on catches. In 1937, some limits were put in place to prevent excessive whale exploitation but specifically to prevent the extinction of the Blue Whale. This was followed in 1946 by the creation of the International Convention for the Regulation of Whaling to 'provide for the proper conservation of whale stocks and thus make possible the orderly development of the whaling industry'. It led to the formation by 15 nations of the International Whaling Commission (IWC) which introduced guidelines for the regulation of whaling, prevented whalers from hunting Grey and Right Whales, developed quotas for the numbers of whales various countries could kill, and designated areas and times of the year when whalers could hunt. But making rules was a lot easier than enforcing them. Too many whales were still being killed. One after another, remaining whale populations were hunted to near extinction as member nations pursued their own self-interests. But, as whale populations diminished, whaling became increasingly uneconomic and many of the whaling nations started to hang up their harpoons.

By the late 1960s and early 1970s, as public environmental awareness increased, the words 'Save the Whales' began to appear on bumper stickers, fliers, T-shirts and petitions. New conservation groups dedicated to the purpose formed; they included ordinary citizens and social radicals whose ideas on how to respond varied widely. A few former whaling countries – and many non-whaling countries – began to push for whale conservation. With Humpback numbers falling rapidly, a ban on killing them was introduced in the mid 1960s covering first the North Pacific population, followed by a ban in Antarctic waters.

❖ ❖ ❖

Increasing public abhorrence of whale killing, a slow recognition by most countries that whaling was unsustainable, a declining market for whale products…and a song…all helped end most commercial whaling. Roger Payne and Scott McVay, two US scientists, recorded and produced the popular *Songs of the Humpback Whale* after their 1967 discovery of whale song among breeding humpbacks. The sounds (then available on vinyl LPs) caught the public interest and imagination, confirming the intelligence of these seaborne giants. Payne described them as 'exuberant, uninterrupted rivers of sound' with long repeated 'themes', each song lasting up to 30 minutes and sung by an entire group of male Humpbacks at once. The songs would vary slightly between each breeding season with a few new phrases added and others dropped. Commenting on the original recording, Paul Winter, the US saxophonist wrote: 'Hearing this album was a milestone experience in my musical life. I was thrilled by the haunting beauty of these Humpback Whale voices, much as I had been when I first heard jazz saxophonists like Charlie Parker.'

In 1979, the IWC banned the hunting of all whale species (except Minkes) by factory ships. In 1982, it adopted an indefinite global moratorium on commercial whaling which came into force in 1986, though loopholes allowed Japan, Norway and Iceland to continue. Russia, too, continued whaling but eventually stopped. Two whale sanctuaries were designated by the IWC, both of which prohibited commercial whaling. The first, the Indian Ocean Sanctuary, was established in 1979; the second was adopted in 1994 and covers the waters of the Southern Ocean around Antarctica. An additional proposal for a sanctuary in the South Atlantic Ocean has been repeatedly submitted to the Commission in recent years but it has so far failed to achieve the three-quarters majority of votes needed to be designated.

Under the terms of the moratorium, whaling is allowed by native peoples if it occurs on a subsistence basis where it has long been part of a local tradition; such subsistence whaling takes place by peoples in Alaska, in part of the Russian Far East, in Greenland, by Inuits, by some very small communities in the Caribbean and by some in Indonesia. Catch limits are set by the IWC; from 1985 to 2012, that total catch was 9,393 whales of which 83 were Humpbacks. Most were Minke and Grey Whales.

The role of the IWC is to control whaling by protecting certain species; designating areas as whale sanctuaries; setting limits on the numbers and size of catches; prescribing open and closed seasons and areas for whaling; the methods and intensity of whaling; the types of gear to be used and maximum catches. All its decisions are supposed to be based on good science. Rather peculiarly, maybe, participation in the IWC is not limited to states currently or previously involved in whaling. Even landlocked states such as Hungary can join and vote – and non-whaling nations eventually gained a majority over the whaling nations. As of July 2013 there were 88 members. Some countries that had been avid whalers, like the US, even became strong proponents of the anti-whaling cause.

Despite the moratorium, loopholes in the IWC convention allow some commercial whaling to continue. Any member country may lodge an objection to an IWC decision and be exempt from that decision. Norway lodged an objection to the moratorium in 1982 and is not bound by it. It continues to hunt Minke Whales in the North Atlantic. Iceland left the IWC in 1992 but rejoined in 2003 with a reservation to the moratorium. It restarted commercial whaling in 2006. Controversially, Japan conducts commercial whaling in the Antarctic and North Pacific under a clause in the IWC convention that allows countries to kill whales for 'scientific research'. It began this 'scientific whaling' in the Antarctic in 1987 and in the North Pacific in 1996. The IWC has repeatedly requested that Japan stops this 'research' but under IWC rules, Japan is free to set its own quotas. And that is exactly what it does in spite of widespread international criticism. At the end of each season it informs the IWC what it has caught. The meat from this 'research whaling' is packaged and sold openly in markets. Between 1986, when the whaling ban came in, and 2012, Japan, Norway and Iceland killed a total of 15,563 whales (the lion's share by Japan), an average of about 600 each year. None were recorded as Humpbacks.

In April 2014, The International Court of Justice ordered a temporary halt to Japan's annual slaughter of whales in the southern ocean after concluding that the hunts are not, as Japan claims, conducted for scientific research. The case had been brought by the Australian government, a long time advocate of banning all whaling. The essence of the judgment was that Japan had failed to prove that their killing – mainly of many hundreds of Minke Whales each year – was needed for 'scientific purposes.' Almost immediately, Japan announced that it would still proceed with a smaller 'research programme' in the northwest Pacific. Japan's Agriculture, Forestry and Fisheries Ministry said the catch from the upcoming Pacific mission would be reduced from 380 whales to 210 and non-lethal research methods would be explored. In a separate statement, fisheries minister Yoshimasa Hayashi said Japan would conduct research whaling 'based on international law and scientific evidence', while maintaining its policy of 'aiming for the resumption of commercial whaling'. Tokyo is making preparations to submit a revised whaling plan for both the Pacific and the Antarctic to the IWC for the 2015/6 season.

Although few people in Japan regularly eat whale meat, many support the controversial whaling 'research programme'. A survey, released by the Japanese newspaper *Asahi Shimbun* in April 2014 found that 60% of respondents thought that research whaling should continue while around 23% said the practice should stop. Almost half of those who thought the research should continue said they didn't eat whale meat; 4% said they consumed whale meat 'occasionally' while 10% said they ate it on 'rare occasions'.

Much like the UN, the IWC can only introduce measures that have the support of the majority of its member states and can only make progress at the pace they determine. 'The IWC whaling moratorium was, and continues to be, a major step forward in controlling whaling,' comments Chris Butler-Stroud, CEO of Whale and Dolphin Conservation, the wildlife charity dedicated to the worldwide conservation and welfare of whales, dolphins and porpoises. 'Before the moratorium, tens of thousands of whales were being killed annually and the number of countries engaged in whaling was significantly higher than today. The moratorium is still a visible and effective inhibitor of new whaling operations emerging in what are currently non-whaling countries. There are thousands of whales alive today because of the moratorium and the work of the conservation initiatives within the IWC.'

'The IWC has some significant inherent loopholes, such as the ability of a member state to take unlimited numbers of whales under so-called "scientific whaling", but members of the IWC are wrestling with how to address these abuses. It has come a long way in 70 years but it's also a prisoner of its past. The conservation work it has undertaken shouldn't be thrown out simply because it needs to be able to do more to control existing abuses,' says Butler-Stroud.

Substantial international disgust at these continued whaling operations has seemingly not influenced those few nations still whaling. But it has spawned some organisations that have taken direct action to try and prevent or reduce the whalers' activities. The most aggressive of these is the Sea Shepherd Conservation Society, a non-profit, marine conservation organisation based in the US which was founded in 1977 by Paul Watson who broke away from Greenpeace because of what he perceived as its lack of more aggressive tactics. It has attracted considerable publicity, substantial private funding and much criticism too. Some governments have labelled its members as 'eco terrorists' and 'pirates' and a few have taken legal action to curb its activities. Its actions have included scuttling and disabling whaling vessels in harbours, shining lasers into the eyes of whalers, throwing bottles of foul-smelling butyric acid onto vessels at sea, boarding whaling vessels and seizing and destroying drift nets. It claims that its aggressive actions are necessary because the international community has shown itself unwilling or unable to stop whaling and unsustainable fishing practices.

❖ ❖ ❖

Humpback Whales have been hunted since the 18th century for their oil, meat and baleen, in early whaling days particularly by the British and Americans. One of the big English whaling companies was Samuel Enderby & Sons, based in London and founded in the late 18th century. The company encouraged their captains to combine exploration with their business activities and sponsored several of the earliest expeditions to the sub-Antarctic, Southern Ocean and Antarctica. It had ships registered in London and Boston, US. The vessels transported finished goods to the American colonists and brought whale oil back from New England to England. Some of Enderby's ships were reportedly chartered for the tea cargoes that were ultimately dumped into Boston Harbour during the Boston Tea Party incident in 1773. An embargo was placed on whale oil exports from New England in 1775 as a result of the American War of Independence. So Enderby decided to pursue the whaling trade in the South Atlantic; by 1785, the company had 17 whaling ships. But with whale numbers falling in the South Atlantic, in early 1786 he lobbied the UK government for the right to go into the South Pacific and in 1788 the whaling vessel *Amelia*, commanded by Captain James Shields, departed London to become the first ship to catch whales in the Southern Ocean. By 1791, the company owned or leased 68 whaling ships operating in the sub-Antarctic region and the Southern Ocean, some of them carrying convicts to New South Wales on their way out.

Captain Eber Bunker of the *William and Ann*, another Enderby ship, not wanting to return to England with an empty vessel, became the first to hunt whales in New Zealand waters in December 1791. Governor Phillip Parker King of New South Wales worked to attract the whaling industry, establishing Hobart as a major centre for the Southern Ocean whale fishery in 1806. It became the greatest whaling port in the British Empire. Over the next 50 years, whaling flourished along the coast of New South Wales, Tasmania, South and Western Australia supported by several shore-based whale processing plants. The main targets were the slower moving Sperm and Southern Right Whales, both of them wanted for their oil. Few Humpbacks were taken.

The introduction of faster ships and the explosive harpoon in the late 19th century changed that. Humpback numbers started to fall as thousands were slaughtered. By the 1930s, there were 41 factory ships in Antarctica with 200 whaling ships that, during the one season of 1930/1, killed 40,000 whales, many of them Humpbacks. The killing continued over the decades into the 1960s by which time the scarcity of whales had reduced the Antarctic fleet to nine factory ships. And because Right Whales had been severely depleted from earlier sailing ship whaling in the late 19th century, Humpbacks were the primary species targeted between 1900 and 1964. According to IWC figures, of the just over two million whales killed in the

Southern Oceans between 1900 and 2005, 213,000 were Humbacks. Well over 40,000 more were taken illegally by the USSR whaling fleet in these waters but not reported to the IWC. The global population of Humpbacks had been reduced by over 90%, with North Atlantic populations estimated to have dropped to as low as 700 individuals.

Wally Franklin, with his wife Trish, runs the The Oceania Project, a research and information organisation dedicated to raising awareness of cetaceans and the ocean environment, off the eastern Australian coast. He reckons that the eastern Australian Humpback population prior to World War II was over 22,000 individuals. In 1952, industrial shore-based whaling started up along that coast and, together with massive illegal whaling in the Southern Ocean in the early 1960s, their population had collapsed by the mid 1960s. When the IWC declared complete protection for southern Humpback Whales in 1963, less than 200 survived there.

❖   ❖   ❖

Humpbacks (and other species) are vulnerable to other threats. They can become entangled in fishing gear, either swimming off with it or becoming anchored by it, causing injury or even death by drowning. Inadvertent ship strikes can injure or kill them too. Dredging of shipping channels, unsustainable fishery developments that can occupy or destroy their feeding areas, recreational use of inshore waters and increased boat traffic may displace whales from an historic area. Acoustic impacts from vessel operation, oceanographic research using sonar, and military operations are all of increasing concern; changes in whale behaviour such as more frequent and unexplained beachings by groups of smaller whales that use echo-location are thought by some to be a result of ships using sonar interfering with whale communication. Pollution and climate change might have a long term impact on whale populations too.

At Hervey Bay on the Australian east coast, Trish Franklin points out that even though Humpback numbers are rising, human activities including increased boat traffic, pollution, aquaculture development and habitat degradation are all increasing rapidly too. 'The Gulf of Maine feeding population is significantly affected by vessel strikes and net entanglements which may be hampering its recovery,' comments Regina Asmutis-Silvia, Executive Director for North America of Whale and Dolphin Conservation. 'Between 2006 and 2010, the annual mortality estimate from fishery entanglements alone was 3%, the same as the assumed rate of increase of the population; this doesn't include mortality caused by vessel strikes so, based on these data, it's likely that the population is in decline,' she adds.

Some populations are also of concern because they are not recovering as fast as others. Across a vast sector of the South Pacific Ocean, Humpbacks are seemingly not doing as well as they are off Australia's east coast. A study led by Dr Rochelle Constantine of the University of Auckland estimated 3,000–5,000 breeding in the region in 2005; it is the least abundant Humpback population in the Southern Hemisphere and it has clearly not been recovering from the enormous whaling losses it suffered – particularly in the 1960s – as rapidly as most others. But why?

'It could be recovering slowly but we don't have the detail in the surveys to be able to detect it. There's little evidence of any sort of impact from ship collisions, net entanglements and so on,' says Dr Mike Noad of the University of Queensland. 'Perhaps they feed in areas of the Southern Ocean that aren't too productive. Another theory is that maybe the east Australian population is acting as a sink for the South Pacific Humpbacks with whales drifting west and joining the east Australian population. But that seems unlikely and there's little evidence of any interchange between them from photo IDs of individuals.'

There are other possible explanations. 'Humpbacks are social animals that congregate annually in tropical areas to breed. If these breeding populations are reduced to very low numbers there might be reasons reducing their ability to recover,' comments Dr Debbie Steel, one of Rochelle Constantine's co-researchers now at Oregon State University's Marine Mammal Institute and Department of Fisheries and Wildlife. 'The ratio of females to males may become strongly biased towards one or other sex, making it harder to find a member of the opposite sex to mate with; the number of whales could be so low that even finding a mate is difficult; or, if the population remains low for a few generations, the whales within it become more and more inbred. So their genetic diversity becomes low and reduced reproductive success becomes more likely,' she adds.

The non-migratory Arabian Sea population remains very small, maybe 80 or so animals; as such this isolated group is categorised as Endangered by IUCN in stark contrast to its assessment of Humpbacks elsewhere in the world's oceans. Although killed illegally by whalers up until the 1960s, no one is clear whether this unique population is now increasing or decreasing in number. Ship collisions and entanglement in fishing gear remain threats.

With these two exceptions, though, sometime since the 1960s Humpbacks across most of the world's oceans started to increase, albeit from very low numbers of perhaps 5,000 worldwide and a trajectory that was otherwise destined to take them to the brink of extinction within a short time. All they needed to increase, in essence, was a cessation of the slaughter they had long endured. In eastern Australia for instance, in the 30 years to 1992, they are estimated to have increased from 200 to 1,900 with a further increase to about 3,185 by 1996. From then to 2009, it continued with an annual growth rate of over 10%.

'When I started helping on Humpback surveys off southeast Queensland in the early 1980s, people didn't think whales were found there. We'd be asked "What are you doing?" and usually get strange looks,' remembers Peter Corkeron. 'Now, during whale migration, you can sit at a coffee shop near where the surveys are still run and see whales in the time it takes to get a cup of coffee. And that's not a reflection on slow coffee service! The story for almost all the Humpback populations in the Southern Hemisphere is really optimistic.'

It is a success story recalled equally by Dr Michael Bryden, formerly Chair of Veterinary Anatomy in the University of Sydney, Australia: 'In 1977, I had discussions with Australian National Parks and Wildlife [ANPWS] about the possibility of doing some surveys to determine whether any Humpback Whales were migrating along our coasts at all. A friend who owned a holiday shack on Stradbroke Island near Brisbane remembered seeing many of them from it as a boy but by then hadn't seen a whale for at least 18 years.'

'In 1979 I spent quite a bit of time there scanning the sea for whales without success. However, during a flight over the area I saw what I was pretty certain was one Humpback and a few weeks later I saw a group of three passing north close to the headland. I got some funding from ANPWS to carry out a survey during the northward migration beginning in 1980 and surveys have continued since; the remarkable recovery of the population followed. We estimated that their rate of recovery, which had barely increased at all between 1963 and 1980, was dramatic after 1980, approximately 12.5% per annum,' he adds.

For a quarter of a century, Wally and Trish Franklin have been recording humpback numbers and identifying individuals at Hervey Bay near Brisbane. They differentiate them from the patterns on their tail flukes.

The bay, a sea area between the Australian east coast and Fraser Island, is a key part of the 14,000 km² Great Sandy Biosphere Reserve. It was accepted by UNESCO in 2009 and incorporates a wide range of coastal habitats. The campaign to get it designated was promoted by FFI because of the outstanding wildlife and habitats in the region, the Humpback Whale being one of the key species. 'They are a good news story in terms of recovery, although the story isn't complete yet. We estimate it will take a further 50 years for them to recover to pre-whaling levels,' says Wally Franklin. 'Hervey Bay is extremely important to the recovery of the eastern Australian and Pacific Humpback Whales and the recovery rate here is one of the highest in the world. Large numbers of Humpbacks stop over from July to October during their southern migration. Between 30% and 50% of eastern Australian Humpbacks use Hervey Bay, that's maybe 10,000–15,000 Humpbacks stopping for a few days en route.'

In many parts of the world – including the coast of Maine and Australia's Hervey Bay – wherever Humpbacks pass close to shore, commercial whale watching has become an important segment of the tourism industry, contributing substantial sums to local economies. Tens, maybe hundreds of thousands of tourists – many of whom have never before seen a whale, let alone seen one close up – get entranced by these remarkable creatures. And Humpbacks, maybe also the sight of a pod of dolphins or porpoises zooming over the waves, are frequently the show-stoppers.

The Humpback Whale is the only example in this book of an animal that has very largely recovered its populations without any human intervention other than a cessation in killing it. And it has done so in half a century. Today there are an estimated 80,000 or more Humpbacks in the world's oceans; up to 20,000 of them in the North Pacific, about 12,000 in the North Atlantic and over 50,000 in the Southern Ocean. That might, or might not, be down a little from their numbers in pre-whaling days but it's a faster comeback than many experts predicted. And although a couple of populations are still struggling to recover, most of the world's Humpback Whales are thriving once again just half a century after the cessation of one of the most barbaric animal killing sprees our human species has ever embarked upon, causing enormous suffering to what we now know to be particularly sensitive animals.

Paul Winter, the US saxophonist, perhaps best sums up their attraction:

'Studying the long, complex songs which the whales repeat again and again, I was amazed by their musical intelligence, and shocked to learn that these magnificent beings were rapidly being hunted to extinction. The whales opened my ears to the whole symphony of nature, and expanded my world forever.'

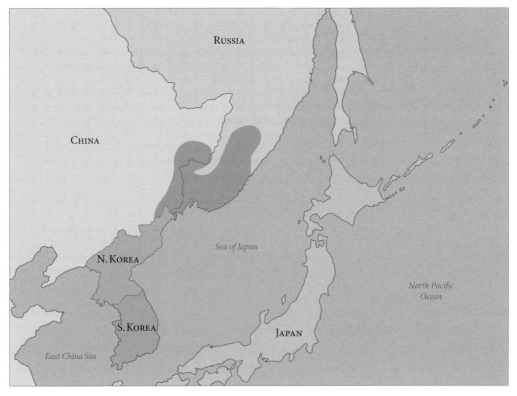

Shaded zone: Siberian Tiger Range

9

BURNING A LITTLE BRIGHTER

SIBERIAN TIGER

Reduced to maybe 40 individuals in the 1930s because of uncontrolled hunting and trapping, the Siberian Tiger population had recovered well until the collapse of the Soviet Union in the 1990s. With no law enforcement and economic chaos, the tiger became an instant cash cow, its body parts worth good money for traditional, but useless, medicines and potions in huge demand across the suddenly porous Chinese border. Illegal poaching remains an enormous concern but Siberian Tiger numbers are now approaching ten times what they were at their low point. More large forest reserves have been designated in Russia and China and both countries seem committed to this magnificent animal's future. How rosy that future becomes depends much on curbing the illegal and still sizeable trade in tiger body parts across Southeast Asia.

When the Supreme Soviet of the USSR signed declaration 142-H at Moscow's Kremlin, formally dissolving the communist state on 26 December 1991, not many people in the West were paying attention. On the previous day – Christmas Day – Soviet President Mikhail Gorbachev had resigned, declaring his office extinct. That same evening, the Soviet flag was lowered from the Kremlin for the last time and replaced with the Russian tricolor. The dissolution of the State also marked a formal end to the Cold War; the so-called Iron Curtain had been dismantled a few years before. Hailed across the West as a vital step towards world peace, democracy and a 'coming in from the cold' of Russia and its former Soviet satellites, the collapse of the Soviet Union led to a severe economic crisis and a catastrophic fall in the standard of living in post-Soviet states and the former Eastern Bloc, worse even than that of the 1930s Great Depression.

In the vast spruce, oak and birch forests of Russia's distant eastern coast facing the Sea of Japan – 7,000 km from Moscow – the people who eked out a living in the few small towns and villages suffered enormous deprivation. With political and economic collapse, rampant inflation and an absence of any law enforcement, with their life savings having to be spent in days – often on useless items – before the money's value disappeared entirely, the inhabitants of this part of eastern Siberia turned to what they always turned to in hard times: the forest.

Legal hunting of tigers within the USSR was officially prohibited in 1947, the first country in the world to give them protection. But after the dissolution of the Soviet Union, illegal deforestation, no enforcement of hunting laws and easy bribery of reserve rangers made the poaching of Siberian Tigers commonplace, putting them yet again at risk of extinction. Along with timber, meat, berries, mushrooms and nuts the local inhabitants could always obtain from the forest that dominated their landscape; the now porous border with China provided a huge new opportunity. The Chinese would pay good money for tiger bones, their skins and their penises. Very good money indeed. Tiger pelts were fetching over $5,000, and bones up to $3,000 per kg, huge sums of money compared with the average annual forestry worker's wage (if he was getting paid at all), making them highly attractive items in such an economically stressed region.

In the 1920s and 1930s the enormous conflicts of the Russian Civil War (1917–1922) and outright persecution of these enormous cats – the biggest in the world – had reduced their numbers to maybe 40 individuals. Both the Russian Red and White armies had, between them, nearly wiped out all the local tigers. In 1925, Nikolai Baikov, a member of the Russian Academy of Sciences with a particular interest in the Siberian Tiger, estimated that roughly 100 tigers had been taken out of the region each year for the Chinese market. But as their numbers dwindled, the few that remained in this vast tract – about a third of a million square kilometres – of isolated forest and mountain, became increasingly difficult to track down. Then, World War II intervened. With many men away fighting and strong law enforcement over subsequent years, there were few incentives to kill tigers unless they came into conflict with people. So by the time the USSR was dissolved at the end of 1991, Siberian Tigers had bred in relative peace and quiet for several decades and their numbers had grown back to around 500. Ironically, then, the end result of *glasnost* (increased openness) and *perestroika* (restructuring), hallmarks of the Gorbachev era, threatened this magnificent animal's future once again.

The Siberian Tiger, an animal revered and feared in equal measure by most of the Russian Far East's villagers, had become during the 1990s a human lifeline for those willing to risk hunting it. The huge area it inhabits is dominated by forests of coniferous trees such as spruce, fir and pine with the addition of broadleaves including birch and oak. They also nurture Amur Leopards, Himalayan Black Bears, Reindeer, Sable (a marten species historically hunted for its fur), Wild Boar, Brown Bears and European Lynx. Edible and medicinal plants, including wild berries, Siberian pine nuts, wild ginseng, other medicinal herbs and mushrooms provide a cornucopia of food and traditional medicines for people many of whom have spent their lives harvesting these forests to supplement any meagre income. Here, long winters where the sun doesn't rise far above the horizon and daytime temperatures well below freezing are standard. Summers are short.

Once found throughout the forests of the Russian Far East, China and the Korean peninsula, Siberian Tigers are now restricted to the Sikhote-Alin range of forested hills and valleys in the Russian Far East (an area about 1,000 km north to south and half that distance east to west) and to small pockets in the border areas of China. Though the climate is far harsher than that experienced by other tiger subspecies further south in Asia where it's generally much warmer, the Siberian Tiger has the advantage that these forests offer the lowest human density of any tiger habitat although the whole area is criss-crossed with logging roads and most of it has been logged at least once. Nevertheless, many of its animal populations have declined long term – some continue to do so – because of poaching and habitat loss. In places, unplanned industrial development, excessive timber harvesting and mining have all diminished or degraded the forest.

❖ ❖ ❖

The Siberian Tiger, also known as the Amur Tiger (named after the Amur river which forms the border between the Russian Far East and Northeast China), ranks amongst the largest cats ever to have existed. With a head and body length up to 1.7 metres for females and two metres for males, the Siberian Tiger – one of six living subspecies – is larger than the better known Bengal Tiger of the Indian subcontinent and the African Lion. Its tail adds another metre.

Siberian Tigers reach sexual maturity at four years of age and they mate at any time of year. A female signals her receptiveness by leaving urine deposits and scratch marks on trees. Born after three or four months, the litter size – tigresses usually give birth every other year – is normally two to four cubs. Born blind in a sheltered den, they are left alone when the female leaves to hunt for food. Female cubs eventually establish territories close to their original ranges while males range farther earlier in their lives, making them much more vulnerable to poachers and fights with other tigers. 'We've found that young adult males have very high rates of mortality, and seem to get into trouble in all kinds of ways,' comments Dale Miquelle, Director of the (US headquartered) Wildlife Conservation Society Russia Program.

In a study between the early 1990s and 2010, Miquelle and his colleagues captured 11 Siberian Tigers, fitted them with radio-collars and monitored them for well over a year in the eastern slopes of the Sikhote-Alin mountains. They found that tiger distribution was closely associated with the distribution of Red Deer, seemingly their main prey, less so with the distribution of wild pigs, Siberian Roe Deer, Sika Deer and Moose. Tigers here also take other prey including Musk Deer, Goral (goat-like mammals), rabbits, pikas (small rodents) and salmon. So managing these prey species is vital for tiger conservation. And prey abundance is almost certainly the main reason why tigers are more abundant in the Russian *zapovedniks* (their strictly protected reserves) than outside them.

Wolves are scarce in Siberian Tiger habitat; they are only found in scattered pockets, and are usually seen travelling as loners or in small groups. First hand accounts of interactions between the two species indicate that tigers occasionally chase wolves from their kills, while wolves will scavenge from tiger kills. Tigers are not known to prey on wolves, though there are four records of tigers killing wolves without consuming them. This competitive exclusion of wolves by tigers has been used by Russian conservationists to convince hunters in the Far East to tolerate the big cats because they limit deer populations less than wolves, and are effective in controlling wolf numbers.

But will the Siberian Tiger kill people? They most certainly can, but there have been very few instances of it happening. They have killed nowhere near as many people as the Bengal Tiger reputedly has. Not that the Siberian Tiger is at all a gentle animal; it can't be to survive. But Miquelle reckons it's largely down to learning…by the tigers that is. 'When the majority of people have no means of defence – firearms – tigers figure that out and include them on the list of potential prey. But where you have a heavily armed population such as here, tigers also figure that out. The implication is that you need to teach people that tigers are dangerous, and you need to teach tigers that people are dangerous,' says Miquelle. Attacks on humans were recorded in the 19th century and there are accounts of several people being killed in some years. Only six cases of unprovoked attacks leading to man-eating behaviour were recorded in 20th century Russia. Provoked attacks are more common, usually the result of botched attempts at capturing them; 50% of tigers that attacked people turn out to have been wounded previously.

In December 1997, an injured Siberian Tiger attacked, killed and consumed two people in the Russian Far East; the story is told in *The Tiger: A True Story of Vengeance and Survival* (Hodder and Stoughton, 2010) by John Vaillant. In it, the author develops a theme, espoused by some local people, that this injured tiger was somehow engaged in a vendetta against its attackers, a claim thought to be highly speculative by tiger experts. The local Russian anti-poaching task force, Inspection Tiger, investigated both deaths, tracked down and eventually killed the tiger.

In January 2002, according to reports in *China Daily*, a man named as Qu Shuangxi was attacked by a Siberian Tiger on a remote mountain road near Hunchun in northeast China. He suffered substantial injuries but managed to survive. The tiger later killed a young woman on the same road. When the attacks were investigated, it turned out that the tiger was horrendously injured by a poacher's snare. In spite of surgery, the tiger died. The first victim admitted to being the poacher who had injured the tiger. After a two year prison sentence, he was made to work clearing forest snares and is now participating in a tiger conservation project in China's Hunchun Nature Reserve.

❖ ❖ ❖

Undoubtedly one of the most recognisable and popular of the world's charismatic animals and known for its enormous strength and beauty, tigers are supreme amongst predators. They once ranged widely across Asia. Over the past century, they have been lost from a staggering 90% or more of this historic range. Their global population in the wild is estimated to number 3,000–4,000 individuals, down from maybe 100,000 at the start of the 20th century, with most remaining populations occurring in small pockets isolated from each other. The main reasons for their decline include habitat destruction and fragmentation as urban areas have expanded and agriculture has intensified. Illegal trapping and shooting continue to take a huge toll.

Featuring prominently in ancient mythology and folklore, tigers continue to be depicted in modern films and literature. They appear on many flags, coats of arms, and as mascots for sporting teams. The tiger figures in literature; both Rudyard Kipling, in *The Jungle Book* (1894), and William Blake, in his set of poems *Songs of Experience* (1789), depict the tiger as a menacing and fearful animal. Other depictions are more benign: Tigger, the tiger from A.A. Milne's *Winnie-the-Pooh* stories is cuddly and likeable. In the Man Booker Prize winning novel *Life of Pi* (2001) a fantasy adventure by Yann Martel, the protagonist Pi Patel, sole human survivor of a ship wreck in the Pacific Ocean, befriends another survivor: a large Bengal Tiger he names Richard Parker. In a poll conducted in 2004 by *Animal Planet*, the US cable and satellite television channel, the tiger was voted the world's favourite animal, narrowly beating the dog. Whether this popularity has helped to provide resources to conserve them, or influenced governments where they still occur to do more to improve their lot is, however, highly doubtful.

The tiger is the national animal of Bangladesh, India, Vietnam, Malaysia and South Korea in several of which, ironically, it is suffering most. It also replaces the lion as 'king of the beasts' in the cultures of East Asia where it represents royalty, fearlessness and wrath. Its forehead has a marking which resembles the Chinese character meaning 'king'. In Chinese myth and culture, it is one of the twelve zodiac animals, often depicted as an earth symbol and equal rival of the Chinese dragon, the two representing matter and spirit respectively. The Tungusic people of eastern Siberia considered the tiger a near-deity and often referred to it as 'grandfather' or 'old man' while the Manchus (a branch of the Tungusic people) considered it as *Hu Lin*, the king.

Some kind of tiger has roamed this Earth since the Pleistocene up to 1.8 million years ago. Its oldest fossil remains were found in China, an irony not lost on tiger enthusiasts who view the country as central to the tiger's demise. From the Pacific coast in eastern Asia – China today – tigers originally spread west as far as the Middle East. At one time they even made it as far west as present day Ukraine. But no further. And they failed to cross the land or ice bridge that once connected Siberia across the Bering Strait to North America, so no tigers ever made it to the so-called New World.

❖   ❖   ❖

There are – or were – nine subspecies of tiger: Bengal, Indochinese, Malayan, Sumatran and Siberian survive; the South China subspecies is probably extinct with the Bali, Caspian and Javan subspecies confirmed as extinct. The species as a whole is classified by IUCN as Endangered and most of its subspecies continue to decline, though not all.

The most abundant surviving subspecies is the Bengal Tiger found in parts of India, Nepal, Bhutan, and Bangladesh with a total population estimated at around 2,500 adult individuals, the majority in India. It lives in valley bottom grasslands, forests and mangroves. In spite of improved attempts since the early 1970s by the Indian authorities to protect populations and reserves, illicit demand for bones and body parts for use in traditional Chinese medicine has placed unrelenting poaching pressure on tigers there. Between 1994 and 2009, the Wildlife Protection Society of India documented nearly 900 tiger kills, considered to be a fraction of the actual poaching and illegal trade in tiger parts during those years. The Sundarbans Reserve Forest – vast mangrove forests in the Ganges delta – is the last stronghold of Bengal Tigers in

Bangladesh; there are claims, strongly disputed by experts, that it supports 300–500 adults. Threats there range from poaching to sea level rise.

In the past, killing tigers was seen as great sport, especially in the early 19th and 20th centuries for the British ruling classes and the maharajas in colonial India. The tiger was one of the 'Big Five' game animals of Asia. A single maharaja or English hunter could claim to kill over 100 tigers in his hunting career. In 1911, Britain's newly crowned King George V went on an elephant-borne tiger hunt in Nepal; he and his retinue shot 39 tigers in ten days. Unfortunately, that was comparatively small fry – the then Maharaja of Udaipur claimed to have shot at least 1,000 of them by 1959. The hunting was sometimes done on foot; others sat in elevated hides with a live goat or buffalo tied out as bait; yet others hunted on elephant-back. In some cases, villagers beating drums were organised to drive the animals into the killing zone. The trade in tiger skins peaked in the 1960s just before international conservation restrictions took effect. In some parts of its range, though, the future for the Bengal Tiger is a little more positive. In Nepal, for instance, a community-based tourism model has been developed with a strong emphasis on sharing benefits with local people and on the regeneration of degraded forests. Today, around 200 tigers roam Nepal's lowland forests.

The Indochinese Tiger subspecies is found in China, Burma, Thailand and with maybe a handful left in Laos. Smaller and darker than Bengal Tigers, they prefer forests in mountainous or hilly regions where their populations are hard to assess; there might be anywhere between a few hundred and a thousand. But all of them are at extreme risk from poaching, from prey depletion as a result of people killing deer and wild pigs, habitat fragmentation, and inbreeding.

The Malayan subspecies of tiger, one of the smallest, lives only in the southern part of the Malay Peninsula. According to official government figures, there might be 500 – in reality there are probably far less – and it is under considerable poaching pressure. A national icon in Malaysia, it appears on its coat of arms and in logos of Malaysian institutions such as Maybank, the largest banking and finance group in the country. Shamefully, none of this veneration has seemingly helped its fortunes; the subspecies is declining because of the usual problems of habitat destruction together with poaching and an added issue: in Malaysia there is a substantial domestic market for tiger meat and tiger bone medicines.

The Sumatran Tiger is confined to the Indonesian island of Sumatra and is Critically Endangered. It is the smallest of all living tiger subspecies, an adaptation to the thick, dense forests in which they live as well as the smaller-sized prey available to them. There are maybe 400–500; in the late 1970s they perhaps numbered 1,000. 'Indonesia has a nationwide logging moratorium that prevents the clearance of new forests, although old concessions can still be operated,' says Dr Matthew Linkie, FFI's Regional Conservation and Development Adviser for Southeast Asia. 'It's not perfect, but certainly offers a more stringent legal framework within which we can operate.' In spite of the tiger having legal protection, a substantial market remains in Sumatra and the rest of Asia for tiger parts and products. TRAFFIC (the wildlife trade monitoring network) estimates that poaching for this trade is responsible for over three quarters of Sumatran Tiger deaths: at least 40 animals per year. As communities expand and tiger habitat declines, human/tiger conflict has become a serious problem in Sumatra; people have been killed or wounded while retaliatory action by villagers often results in yet another tiger being killed. Between 1998 and 2000, 66 tigers were killed; that's nearly one fifth of the total population.

Two tiger subspecies from this part of Southeast Asia are already extinct. One is the Bali Tiger; only ever found on the Indonesian island of Bali, it was a very small tiger that was hunted to extinction, the last one killed in 1937. Ironically, it continues to play an important role in Balinese Hinduism. The other is the Javan Tiger, found only on Java and seemingly still in existence until the mid 1970s or into the 1980s. By that time, almost all the island's forest had been cleared and the human population had burgeoned. Poisoning and hunting did the rest. The Javan Tiger stood no real hope of surviving from the first day that people arrived there.

Yet another extinct subspecies is the Caspian Tiger, once found in the sparse forests and reed-filled river valleys west and south of the Caspian Sea, and east of there as far as western China. In the late 19th century, Caspian Tigers were ruthlessly persecuted by large parties of sportsmen and military personnel who hunted wild pigs and tigers with reckless abandon. At the same time the extensive riverside reedbeds were converted to cotton plantations and other crops that did well in the rich silt. There were scattered tiger sightings until the 1970s; since 1990 there have been none. However, the Siberian and Caspian Tigers are now considered to be genetically identical and it is likely that the two evolved from a common ancestor that probably inhabited much of central and eastern Asia. In consequence, consideration is being given to translocating some Siberians from the Russian Far East and releasing them in the extensive tiger habitat that remains in Kazakhstan. 'Taking Siberian Tigers from the Russian Far East to form another population is certainly realistic,' comments Dale Miquelle. 'The question is whether there is a suitably large area with quality habitat, low human impacts, and sufficient prey to support a large tiger population there. I'd argue it would not make sense to create a small population just to say you did it. You want to be sure it could be a large, more or less self-sustaining population.'

Another subspecies, the South China Tiger, is the most critically endangered subspecies of those still officially regarded as alive though it has not been seen by any reputable observer for several years and it might well be extinct. In the 1950s, there were more than 4,000 South China Tigers. But, alongside sparrows and rats, they became the target of large-scale government 'anti-pest' campaigns which were part of Mao Zedong's disastrous, ineptly-named 'Great Leap Forward', 1958–1961. The effects of this state-sanctioned, uncontrolled hunting were compounded by extensive deforestation, poaching, the probable killing of potential tiger prey, and large-scale forced relocations of urban populations to rural areas. Ironically, in 1977 the Chinese government, recovering from the setbacks and deprivation caused by the 'great leap' that wasn't, belatedly passed a law banning the killing of wild tigers. It had no effect. By 1982, only an estimated 150–200 South China Tigers remained; by the 1990s, there were maybe 30. Since then there have been no reliable records. There is a small chance that some individuals still hang on but it is unlikely.

In May 2007, the government of China reported to the CITES Secretariat that there was no confirmed presence and declared its goal of eventually reintroducing captive-bred South China Tigers (of which there are around 60) back to the wild. Short-term, there might not be any large enough areas of good tiger habitat with sufficient prey left in South China so any immediate prospects don't look good. Longer term, though, that might change. A quarter of China's people lived in urban centres in 1990; by 2012 that was up to 53% and by 2035 some commentators suggest it might be 70%. It has huge implications for wildlife. Vast areas of once agricultural countryside, often intensively managed with little or no room for wild animals, will revert slowly to natural habitat, much of it forest. That will provide potential habitat for reintroduced tigers, not just South China Tigers but Siberian Tigers too. As Linkie says: 'This is what happened in Italy in the 1970s and 1980s and enabled the wolf population to expand by recolonising countryside vacated by people.'

❖   ❖   ❖

With an average male tiger weighing around three times that of a human, and with what is to a tiger relatively slow moving prey compared with, say, a lively deer, it isn't difficult to imagine why people are sometimes attacked and killed by these huge and exceedingly powerful animals.

It is the Bengal Tiger that is the source of the largest amount of direct conflict between tigers and people. Not because the Bengal subspecies is innately more aggressive, but because many of its populations exist close to large human settlements where people farm the land, use forests daily to collect firewood and live in villages where their livestock are easy prey. Separating out man-killer myth from reality isn't easy, but a study in and around one tiger reserve in central India led by Harshawardhan Dhanwatey of the Tiger Research and Conservation Trust in Nagpur published in 2013 recorded 132 cat attacks on humans in six years, 71 of them lethal. Three-quarters of the attacks were by tigers; the rest by leopards. Most victims were attacked as they collected firewood or other forest products and many were attacked when they were bending down to pick things up off the ground. Big cats, it seems, are less likely to attack a human standing upright. Utilising alternative sources of fuel – such as dried cow dung – or not going alone to collect wood in forests have been proposed to reduce these human tragedies and, thereby, reduce the reprisal kills of tigers that almost inevitably follow.

Jim Corbett (1875–1955), the legendary tiger hunter who turned conservationist, documented many cases of human kills. Corbett was a Colonel in the British Indian Army who was often called in when a man-eating tiger or leopard needed shooting. He hunted alone and on foot, usually with his dog; he was enormously brave and highly respected. Between 1907 and 1938, Corbett tracked and shot a total of 33 man-eaters, though only about a dozen of these events were well documented. It is claimed that these big cats had killed more than 1,200 men, women and children. But when the bodies of these tigers were examined, almost all were found to have previous unhealed injuries such as gunshot wounds or septic sores from porcupine quills; the suggestion was that such injuries encouraged tigers to catch prey that was easier to obtain and readily available – people.

The most comprehensive study of documented tiger kills was compiled by a group led by Philip Nyhus (an expert in human/wildlife conflict) of Colby College in Waterville, Maine, published in 2010. Nyhus and his co-workers had sifted out any reports they considered unreliable so what they ended up with is a conservative figure. They concluded that at least 373,000 people died due to tiger attacks between 1800 and 2009, the majority of these in South and Southeast Asia. There was evidence that attacks have gradually declined in most areas after peaking in the 19th century but that attacks in South Asia have remained high, particularly in the Sundarbans.

❖   ❖   ❖

China came rather late to protecting tigers. During the early 1970s it rejected the views of the West-led environmentalist movement pressing for tiger protection, considering it as a restriction on its right to make full use of its own resources. Many people in China and other parts of Southeast Asia have a long established, traditional belief that various tiger parts have medicinal properties, although there is no scientific evidence to support that view. The use of tiger products and their medicines is seen as a symbol of high status and wealth. In addition, in recent years there has been a resurgence in traditional practices fundamental to the history of Chinese society fuelled by cultural pride and a growing sentiment that western medicine contains some shortcomings in treating illness.

Endangered tiger parts such as bones, eyes, whiskers and teeth are used to treat ailments and disease ranging from insomnia and malaria to meningitis and bad skin. Tiger claws are sometimes used to cure insomnia; tiger bone to reduce inflammation; even a tiger whisker inserted into a painful tooth cavity is supposed to cure toothache. In Hong Kong, China, Taiwan, South Korea, Japan and Vietnam and in Chinatowns across Europe and North America, some Chinese medicine stores sell tiger wine, powder, tiger balms and tiger pills. Most are unrecognisable as tiger parts so it has proved very difficult to take legal action to stop the trade.

During the 1980s as China emerged from diplomatic isolation and wanted normal trade relations with Western countries, its stance on tiger parts in traditional medicines altered. China became a party to CITES in 1981, bolstering international efforts to conserve tigers. In 1988, it passed a Law on the Protection of Wildlife, listing the tiger as a Category I protected species and, in 1993, it banned trade in tiger parts which led to a drop in the number of tiger bones used in traditional Chinese medicine.

Just as one poaching door was closing, however, another opened even further: the trade by Tibetan people in tiger pelts, an increasing market as Tibetan wealth improved. Coats or other clothes made from them are worn at weddings, at horse races and just for show. In 2003, Chinese customs officials in Tibet intercepted the skins of 31 tigers, 581 leopards and 778 otters. A single tiger pelt can sell for $20,000; compare that with an average working man's annual income in Tibet of $100 or $200. FFI, together with other conservation organisations, ran campaigns against this horrendous trade and attempts to confront the Dalai Lama to get him to condemn it, initially spurned, eventually succeeded. As a result of his condemnation, the trade seemingly collapsed although the Environmental Investigation Agency (an independent

US campaigning group) covertly filmed trade in a variety of cat skins, including tigers, in some Chinese and Tibetan markets in 2009. Although supposedly illegal, most purchases were made quite openly by wealthy Chinese businessmen. Policing such illegal sales seemed non-existent.

In China, snares – cheaply obtained and indiscriminate killers that function for years – are a bigger problem than firearms; in the 1,000 km² Hunchun Reserve in northeast China established in 2002, more than 10,000 snares have been removed and there is evidence that tiger prey are increasing as a result. Between three and five Siberian Tigers inhabit the reserve (a quarter of China's remaining Siberians) and it abuts larger populations over the Russian border.

A great many Siberian Tigers are held in captivity, most in zoos scattered around the world, but especially in China and the US. So can captive breeding and release have any role to play in tiger conservation? According to the *Travel China Guide*, Harbin Tiger Park in northeast China (built in 1996) holds an incredible 500 Siberian Tigers of which 100 are 'visible to the public' in only 143 ha of land. It goes on to describe some of their tigers as 'unruly' – what a surprise that must be. The Heilongjiang Northeast Tiger Forest Park, near the Russian border in the northeast of China, contains 500–800 Siberian Tigers, reportedly bred from just eight animals when it was founded in 1986. Here, in what is much more an entertainment venue than a conservation initiative, visitors to the park are encouraged to buy live rabbits, goats, pigs, chickens, even oxen to feed the hungry cats.

When the park at Heilongjiang was created, selling tiger parts in China was legal and it is frequently suggested that the park is pressing for the 1993 ban to be lifted or modified so that it can restart sales. It even has a large number of frozen tiger corpses kept for such a time. Short of investment and with such unnaturally high numbers of tigers in a small confined area, the temptation is all too obvious. Controversy rages over whether revoking the ban and supplying this traditional market – abhorrent to many – with captive-bred tiger parts will increase or decrease illegal poaching of wild Siberian Tigers, akin to the debate over rhino horn (see Chapter 3). 'We [the local tiger protection authority] have not received any word of lifting the ban from the central government so far, and the ban has not changed,' said Tao Jin, an official with the Heilongjiang forestry department in 2014. Selling tiger parts might be banned in China but enforcement is lacklustre. In 2008, John Vaillant noticed Tibetan street vendors in the city of Harbin openly selling the paws and penises of tigers, a short walk from the city's main train station.

In the Russian Far East there are over 60,000 registered hunters within the Siberian Tiger's range. So getting their cooperation, and altering their view that tigers are in competition with them for killing deer and other game, is essential for conserving tigers. WCS is working with hunters to increase prey density overall in the forest; that way both hunters and tigers benefit. Since 1995, the responsibility for hunting concessions in Russia was transferred from state level to local individuals or groups, so local people for the first time have a personal interest in managing a resource they need to sustain. This vast area of land is impossible to police effectively and powerful guns are readily available. The Russian nature reserves have their own inspectors; outside these, enforcement is down to a Committee for Hunting Management based in Vladivostok, the capital of this Russian Province, and which commentators believe is understaffed and underfunded. 'Punishment for poaching has been made much tougher. Those who kill tigers will receive both criminal penalties and fines with all the consequences,' says Yury Darman, Director of the Far Eastern branch of the Russian regional World Wildlife Fund (WWF) office. 'The hardest thing was that we could not punish those who did not kill a tiger themselves but were caught selling its skin, bones and so on. Such a law was adopted this year. Now everyone who keeps a tiger's skin at home or tries to sell it will be punished.'

All the same, poaching has not been eliminated. Sergei Bereznuk, founder and director of the Phoenix Fund, a Vladivostok-based NGO promoting wildlife and forest conservation, said: 'Detecting poaching cases is extremely difficult, so any that are detected could represent just a small percentage of the actual number of poached animals. The tip of the iceberg. Recent monitoring suggests that tiger numbers are declining and these events suggest poaching is the main culprit.'

'Most worrying of all are clear indications that poaching is becoming better organised and more international in nature. It is crucial to maintain protection on the ground but it is also important to tackle the demand for tiger parts which still comes primarily, though not exclusively, from China,' says Sarah Christie, tiger conservation expert at the Zoological Society of London.

❖   ❖   ❖

In the 4,000 km^2 Sikhote-Alin Nature Reserve in the Russian Far East, conifer forests with a scatter of birch, maple and other broadleaves dominate the mountains and valleys. This area gained protection in 1935, in order to conserve the Sable (an animal related to the Pine Marten), whose numbers had been decimated as a result of over-hunting for the international fur market. At that time, the reserve was several times larger than it is today. It was here in 1992 that the WCS in cooperation with Russian scientists and conservationists began intensive studies of tiger ecology; it has proved to be a productive and long-lasting partnership. The Siberian Tiger Project, today the world's longest running radio-telemetry based tiger research and conservation effort, had begun. 'The idea was simple enough,' comments Dale Miquelle, its director. 'Combine the technical expertise of scientists from the US with the local knowledge and natural history skills of Russian biologists to develop a better understanding of Siberian Tiger ecology.'

There was already a long history of tiger surveys in this part of Russia such as that by Lev Kaplanov, an outstanding zoologist who warned that only 20–30 tigers were left in the 1940s in the Russian Far East. Too much hunting in the 1920s and 1930s had sent them into what could well have been a terminal decline. As a result of Kaplanov's efforts, though, tiger hunting was made illegal and the completely unnecessary collecting of cubs for zoos worldwide was reduced in scale. Tigers increased in number right up to the late 1980s and they would have continued to do so had it not been for the free-for-all that resulted from the break-up of the USSR in the 1990s that fuelled an orgy of tiger killing to supply the Chinese tiger parts market. Thanks to an international outcry soon after, law enforcement was upped, the orgy eased and tiger numbers eventually stabilised at somewhere around 450.

Tigers are notoriously difficult to survey; they are rarely seen in daylight and each one occupies a huge territory in which access is often treacherous. Most surveying relies on spotting tiger tracks (in snow especially), kills and faeces, much of the information being supplied by hunters. It is little wonder, then, that different surveys at similar times came up with very different numbers. But by refining the survey methods and testing them thoroughly, the WCS team believe they now have a more accurate idea of the number of Siberian Tigers; 430–500 individuals according to the 2005 survey, the most thorough so far.

By radio-tracking more than 60 Siberian Tigers that have been captured, sedated and fitted with radio collars over the last two decades, the project has studied their social structure, habitat and food preferences, reproduction, mortality, and their relationship with other species, including humans. They found that pine and oak forests were their most favoured habitats so the retention of these, both within and outside protected areas, is vital. And they also found that, between 1995 and 2005, Siberian Tigers spread north, for the first time in 70 years crossing the Amur River, maybe in response to climate warming.

Numbers of tigers in northeast China and the northern part of North Korea (effectively a closed country), both bordering the Russian Far East, are very much more difficult to ascertain. A 1974 survey in China estimated around 85 Siberian Tigers; by 1999, evidence for somewhere between nine and 13 was almost certainly the result of occasional wanderings by Russian tigers. There was no evidence of any tiger breeding in China where they were once well distributed. Their absence did, however, eventually spur the Chinese government into developing a plan to encourage their return. Now, there is much more positive information. In 2014, the State Forestry Administration in Harbin, authenticated foot marks and tracks found the previous year in Hunchun Forest (but outside the Hunchun Reserve) in northeast China as those of a female Siberian Tiger and three cubs. At least 20 km from the Russian border, this is the first clear evidence of tigers breeding in China. 'We have tried repeatedly to engage with the North Koreans, without much success, whether me directly or through Russian collaborators,' says Dale Miquelle. 'We actually provided a grant to the North Korean Academy of Geography to conduct a survey of tigers in 2002 but they didn't find any. And since there are few, if any, tigers across the border in China, it's unlikely that any remain in North Korea where people specialise in snaring wildlife.'

The WCS research has found that about 80% of tiger mortality in Russia is caused by humans; roughly half of all tiger cubs die before reaching one year of age, many of them starving to death because their mothers are killed by poachers. And mortality is significantly greater near roads than in the more remote parts of the reserve because access is so much easier. Large numbers of villagers in the Russian Far East hunt wild game, deer in particular, to supplement their family's diet. It is perfectly legal, but some hunters exceed their legal quota and a few, if they come across a tiger, might shoot it to sell. And it's all too easy for anyone who has not lived and eked out an often very basic living in places where tigers roam to dismiss fears about them. They are powerful, frightening and unpredictable large mammals and everyone knows that they can kill people; indeed many rural forest dwellers know someone who has been either badly mauled by one or killed. Only a fool underestimates the stealth and the enormous strength of a tiger.

Siberian Tigers aren't difficult to accommodate; they are habitat generalists and will adapt to a range of environments provided they can find enough prey. So tiger conservation is not inherently difficult. Tigers can easily look after themselves, provided they have very big areas of largely unexploited and undisturbed habitat that is rich enough to support plenty of prey. In the Russian Far East, the WCS/Russian research has established that each breeding female needs an exclusive area of about 400 km² to rear cubs. That's why a protected area such as the Sikhote-Alin Nature Reserve, at 4,000 km², is not going to support huge numbers. The bulk of the Russian Far East has to have tiger-friendly land use management if large numbers of Siberian Tigers are to thrive there once again.

Armed with such knowledge, by 2006 Russian authorities in parts of the Far East had adopted a plan to link up existing protected areas, including national parks and reserves, with large forested corridors to enable tiger movement – though a great deal of practical action is still lacking. Only about 15–20% of the potential tiger habitat in the Russian Far East has formal protection. Russia created a new national park in 2012 called 'Land of the Leopard' National Park that combines three existing protected areas plus other forest to give a total area of around 2,600 km², mostly along the Russian side of the Chinese border abutting China's Hunchun Reserve created to protect tigers. That brings to seven the number of national parks and reserves in the Russian Far East. Not all of it is strictly protected; an 'economic development zone' of 380 km² is included within it. Nevertheless, its designation is being welcomed. 'This is tremendous news for big cat conservation,' said Peter Zahler, WCS Deputy Director for Asia, when it was announced. 'The creation of this park greatly increases the amount of land protecting critical populations of two of the world's big cats [the Amur Leopard and the Siberian Tiger], and it will go a long way to securing their future.'

For Northeast China, WCS has devised a plan, starting with the proposed establishment of forested 'beachheads' adjacent to known Russian areas across the border supporting tigers, followed by a series of protected forest zones and interconnecting habitat. The proposals are under consideration by the Chinese authorities as part of a Tiger Action Plan. In 2013, the Chinese government announced the setting up of two more reserves (in addition to Hunchun) together with the claim that their Siberian Tiger population had risen to 20 animals. It is all a positive development though there is concern that the Chinese protected areas are poorly funded. 'With a group of relevant experts, we have carried out a study of the potential tiger habitat in the Changbaishan area of China [on its border with North Korea],' says Quanhua Shi of WWF China. 'It shows that there is over 120,000 km² of forest suitable for Siberian Tigers. It could support several hundred tigers. Rural people moving to cities are no doubt an important reason for habitat improvement. Another important reason is that China's government initiated a natural forest protection project since 1998; logging has reduced by more than 70% and Jilin Province just announced that it will have no logging within two years.'

Since signing an agreement in 2010, China and Russia have improved their cooperation in protecting areas near their mutual border to enhance the populations of both the tiger and leopards. China has undertaken a series of public awareness campaigns promoting greater respect for tigers and is attempting to reduce illegal demand for tiger parts. 'We have helped the Chinese government to develop national and province level tiger conservation plans, pilot tiger prey recovery and habitat programmes in northeast China and our goal is to double our Siberian Tiger population by 2022, that's to 50 tigers, by the next Chinese Year of the Tiger,' says Zeng Ming of WWF China. WWF China also plans to conduct an overall Siberian Tiger population survey in 2016 to check on progress. Early in 2014 the Chinese government announced that it is considering a plan to expand its Hunchun National Siberian Tiger Reserve and move out half of the local residents. The move aims to reduce tiger disturbance in the reserve by ending locals' deforestation and frog breeding businesses (currently a third of the reserve's land is privately owned). Unless there is full and appropriate compensation for this human exodus, it is not a strategy that engenders community support for the tiger's cause.

In spite of long periods when their very existence has been in question, in recent decades the Siberian Tiger has been faring the best out of all the remaining subspecies. They were down to around 40 animals in the 1930s and came close to extinction in the wild, but today they number at least ten times that, probably about 450, although that is down a little from around 500 in the late 1980s and has to be compared with an estimate of maybe 1,000 before the significant impact of forest felling and hunting in this remote part of eastern Asia. Both the Russian and Chinese governments are designating more protected areas for these magnificent animals; they are being given better protection from poachers; the horrendous trade in tiger parts is declining, albeit very slowly; and both governments are paying more attention to the need to consider tiger requirements when they are considering major land use decisions. At the same time, research and the consequent sound advice – especially from NGOs – combined with unrelenting international pressure, public opinion and the constraints of international conventions signed by both governments, means that the prospects for the Siberian Tiger look more positive than ever.

The Siberian Tiger population is the largest unfragmented tiger population in the world. It has been brought back from the brink by an enormous effort on the part of a huge range of conservationists with Russian and Chinese governmental and international support. There is enough habitat now to support a growing population and, long term, the continued urbanisation of the Chinese human population will result in what is likely to be a considerable area of suitable habitat developing. Whether Siberian Tigers continue to increase depends on better protection against poaching, a higher standard of living for the people inhabiting this vast region so that poaching becomes unnecessary, and a strident public campaign together with effective law enforcement to discourage the trade in, and use of, tiger parts in those countries where it continues. If that all works out, the fortunes of the Siberian Tiger will be burning a little brighter in the future too.

Above: Arabian Oryx in desert in the United Arab Emirates (courtesy of Dr David Mallon)

Below: Gravel plains and stunning, folded dunes; the harsh Saudi desert inhabited by Arabian Oryx

Black Rhino, South Africa (courtesy of Rob Brett, FFI)

Fitting a transmitter in a sedated rhino's horn
(courtesy of Pamela Sherriffs, WWF, Cape Town)

Wild Turkey Tom displaying (courtesy of Department of Game and Fisheries, Virginia, US)

(inset) Turkeys get on car plates in Virginia, US

(left) European Bison in a Polish winter (courtesy of Dr Rafal Kowalczyk)

(below) Bialowieza Forest in Poland/Belarus has the largest herd of bison in Europe

Florida Manatee (courtesy of Dr Patrick M Rose, Save the Manatee Club)

Wayne Hartley monitoring manatees, Blue Spring, Florida.

(above left) Houbara displaying on Lanzarote, Canary Islands (courtesy of Gustavo Peña Tejera)
(above right) Houbara killed in falconry in the UAE (courtesy of Khalfan Butti Alqubaisi)

Humpback Whale at Hervey Bay, eastern Australia (courtesy of Trish Franklin, Oceania Project)

Siberian Tiger in the Russian Far East (courtesy of Dr Dale Miquelle)

White-rumped Vulture in a breeding enclosure, India (courtesy of Ami Vitale)

Dead cattle carcasses dumped in the absence of vultures (courtesy of Ami Vitale)

Controlled tourism and Mountain Gorilla conservation go hand in hand (courtesy of David and Jane Phillips)

Mountain Gorilla (courtesy of Juan Pablo Moreiras, FFI)

Whooping Crane at Aransas, Texas (courtesy of Reinier Munguia)

Iberian Lynx in the Sierra Morena, Spain
(courtesy of Manuel Moral, Life Iberlince
Project, Junta de Andalucia)

Above: Rodrigo Serra at the lynx breeding enclosures in the Algarve, Portugal

Below: Muskeg in a Canadian summer, the breeding habitat of Whooping Cranes
(courtesy of James Crippen)

(left)   Juvenile Zino's Petrel being ringed on Madeira (courtesy of Dr Frank Zino)

(below)   The precipitous mountains of Madeira; the breeding place of Zino's Petrel

Large Blue Butterfly in southwest England (courtesy of Neil Hulme, Butterfly Conservation)

Caroline Kelly searching painstakingly for Large Blue Butterfly eggs on thyme

Mauritius Kestrel (courtesy of Jacques de Speville)

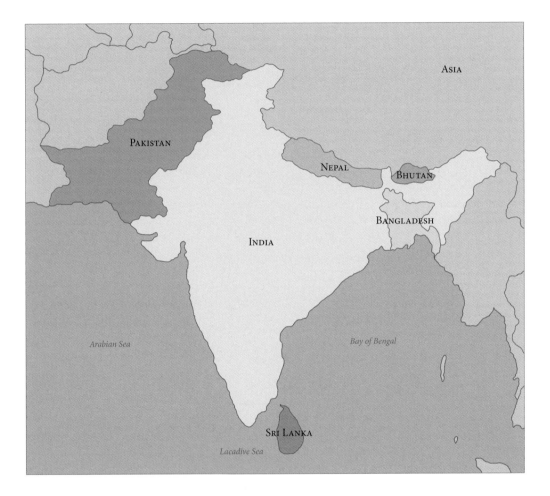

10

THE SCAVENGERS SET TO RETURN

INDIA'S VULTURES

The millions of vultures that until the 1990s soared and scavenged throughout the vast Indian subcontinent have been poisoned by a common painkiller, driven to the verge of extinction in one of the greatest wildlife catastrophes ever witnessed. Their demise at first went unnoticed. Very soon, though, its scale not only staggered conservationists but also the vultures' disappearance undermined the practices of one of the world's oldest religions and caused an increase in life-threatening diseases. Some of the remaining few vultures – of three different species – have been captured and are being bred successfully in aviaries; very soon, the first to be released will once again be performing their role as free sanitary engineers.

The world over, there are very few instances in recent times of an animal that was superabundant being driven to extinction. The hapless passenger pigeon of the Americas was one. An estimated three to five billion lived on the continent when Europeans first entered America. They lived in enormous flocks that reputedly blackened the sky when they flew over, sometimes taking hours to pass. Vast numbers of them were shot for food, to protect crops from their ravages and for sport. Pigeon meat was sold in the 19th century as cheap food for slaves and the poor. By 1896 just one massive flock of these highly gregarious birds survived. A few individuals lingered into the first months of the 20th century and on 1 September 1914 the very last passenger pigeon died in Cincinnati Zoo, Ohio.

Compared with the passenger pigeon, the demise of most of the Indian subcontinent's vultures is different in two ways. One is the incredible and seemingly unprecedented speed with which they declined, plummeting from superabundance to rarity in little over a decade. The other difference is that – thanks to the actions of a small number of conservationists – the vultures didn't become another extinction statistic. Not quite. And if they hadn't acted quickly to identify the baffling cause of this disaster and capture some of the last wild birds for aviary breeding, there is little doubt that extinction would have been the result.

This is not, though, a story about one species of vulture. At least three different vultures – the White-rumped Vulture, the Indian Vulture and the Slender-billed Vulture – across the vast area of India, Pakistan, Nepal and Bangladesh, are now so rare, it isn't easy to find one. All three are listed as Critically Endangered by IUCN, its highest category and indicative of a high risk of global extinction. What is more, this wasn't only a catastrophe for the birds themselves their loss has caused enormous turmoil amongst the adherents to one of the world's oldest religions, and still threatens an upsurge in human disease in one of the most disease-ridden parts of the world.

For all of human history, vultures have served the countries of the Indian subcontinent extremely well. They scoured the countryside clearing fields of dead cows, water buffalo or any other dead animals, wild or domesticated. Every year, five to ten million cow, camel and buffalo carcasses disappeared neatly down the gullets of India's vultures. A whole cow carcass would be consumed in less than half an hour leaving only the cleaned skeleton behind. They soared over the cities in search of road kills, congregated on farmland if they spotted any dead livestock and picked through the squalor of town and city refuse tips. Vultures were a natural and efficient disposal system, more comprehensive than anything the public authorities seem to be capable of supplying across this huge subcontinent. They were everywhere. Fading old sepia photographs show thousands at refuse tips; hundreds thrashing at each other to devour a cattle corpse. But everyone took them for granted; they were effectively invisible to most passers by.

❖   ❖   ❖

This fateful story has its origins in the beautiful Keoladeo National Park, 140 km south of New Delhi. Thirty square kilometres of wetlands, pools, grasslands and woodland, Keoladeo was originally a duck-hunting reserve of the Maharajas but is now a UNESCO World Heritage Site of huge importance for its wildlife. Keoladeo is packed with wildlife at almost any time of year. The raucous calls of Rose-ringed Parakeets compete with the howling of Golden Jackals. Flocks of elegant, red-faced Sarus Cranes strut across the grasslands. Black Drongos pick insects off the backs of wild antelope. And birds of prey – from snake-eating Crested Serpent Eagles to delicate Black-shouldered Kites – soar in the warm air.

Dr Vibhu Prakash, then Principal Scientist with the Bombay Natural History Society (BNHS) and now Deputy Director, takes up the story. 'In the mid 1980s I had been studying Keoladeo's birds of prey, including its vultures. There were about 300 breeding pairs of White-rumped vultures nesting in the park's tall kadam and acacia trees. When I returned in 1996 I noticed that there seemed to be far fewer of them. And, unusually, I saw some dead vultures on the ground and others tangled in the thorns of acacias as if they had suddenly fallen dead in the trees. I knew something was wrong,' he continues. 'So I recounted their nests. There were only 150 breeding pairs, half the number that were there in the mid 1980s.'

In the 1980s and into the 1990s it was all but impossible to look into the Keoladeo sky without seeing a vulture circling languidly above. Today they have all gone. At first their deaths were thought to be some local problem, an outbreak of disease perhaps or deliberate poisoning by farmers. Then anecdotal information about vulture declines in other parts of India started to reach the BNHS in Mumbai. 'I first got involved in 1999,' says Dr Debbie Pain, then Head of International Research at the RSPB and currently Conservation Director at the UK's Wildfowl and Wetlands Trust. 'We were alerted because the BNHS thought there was a problem India-wide. A survey of India's birds of prey had been done between 1991 and 1993. It recorded these vultures as superabundant across the country. So we paid for the survey to be repeated in 2000. The result was incredible. It showed a decline of nearly 96% in White-rumped and over 92% in Indian Vultures. In less than a decade. I was absolutely shocked. I just couldn't think of any other bird – or any animal at all – known to have declined so rapidly.'

Very soon it was obvious that it wasn't only in India that vultures were in dire trouble. Between 2000 and 2003, White-rumped Vulture numbers dropped by an incredible 92% in the Punjab province of Pakistan, almost a wipe-out of an abundant bird. In Nepal, they had declined by as much, though over a longer time period. Red-headed and Egyptian Vultures had declined enormously too. 'Our first thought was disease,' says Dr Pain. 'Vultures are communal birds so, if there was some contagious disease to which they had no immunity, they could all get it.'

Around the same time, another conservation charity, The Peregrine Fund from Idaho, US, collaborated with the Ornithological Society of Pakistan – where vulture numbers had also plummeted – to try and find the cause. It is a fundamental principle enshrined in the IUCN guidelines that understanding what is causing, or has caused, a species decline is essential before thinking about protecting the rapidly dwindling numbers left alive. The issue with the vultures was clear; the birds were dying off so quickly, conservationists feared that they might become extinct across this vast land area before the cause of their deaths had been determined. Certainly before anything could be done to correct it.

In both countries post mortems showed accumulations of white uric acid crystals around vital organs in the vultures' bodies. The birds had died of some type of gout following kidney failure and there was no evidence of any infectious disease. 'Having ruled out infection,' commented the late Dr Lindsay Oaks at the time, then a leading microbiologist and vet with Washington State University who led the Pakistan work, 'We ran tests of all the obvious poisons such as pesticides, PCBs and heavy metals. None showed up in anywhere near lethal quantities. So it made sense to examine what veterinary drugs were used for farm livestock because dead cattle and water buffalo are the vultures' main food. The non-steroid painkillers were good candidates. They're known to sometimes cause kidney problems as a side effect. Really they were the only likely ones. And just one, diclofenac, was commonly used by farmers to treat livestock lameness and mastitis.'

Across this huge subcontinent, millions of farmers rely on cows for milk and water buffalo for muscle-power. Without them they can't easily farm at all. And when a cow or water buffalo eventually died, the farmer would know that the local vultures would spot the corpse and devour it in quick time. He only had to dispose of the bones. It was rapid, free and hygienic. But it was an inter-dependence that required a regular supply of dead livestock and an abundance of vultures.

Closely related to ibuprofen, diclofenac is one of many non-steroidal anti-inflammatory drugs (NSAIDs). Ibuprofen and aspirin are both NSAIDs. Diclofenac was first marketed in India during the late 1980s – and in Pakistan from 1989 – as a painkiller for veterinary use. It is commonly used as a human medicine, too, both in Southeast Asia, in Europe and the US, often under the name Voltarol. Oaks and his colleagues found that more than 80 outlets they investigated in Pakistan sold diclofenac. Over 90% of them sold it daily. And it cost just 10 rupees (20 US cents) a shot.

Doing the post mortems, they found residues of diclofenac in the kidneys of all the vultures that had died of visceral gout. But not in any of the vultures known to have died of other causes. The clincher came when they fed healthy captive vultures meat from livestock treated with normal doses of diclofenac. They all died of gout. Further checks found diclofenac to be the cause of the vulture deaths in India and Nepal too. It was the first time that a pharmaceutical – in this case a common painkiller – had been identified as the cause of an environmental disaster.

What no one knew – and could not have predicted – was that vultures were incredibly susceptible to a side effect of the painkiller, one that paralysed them with acute gout from feeding on the corpses of any animals treated with the drug before they died. For the vultures, very unusually, it was lethal. Why the drug doesn't appear to kill other carrion feeders – kites and crows for instance – no one knows. Tests on some birds like chickens – and even on Turkey Vultures in North America (though they look similar, American vultures are not closely related to European and Asian species) – have found considerable tolerance to the drug. Conversely, some Old World (Europe, Asia and Africa) vultures and several eagles have proved surprisingly sensitive to its effects. Such varying reactions to the same NSAID drug are not unusual. The most striking example is the differing toxicity of aspirin to different mammals. For humans and many other mammals, aspirin is a generally safe and reliable painkiller yet doses that we would take for a mild headache are highly toxic to cats.

Each year in India alone, perhaps five million cattle and buffalo were being treated with diclofenac out of a total population estimated at 500 million. That was more than enough, according to computer modelling by the RSPB, to cause these catastrophic vulture deaths. The finding that a particular drug was causing such massive vulture mortality, though, doesn't mean that other causes should be ignored. With the now tiny population of vultures left across India and adjacent countries, any additional causes of mortality – diseases, deliberate killing, collisions with vehicles or overhead cables for instance – could make an already desperate situation terminal.

It is sometimes suggested that the decline of vultures in the Indian subcontinent is acceptable because it represents a fall from abnormally high numbers supported by the huge and unnatural food supply provided by hundreds of millions of domesticated buffalo and cows. It is certainly likely that the amount of food for vultures in the late 20th century was at an all-time high, and higher even than it was when wild mammals were naturally abundant here before the advent of pastoralism and agriculture thousands of years ago. However, the impact of diclofenac has meant that the vulture population in the subcontinent has declined so drastically that it is now probably very much lower than it has been at any time since the end of the last Ice Age.

❖　❖　❖

Up until the mid 1990s, the White-rumped Vulture was the most abundant large bird of prey in the world. For every 1,000 recorded in India in 1992, only one remains today. Indian Vultures used to be almost as common as White-rumped, while the other decimated vulture, the Slender-billed, was found only in northern India around the foothills of the Himalayas. Estimates put India and Nepal's combined total of all three in 1990 at around 40 million. Today it is about 10,000 – a 99.9% drop!

The White-rumped Vulture once had a range extending from eastern Iran through Pakistan, India, Bangladesh and Nepal to Myanmar. A little under a metre in length with a wingspan up to 2.6 metres, this is by no means the largest of vultures and it isn't an aggressive species: White-rumps usually wait their turn at carcasses while more ferocious vultures such as the Indian take precedence. Very dark in colour with partially white under-wings, they nest in trees, either in solitary pairs or in colonies. Each pair builds a large, scruffy structure of branches and twigs anywhere between 15 and 100 feet up. The same nest is often used year upon year, 'renovated' with a few green branches each spring. Before they were decimated by diclofenac, it was possible to find breeding colonies of 1,000 or more breeding pairs of White-rumped. Many colonies were located close to villages, towns, and even the edges of cities where good feeding on food scraps and animals killed on roads could be guaranteed. Now it's all but impossible to find a colony of any size. Even single nests are few and far between.

Formerly equally widespread, Indian Vultures are slightly larger and much lighter brown in colour with dark necks; they too were avid feeders at cattle and buffalo corpses where they frequently accompanied White-rumped Vultures. But unlike their cousins, Indian Vultures nest in small colonies on cliff ledges where they build a haphazard nest of sticks topped with somewhat more comfortable leaves and grasses. Slender-billed Vultures are similar in size to Indian Vultures but have – as you might assume – a more slender beak and an almost black neck.

India and adjacent countries are home to other vultures too, though the degree to which they have proved susceptible to the killer effects of diclofenac isn't clear. Many of them do not actually feed much on animal carcasses so might be largely unaffected. Most impressive among these is the Lammergeier or Bearded Vulture with a wingspan approaching three metres. Dark grey above but a striking orange-brown underneath with a prominent black band across its eyes and, unusually for a vulture, a fully feathered neck, it is a stunning bird. Reasonably common in the mountainous north of the subcontinent, it's the only bird known to feed mainly on bone marrow. Smaller bones it can swallow and digest whole in its highly acidic stomach; larger ones – even near the weight of the vulture itself – it has learnt to drop from a height on to rocks to break them open and then descend to eat up the marrow. It's why the Lammergeier is sometimes called the 'bone breaker'.

The Egyptian Vulture, found across much of the Indian subcontinent, is also visually attractive. Black and white with a yellow head, it is a diminutive vulture hardly bigger than a raven. Egyptian Vultures not only feed on dead animals but also consume decaying fruit and vegetables in household waste at rubbish tips. They'll eat insects and take birds' eggs too. And they have an unerring penchant for excrement; any excrement, be it from cow, goat, sheep, dog or even human. It might sound revolting. But new research suggests that there is more to their dung eating than some warped vulturine pleasure. The dung is rich in protein from the eggs, and subsequent larvae, which dung beetles and flies lay in it. The healthiest Egyptian Vultures are the ones eating most dung. And cow, goat and sheep excrement contains a yellow pigment that the birds can't produce for themselves. It keeps their head feathers canary-coloured; the brighter the head colour, the more attractive an adult Egyptian Vulture seems to be to its mate.

There are three other vultures in this part of the world too. The large, very dark Cinereous Vulture likes to spend the winter in much of Pakistan and northwest India, though it breeds in mountainous areas further north. It has not been significantly affected by diclofenac. The Red-headed Vulture, a smaller, dark-plumaged bird with a naked reddish head and a fringe of fluffy-looking white feathers at the base of its bare neck is – or rather was – a bird of open country rather than towns and villages. It was once widespread and abundant, numbering hundreds of thousands across the subcontinent, but it has suffered a massive, diclofenac-induced decline. The Red-headed is now classed by IUCN as Critically Endangered. There are few left except in parts of the Himalayan foothills where livestock carrion is probably not a major food item for them. And, lastly, the Himalayan Griffon, a large, creamy brown and white vulture with a three metre wingspan is, as its name suggests, a vulture of the high mountains in the very north of India and Nepal. It has not declined, almost certainly because it is much less dependent on cattle corpses in its mountain habitat. Much of its diet consists of the flesh of dead yak, which are not treated with NSAIDs. The Himalayan Griffon is the most common vulture that eats human bodies in the so-called sky burials still practised on mountaintops by Buddhists in Tibet where, presumably, NSAIDs are not widely administered to people.

In addition to vultures, there are many other birds of prey across this vast subcontinent too. Add together an array of eagles, buzzards, hawks, harriers and kites – even forgetting to add in a goodly number of owls – and you have arguably the greatest concentration of different birds of prey to be found anywhere in the world.

❖ ❖ ❖

With cheap and readily available diclofenac – obtainable from veterinary pharmacies throughout the subcontinent – identified as the cause of the vast number of vulture deaths, Indian and international conservation organisations pressed for the drug to be banned for animal treatment. In 2006, the Indian government started to take action. Its Ministry of Environment and Forests produced *An Action Plan for Vulture Conservation in India* with recommendations to ban the veterinary use of diclofenac; to urgently set up captive breeding centres for the three main species of vulture affected; and to find a safe alternative to diclofenac for farmers to use. Between then and 2008, the Indian government legislated to phase out the veterinary use of diclofenac, its manufacture, sale and import. Nepal and Pakistan soon followed suit. A letter from the Drug Controller General of India in 2008 warned more than 70 drug firms not to sell the veterinary form of diclofenac and to mark human diclofenac containers 'not for veterinary use'. In October 2010, the government of Bangladesh banned the production of diclofenac for use in cattle, and the sale of the drug was banned in 2011.

But banning the drug has not been plain sailing according to SAVE (Saving Asia's Vultures from Extinction), a consortium of regional and international conservation organisations created to oversee and coordinate conservation, campaigning and fundraising to help the plight of South Asia's vultures. While the bans have led to a reduction of diclofenac use for treating cattle and buffalo, the drug is still being used illegally. SAVE's concern stems from a study by Dr Richard Cuthbert of the RSPB with several Indian colleagues, published in 2011 in *Oryx* (*The International Journal of Conservation* published for FFI), which found that over a third of Indian pharmacies continued to sell diclofenac to livestock farmers in spite of the ban. It seems that most of this is diclofenac produced perfectly legally for human use and conveniently manufactured in large vials (cattle and buffalo require much larger doses than people), though some appears to have been illegally manufactured specifically for veterinary use. The research was conducted in over 250 veterinary and general pharmacy shops in 11 Indian states between 2007 and 2010. The undercover researchers asked if they could buy NSAIDs for treating cattle. Diclofenac was provided in over a third of them. 'The ban is still quite easy to avoid because human formulations are for sale in large vials and these are clearly not intended for human use. Preventing misuse of human diclofenac remains the main challenge in halting the decline of threatened vultures,' said Cuthbert. As a result of this shocking circumventing of the ban on their sale for animal treatment, SAVE is calling for all diclofenac for human use to be available only in small vials, for the pharmaceutical and veterinary industries to act responsibly and for the Indian and other governments to take firm action against retailers flouting the law.

There is also evidence that NSAIDs untested for vulture toxicity are more widely available and ketoprofen, an alternative that is known to be deadly to vultures, has still not been banned. It was on sale for veterinary use in a little under a third of pharmacies in Cuthbert's study. Not surprisingly, SAVE wants to see all NSAIDs banned unless they have been tested and found not to be harmful to vultures. 'We realise this is a big ask, and the only way to make this happen is by establishing a government endorsed testing system. This is what we are working towards,' comments Chris Bowden, SAVE Programme Manager. 'It's essential that all such drugs are tested thoroughly so that there's no chance of another drug being introduced which causes equal problems or we're back in the same mess,' said Professor Ian Newton, SAVE Chairman, in 2012. Safety testing has found that an alternative NSAID, meloxicam, is not toxic for vultures and other scavenging birds but is equally effective for treating livestock. What is more, it is manufactured in Asia, out of patent and is, as a result, cheap. Encouragingly, the research showed that 70% of the pharmacies surveyed stocked it.

Happily, in spite of some continued illegal use of diclofenac, there is, in some parts of their former ranges, recent evidence that the declines of wild-living vultures have either slowed or, maybe, stopped. In southeastern Pakistan, Jamshed Chaudhry has been collecting nesting information on Indian Vultures before and after the diclofenac ban. In the three years before the 2006 ban, their abundance fell by 61%. After the ban, numbers increased by 55% over the subsequent two years and have remained stable since. He has also found stable trends in the number of occupied White-rumped Vulture nests. There are some similarly encouraging results from India while in western Nepal a survey found that White-rumped Vultures declined by over a quarter between 2002 and 2009 but that they increased by nearly a third over the two years since 2009. In much of Nepal, though, there are so few birds left of any of the three species that drawing conclusions about changes in their abundance verges on the meaningless.

Yet, amongst all this good news it seems barely believable that the very same drug was licenced in 2010 and 2013 for veterinary use in Italy and Spain respectively. It is also legally available in Turkey and Kazakhstan. Seemingly, it is all being manufactured in Brazil. In countries with a legal obligation under EU Directives to protect vultures (and much other wildlife beside), it may well sound bizarre. Spain holds 80% of Europe's vulture population; the Egyptian Vulture is threatened with extinction and is listed as Endangered by IUCN while the Cinereous Vulture is listed as Near Threatened. The Griffon Vulture and Bearded Vulture have recently recovered from very low populations after decades of conservation efforts. 'It is shocking that a drug that has already wiped out wildlife on a massive scale in Asia is now put on the market in countries crucial for vulture conservation such as Spain and Italy, especially as the total ban on diclofenac in India has produced the first signs of recovery,' said José Tavares, Director of the Vulture Conservation Foundation, the leading European vulture conservation NGO. Not surprisingly, an array of wildlife NGOs across Europe are calling for an EU-wide ban and are currently (2014) in discussion with the European Commission and Member State governments. A European ban would also send a crucial signal encouraging African countries to stop the spread of diclofenac, which is already affecting some highly endangered populations of African vultures. A decision by the Commission is awaited.

❖ ❖ ❖

This enormous decline in once abundant birds has not been an issue solely for conservationists; it has also challenged the fundamental beliefs of the adherents to one of the world's oldest religions. Mumbai has the single largest community of Parsis in the world, around 46,000 believers in the Zoroastrian faith, a tenet of their belief being that their dead must not pollute land, air or water. For millennia they had carried on their tradition of laying out their dead for the sun to dry their bodies and for vultures, or other carrion eaters, to devour them naturally. In India the process became ritualised at stone towers built specially for the purpose of encouraging vultures to consume their dead quickly. After all, vultures were always incredibly abundant, perfect for the form of body disposal central to their faith. When vultures were abundant at what became known as Mumbai's Towers of Silence, a lain body's flesh would have been consumed within an hour, leaving the skeleton to desiccate in the hot sun. After a few weeks the Nassesalars (the corpse bearers employed to place the bodies) would return to sweep the brittle, powdering bones into the tower's central pit where they would join those of thousands of other Parsis. The process was rapid, hygienic and non-polluting. The vultures would have needed no encouragement to stay. In Mumbai, the Parsi community is slowly depleting as its population ages and because it never accepts converts to the faith. Up to 900 Parsis die annually in the city, so bodies are being laid out on the top of the stone towers at the rate of two or three a day.

Noshir Mulla, a Mumbai Parsi, bursting with energy in his draper's shop, is keen to describe for me the traditional ritual. He remembers his grandmother's funeral as if it had just taken place he says. Tears well up in his eyes as he recalls the occasion. 'I was 14 then and asking lots of questions,' he says. 'When the Nassesalars carried her body and we walked behind in procession, there were many vultures in the air. They seemed to follow us to the tower, landing on the stone parapet around its edge; perhaps seventy or more. Once they had left her body on the tower, the Nassesalars clapped their hands. It was the sign for the vultures to descend to gorge themselves. They took less than an hour. They had done their work perfectly according to our Parsi tradition,' he adds. The year was 1957. Exactly the same funeral ritual had taken place at Mumbai's Towers of Silence almost every day since. That is, until the early 1990s, when the last vultures disappeared. Only crows and black kites remain there today and they take days to devour a human body. Slow decomposition produces odours, unacceptable to Parsis and nearby residents alike.

'I suspect that the first vultures [in India] to die were those feeding on the bodies of the Parsis,' comments Jemima Parry-Jones, Director of the UK-based International Centre for Birds of Prey and a vulture expert. 'It seems that vultures at the towers had been declining since the 1970s which would be about right because diclofenac was introduced as a human drug in the 1960s. It was not used as a veterinary drug until the late 80s.' Most experts agree that although diclofenac breaks down within days in any animal, breakdown stops at death. So livestock or humans given the drug shortly before death to relieve pain can retain enough in their vital organs to kill vultures.

In the absence of vultures to dispose of their dead, Mumbai's Parsi Punchayet (its governing body), decided to go for a novel – and controversial – solution. Solar reflectors have been installed on three of the four towers to concentrate the sun on the bodies in order to desiccate them so that there is no smell of slow decomposition. Some leading Parsi scholars like Khojeste Mistree, a Punchayet member, have been critical, contending that the bodies burn, contrary to Parsi beliefs. But many Parsis I've spoken to are seemingly resigned to using the reflectors as a necessary alternative.

Mistree, though, has long advocated building an aviary around one or two of the towers to house vultures there, a kind of breeding centre in the middle of sprawling Mumbai where the birds were previously abundant. For obvious reasons, their food supply would be guaranteed. 'Construction is scheduled to begin soon,' commented Dinshaw Rus Mehta, Chairman of the Bombay Parsi Punchayet in November 2012. 'If all goes as planned, vultures may again consume the Parsi dead. Without the vultures, more and more Parsis are choosing to be cremated. I have to bring back the vultures so that the system is working again.' The plan is the result of six years of negotiations between Parsi leaders and the Indian government. The cost of building the aviaries and maintaining the vultures is estimated at $5 million over 15 years. 'Most vulture aviaries have to spend huge sums to buy meat, but for us that's free because the vultures will be feeding on human bodies — on us,' Mr. Mehta said. Desperate to maintain one of their most important rituals, Parsi leaders have yet to receive formal approval before beginning construction.

Jemima Parry-Jones, though, doesn't think any of this is feasible. 'For the Parsis to be able to guarantee that none of their dead will have been treated with a NSAID that could be toxic to the vultures is I think not only impossible, but actually morally wrong, because they would have to withhold pain relief from dying people. Originally, when the birds were wild here, they had the option of flying off to eat other food. To keep them in a large aviary and feed them nothing but dead humans is not acceptable. To have enough vultures to consume all the Parsis that die is not going to be possible; it would need to be in the hundreds. They need a mix of foods; they need clean baths; they need expert care. If the staff upset them when cleaning, they will vomit human flesh, which will be very unpleasant for the keepers. The project has not been thought out properly,' she says. So far, no construction has begun at the towers.

The demise of the subcontinent's vultures also has potentially worrying consequences for public health across this vast land area where people already endure a range of deadly and debilitating diseases, some of them poorly recorded in health statistics. When vultures were abundant, they kept all other carnivores at bay when they were feeding on cattle carcasses. Now, corpses hang around for days and feral dogs hold sway with rats, jackals, feral pigs, crows and a plethora of insects feeding on them. The threat of diseases such as bubonic plague spread by rat fleas, typhus, and even anthrax, together with all manner of bacteria washed into water supplies in the monsoon season, is likely to add more ill health. Since the vultures disappeared, feral dog numbers in India have burgeoned. No country has as many stray dogs and no country suffers as much from them. Packs of strays lurk in public parks, guard alleyways and street corners and howl nightly in neighbourhoods and villages. Joggers carry bamboo rods to beat them away, and cyclists fill their pockets with stones to throw at them. In India, an estimated 30,000 people die every year from rabies infections; that's more than a third of the global rabies toll. There have even been incidents where village children have been killed and partly eaten by dogs near carcass dumps.

Unfortunately, no statistics show whether or not such diseases are on the increase because there is virtually no recording, especially amongst poor rural communities where the risk is greatest. But research by Dr Anil Markandya and colleagues at the University of Bath, UK, has calculated that the decline of vultures resulted in at least 5.5 million extra feral dogs in India between 1992 and 2006. During this period, they estimate, these extra dogs would have been responsible for at least 38.5 million human bites. National surveys show that in India 123 people die of rabies per 100,000 dog bites, suggesting that a minimum of 47,300 people may have died as a result of the vulture die-off. Taking account of the cost of treating bite victims and dealing with the extra deaths (if all these victims were treated), the researchers calculate that the use of diclofenac has indirectly cost India an unforeseen $34 billion in extra health costs.

❖   ❖   ❖

In part, the impetus to have an aviary at Mumbai's Towers of Silence is a result of the successful breeding of all three severely depleted vulture species in purpose-built breeding centres across the subcontinent. Their urgent establishment was to enable some of the last birds to be brought into captivity away from the risks of getting poisoned by NSAIDs. Vulture survival could not be chanced upon the diclofenac ban; if enough of the killer drug was still in use illegally, there might not have been any vultures to save. First, though, after the relevant government permissions were obtained, vultures had to be captured to form the basic breeding stock – not the easiest of tasks. Birds of all three rapidly declining species had to be located; capture had to be done by trained teams with vets on hand; and the adults had to be captured outside the breeding season to make sure no eggs or youngsters were jeopardised. The welfare of captured birds was paramount. Nestlings of all three species were collected too. Experienced climbers placed nestlings in cotton bags and lowered them to the ground from tree-top or cliff nesting sites. Genetics experts have advised that around 300 vultures of each species are needed in order to breed populations with a good range of genes, thereby giving them a better chance of surviving some untold future catastrophe whenever they are safely released into the wild. Finding and capturing that many vultures has proved extremely difficult.

The first captive breeding centre was built in Haryana State in North India with financial support from its state government. About 200 adult vultures are currently housed there; mainly White-rumped and Indian with smaller numbers of Slender-billed Vultures. A second centre in West Bengal currently houses about 100 adults of all three species and another in Assam has at least 50 adults but no Indian Vultures. All three centres are managed by the BNHS. Nepal has one breeding centre with 60 White-rumps, while the centre in Pakistan currently houses about 30 of the same species. Five more conservation breeding facilities in India are planned. 'Usually only one species is kept in an individual aviary but if there is a problem of space than we do keep two species together,' comments Vibhu Prakash. 'These three species are not very close genetically so the possibility of inter-breeding is unlikely but pairs can be established between species if they are kept together and that would be a waste. We keep a very strict eye and do not let it happen.'

The first successful captive breeding – two White-rumped chicks reared in 2008 and two young Slender-billed Vultures plus another three White-rumped the following year – was a much-welcomed bit of positive news. By 2012, the captive breeding centres reared a total of 26 young birds, although this includes just three Slender-billed youngsters. Indian and Slender-billed vultures had never before been bred in captivity. More have been reared since.

Like all other large birds of prey, vultures are slow breeders. The White-rumped, for instance, is not sexually mature until four or five years old and an adult female will lay just one egg per year after that. It takes around 50 days of incubating before the vulture chick hatches, a lesson in endurance. But vultures do have the advantage of a long life; 20–30 years in the wild, 40 or so in captivity. So breeding large numbers for future releases is never going to be a rapid process. It is a huge irony that these vultures were killed off so quickly; building their numbers back is going to take decades at best. In order to accelerate productivity at least a little, eggs laid by some vultures in the breeding centres are removed from their nests soon after laying to induce the female to re-lay. The removed eggs, and any abandoned by their parents, are then hatched in incubators; the young birds are later placed back with their parents.

Breeding vultures in captivity has been previously well tried and tested. It was done successfully to rescue the Californian Condor, to reintroduce the Lammergeier to the European

Alps and the Eurasian Griffon Vulture to parts of France. Much of the initial practical advice on rearing these three species of Asian vultures came from Jemima Parry-Jones and her staff. 'We designed the first aviaries and started the breeding programme. Although similar vultures had been bred in various zoos around the world, never had anyone put so many birds together in one place before, so the whole thing was a learning experience,' says Parry-Jones. 'Much of our continuing involvement with the breeding centres has been in training staff in husbandry techniques with the vultures, training them to use incubators for the eggs and chick rearing; but also answering queries, sometimes any time of day or night! The experience of the on-site staff has increased enormously,' she adds.

Setting up breeding aviaries is not a simple – or cheap – job. Each one costs a minimum of $39,000 to build and equip with the facilities they need: a variety of perches, nesting ledges, bathing facilities with fresh water, egg incubators and plenty of branches and other suitable materials for nest building. Aviary running costs are high; they need expert staffing, a copious supply of uncontaminated meat for the birds and regular cleaning plus vets on call for health checks and any illness. Staff need to be accommodated and trained in feeding and handling the birds, in incubating eggs and in basic veterinary care for sampling blood and other health checks. It costs $524,000 a year to run the breeding centres in India alone. Most rely on goat meat for feeding to their vultures because goats are less likely to have been treated with NSAIDs by farmers and – if they are – the drugs pass though their bodies more speedily. Vultures consume a lot of meat; up to 5% of their body weight in a day. A diet of finely minced or chopped meat – usually rats or rabbits – is suitable for newly hatched vulture chicks. Meat from goats, cattle, buffalo, horses and donkeys (if the source is known and the animal is completely free of drugs) can also be used but, in the case of the large animal food, crushed bone must be added.

So who pays for all this? The governments in the countries hosting the breeding centres have contributed some of the capital and feeding costs but most of it comes from those voluntary organisations involved, the RSPB especially. Ironically there is no contribution being made by the drug companies that have, in all probability, made considerable profits from sales of diclofenac in the past and who will do so in the future from selling alternative NSAIDs.

❖   ❖   ❖

With a captive population increasing in number, but many more young vultures needed before any can be released, conservationists have begun to turn their attention to establishing a network of 'vulture safe zones' into which birds can initially be released knowing that these areas are clear of diclofenac or other NSAIDs. The IUCN's *Guidelines for Reintroductions and Other Conservation Translocations* is very clear that 'there should generally be strong evidence that the threat(s) that caused any previous extinction have been correctly identified and removed or sufficiently reduced', in this case the chances of poisoning from cattle and buffalo corpses having toxic NSAIDs in their flesh. The SAVE team are well aware of these requirements; they have to assure themselves that no new NSAIDs toxic to vultures have been introduced for cattle and buffalo treatment before vultures are released into safe zones. Or, if there is still a residual level of toxic NSAID use when birds are released, that it is at such a low incidence to be of no significance for the reintroduced birds.

These are, of course, difficult decisions that have to be made with frequently imperfect information. Having spent years, considerable effort on the part of many dedicated individuals – and much money – breeding vultures ready for release, the last thing the SAVE team want to experience is more vulture deaths. Furthermore, the availability of cattle carcasses has altered in the countryside into which they will eventually be released; many are now disposed of in other ways since the vultures disappeared. Consequently, there is unlikely to be the quantity of carrion that was available in the past.

SAVE's thinking is that the vulture safe zones will each cover an area of 30,000 km². One has been identified in Nepal and is considered diclofenac-free. Seven zones have been provisionally identified in different parts of India, and memoranda of understanding have been signed between the RSPB, the BNHS and the state governments concerned. The safe zone in Nepal is the most advanced, and the largest so far. Expanded by 2013 to cover the whole southwest of the country, it has government support and incorporates feeding places where diclofenac-free meat is put out; a diclofenac-free pledge by all vets in the area; and good public support. It links up physically with another zone across the Nepalese border in India. NSAID monitoring in veterinary pharmacies and in cattle corpses has begun in some potential safe zones together with promotion of alternative drugs to farmers. One of the zones in India is already diclofenac-free, helped by its state government giving the safe alternative, meloxicam, free to vets. Key to the success of these initial reintroduction zones will be the employment of local, dedicated teams to do the testing; to work with state officials, vets, drug distributors, local farmers and veterinary colleges in the area; to monitor vulture populations; and, in the early stages, to provide safe meat to encourage the released vultures to stay within the zone. It's an expensive undertaking.

The vulture population will take many decades to rebuild itself in the wild because their reproduction rate is slow and food resources will be more restricted, and they will probably never reach the numbers that existed in the 1980s and before. But, as the captive population slowly expands, as diclofenac and other toxic NSAID use is eliminated, as the vulture safe zones receive their first released birds, the vultures of the Indian subcontinent will begin their long return journey. And, whether it's by Parsis, conservationists, millions of farmers or public health professionals, these essential scavengers are unlikely to be taken for granted again.

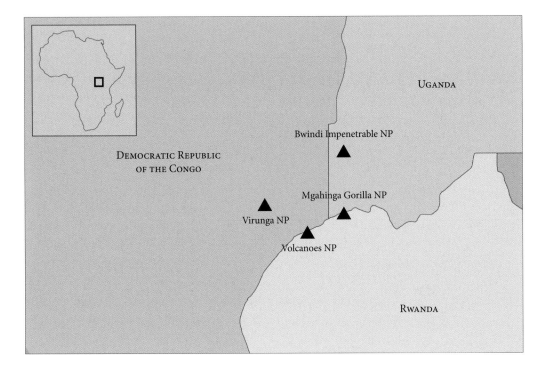

11

COMING OUT OF THE MIST

MOUNTAIN GORILLA

Inhabiting forests in the heart of Africa, Mountain Gorillas have had to endure hunting, forest destruction, trapping of their infants for an illegal 'pet' trade, horrific injuries caused by snares and periods of armed conflict around them. By the 1980s, maybe 500 survived and their prospects looked bleak. Protected, when military conflicts have allowed, in four national parks in Rwanda, Uganda and the Democratic Republic of Congo, by 2011 their numbers had risen to 880 and seem set to rise further. In the front line of their protection are local rangers, several of whom have lost their lives. Carefully managed tourism remains the key to continued success, bringing in cash to provide for gorilla and habitat protection and improving the living standards of the local people upon whom the destiny of one of our closest relatives depends.

*I*t all sounds rather forbidding: 'viewing time limited to an hour; keep seven metres away; if you cough, cover your mouth and turn away; talk quietly; don't make any rapid movements'. But these 'Gorilla Guidelines' issued by the Rwanda Development Board are not some exercise in over-the-top bureaucracy; they are a small but essential part of the enormous effort to protect one of the rarest mammals in the world, the Mountain Gorilla of *Gorillas in the Mist* fame. Central Africa hosts two major populations of Mountain Gorillas. One is in the Virunga volcanic mountains within three national parks that connect to each other across three international boundaries: Mgahinga in south-west Uganda; Volcanoes, in north-west Rwanda; and Virunga in the eastern Democratic Republic of Congo (DRC). Together they total about 15,000 km^2 (with Mgahinga by far the smallest), an area smaller than Kuwait. In 2010, there were 480 Mountain Gorillas living there. The other population, isolated from the previous one by large expanses of farmland, is found in Uganda's Bwindi Impenetrable National Park (a forested area of about 330 km^2, about the size of Malta) north of Mgahinga. It has 400 Mountain Gorillas.

Mountain Gorillas were unknown to westerners until 1902 when a German Army Captain, Friedrich Robert von Beringe, leading an expedition into the Virunga Mountains, shot two of them. Transported to the Natural History Museum in Berlin, it was thought then to be a new species and – as *Gorilla beringei* – named after him. In his journal, von Beringe recorded:

> From our campsite we were able to watch a herd of big, black monkeys which tried to climb the crest of the volcano. We succeeded in killing two of these animals, and with a rumbling noise they tumbled into a ravine. After five hours of strenuous work we succeeded in retrieving one of these animals using a rope. It was a big, human-like male monkey of one and a half metres in height and a weight of more than 200 pounds. His chest had no hair, and his hand and feet were of enormous size. Unfortunately I was unable to determine its type; because of its size, it could not very well be a chimpanzee or a gorilla, and in any case the presence of gorillas had not been established in the area.

No one had any idea how many Mountain Gorillas existed at that time but what is clear is that over the ensuing century, a combination of hunting and habitat destruction drove them to the verge of extinction. In the first two decades after their discovery, European and American scientists and trophy hunters killed over 50.

But for the intervention and dedication of a handful of people, the Mountain Gorilla would surely already be extinct. Carl Akeley (1864–1926), an American who is now considered the father of modern taxidermy, became a convinced conservationist after seeing the plight of Mountain Gorillas in the Virunga Mountains. Having 'collected' several for display in zoos, his attitude fundamentally changed and for the remainder of his life he worked for the establishment of a gorilla reserve in the Virungas. In 1925, greatly influenced by Akeley, King Albert I of Belgium (the DRC was then part of Belgium's colonial empire) established the Albert National Park, since renamed Virunga. It was Africa's first national park.

George Schaller, mammalogist and one of the world's leading field biologists, spent a few years in the early 1960s living close to the Mountain Gorillas in the Virunga Mountains and studying their lives. Very little was known about their life in the wild until the publication of his book, *The Mountain Gorilla: Ecology and Behavior* (University of Chicago Press, 1963), which first spelt out how profoundly intelligent and gentle gorillas are, contrary to then common beliefs to the contrary. And it was Schaller's research that Dian Fossey built upon when she spent 18 years from 1967 studying part of the Virunga population. Schaller and Fossey were instrumental in dispelling the public perception of gorillas as brutes by demonstrating the deep compassion and social intelligence evident among them and how very closely their behaviour parallels that of humans.

But it is the people of the Democratic Republic of Congo (DRC), Rwanda and Uganda, for the most part unsung heroes, who deserve the credit for ensuring the survival of the Mountain Gorilla, and who offer the greatest hope for its continued survival. The protection, monitoring and management of their populations and habitat have demanded huge commitment and have cost many lives. In the DRC's Virunga National Park alone, 190 park rangers have been killed in the last 15 years. The dedication of park staff in the three countries is the chief reason why Mountain Gorillas are thriving today.

At their lowest point, in 1981, there were probably 250 or fewer Mountain Gorillas left in the Virunga forested mountains (across the three countries involved) though, by 1989, they had increased to about 320 and by 2003 there were 380 of them. Adding in the 320 Mountain Gorillas in Bwindi Impenetrable National Park in Uganda in 2002, it brought the total world population to 700 individuals. By 2011, there were 880 or more and the expectation is that their numbers will rise further. There is certainly more habitat – today better protected and with more local community support – available for them to expand into.

❖　❖　❖

Of the more than 400 species of primate in the world – and new species are still being discovered – apart from chimpanzees and our very own human species, gorillas are arguably the next best known. Their name was first used by Hanno the Navigator, a Carthaginian explorer who led a huge seaborne exploration of the West African coast around 500 BC. At some point he found an island heavily populated with what he described as hirsute and savage people. Attempts to capture the males failed, but three of the females were taken. These were so ferocious that they were killed, and their skins preserved for transport home to Carthage. His interpreters called them gorillae, and when European explorers first encountered gorillas in the 19th century, the apes were given this name on the assumption that they were the 'people' Hanno had described.

They are the largest of all primates; they live on the ground; they are predominantly vegetarian; and they inhabit the tropical and subtropical forests of central Africa. Their DNA is very similar to ours and they are our closest living relatives after the chimpanzees. Gorillas, chimpanzees and humans all diverged from a common ancestor about seven million years ago. Gorillas further diverged into their separate species and subspecies during the Ice Age, which began about 2.6 million years ago when their forest habitats shrank and became isolated from each other. Mountain Gorillas have been isolated from Eastern Lowland Gorillas for about 400,000 years and these two separated from their western counterparts approximately two million years ago. So gorillas have a patchy distribution but they have adapted to live in a wide range of forests from sea level to high mountains. There are just two species of gorilla. The Western Gorilla is divided into two subspecies, the Western Lowland Gorilla and the Cross River Gorilla; the Eastern Gorilla is subdivided into the Eastern Lowland or Grauer's Gorilla and the Mountain Gorilla. Some experts refer to the Bwindi population of the Mountain Gorilla as another subspecies of the Eastern Gorilla.

Although the population of the Western Lowland Gorilla is larger than all the other subspecies, and a figure of 95,000 is often quoted as its likely number, IUCN assessments conclude it is far less common because that figure is based on population densities in intact habitat in Gabon in the 1980s. Since then, commercial hunting and outbreaks of deadly Ebola virus – both of which have increased – have greatly reduced their numbers and pose a huge threat to remaining populations. IUCN classifies them as Critically Endangered. Even if the threats to their survival cease – highly unlikely anyway – their slow reproductive rate means that they would take many decades to recover their populations.

While Western Lowland Gorillas live in swamp and lower elevation forests, its nearest relative, the Cross River Gorilla, is restricted to the forested hills and mountains of the Cameroon-Nigeria border region. Surveys suggest that 200–300 Cross River Gorillas remain, distributed now in up to ten small groups desperately hanging on in scattered and frequently isolated pieces of forest, most of them unprotected. They are classified as Critically Endangered. It is the most threatened of the African apes and has been in decline for years due to hunting and continuing small-scale forest clearance for crop growing. Ebola has not been reported in their populations but their close proximity to dense human communities puts them at high potential risk. More positively, in 2008 the Cameroon government created the Takamanda National Park on the border of Nigeria to attempt to protect them. It connects to Nigeria's Cross River National Park, safeguarding an estimated 115 Cross River Gorillas – at least a third of their population – along with other rare species. In southwest Cameroon, FFI is working with local partners and Cameroon's Ministry of Forests and Wildlife to try to protect another population of these gorillas discovered there in 2004 by securing the protection of the proposed Tofala Hill Community Wildlife Sanctuary. It is also working with developers already awarded concessions for nearby logging and oil palm plantations to protect corridors of habitat so that the sanctuary doesn't become another isolated piece of habitat.

The Eastern Lowland Gorilla, found almost entirely in the east of the DRC, is classified as Endangered and has declined substantially over several decades. The largest of the gorilla subspecies, their numbers are thought to be below 5,000 and falling. They have been killed for bushmeat, their forest habitat is often logged or cleared for farming and mining, and they are sometimes killed or seriously disturbed because of frequent civil unrest and fighting in the region. The Mountain Gorilla has been classified since 2008 by IUCN as Critically Endangered because of its small numbers and because of illegal killing in recent decades, political instability and civil war in the DRC and the risk of disease transmission by humans. With more stability in the region and growing numbers, it is possible that this most famous of gorillas might soon be upgraded to Endangered from Critically Endangered.

❖ ❖ ❖

The fur of the Mountain Gorilla, often thicker and longer than that of its relatives, enables them to live in colder conditions. Males, at a mean weight of 195 kg (two to three times the weight of a mature man) and an upright standing height of 1.5 metres, usually weigh in at twice that of females. Primarily terrestrial and using all four legs to walk, Mountain Gorillas will climb into fruiting trees if the branches can carry their weight. They can also run short distances on two feet, and, like all great apes other than humans, their arms are longer than their legs. All gorillas move by knuckle-walking, supporting their weight on the backs of their curved fingers rather than on their palms although they sometimes walk upright for short distances if they're carrying food or defending their compatriots.

Each gorilla builds a nest from the surrounding vegetation to sleep in, constructing a new one every evening. Only infants sleep in the same nest as their mothers. It's this nest building that gives rangers the ability to get an accurate count of how many gorillas there are. They count the nests and collect gorilla dung from it; genetic information extracted from the dung gives each individual a unique genetic fingerprint to make sure the same gorilla is not counted twice. They leave their sleeping sites when the sun rises; but not if it's cold, misty and overcast, which it often is; then, just like us, they might have a lie in.

Rather like most humans too, Mountain Gorillas are highly social and live in relatively stable, cohesive groups held together by long-term bonds between adult males and females but led and protected by one older, distinctly dominant male – the silverback – who will fight to the death to protect his charges. Two thirds of these groups, whose size varies from five to 30 with an average of ten individuals, consist of one adult male and several females bonded to the silverback; a third contain more than one adult male. There will also be from three to six juveniles and infants. Younger males often act as sentries. But the groups are not territorial; a silverback generally defends his group rather than his territory and a dominant silverback might hold sway on average for five years. Outside the groups, the remaining gorillas are either lone males or are in exclusively male groups usually made up of one mature male and a few younger ones.

Most males, and maybe two thirds of females, eventually leave their natal group. Males leave when they are about 11 years old and the separation process can be gradual. They spend more and more time on the edge of the group until they leave altogether, travelling alone or with an all-male group for a few years until they can attract females to join them and form a new group. Females typically leave when they are about eight, either transferring directly to another established group or beginning a new one with a lone male.

The dominant silverback generally determines the movements of the group he controls, leading it to appropriate feeding sites throughout the year. He also mediates conflicts within the group and protects it from external threats. When the group rests, the silverback is the centre of attention and young animals frequently stay close to him and include him in their games. If a mother dies or leaves the group, the silverback is usually the one who looks after her abandoned offspring, even allowing them to sleep in his nest. When a dominant silverback dies or is killed, the family group is usually severely disrupted. Unless he leaves behind a male descendant capable of taking over his position, the group will either split up or be taken over in its entirety by an unrelated male. When a new silverback takes control of a family group, he might kill all of the infants of the dead silverback. Grotesque as it might seem, such infanticide is an effective reproductive strategy because the newly acquired females are then able to conceive the new male's offspring. Potentially immensely strong and powerful, gorillas are usually gentle and shy. Within their stable groups they rarely exhibit severe aggression but when two Mountain Gorilla groups meet, the two silverbacks can sometimes engage in a fight to the death using their canines to cause deep, gaping injuries.

They spend many of the daytime hours eating; large quantities of food are needed to sustain such a massive bulk. Adult males can eat up to 34 kg of vegetation a day, chomping away at leaves, shoots and stems from a huge range of different plants. When fresh bamboo shoots are available, they spend a fair amount of time in bamboo-dominated forests. Bark, roots, flowers, fruit and small invertebrates make up the rest. Eating stops for a while at the midday rest period, an important time for establishing and reinforcing relationships within the group. Mutual grooming reinforces social bonds and helps keep their hair free from dirt and parasites. Just like human children, young gorillas play much of the time and are more arboreal than the large adults. Playing helps them learn how to communicate and behave within the group; it includes wrestling, chasing and somersaulting, which the silverback and his females tolerate, and even participate in, if encouraged sufficiently.

Mountain Gorillas call to communicate within the group. Twenty-five distinct calls are recognised, many of them used primarily for group communication within dense vegetation where they often can't see one another. Grunts and barks are heard most frequently while a group is travelling; they're necessary to keep group members in contact. They may also be used during social interactions when discipline is required. Screams and roars signal alarm or warning and are produced most often by silverbacks while deep, rumbling belches suggest contentment and are heard frequently during feeding and resting periods.

Mountain Gorillas appear to have rather irrational phobias, just like many humans. They seem naturally afraid of certain small animals like reptiles and they will go out of their way to avoid chameleons and caterpillars. They are also afraid of water and will cross streams only if they can do so without getting wet; using fallen logs to get across for instance.

❖ ❖ ❖

If there is ever a name that will always be associated with the Mountain Gorilla, it's that of Dian Fossey (1932–1985). An American zoologist, she devoted 18 years to their study in the mountain forests of Rwanda, initially at the request of the anthropologist Louis Leakey who believed in the importance of long term research on the great apes – something that was lacking when Fossey started in 1967 – before they became extinct as he and others thought they undoubtedly would. In 1967 she founded what is now a much larger research centre at Karisoke, a remote rainforest camp high in the forested saddle between two extinct volcanoes. Here, she became known by locals as Nyiramachabelli, roughly translated as 'the woman who lives alone on the mountain'. With heavy rainfall much of the year and cool temperatures, often head-high vegetation and constantly muddy conditions, it is not an easy part of the world to work in. Many research students left because they couldn't cope with it.

But Fossey was nothing if not incredibly determined. She identified three distinct Mountain Gorilla groups in her study area but could not get physically close to them. She eventually found that mimicking their actions and making grunting sounds reassured them, together with submissive behaviour and eating the local plants. Fossey later attributed her success with habituating gorillas to her previous experience in the US working as an occupational therapist with autistic children.

While poaching had been illegal in the Volcanoes National Park since the 1920s, the law was rarely enforced; park rangers were often bribed by poachers. Using international funding, she financed patrols to destroy thousands of poachers' traps, while the national park rangers didn't eradicate any. On three occasions, she witnessed the aftermath of the capture of infant gorillas at the behest of the rangers to supply zoos; since gorillas will fight to the death to protect their young, the capture would often result in up to ten adult gorillas being shot. Famously, in

1978 she attempted unsuccessfully to prevent the export of two young gorillas from Rwanda to Cologne Zoo in Germany. During the capture of the infants, 20 adult gorillas had been killed. Shipped to Germany, these two lived just nine years in captivity. If they weren't capturing youngsters for zoos, poachers would kill gorillas and cut off their hands as food delicacies, magic charms or to make ashtrays. Gorilla heads decorated the walls of the city wealthy.

Fossey also endured the loss of several of the gorillas in her study group because of poaching aided by the national park rangers. Seemingly it was these deaths in particular that made her devote more of her attention to preventing poaching and less to scientific research. Her anti-poaching activities became increasingly intense and bizarre: she and her staff cut animal traps almost as soon as they were set; frightened, captured and humiliated the poachers; held their cattle for ransom; burned their hunting camps and even mats from their houses as well as constantly challenging local officials to enforce the law and assist her. It was not a strategy that endeared her to many locals.

She also strongly opposed wildlife tourism, bringing herself into often irascible conflict with a number of organisations who saw carefully managed tourism as the means of attracting funding and getting local people on side. Her opposition was based partly on the need to keep humans and gorillas apart in case of the spread of disease. But she also believed that the Mountain Gorilla habitat should not be disturbed in any way... nor her own research. Today, however, the Dian Fossey Gorilla Fund International recognises the importance of tourism in helping to create stable and sustainable local African communities dedicated to protecting the gorillas and their habitat. Her book, *Gorillas in the Mist* (Houghton Mifflin, 1983) combines her scientific study of the Mountain Gorilla with her own personal story. It was adapted into a popular 1988 film of the same name directed by Michael Apted and with Sigourney Weaver as Fossey.

In 1985, Fossey was discovered murdered in the bedroom of her cabin. She is buried at Karisoke in a cemetery that she had made herself for her deceased gorillas. It is a fitting resting place for an albeit controversial woman without whom few people would have been aware of the plight of the Mountain Gorilla and because of whose work we know far more about their day to day lives.

❖　❖　❖

Even though Mountain Gorillas are increasing in number, their future still remains precarious because of a number of possible threats.

Except when there is armed conflict and hungry militias and refugees become the norm, Mountain Gorillas are not usually hunted for bushmeat, but they are frequently maimed or killed by traps and snares intended for other animals. 'The success of intensive awareness-raising campaigns in recent years means that it has become virtually taboo to hunt and kill a gorilla for bushmeat,' says Daniel Pouakouyou, FFI's former Programme Manager for Central Africa, though there is active killing of many other animals, including primates. 'The ongoing struggle to reduce the impact of bushmeat consumption is a cornerstone of FFI's primate conservation strategy in Africa. We are addressing it by supporting national wildlife authorities and sometimes by providing alternative sources of protein and income to those involved in the hunting and the trade. That might be controversial but FFI's approach is pragmatic and daring; it recognises that there's a cultural dimension to bushmeat eating that can't be ignored,' he says.

'In Uganda it is taboo to eat primates so there is no deliberate effort to kill gorillas and this, coupled with public sensitisation about the conservation status of gorillas, means that poaching is not targeted at them,' says Pontious Ezuma, Chief Warden of the Bwindi National Park. 'There are isolated cases of poaching of Duikers [small antelope] or bush pigs for food using wire snares. Any animal that passes by gets caught up in them; in the ten years to 2014 we had eight cases where gorillas have got into such snares and get maimed. With increased public awareness, though, these incidences have greatly reduced of late and we are looking forward to a time when the park will be free of them.' Ezuma adds, 'Because of our community conservation efforts with support from conservation NGOs, more and more people are giving up poaching and are turning to agriculture to earn a living. A total of 48 poachers surrendered last year in the southern part of Bwindi and we are working with about 30 this year to do the same.'

Up until the 1970s, infant and juvenile gorillas were captured for sale to foreigners as trophies and captive specimens; they are reckoned to have been worth many thousands of US dollars. None survived in captivity. Thankfully, that now rarely happens, but the illegal capture of infants 'commissioned' by unscrupulous dealers remains a real threat. Regular armed patrols by rangers, good relations with local communities acting as 'eyes and ears', and more tourism are all factors that discourage it. In 2002, poaching attempts occurred in all three countries, two of them successful. In Rwanda, two adult females were killed and one baby stolen. A second infant was found next to its dead mother and reintroduced to the group. In the DRC, four gorillas from one group were killed. A three-year old infant, believed to be part of this group, was found alive in Rwanda but died later in captivity. Park guards thwarted two further attempts, in Rwanda and Bwindi respectively. Security throughout the parks has since been increased. In 2004 another infant was confiscated from poachers by the Rwandan authorities; this one is currently under the care of the Mountain Gorilla Veterinary Programme (MGVP). In June 2007 an adult female was shot in DRC and her two month old infant recovered and put under MGVP care. Constant vigilance is obviously a necessity.

In this part of Africa, human population growth is relentless. It brings with it more chance of forest felling to clear land for crop growing and more illegal hunting of edible animals. And because of shifting slash-and-burn agriculture, moving on from one exhausted piece of land to clear another, villages in forest zones cause fragmentation and degradation of habitat as they go. In the late 1960s, a huge area of forest within Rwanda's Volcanoes National Park was cleared to grow pyrethrum causing a massive reduction in the Mountain Gorilla population by the mid 1970s. And NASA satellites showed a significant amount of deforestation in the DRC's Virunga National Park between 1999 and 2008, probably due to a combination of slash-and-burn farming, charcoal burning and conflict between rebels and government forces at different times. Apart from the obvious loss of habitat, large clearances like this tend to isolate gorilla groups from one another leading to inbreeding, reducing their overall genetic diversity.

It also results in an increased likelihood of gorillas raiding farm crops for food, raising the antipathy stakes with local communities.

The ever-present threat of catastrophic disease spread is another concern; Ebola has decimated several populations of other gorilla subspecies. A serious outbreak amongst the human population of Guinea in 2014 has spread into adjacent countries and beyond. And there is always a risk of disease transfer from visiting tourists to gorillas – hence the stringent tourist rules – or from domestic livestock.

War and civil unrest continue to be a threat. Rwanda, Uganda and the DRC have been politically unstable and beleaguered by war and fighting at different times over the last decades. In times of such conflict there are a whole set of consequences including: a higher risk of killing of any bushmeat by hungry, displaced people; an obvious breakdown of law and order; forced withdrawal and weapon surrender of national park rangers; forest felling to provide firewood; and mines, frequently placed along trails, triggered by passing gorillas.

The consequences are typified by what has happened within the DRC's Virunga National Park. Designated in 1925, for its first 35 years poaching was kept to a minimum and sustainable tourism thrived due to the work of a large number of Congolese rangers and dedicated wardens. They started to improve relations with local communities. When Congo gained independence in 1960 the new state deteriorated rapidly, and so did the park. Only in 1969 did things revive with then President Mobutu taking some personal interest in conservation. The Congolese Wildlife Authority was established. Virunga fared well for the better part of the 1970s. Foreign investment helped to improve the park's infrastructure and training facilities and it became a popular destination for tourists, receiving over 6,000 visitors a year. In 1979, UNESCO designated it a World Heritage Site. In the mid 1980s, the country began a long slide into chaos. The park suffered terribly; poaching depleted its large mammal populations, infrastructure was destroyed and many of its rangers were killed. The Congolese Wildlife Authority slowly lost control. Over the next 25 years, Virunga staff endured an almost uninterrupted series of problems that included a refugee crisis from the Rwandan genocide in 1994 that unleashed a flood of more than one million refugees, placing tremendous pressure on the park's forests and wildlife.

The 'Second Congo War', 1998–2002 (the first was 1996–1997), devastated the DRC, killed over five million people (most from disease and malnutrition), involved nine African nations and 20 armed groups. Many Virunga park rangers lost their lives. Then came the Kivu conflict (2004–2009) between the DRC military and the Democratic Forces for the Liberation of Rwanda, which centred on the park with rebel forces occupying its headquarters and evicting the park's staff. In 2007, members of an illegal charcoal mafia murdered a family of Mountain Gorillas. The event was arguably the Virunga's darkest hour in over a decade. Their motivation was simple: kill the gorillas and there will no longer be a reason to protect the park. By the end of the year, nine gorillas had been killed. From 2012 to 2013 armed conflict flared up yet again – the so-called M23 rebellion – with mutinied Congolese soldiers fighting DRC forces. Some of this conflict took place in the Virunga National Park, where large parts were controlled by irregular armed groups and the DRC army. The rangers had fled for their lives and local communities had taken over some areas to live in and grow crops.

The M23 rebel military group surrendered in November 2013. Slowly, the political situation has improved since then. Rangers have returned, gorillas are being monitored again and anyone involved in criminality prosecuted; staff training and discipline was slowly restored and rangers got paid, if not by their governments, by the International Gorilla Conservation Programme (IGCP) which was then funded by FFI, WWF and the Africa Wildlife Foundation, AWF. 'At the height of the conflict, the best IGCP could do was support the staff on the ground in the national parks so that they could continue to operate as safely as possible. It has been extremely hard for so many of them. Yet it is due to them that the gorillas are still there, and that the parks are still intact,' recalls Eugène Rutagarama of IGCP.

Today, Virunga National Park is managed once again by the Congolese Wildlife Authority, together with its partner, the UK-based Africa Conservation Fund. International donors are investing in the development of its infrastructure and tourist numbers increased from zero in 2008 to a few thousand by 2014 as new tourist facilities are developed. At the same time its population of Mountain Gorillas has more than doubled since the late 1980s.

But another potential threat has appeared in recent years: oil exploration. WWF and UNESCO have expressed alarm over a provision in a draft DRC Parliamentary Bill that proposes to strip national parks of the protections afforded them under the country's constitution. They have urged the DRC government to uphold the rule of law and its treaty obligations. FFI believes that, as a World Heritage Site, Virunga National Park should be excluded from any form of prospecting for the extractive industries. But some oil concessions have already been offered; SOCO, an international oil and gas exploration and production company headquartered in London, for instance, was proposing to do a seismic survey on Lake Edward at the eastern edge of the national park, which could lead to test extraction of oil if reserves are indicated. 'The block assigned to us doesn't include any Mountain Gorilla habitat and the seismic survey might not even identify any oil reserves. Nevertheless, we have withdrawn from Virunga', says Carol Fan, SOCO Deputy Company Secretary. WWF had argued that even under ideal circumstances, pollution-free oil extraction is impossible to guarantee and that operating in areas of weak governance makes it even more challenging; that the environmental, social and economic impacts of oil extend far beyond the area of extraction; and that roads and infrastructure needed to facilitate drilling, extraction and oil transportation can make remote areas more easily accessible.

❖　❖　❖

It isn't long ago that tourists being allowed to see rare wild animals, let alone encouraged to, was anathema to most conservationists. But those were days when baby wild gorillas could still be legally snatched and put into zoos! Times – and attitudes – have changed, and rightly so. Carefully managed tourism has become a vital element in conserving Mountain Gorillas. Managed well, there is no reason why tourism should cause damage, pose a threat to the very places and species people come to see, or spread disease to rare animals. It helps build an international public support base for the places and the species themselves and it engenders a sense of national pride and increased commitment in the host country. The key, though, is that it has to be done in collaboration with local communities in the area and has to bring them tangible benefits too.

It's all too easy to get it wrong. When the Bwindi National Park in Uganda was designated in 1991, there was little community consultation and its new status prohibited local people from obtaining any resources from within the park, thereby limiting their economic opportunities. Not surprisingly, local people saw its imposition as a threat. A number of forest fires were deliberately lit and threats were made to the gorillas. To address the issue, the national park started involving local communities in its management, local people were allowed to use some forest resources and part of the tourism income was channelled into community development to benefit them. Subsequent surveys of community attitudes at Bwindi show a steadily increasing proportion of local people in favour of the park; there have been no cases of deliberate burning since and the number of snares put out to catch wild animals for food (which could equally well injure a gorilla) has reduced.

In 2010, IUCN published *Best Practice Guidelines to Great Ape Tourism*, building on years of experience in different parts of the world. These are being implemented in all three Mountain Gorilla countries. For Mountain Gorillas, they recommend that tourist groups, always with a guide, should be restricted to six (not eight as at present) and that regulations about personal cleanliness, no smoking, no loud noises, keeping a seven metre distance, leaving all food and drink behind, disinfecting boots, staying a maximum of an hour, no mobile phones and more must be adhered to rigorously. Any chance of disturbance to the gorillas and any risk of disease passed to them (especially flu and common colds) must be kept to an absolute minimum.

Mountain Gorilla Regional Tourism Policy Guidelines published in 2014 by the International Gorilla Conservation Programme – a consortium of FFI, WWF and the African Wildlife Foundation (who withdrew during 2014) with the Rwanda, DRC and Ugandan governments – state:

> Tourism has been used for three decades as a tool to enhance the conservation status of Mountain Gorillas. During this period, gorilla tourism has served as a primary draw to attract visitors to the region, turning the Mountain Gorilla range states into premier tourist destinations earning significant funding for conservation with associated revenue generation for local and national economies. Policy makers in the three countries attribute value to the gorillas as a source of revenue and national pride which contributes to the commitment to maintain their protected status and the conservation of their habitats in national parks. During this period, the level of conservation effort applied in the national parks has resulted in a continual growth of the Mountain Gorilla populations, a remarkable feat given the recurrent episodes of insecurity and wars in the region. The overall conclusion is that tourism, when appropriately managed, has served as an effective tool for Mountain Gorilla conservation.
>
> Mountain Gorilla tourism, however, can also pose a threat to the gorillas. A large number of negative impacts of tourism affect not only the apes, but also local communities and the environment. Due to the associated risks, gorilla

tourism cannot be exploited without limit, and an over-reliance on gorilla tourism to attract revenue may result in unsustainable growth in the programme which runs counter to principles of conservation. It may also turn tourists away, as many are only willing to pay the high price of gorilla tourism if it is exclusive and conservation-centred. A gorilla tourism programme must be kept small and tightly controlled, with emphasis on mitigating its negative impacts. Only if all these prerequisites are met can the risks associated with gorilla tourism be mitigated so that it does not itself become a conservation threat.

Only a limited number of gorilla groups are seen by tourists; these are so-called 'habituated' groups; animals that have slowly got used to people being reasonably close and looking at them, a process that takes up to two years before the animals are comfortable. 'At the beginning we had only two gorilla groups habituated for tourism. Now [2014] there are eleven habituated groups. Visitor numbers have grown annually. We stick to ecotourism principles and allow a maximum of eight tourists visiting a gorilla group per day. With full occupancy, the maximum number of tourists to visit Bwindi would be over 30,000 a year but at present it's around 22,000,' comments Pontious Ezuma. 'Each habituated group varies in number but overall there are 156 habituated individuals out of our 400 Mountain Gorillas, 39% of the total population. So the majority never experience tourists, the rationale being that the wild ones remain completely wild so should anything go wrong with the habituated groups this wild reserve is in place for continuity of the gene pool'. Dr Chloe Hodgkinson, Programme Manager for Conservation Capacity and Leadership at FFI confirms that '*The Mountain Gorilla Regional Tourism Policy Guidelines* recommends no more than 50% of the Mountain Gorilla population should be habituated for tourism or research.' So the arrangements at Bwindi are well within the guidelines.

Probably because habituated gorillas are more closely guarded by field staff and they receive veterinary treatment whenever necessary, these groups have higher growth rates than unhabituated gorillas. Unhabituated groups, being totally wild, are seen by rangers much less often. If they get injured in any way, it might not get noticed, at least not for some time. There is, though, a potential downside to gorilla habituation in a region like this where armed conflict might easily reoccur; habituated animals are just as likely to stay put and allow armed militias to get as close to them as tourists. So taking a pot-shot for 'fun' or killing one for food would be all too easy. It is a distinct risk.

For poor African countries the income generated by managed gorilla tourism is substantial; IGCP estimate the annual revenue earned directly from Mountain Gorilla tourism at $3 million. When combined with the additional income received by, for example, hotels, lodges and restaurants, the total might exceed $20 million a year shared between the three countries. The national parks are also broadening the tourism base to include cultural interests and some of the other stunning wildlife on visitors' itineraries in this part of central Africa. 'Conservation may become irrelevant to communities in Africa unless it pays for itself,' argues Pontius Ezuma at Bwindi. 'It's the only way conservation can be relevant to poor local communities. Tourists pay to see the gorillas and local communities benefit through 20% of the gate collections and $5 from each trekking permit that then gets ploughed back into community projects. As our tourist numbers increase, so more money gets invested in projects the surrounding communities need, proportional to their community inhabitants. This works very well and no complaints are raised as the formula was jointly developed with the communities themselves.'

Gorilla tourism certainly doesn't come cheap. A permit costs $750 per person in Rwanda's Volcanoes National Park; that includes park entry, the trek and a guide. 'Due to market forces, the cost of the gorilla permits vary between countries and seasons. However, the *Tourism Policy Guidelines* recommend that pricing should be harmonised across the three countries,' says Chloe Hodgkinson. But tourism-generated cash doesn't always help improve the lot of local communities as well as it might. For instance, a study published in 2012 of the Bwindi National Park scheme by David Mwesigye Tumusiime and Paul Vedeld of the Department of International Environment and Development Studies in Norway concluded that there was a lack of real local participation; an insignificant economic return to local people relative to costs; and that it was too complex.

Mountain Gorillas and tourism are inextricably linked. Arguably, neither has a future without the other, but reconciling the demand for tourist dollars with the needs of the gorillas and of local communities is a delicate and challenging balancing act. It will continue to be so.

Will Mountain Gorilla numbers increase further? Pontious Ezuma is upbeat. 'The last census showed at least 400 gorillas in Bwindi. Currently, we have a study we hope will start soon aimed at understanding the carrying capacity of the park for gorillas. However, my intelligent guess is that the park could still accommodate more, for example in the northern part of the park where the habitat is intact. No gorillas had been in this area until the last two years when one of the habituated groups has moved to this virgin area. It's a good sign,' he says.

It might be optimistic in a part of Africa where armed conflict has been all too commonplace, but given greater political stability, no more conflicts or habitat loss, and provided that the continuing benefits of controlled tourism support local communities and fund national park and gorilla protection, there is every reason to assume that Mountain Gorilla numbers will rise further. Local people and communities must be at the forefront of their protection, gaining from the carefully managed tourism that these animals will continue to generate and the enormous international support they attract. Conserving Mountain Gorillas requires local community support and those communities have to see tangible benefits from doing so.

In the final analysis, though, conserving gorillas should be a natural human instinct. This is what George Schaller, the veteran field biologist said of Mountain Gorillas after living close to them: 'No one who looks into a gorilla's eyes – intelligent, gentle, vulnerable – can remain unchanged, for the gap between ape and human vanishes; we know that the gorilla still lives within us.'

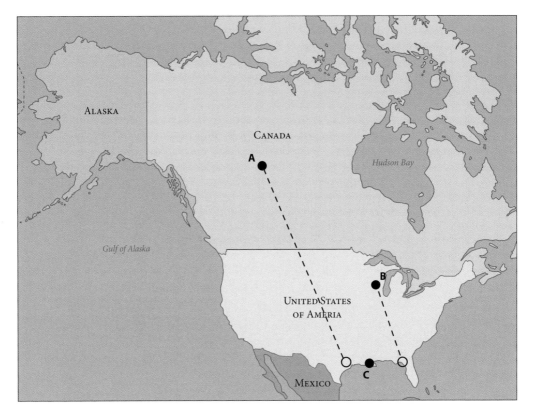

A   Wood Buffalo/Aransas population
B   Wisconsin/Florida population
C   Louisiana non migratory population

●   Whooping Cranes breeding
○   Whooping Cranes wintering

12

AN ELEGANT RECOVERY

WHOOPING CRANE

Before white settlers ploughed, drained and shot their way across North America, the continent had around 10,000 breeding Whooping Cranes, one of the most elegant birds in the world. By the 1940s and 1950s they were down to about 20 and extinction was looming fast. Since then, concerted efforts by Canadian and US federal and state agencies, NGOs and others have slowly built up the one remaining natural population to around 300 individuals. Reintroductions of captive-reared birds to historic sites, plus the innovative use of microlight aircraft to guide newly released young birds on their first migration, has added another 300 cranes. Low breeding success in the reintroduced populations remains an issue but the Whooping Crane is back from the brink and on an albeit bumpy road to recovery.

On a warm and sunny January day in the shallow waterways of the Aransas National Wildlife Refuge on Texas's southeast coast, Jay Tarkington, the skipper of our boat, was the epitome of Texan helpfulness and bonhomie. 'All right folks, we're going to boogie on up now cos there's a family group of those guys on the marsh to the left over there. You'll all happy to do that?' The 'guys' Tarkington was looking at were one of the world's rarest bird species, America's tallest and, just a few decades ago, a bird whose very future rested on a knife-edge: Whooping Cranes.

And a kilometre or so ahead in the saline marshes alongside the waterway stood two snow-white adults with their characteristic scarlet faces accompanied by an almost fully grown, brown and white youngster. It was a family group all right; whoopers rarely raise more than one chick at a time. And here they were, stepping carefully and elegantly through the shallows, searching for food, plunging down with those red faces dipping into the water each time they spotted another tasty morsel.

It is here on the extensive tracts of saltmarsh and shallow brackish waters supporting a cornucopia of invertebrate life that the only naturally migratory Whooping Cranes in the world spend their winter months. These saline and brackish marshes support a huge diversity of wildlife including more than 400 species of birds. There are herons and egrets, pelicans, numerous ducks, waders, gulls and terns as well as alligators and turtles. Birds of prey such as Northern

Harriers quarter the ground and attractive Crested Caracaras are on the lookout for carrion and small mammals Salt-tolerant plants provide habitat for hermit crabs and juvenile fish. The brackish waters are nurseries for young fish and are teeming with blue crab and shellfish, food for Whooping Cranes, herons and other wildlife. And the freshwater marshes on their land-ward side are a haven for alligators, turtles, frogs, snakes and many other animals. Beyond the refuge's marshlands, the oak savannahs and sandy grasslands are important for wild flowers as well as for pollinators like bees and butterflies. In spring, White-tailed Deer can be seen grazing on tender grasses; in autumn they move into the refuge's woods to feed on acorns.

But it is the rare and elegant Whooping Cranes that most people come here to see. They have become a huge attraction for the small twin towns of Rockport and Fulton nearby. It's from the little harbour at Rockport that tour boats leave to do bird and dolphin trips in and around the Aransas Refuge. 'The Whooping Cranes are a huge winter tourism attraction in the Rockport-Fulton area. Over 8,000 visitors from around the world come to view these rare birds each year; it's a great boost to our local economy,' comments Sandy Jumper, Director of Tourism and Events for Rockport/Fulton Chamber of Commerce. 'The whoopers arrive in what would normally be the off-season for tourism. So that's helpful for us. As a result, the visitors who flock to the coast to get a glimpse of this endangered bird also stay in our hotels, eat in our restaurants, shop in our stores and visit other attractions in the area. The birds start to arrive in November, just as the summer tourism season is coming to a close and they don't begin their northern migration until late March to mid April, so international tourism is a year-long affair for our area.'

❖ ❖ ❖

All of the whoopers wintering in and near Aransas on the Texas coast breed in the muskeg in and around Canada's Wood Buffalo National Park; at 44,000 km² it's the second largest national park in the world and bigger than the Netherlands. It straddles the north of Alberta and into Canada's Northwest Territories, much of it inaccessible on foot. Muskeg, a vast wilderness of boggy pools and marsh developed over deep peaty soils, is a permanently waterlogged landscape frozen solid in the long Canadian winter. The annual migration, nearly 4,000 km each way, is a massive journey fraught with risks.

Whooping Cranes are found only in North America. In January 2014 the 500 km² Aransas National Wildlife Refuge, and other habitat nearby, was home to just over 300 Whooping Cranes, its largest number ever. Today, in addition to this natural migratory population moving between Wood Buffalo and the Texas coast, there are other reintroduced populations elsewhere in North America; making the total wild population by 2014 approaching 500 birds. Another 160 or so are in five captive breeding centres in the US and Canada giving a total of around 660 whoopers in North America. Although that's not yet enough to change the Whooping Crane IUCN status, if their population continues to increase – and other populations become established in North America – their category could well be upgraded from Endangered to Vulnerable.

No one is very sure how many of these tall birds – adults reach 1.5 metres in height – originally used to grace the wetlands, fields and marshes of this vast continent. But extrapolating from the breeding densities of today's Whooping Cranes at Wood Buffalo, it is possible – according to the International Recovery Plan for the species (jointly produced by the US and Canadian authorities) – that more than 10,000 Whooping Cranes once roamed across North America. Some estimates put the figure even higher. A couple of centuries ago as white settlers moved further and further west across the US, they hunted and shot Whooping Cranes and collected their eggs for food, just as they did with Wild Turkeys (Chapter 4). Their habitat was disappearing too; settlers ploughed up vast areas of the prairie grasslands and drained as much marshland as they could for farming.

Although Whooping Cranes may never have formed large flocks and were thus reported infrequently, prior to the influx of white settlers they ranged widely and utilised the vast wetland acreages available. Their major nesting area during the 19th and 20th centuries extended over a much larger area of central Canada and down into the north-central US as far south as Iowa. Some nesting apparently occurred at other sites out in the west of the US in the 1900s but there is little detail documented. At that time, whoopers wintered in a range that extended from southwest Louisiana through the Gulf Coast of Texas (including Aransas) and west to northeast Mexico. Seemingly, the cranes weren't wintering only along the coast (as they mainly do now) but inland into central Mexico and Texas where they mixed in with thousands of smaller, pale grey – and very much commoner – Sandhill Cranes. There are records from further afield too. Small flocks were recorded in Florida up to 1911 and the last record there is of one in the north of the state in 1927. There are records from other areas of the US interior: Alabama, Arkansas, Missouri and Kentucky though it's not clear whether these represent wintering locations, remnants of a non-migratory population, or wandering birds. Much of the information is anecdotal and there are few written records.

In 1918, the passing of the US Migratory Bird Treaty Act made it illegal to hunt Whooping Cranes but, despite this and other early protection efforts, these magnificent birds continued to decline. By 1870 they were almost certainly much depleted, probably down to about 1,300 or 1,400 individuals at best; some estimates give a smaller total. The Whooping Crane disappeared from the heart of its breeding range in the north-central US by the 1890s and the last reported breeding in the resident Louisiana population was in 1939. Their numbers fell to an all-time low of just 16 wintering at Aransas in the winter of 1939/40; add in the six then still holding out in Louisiana and its total world population was down to just 22 birds. By 1954/5 their fortunes had not improved; there were 21 wintering at Aransas but the Louisiana birds had been killed a few years previously by a hurricane. Very obviously, the Whooping Crane, America's tallest bird, was on the verge of extinction.

Since then, protection of their Canadian breeding site, their Texas wintering site and protection en route at their known stopover locations between the two, has very slowly resulted in an increase in numbers. By 1983, there were up to 105 birds and by 1990 they had increased to 159. With reintroductions elsewhere to some of their historic breeding areas, by 2005 there were over 340 Whooping Cranes in the wild, which by 2014 had risen further to around 450.

Looking out over the extensive Aransas marshes with Wade Harrell, Whooping Crane Recovery Coordinator for the US Fish & Wildlife Service, we watch a pair of adults with its single youngster. Standing maybe half a metre shorter than its parents, its brown and white plumage allowing it to blend in more with the surrounding saltmarsh vegetation, the three are feeding together about a kilometre away from us. 'They eat mainly blue crabs, fruits of wolf berry [a shrub common on the higher coastal marshes], small clams, fish and lots of different crustaceans but they'll also take oak acorns, insects, small mammals and reptiles that become exposed on burnt areas of vegetation when we do controlled burning here. We do that to keep an open habitat and to slow scrub encroachment; otherwise, the area of open marsh would shrink,' comments Harrell.

We talk and watch the family group, three of what must be some of the most elegant birds in the world. 'They do have predators, though not many seem to get killed. But Bobcats and alligators will kill them and we always get any dead cranes we find checked to find the cause of death,' says Harrell. 'Every winter here we have a small team capturing some of the cranes so that we can attach leg colour bands that can be seen from a distance. That's how we can recognise individuals. And we fit a telemetry device to some so we can monitor their migration routes and know where they stopover on those routes. It helps us know what kind of places they use as stopovers too.'

They begin their huge journey south from northern Canada from early September to late October. In 2012, their near 4,000 km flight took an average of 46 days. No less than 261 stopover locations, where some or all tracked birds stopped for one night or longer, were recorded along their migration corridor south to the Texas coast. Not all of these were protected wildlife sites of course; many were on private land. But most landowners are positive about the return of this magnificent bird.

In response to my question about whether he thinks there is more suitable wintering habitat outside the Aransas Refuge along the Texas coast, Harrell is certain there is. 'That's one of our big planning efforts; trying to make sure we can protect more habitat by expanding Aransas and other protected areas along the coast here. Maybe we need to be looking away from the coast too because these cranes are probably more adaptable than we previously thought; they turn up at pools and even some reservoirs inland if there's a drought here in winter. They're not as confined to coastal marshes as we used to think they were,' he says.

❖   ❖   ❖

Cranes – there are 15 species worldwide – are amongst the most graceful of any birds. They are incredibly tall – the tallest, the Sarus Crane, stands 1.8 metres high – and have renowned courtship dances at their nest sites. Almost all of them have ornamental inner wing feathers that hang down over their short tails, giving them the appearance of an Edwardian lady's bustle. Among the most ancient and distinctive families of birds on Earth, their great size and beauty, unique calls, and complex behaviours have for centuries commanded the attention and respect of people on the five continents on which they are found. Wary residents of wetlands and grasslands, cranes have also long symbolised natural grandeur and the special quality of wild places. Few groups of animals have had so strong a claim upon the human mind, heart and imagination. They appear in the artwork and literature of several early civilisations, in

Ancient Egypt, Greece and Rome. In the East, in China and Japan in particular, they have always been associated with longevity (most cranes live long lives), happiness, luck and peace.

Veneration, though, has certainly not always secured their populations. Six species are considered to be Vulnerable; two species are Endangered and one Critically Endangered. Big birds flying in groups make an easy target for hunters while the marshes in which most of them breed have long been the object of drainage and conversion to pasture or to paddyfields for growing rice. And while they are a protected species in virtually every country in which they either pass through on migration, breed or overwinter, the rate of killing and trapping is still high in several countries; some of it is for food but much of it is not.

Hunting is a significant concern for the populations of Demoiselle Cranes, slender pale grey and black birds that mostly inhabit grasslands in central Asia but migrate through Afghanistan and Pakistan. Particularly in the North Western Frontier Province of Pakistan, catching live cranes is a favourite sport. It's a local tradition and a symbol of social status. Camps are set up and decoy cranes put out to attract migrating demoiselles down. Captured demoiselles are given to guests to adorn their lawns and courtyards. The hunting season falls between October and November when the birds migrate south from their breeding grounds to winter, and from March to April when they return north. They are often also trapped at night using a *soya*, a long, thin, silky rope with a lead ball at one end. As the unsuspecting birds fly over, the hunters simulate their calls; some cranes fly down and are hit by the *soya* thrown up like a projectile. The alighting birds are then trapped and about half of them are injured in the process. Common Cranes and the Critically Endangered Siberian Crane are also affected by this 'sport'. As many as 5,000 cranes of all three species (10–15% of the total population of migrating cranes) have been shot or captured in Pakistan in a single season, and, in spite of efforts to stop the practice, the popularity of the sport doesn't appear to be diminishing.

Cranes that breed in northern locations – the Whooping Crane for instance or the Common Crane of Russia and Scandinavia – migrate long distances south for the winter. It is on these huge journeys that they are at their most enigmatic and inspiring, with large groups of them gliding from one high thermal to another before setting down for the night on grain fields or wetlands en route, their loud trumpeting calls audible from a distance as they come in to land on stick-like legs. It is on these long flights, too, that records are set; many of the Common Cranes from Russia fly over the Himalayas to India and Pakistan at airliner altitudes: 10,000 metres. They are some of the highest-flying birds in the world.

Cranes are monogamous and long-lived, partners remaining together for many years and returning to the same nesting area to breed. In captivity, some live into their seventies or eighties. At the nest site there is much synchronised calling between the two as well as exuberant dancing: jumping in the air, wingspreads, elaborate bowing to each other, uprooting plants and tossing them in the air are all part of many cranes' annual courtship routines. This behaviour reinforces their pair bond, just as going out together for dinner does in a loving human partnership. Most cranes nest in marshes of some description, often pretty inaccessible places, and they build up a bulky mound of vegetation above water-level on which to lay eggs:

usually two, maybe three at the most. The Wattled Crane of African wetlands south of the Sahara almost always lays just one egg but that's less usual.

Cranes share breeding duties; males often incubating in daylight with females taking the night shift. The hatched chicks leave the nest early to follow their parents, sticking with them for maybe a year. More successful species, such as the Sandhill Crane of North America and the Common Crane of northern Europe, sometimes raise two chicks at a time but, ironically, the rarer species – including the Whooping Crane – almost always rear just one. If they are species that migrate, the youngsters learn the route by accompanying their parents, once to their wintering ground and, maybe, once back again. After that, they're on their own; they will need to have memorised the route.

Two species inhabit drier places and don't breed in wetlands; these are the comparatively small but very aggressive Blue Crane of southern Africa, which inhabits pastureland, and the Demoiselle Crane – the smallest of all – which breeds from eastern Europe across to China in arid areas and pastureland, albeit sometimes quite close to streams. The two Endangered species are the Whooping Crane and Asia's Red-crowned Crane. The Red-crowned Crane breeds in eastern Russia and northeast China and winters much further south while a smaller population in Japan is effectively resident all year. Due mainly to habitat degradation and destruction in Russia and China especially – maybe also to some heavy metal poisoning – there are less than 3,000 left and its future looks bleak.

The almost all-white Siberian Crane that breeds across northern Russia is down to around 3,500 individuals, most of them wintering at Poyang Lake in China. Shot and trapped on migration, they are in serious decline and are now the rarest of all crane species, listed as Critically Endangered by IUCN. Adding to the woes of the Siberian Crane is its dependence on eating the fleshy roots and tubers of aquatic plants; it has not adapted to making use of farmed habitats on migration, limiting it yet further. Cranes are omnivorous and take a wide range of foods: fish, frogs and crustaceans, plant tubers the larger species dig for, insects, ripe seeds and berries plucked off shrubs. In more recent times with much of their traditional wetland habitat gone, many species have adapted well to farmed fields and grain stubbles where they pick up insects and spilt seed, cashing in on what food resources are more readily available.

As ground nesters, they are all vulnerable to predators. For the Whooping Crane this can include American Black Bear, Wolverine, Grey Wolf, Red Fox, Canada Lynx, Bald Eagle and Northern Raven; maybe others too. In Florida, Bobcats have caused the great majority of mortalities among whoopers; researchers believe that this is due to an overpopulation of Bobcats caused by the absence or decrease in larger predators (the endangered Florida Panther and the extirpated Red Wolf in particular) that formerly preyed on them. American Alligators have taken a few Whooping Cranes in Florida too. In Wood Buffalo, Mark Bidwell, Canadian Whooping Crane Recovery Coordinator for the Canadian Wildlife Service, says that ravens are the most common predator of Whooping Crane eggs. Omnivorous, intelligent and highly opportunistic, ravens adapt their diet with location, season and serendipity. Scavenging dumps, animal and bird carcasses, taking other bird's eggs or nestlings and even catching small mammals are all part of the raven's successful survival strategy.

❖ ❖ ❖

Little wonder that North America's Whooping Cranes were something of an enigma for much of the year. They were visible and obvious in their coastal Texas wintering quarters. They made themselves pretty obvious, too, on their huge spring and autumn migrations and at numerous 'refuelling stops' en route. Ornithologists knew that they nested somewhere well to the north in Arctic Canada. But where in this vast land area of lakes, forests and marshes were they breeding? No one knew. As their numbers continued to dwindle year upon year into the 1940s in their Texas coast wintering marshes, it became more and more frustrating that their breeding site or sites somewhere in northern Canada had still not been found. With less than 30 birds left, and the Canadian wilderness being explored for metal ores, oil, timber and any other resources that might be useful for mankind with little or no consideration of its impact on wildlife and the pristine habitats involved, finding the summertime whoopers became a priority. Searches in 1945 and 1946 failed.

Until, that is, the National Audubon Society brought in its most tenacious ornithologist, Robert Porter Allen. Even then, nine years of occasional searches by small airplane, some ground searching and much following up of anecdotal records from a range of people who reckoned they'd seen or shot whoopers, produced no definitive idea of where the breeding area was. Until 2 July 1954, when a letter from the Canadian Wildlife Service in Ottawa said that their mammal expert, Dr Bill Fuller, had reported spotting four or six whoopers – including a few youngsters –from a helicopter taking out firefighting gear into the Wood Buffalo National Park. Fuller was pretty sure that they must have been breeding nearby. They hadn't been seen there before because the place was so difficult to access on the ground. In late spring the following year, Fuller managed to get a ride in a plane over the area and spotted an adult whooper sitting on a nest. It triggered a ground survey run jointly by US and Canadian biologists, and led by Porter Allen. The site was confirmed after many weeks of gruelling exploration on foot and by canoe, camping rough every night in this vast, remote region. The whoopers had chosen their nesting grounds well; it was the summer of 1955 and it had taken a decade to find them.

❖ ❖ ❖

While the Wood Buffalo/Aransas population remains the only self-sustaining population in North America, their total wild population includes some cranes that have been reintroduced to locations within their historic breeding range, done so because of their low numbers in the wild and biologists' fear that their one natural and migratory population might be wiped out, perhaps by a hurricane on migration or a disease.

The first attempt to do this was carried out in the mid 1970s by the US Fish and Wildlife Service and the Canadian Wildlife Service; they began to establish a new breeding population in the midwest of the US at Gray's Lake National Wildlife Refuge. It involved taking the second egg from Whooping Crane nests in Canada and using much more common Sandhill Cranes to incubate them. Nesting whoopers invariably lay two eggs but only ever raise one chick. Consequently, the second egg in each nest is effectively surplus to requirements. It can be removed and incubated without affecting the breeding pair from which it's taken. The Gray's Lake population of Sandhill Cranes numbered many thousands and all of them headed south in autumn to winter in New Mexico. The Sandhill Cranes hatched and raised 85 whooper chicks from 289 eggs transplanted into their nests. And 77 juvenile whoopers learnt to migrate south in winter to New Mexico accompanying the sandhills and to forage on drier ground with them too. And they learnt the migration route, repeating it each spring and autumn.

It was a clever idea, which might have worked…but it backfired. The raised whoopers imprinted on the sandhills as if they were young sandhills; some even crossbred with them. And none of the whoopers mated with each other. It was an early lesson in the need to make sure that animals raised in captivity do not imprint on any other creature and then follow them instinctively as if they are the young animal's parents. The Whooping Cranes had imprinted on their sandhill foster parents as if they were their actual parents. Other young whoopers disappeared during migration, presumably killed or dying naturally, and the programme was stopped in 1989. None of these birds survive today. Fifteen or so years and millions of US dollars had been wasted.

At the time, imprinting was not well understood. Konrad Lorenz (1903–1989), the Austrian ethologist and zoologist, had discovered that newly hatched birds assume that the first thing they see close to them is their parent, and follow it wherever it leads. His classic research was done with newly hatched ducklings that imprinted on him – more precisely his wellington boots – and would follow them anywhere. Likewise the whoopers had imprinted on their foster parents, the Sandhill Cranes, and there was no way of weaning them away from their assumed parents. But it gave Dr Robert Horwich, then a research associate at the US-based International Crane Foundation an idea. He had noticed from trials with sandhills that young birds kept isolated from any human contact readily joined wild sandhills, migrated with them and returned to their breeding areas come spring.

So he decided to raise young whoopers from hatching without seeing any humans or hearing any human conversation. Instead, they were exposed to models of adult whoopers, to recorded whooper calls, adult whoopers in adjacent enclosures and to hand puppets that resembled the red-marked face, sharp beak and long white neck of an adult whooper held by staff dressed entirely in white (with their faces hidden) to resemble cranes. They were also conditioned to seeing and hearing the engine of a microlight aircraft kept close by. In this way, young whoopers had been conditioned by imprinting to follow the microlight – which broadcast whooper flock calls – and its whooper-lookalike pilot dressed in white, on a journey from Necedah National Wildlife Refuge (NWR), Wisconsin in the northern US, south to the extensive Chassahowitzka NWR on the west coast of Florida and to other locations in northern Florida.

The idea of conditioning the birds to follow a microlight was a natural progression from successful microlight-led migration of Canada Geese in the late 1980s and early 1990s by Bill Lishman and Joe Duff, founders of Operation Migration. In 1993, they helped 18 geese migrate from Ontario in Canada to Virginia in the US, nearly 2,000 km. If it could be done for Canada Geese, why not for Whooping Cranes? Today, Operation Migration is staffed by a small group of committed engineers, pilots and biologists plus volunteers, all of whom have to work incredibly long hours in disguise feeding the young birds, teaching them to fly and, eventually, to follow a microlight on a journey three quarters of the way down the US.

In 2001 the first autumn flight took off with five cranes following and, with lots of feeding-up stops (for cranes and pilot) en route, took 49 days and covered nearly 2,000 km before it arrived at its destination. The establishment of a second migratory flock of Whooping Cranes in North America had begun; it became known as the (not very catchy) Eastern Migratory Population. Weaned slowly from their microlight and crane-costumed pilot, all five survived the winter and returned to summer in central Wisconsin independently, having memorised the route in one go. They returned to Florida for the subsequent winter on their own too. In 2005, the microlight-led migration was supplemented with some young, captive-bred cranes that were released in small groups with wild whoopers with the intention that they would learn the migration route from these older, more experienced birds. And they did. By 2006 the first chicks had hatched from wild adults in this new population in Wisconsin.

But over the next four or five years many of the nests in Wisconsin were abandoned or incubation failed. Research began to try to find out why and focussed on crane behaviour and on potential factors influencing incubation length, including food availability and bothersome black flies. And it was the flies that were the cause of most of the problem. Studies found that the success rate for pairs that nest early and face hordes of black flies was only 0.5%, whereas pairs that re-nested after the blackflies had gone had a 30% success rate. They seem to concentrate in large numbers in spring on and around incubating birds, often causing them significant distress and biting injury. Anyone who has experienced clouds of blackflies or mosquitoes knows all too well how unbearable they can be! Whooper nesting success improved once control measures were put in place to reduce blackfly numbers and more recent releases of young birds have been moved to a couple of other sites further east in Wisconsin where there is less of a blackfly problem.

Interestingly, at Wood Buffalo, whoopers don't have to cope with blackflies; there, breeding is generally successful. Predators taking eggs, and the impact of severe weather, might be other reasons for a lower rate of nesting success at Wisconsin than at Wood Buffalo. Research examining their reduced breeding success includes an experiment, begun in 2013 and likely to last two or three years, to test whether chicks raised by adult whoopers in captivity – rather than by a costumed caretaker – will be more fit and thereby better at surviving when they are released into the wild. Up to 2012, 207 cranes have been released into the wild in this Eastern Migratory Population and by December 2014, 97 cranes had survived.

As more knowledge is gained about Whooping Crane reintroductions – and from monitoring the wintering locations of the natural Aransas/Wood Buffalo population – it is becoming clear that these birds are certainly not as fixed to traditional wintering sites as was previously thought. 'I guess in general I would say we don't fully understand what "normal" behaviour for Whooping Cranes is given the fact that the population has been very low since we started monitoring them,' comments Wade Harrell. 'So we would expect that a larger population would behave differently than a very small population. We are also seeing this with the growth of the Aransas wintering birds; some are now overwintering well over 200 km north of Aransas. In any given year, only about half the Wood Buffalo/Aransas birds now actually overwinter within the boundaries of the Aransas NWR.'

❖ ❖ ❖

All captive-reared birds used in these reintroductions were obtained originally from second eggs laid at the Canadian breeding grounds at Wood Buffalo. Beginning in 1967, these 'spare' eggs were transferred to the Patuxent Wildlife Research Centre in Maryland. By 1975, the population of captive bred whoopers reared from them had themselves produced eggs and the population had grown year on year. In 1989, the captive flock was split and over 20 whoopers were sent to the International Crane Foundation (ICF) in Wisconsin. Splitting them up further to greatly reduce any chance of a catastrophic infection, by 2013 there were 157 Whooping Cranes in captivity in five breeding centres, most of them at Patuxent and at the ICF with much smaller numbers in several other wildlife parks and zoos.

In addition to being used to establish the Eastern Migratory Population (Wisconsin/ Florida), captive-reared whoopers have been used to establish a reintroduced but non-migratory population in Florida; Whooping Cranes were present historically in Florida and other southern states year round, where there is no need to migrate south to avoid cold winter weather. Between 1993 and 2006 nearly 300 whoopers, isolation-reared at some of the captive breeding centres, were released in central Florida, primarily in the floodplain of the Kissimmee River where there's about half a million hectares of freshwater marsh and grassland, the grasslands used for livestock grazing but also by the cranes for foraging.

But survival and breeding productivity of these released birds proved to be low from the start, partly perhaps due to an unfortunate series of drought years and to disease and predation, mostly by Bobcats. The Florida population also initially suffered from metal ingestion, a reminder of the often unpredictable issues that arise when reintroductions such as this are undertaken. Seemingly, the reintroduced cranes took to roosting on dry land rather than in wetlands, a habit which immediately put them at greater risk of predation. Here, too, they ingested bits of discarded metal from chain link fence construction and suffered zinc poisoning. It necessitated recapture and X-rays of the birds to remove metal fragments by surgery. The first Florida nest got built in 1996 but no eggs were laid; two pairs produced eggs in 1999 but the first chick didn't survive to fledging until 2006, albeit the first in the US to do so since 1939. It was painfully slow progress. By 2014 the population had steadily dwindled to about a dozen adults and any further reintroductions were stopped. It was another setback. Decisions will need to be taken on whether to move the remaining birds or to leave them where they are and harvest their eggs for captive breeding or other reintroductions.

In 2010, a consortium of experts from the US and Canada began a new reintroduction at a state-owned Conservation Area in Louisiana on the south US coast where Whooping Cranes nested until the 1950s. It has large areas of freshwater and estuarine marsh. In the four years up to and including 2013, 50 captive-bred cranes were released; all so-called 'soft releases' where they are kept in an enclosed, netted pen and then released after slowly acclimatising to their new environment. The released cranes also utilise farmed land nearby, often rice and crawfish-rearing water fields. Most of the land on which they breed and feed is privately owned and landowner support for this project is notably high in the region. Survival of the released cranes was low in the first year, but has improved since. Most of the released whoopers have not reached breeding maturity yet, but the first nest was documented in the spring of 2013 and the population stands at about 30 adults. As for the success of the project, it's still too early to tell, says Wade Harrell. 'The goal is to establish a self-sustaining population of the birds, but it might take eight to ten years for a mating pair of Whooping Cranes to reach full productivity. With whoopers you have to have a longer-term project to judge success; we are still very early into it,' he added.

As if Whooping Cranes don't face enough challenges, there have been shooting incidents in recent years in spite of their protected status and huge amounts of publicity about their plight. Nineteen were shot between 2001 and early 2014, losses the population can ill afford. In February 2014, two cranes were found shot in southwest Louisiana; they turned out to be the oldest pair among the newly reintroduced Louisiana population. The birds, which had been tagged and were monitored by Louisiana officials, were expected to produce a chick in a few years. 'It's a devastating setback and such a senseless act,' said Robert Love, Louisiana Department of Wildlife and Fisheries administrator. 'Don't shoot big white birds. It's that simple.' Officials said they could offer a $15,000 reward for information leading to an arrest. Since that incident, two more were shot in the state in February 2014; one survived but might not fly again.

In January 2014 federal wildlife officials in Kentucky announced a $7,200 reward – later increased to more than twice that – for information about a Whooping Crane pair shot in November 2013. Hunters often claim to confuse the much bigger and whiter whoopers with Sandhill Cranes, which can be legally shot in most states during certain months. Shooting a whooper can lead to a $100,000 fine and a year in federal prison. In 2013, a 26-year-old South Dakota man pleaded guilty to killing a Whooping Crane and was sentenced to two years' probation and an $85,000 fine according to the US Attorney's office. But experts have said that bringing federal charges isn't easy. In one case, a juvenile who admitted shooting a whooper was charged in the Indiana State Court with a misdemeanour and eventually fined $1, a punishment that rankled animal rights groups. Joe Duff, Operation Migration's co-founder and CEO said that breeding the birds and teaching them to migrate costs $100,000 apiece on average and that his group relies on private donations. 'These shooters, they are not real hunters but they are vandals with a gun who just want to destroy something or take their anger out,' he said. 'It's unbelievably selfish.'

Large birds like whoopers are bound to be vulnerable on their long migratory journeys whether they are part of the natural Wood Buffalo/Aransas population or the reintroduced Wisconsin/Florida migratory population. Such huge journeys are fraught with potential problems other than someone illegally taking a potshot or claiming to mistake them for a sandhill crane. Collisions with overhead power transmission lines – many of which still have no bird-warning markers on them – and wind turbines, communication towers and even fences (especially in misty weather) can be another cause of injury or, rarely, death.

❖ ❖ ❖

In 2013, a total of 74 nesting pairs of whoopers were counted in the vast Wood Buffalo National Park, the second highest (after 77 in 2011) ever. And that number has increased steadily over the years; in the 1990s it was averaging below 50 pairs annually. Over 20 other territorial pairs were recorded, not yet breeding but suggesting great potential for population expansion in future years. Eight of the nesting pairs were outside the national park, one or two about 20 km outside, an indication that plenty of breeding habitat exists in this part of Canada. 'Most of the suitable breeding habitat is in the national park, but several pairs breed outside it most years,' says Mark Bidwell. 'A study in 2003 estimated that there's enough total suitable habitat inside and outside the park to allow 107–472 nesting territories; the large range is due to different assumptions about territory size.' That gives plenty of room for a growth in numbers.

A decade or so ago virtually all the birds wintering on the Texas coast spent their time within the Aransas Refuge. But not these days. Increasing numbers are found in other locations, some in similar coastal marshes but others at locations no one ever predicted in previous years – pastureland, lakes and even the shallows of reservoirs well inland. Studies in Texas show that over half of the current wintering population is using habitat outside the Aransas National Wildlife Refuge boundaries. 'I think the future growth of the Wood Buffalo/Aransas population will involve them wintering in coastal wetlands away from Aransas, inland into rice prairie wetlands and perhaps other inland sites. But we don't know if whoopers wintering in non-traditional inland sites have as much breeding success as coastal wintering birds,' comments Lee Ann Linum, who was Texas Parks and Wildlife's wildlife biologist for 30 years. And if the more recent Louisiana reintroduction proves successful, it's possible that resident Louisiana cranes might well mix with wintering Aransas birds. They are, after all, 'only' about 500 km apart, not far in crane flying terms. 'While the potential for the two populations mixing may exist, I don't think that consistent overlap will occur for many, many years,' adds Linum.

So what does the future hold for Whooping Cranes? A study published in 2013 by Matthew Butler, Grant Harris and Bradley Strobel of the US Fish and Wildlife Service modelled the known 70+ year time series of numbers breeding in the Wood Buffalo/Aransas population and simulated its future growth. What they found is extremely positive. Although they identified periodic declines of the population, they predicted that this core population should reach more than 400 birds by 2025 and continue increasing.

Over the last 50 years, a combination of strict legal protection, habitat protection and continuous international cooperation between Canada and the US has allowed the only remaining wild population to increase steadily from a historic low. Growing public interest and concern about this impressive bird, combined with landowner interest, has also been central to the conservation efforts. With the enormous commitment by a range of biologists and volunteers over the last few decades set to continue, the prospects for a second migratory population establishing and migrating between Wisconsin and Florida seem reasonably good in spite of relatively low nesting success at the present time. And the non-migratory population establishing in southern Louisiana where it existed naturally until the 1950s, is spreading out to breed in other parts of the southeast US too. It has also become increasingly notable that wintering birds are adapting naturally to new locations and to a broader range of habitats. All of which suggests strongly that, in spite of occasional setbacks, the elegant and charismatic Whooping Crane of North America is not only back from the brink, it's on the road – albeit a bumpy one – to further recovery.

It was Robert Porter Allen (1905–1963) who pressed for the Whooping Crane's winter habitat at Aransas to be protected, who led expeditions to find their Canadian breeding sites and who travelled across America firing up the country with never-before-seen enthusiasm for an environmental cause. And it was he who wrote:

> For the Whooping Crane there is no freedom but that of unbounded wilderness, no life except its own. Without meekness, without a sign of humility, it has refused to accept our idea of what the world should be like. If we succeed in preserving the wild remnant that still survives, it will be no credit to us; the glory will rest on this bird whose stubborn vigour has kept it alive in the face of increasing and seemingly hopeless odds.

13

THE RABBIT KILLER RETURNS

IBERIAN LYNX

The diminutive Iberian Lynx was once found across all of Spain and Portugal. Killed for their beautifully marked pelts and hunted and trapped as vermin, in more recent times increasingly intensive farming has destroyed and fragmented much of their habitat. By 2004, only 100 or so survived in two locations in southern Spain. The likelihood of a relatively prosperous EU country in the 21st century allowing the only cat to become extinct since the demise of the Sabre-toothed Tiger 10,000 years ago belatedly spurred Spain's government, and that of Portugal too, into action. Today, while the lynx still faces huge problems, particularly that of reduced numbers of rabbit (its main prey) due to disease, substantial EU funding has enabled over 300 Iberian Lynx to hunt again.

Standing with Rodrigo Serra on a rocky bluff overlooking rows of high-fenced, secure enclosures kitted out with an array of video cameras, it is something of a shock at first to realise that the future of the rarest cat in the world depends on a high security facility such as this. But Portugal's National Centre for the Reproduction of the Iberian Lynx, tucked away in a quiet rural area towards the north of the Algarve, is a key part of a joint Spanish/Portuguese initiative that is slowly and successfully increasing the population and distribution of this gorgeous animal. 'We have 39 lynx here at present; nine adult males, seven adult females, six juveniles and 17 cubs. We are at full capacity,' says Serra, the centre's charismatic director when I meet him in 2013. 'Our breeding has been very successful and this year, of the 17 cubs born, all of them survived.'

We watch with binoculars from above. No one – except a very limited number of trained and camouflaged keepers – is allowed close to the lynx so they don't get used to seeing people. I stand transfixed as an adult roams around its large enclosure; its short bob tail, spiky ear tufts and dark-spotted, creamy brown coat even more attractive than I had imagined. In another enclosure, two juveniles are playfully jousting with each other; and in a third, an adult sleeps contentedly in the warm noon sunshine. I get a closer view from inside the centre's 'control room' where a set of monitor screens are linked to the CCTV cameras mounted at each enclosure. From here, Serra's highly committed staff can watch every movement of each lynx any time of the day or night, spotting any sign of fighting that could cause injury or an early indication of illness. 'We started with our first lynx in 2009 with founders captured in the two main areas where they still have their strongest populations. That's the Sierra Morena [the long chain of partly forested hills across central southern Spain] and from the Doñana [the extensive wetland and forest on Spain's southwest coast],' says Serra, a vet and biologist with considerable international animal management experience.

They are fed live rabbits – it's no use being squeamish here – because rabbits are an Iberian Lynx's main prey and they have to learn to catch them from a young age if they are to survive once they are reintroduced in the wild. So the centre has to be guaranteed a daily supply of rabbits; some are wild-caught, others domestic. The fenced runs the lynx occupy are kitted out with plenty of places for the rabbits to hide, a ploy to make it harder to catch them, a skill essential for lynx to survive in nature.

There are three other similar breeding centres, all in southern Spain plus a small breeding population at Jerez de la Frontera Zoo. Expensive to run, they require expert staff including permanent veterinary supervision, CCTV monitoring facilities, high levels of physical security and much else. The stud book containing the vital information recording which animals are located at which centre plus how – or if – they are related to one another is kept at Jerez Zoo. Ensuring that related lynx don't interbreed is essential in order to make sure that the captive animals are as genetically diverse as possible. And the captive breeding centres for lynx in Spain and Portugal are not, of course, an end in themselves. The young Iberian Lynx they are breeding are already being reintroduced and monitored in the wild in parts of Spain. The intention is to reintroduce them into Portugal too.

❖   ❖   ❖

Up until the early 19th century, the Iberian Lynx was found quite commonly in Spain, Portugal and even in the south of France. Then, they started to decline, initially because of the fur trade; their pelts were sought after and plenty of hunters obliged. In the 1880s, one estimate suggests that 200–300 pelts annually were being sent from central Spain to Madrid fur dealers. The trapping continued well into the 20th century when some sources put the number of pelts obtained as high as 500 or 600 a year. Increasingly intensive agriculture – crop-growing especially – fragmented the scrub and forest habitat that lynx require and made large areas uninhabitable for them. Conversion of natural forest to quick growing plantations of trees reduced their habitat even more. By 1910, Iberian Lynx were confined to the southern half of Spain and Portugal. Then, in 1953, a decree was published which required the creation of 'Provincial Boards for the Extinction of Vermin'; over 150 Iberian Lynx kills were recorded in Spain between then and 1961. The kills were recorded only in western and southern Spain, probably indicating that elsewhere the lynx was already a rare animal. There's little doubt that these provincial boards contributed to the extinction of many of the mammal's small and scattered populations.

The other factor that hastened their decline was the humble rabbit. Rabbits have always occurred naturally throughout Iberia, maybe along the French Mediterranean coast too. In the Middle Ages they were introduced all over Europe (and later over much of the world) initially as a source of food; in many places they became agricultural pests as their populations grew to almost epidemic levels. The Iberian Lynx is a rabbit killing specialist; they comprise as much as 90% of their diet. And that brings very serious problems when rabbits get struck down with disease. Myxomatosis, a killer disease for rabbits, was introduced to Europe in the 1950s as a misguided and ill-informed way of reducing rabbit numbers. Today it is endemic in the population, sweeping through at different times, killing any that haven't developed resistance to it. These days, though, at least a third of infected rabbits survive it. But rabbits face a double whammy. Rabbit haemorrhagic disease (RHD), another easily transmitted and virulent infection, appeared in the late 1980s and stormed through the Spanish and Portuguese rabbit population like a tornado, killing most of them. While rabbit numbers recover temporarily, these diseases periodically wipe out large numbers in killer cycles. Also, hunting of rabbits by people for food probably didn't deprive lynx of their main food source when there were plenty to go around. But when their numbers had been decimated by disease, sport hunting probably could easily have taken the last few in local areas, condemning lynx to near starvation.

By the 1960s there were estimated to be maybe 3,000 Iberian Lynx surviving in a tenth of Spain's land area. Under siege from yet more intensive farming, extensive planting of fruit crops, pesticide-laden cereal growing, tourist and urban developments around the coast and a general fragmentation of their habitat, they declined even further. Lynx hunting was banned in 1973 but the other causes of their decline remained; some were even accelerating. And there is evidence that lynx poaching continued in spite of the ban; they are sometimes found trapped in deadly snares set for other animals too.

Surveys in the 1980s indicated that the lynx in Spain was distributed in less than 50 small and unconnected populations totalling maybe 1,200 individuals. With their population dwindling, a series of deaths on public roads criss-crossing prime lynx habitat – especially around the Doñana National Park in southwest Spain – started to become a national embarrassment and a trigger for public outcry. By 1990, little over 1,000 lynx were estimated to survive in Spain and maybe 40 in Portugal. A 2004 study found just 100 adult Iberian Lynx remaining in the wild, concentrated in two populations (the eastern Sierra Morena and at Doñana) in southern Spain. And of those, only 25 were breeding females. There were none in Portugal.

IUCN's assessment in 2007 stated what had become all too obvious; that their numbers were not sufficient for the survival of the species in the long term, putting the Iberian Lynx on the brink of extinction. They were classified as Critically Endangered. The prospect was looming that the rarest cat in the world was set to become the first cat on the planet to become extinct since the demise of the famed Sabre-toothed Tiger 10,000 years ago! The Portuguese Ibex had become extinct in 1892; the Pyrenean Ibex or Bucardo (both subspecies of the Spanish Ibex) as recently as 2000. The prospect of yet another extinction, this time of an enigmatic small cat, in two prosperous countries within the EU in the 21st century galvanised their governments into action. Money started to flow for some serious measures to be put in place not only to 'rescue' the Iberian Lynx but to begin its long path of rehabilitation.

❖ ❖ ❖

Lynx: the names derives from a Greek word for light or brightness, thought to be a reference to the luminescence of its reflective eyes. There are, though, some cats with lynx in their name that taxonomists don't count as true lynx species. So it is that the Caracal, often called the Desert or Persian Lynx, and the Jungle Cat, often referred to as the Swamp Lynx, are not true lynx at all. They are, of course, cats. Of the true lynx, there are just four species: the Eurasian Lynx (larger than its Iberian cousin), the Canadian Lynx, the Bobcat and the Iberian Lynx. Depending whose expert view you accept, either all of them, or three of them other than the Bobcat (which might pre-date the others), evolved from a common ancestor, known as the Issoire Lynx.

The four lynx species are characterised by their short tails and characteristic tufts of black hair on the tips of their ears; long whiskers and, under the neck, a ruff of fur giving the appearance of a small beard or exaggerated sideburns. Their body colour varies from medium brown to almost gold or beige-white and is marked with dark brown spots, especially on the limbs. All species of lynx have white fur on their chests, bellies and on the insides of their legs; the amount of fur – the thickness of their coat – gets progressively thicker (for warmth) in the more northerly dwelling species. The smallest species are the Bobcat and the Canadian Lynx while the Eurasian Lynx is the largest. But there is considerable size variation within species.

The Eurasian Lynx is native to European and Siberian forests and while it's now very uncommon in Western Europe (where it is being reintroduced) it remains widespread across Eastern Europe, Russia and much of Asia. A strict carnivore, its favourite prey is Roe Deer but it will take almost any animal it can get. The Canadian Lynx inhabits forest and arctic tundra across Canada and into Alaska as well as some parts of the northern US. Its diet is almost exclusively Snowshoe Hares but it will also kill other medium-sized mammals and birds if hare numbers fall. The Bobcat is common throughout southern Canada, the US and northern Mexico. An adaptable predator that inhabits most types of woodland, unlike other lynx it will live in swamps, desert, mountainous and agricultural areas. Though it prefers to eat rabbits and hares, it will hunt anything from insects, chickens, small rodents, and even young deer.

Rabbits comprise 80–90% of an Iberian Lynx's diet – with hares and rodents accounting for most of the rest – though they will sometimes take birds, reptiles, amphibians and young deer. A male requires one rabbit a day; a female bringing up cubs will eat three or four rabbits per day and, very frustratingly, there is no evidence that they will adapt well to taking alternative prey. They continued to rely on rabbits for the majority of their diet even after the rabbit population was decimated by myxomatosis and RHD; contributing to lynx decline as starvation took its inevitable toll. Why Iberian Lynx are so fixated on rabbits for food isn't completely clear but probably has distant origins. The two probably evolved together, the lynx becoming a specialist predator adapted to an abundant and easily obtained rabbit diet. It is no surprise that lynx were perceived as competitors by people who often trapped and killed rabbits for food. As a direct result, lynx were often trapped and shot too.

Rabbits are famed for their reproductive capabilities. Although certainly not the strongest, fastest, or smartest mammal, they have carved out a strong ecological niche because of the ease with which they get pregnant. This Olympic-style reproductive capacity has frequently made the rabbit public enemy number one, devouring vast quantities of greenery at the expense of other animals, livestock included. In Australia, where the 20 or so rabbits first introduced in 1859 by estate owner Thomas Austin had multiplied in the absence of any predators to over 600 million in less than a century, they have long been public enemy number one.

Iberian Lynx, like their cousins, are solitary hunters, stalking their prey or lying in wait for hours behind a bush or rock until the prey is sufficiently close to pounce in less than a few strides. Lynx don't give chase; they are not designed for fast bursts of speed or long runs like cheetahs. Instead they are the essence of patience and camouflage, pouncing and grabbing their victim – almost always a rabbit – close-up and undetected.

Younger animals, especially, roam widely, sometimes as far as 100 km. Just occasionally, it seems, they move much further than anyone imagined – and through some pretty unappealing habitat en route too. In 2009, an old, radio-collared female called Nuria from the Doñana population embarked on an unexpectedly long trip. Expelled from her territory by her daughter (a common fate for an elderly lynx), Nuria headed east. She was soon confronted by stark expanses of olive groves, where, against all the odds, she settled. Nuria has since made three long forays east, twice covering more than 100 km and once scaling rugged mountains en route. She has covered more than three times this distance during her wanderings; had she set off west instead of east she could have been in the Sierra Morena in prime lynx habitat within 200 km. But this wandering is great news; Iberian Lynx will seemingly adapt to different habitats more readily than anyone dared hope. If only their dietary interests were as adaptable!

Iberain Lynx territory, an average of perhaps 10–20 km^2, is very dependent on how abundant rabbits are. If rabbits are thriving, lynx ranges tend to be stable in size over many years, their boundaries often being along man-made roads and trails they mark with their urine or faeces and with scratch marks on the bark of trees. Their habitat preference is for a mix of open grassland with dense shrubs such as strawberry tree, mastic and juniper and trees such as holm oak and cork oak. But research shows that they tend to avoid croplands, intensive fruit-growing areas and plantations of trees, especially trees not native to Iberia such as eucalyptus. Happily, rabbits shun these places too. And while the largest population in Spain occupies a mountainous area of forest, scrub and grassland, they also seem to thrive in lowland pine forest and scrub, hence the Doñana population living in the extensive dry scrublands and the umbrella-domed Stone Pines that typify much of that region.

Iberian Lynx cubs are born between March and September with a peak of births in March and April, a litter consisting of two or three (rarely one, four or five) kittens that weigh no more than 250 g each. Incredibly attractive, it takes the best part of ten months before they are weaned and independent. They then remain close to mum, learning patience, hiding and pouncing skills until they are not far off two years old. Presumably, they can be taught very quickly how to recognise a rabbit; there isn't much else to confuse them with except the occasional hare. Youngsters look incredibly cuddly but young sibling kittens are frequently aggressive towards each other and deaths are not infrequent. Why this happens isn't completely clear; it might be either related to a change in hormones when a kitten switches from its mother's milk to meat, or to establishing a hierarchy in lynx society.

Adult Iberian Lynx are extremely intolerant of other carnivores, at least of those smaller than themselves. In the Doñana where lynx have long been studied, they often kill – but don't eat – Red Foxes, domestic cats, Egyptian Mongoose and Common Genets (a long-tailed, mostly nocturnal cat-like mammal introduced in Iberia). Mongoose and genet are between ten and 20 times less abundant in places inhabited by lynx compared to places where lynx are absent. Yet more surprisingly, rabbits – the dominant lynx prey – are generally more abundant in areas where lynx are common. This is apparently because lynx reduce the numbers of these other carnivores that also kill rabbits.

Lynx are not easy to survey. They are mainly solitary and they venture out almost exclusively around dawn and dusk, often staying out to hunt in the night but sleeping by day. So they are hard to see, even where they are reasonably common. Sometimes their tracks or their droppings can be identified but that requires expert knowledge. And casual sightings by members of the public can be misleading; they sometimes get mixed up with domestic tabby cats or wildcats.

❖ ❖ ❖

Serious action to stop the decline of the Iberian Lynx, with a long-term aim of increasing its numbers and distribution, began in 2000. It was led by the Andalusian Regional Ministry of Environment in Spain with financial aid from the EU in recognition of the European (at least) importance of this mammal. Initial actions centred on getting an accurate picture of the range of the remaining lynx and carrying out monitoring of both rabbit and lynx populations. Within two years, the distribution of the surviving lynx was much better known and accurate ways of monitoring their populations had been devised. By 2002, a more ambitious, part EU funded programme of work began, led still by the Andalusian ministry but now involving a range of conservation, hunting and land owning interests. Eighty percent of the land still inhabited by lynx was privately owned for hunting, so getting support from hunters was essential if the lynx was to be saved. The programme, funded until 2006, started to address a whole range of issues: expanding the residual two lynx populations at Sierra Morena and Doñana; improving habitat around these isolated populations to help them expand; reducing non-natural mortality such as road kills; signing agreements with landowners to help protect the remaining animals; boosting rabbit populations and getting public support for the species. By 2006, well over 100,000 ha of land had been signed up into management agreements with landowners who then had to undertake measures to protect lynx on their property. Getting hunters to shoot fewer rabbits was also a priority. Improving the habitat, both for lynx and for rabbits, consisted mainly of clearing scrub off meadows and providing increased shelter for rabbits in the form of artificial burrows and hiding areas. In places where rabbits were at a density of less than one per hectare – considered the minimum to support a sustainable lynx population – they were bred in captivity and released to boost their numbers or bred in fenced enclosures that agile lynx could jump into but most other carnivores could not.

It wasn't long before this set of measures started to pay dividends. The number of lynx territories established in the Sierra Morena rose from 18 in 2002 to 40 in 2008; there were 38 adults (out of a total of 53 animals) there in 2002 but, by 2008, their numbers had risen to 95 adults out of 160 total animals. Lynx were making a comeback. The number of individuals in the Doñana population over the same period didn't increase but the previous decline had been stemmed and numbers remained stable at just over 30 adults. However, this masked an increase in the number of territorial females from ten to 19 between 2002 and 2008 while the total number of males decreased because more males were killed by an outbreak of deadly feline leukaemia in 2007.

In the Doñana, road kills were an ever-present threat, especially it seems to young lynx dispersing from their parents. One of the biggest problems occurred on the generally straight section of the small but popular road between two villages, El Rocio and Villamanrique de la Condesa, where it cuts through an extensive area of umbrella-topped Stone Pine forest. This road used to be a forest track. But it soon became a speedway between the two villages after it was re-laid with tarmac by the regional government. The problem was that the pine forest grew up to the road on both sides so lynx travelling at night sometimes got killed as they crossed. Today, the pine forest and underlying heath has been cut back on both sides, high fences are installed along the road and underpasses have been built at frequent intervals to allow lynx (and other animals) to cross. The road is fitted with rumble strips, signs and speed humps to slow traffic down above the underpasses. Even more impressively, on the main dual carriageway that runs north/south against the western edge of the Doñana National Park, two huge, arc-shaped bridges have been built over the busy roadway, each of them covered in natural vegetation and designed as overpasses so that lynx can move from habitat on one side of this busy road to the other. The under and over-passes seem to have worked; very few lynx are killed on these roads nowadays.

Getting hunters to respect the need to boost lynx numbers has helped control illegal hunting methods; the number of leghold traps and snares has seemingly reduced, and the general attitude of most hunters has changed in line with that of the wider population, due in good part to a very positive communication strategy promoted by the regional government. Nevertheless, illegal killing does occur. During 2012, 21 lynx were found dead, 16 in Sierra Morena and five in Doñana. Of these, over 60% had been shot or caught in traps; 14% had died in fights with other lynx or with other carnivores; 10% died of disease and in 14% of cases the cause couldn't be found. There is obviously no justification for complacency; illegal trapping (with traps often meant for other victims such as foxes) and killing remains a threat.

❖   ❖   ❖

With such small numbers of lynx remaining in the wild in just two populations, it had long been considered essential to establish a captive population to start breeding them for a reintroduction programme. The Iberian Lynx captive breeding programme was developed by Dr Astrid Vargas, a charismatic Puerto Rican conservationist who was part of the team that restored the Black-footed Ferret to the prairies of the US (Chapter 17). Lynx are not difficult to breed in captivity – it had been done successfully for European Lynx – so the prospects for rearing wild-caught Iberian Lynx were good. Between 2002 and 2008, 36 lynx were captured (six from Doñana and 30 from Sierra Morena) and brought into captivity in a breeding centre built within the Doñana National Park. From these, 24 lynx were specifically identified for breeding; the others were captured because they were injured or diseased. In 2005, to much local celebration and a considerable amount of international publicity, the first ever Iberian Lynx was born in captivity. It would be the first of many. In the 2013 season, 44 kittens were raised in the centres – the highest number yet – exceeding expectations and mainly due to an increase in their survival rate. The mean litter size has increased too.

Iberian Lynx possess limited genetic diversity. As with the European Bison (Chapter 5), this could make the whole population vulnerable to a new disease or a major change in environmental conditions to which the population might not adapt. But when researchers compared present day lynx DNA with that from lynx fossils spanning the last 50,000 years, they had a surprise: both ancient specimens and today's animals showed low genetic variation. 'This is the first species, as far as I am aware, where such low genetic diversity has been seen recently and over such a long period of time,' said Professor Mark Thomas, an author of the research (published in *Molecular Biology*, 2011) from University College London. 'Usually, animals alive today that have a low genetic diversity had a much higher level of genetic variability thousands of years ago. But the Iberian Lynx is different.'

'This type of low diversity has not really been observed in any other species,' commented Dr Love Dalen, from the Swedish Museum of Natural History and a co-author. 'Usually this would lead to inbreeding and a reduced potential to adapt to changes in the environment.' But, he added, 'there is a difference between being inbred and suffering from it. In most cases, inbreeding leads to a decrease in fitness – genetic problems such as deformities, or lower litter sizes. But there is a possibility that some species can handle that.' And handling it the Iberian Lynx seems to be doing, unless some unpredictable catastrophe comes their way.

Even though there were no captive-bred animals available at that time for release, an assessment of potentially suitable land areas for lynx reintroduction began as early as 2002. It took into account the availability of suitable habitat, the abundance of rabbits, whether lynx had been there historically and the degree of protection that would be provided by local landowners and hunting interests in order to comply with the IUCN guidelines for reintroductions. Three mountainous, partly forested areas in the Sierra Morena distant from the existing lynx territories in the same mountains were selected as the first reintroduction sites. Both of these were judged to have good lynx habitat, high numbers of rabbits and local support.

In 2009 and 2010, the first reintroductions took place. Initially these were with lynx captured in the existing Sierra Morena population. Experience with European Lynx in northern Europe had found that establishing a new population is more successful initially using translocated animals followed by captive-reared lynx in subsequent years. Between 2010 and 2013, 17 adult lynx were translocated. Captive-bred lynx have since been released to boost these newly established populations; the first (two adults) in 2011 followed by 14 in 2012 and 18 in 2013.

The reintroductions have proved successful. By 2012, the Sierra Morena population had increased to around 190 animals with 53 occupied territories while the Doñana population had reached 86 animals and the number of territorial females had more than doubled to 23.

The lynx released from captive bred or translocated populations are fitted with lightweight tracking devices so that their locations and survival can be monitored. So far, they are doing well in their new wild homes. By 2013, there were well over 300 wild-living Iberian Lynx in Spain and another 150 animals in the breeding centres, many of them waiting their turn to be reintroduced. The huge effort made by governments, NGOs, landowners and hunters is paying off. It has probably cost over 100 million EUR ($135 million) so far (the bulk of that from the EU) but the Iberian Lynx is certainly back on the map and its populations are more secure than they have been for a century.

While this multi-pronged strategy for boosting Iberian Lynx numbers has very wide support, it does have its critics. Dr Alejandro Rodríguez of the Department of Conservation Biology at the Estación Biológica de Doñana claims that there is a lack of consistency in some of the work, that what is done varies over time and location. So proving what actions are effective – and what aren't – is impossible. He also considers that reintroductions would be better targetted in fewer but larger land areas and that there are plenty of suitable large areas in southern Spain and Portugal. 'I believe that lynx populations occupying areas larger than 500 km^2 are more resistant to extinction that those occupying smaller areas so we should have fewer larger areas set aside for lynx,' he says.

❖   ❖   ❖

Until 2003, not much attention was being paid to bringing back lynx in Portugal. But it was then that FFI got involved, invited in by Portuguese scientists eager to begin looking at its feasibility and building on early Spanish success. 'We put in £400,000 to fund Liga para a Protecção da Natureza [League for the Protection of Nature, LPN], a leading Portuguese NGO, to get surveys done and to pay for the first land protection agreements with landowners. They've always been so enthusiastic about the project,' says Paul Hotham, FFI Eurasia Programme Regional Director. 'We helped draft the original plans to create habitat in eastern Portugal with a longer term goal of getting lynx back there.' Iberian Lynx have not been present in Portugal since the turn of the millennium except for one or two long distance wanderers that have turned up in recent years and came from the Doñana.

With two released in Southern Portugal in December, 2014 that's changed. To prepare for that, with EU funding LPN had been busy improving habitat to make it more suitable for lynx. 'We had a budget of 2.6 million EUR [$3.5 million] over the four years of the current programme,' comments Eduardo Santos, LPN's coordinator of the programme. Threequarters of the funding comes from the EU, a quarter from the Portuguese government.

They are working in several different areas in this part of Portugal, all of them selected for a combination of features such as the amount of remaining lynx habitat, the presence of good rabbit populations and acceptance by local farming communities. Standing in one such area near Moura – not far from the Spanish border – with Eduardo Santos and his field technician,

Nuno Curado, we are looking at the area most recently inhabited by lynx in Portugal before they died out, and one of the most important places to try and re-establish them. It is also physically connected to the lynx stronghold in the Sierra Morena mountain range to the east just over the border in Spain. All around us are manicured olive groves with little or no flowers and grasses between them – often just bare soil – and not a shrub in sight. It is not the kind of habitat that lynx, or much other wildlife for that matter, would feel at home in. But we are standing alongside a corridor of land that is very different. Between the mature olive trees here is a dense scrub of aromatic Rosemary bushes, shiny-leaved Strawberry Trees, resinous Mastic shrubs, white-flowered cistus, Kermes Oaks with their spiny, serrated leaves and much else. It's a wildlife-attracting corridor that stretches away into the distance linking one small, scrub and tree-covered hilltop to another, a lifeline for plants, birds and animals in an otherwise none too attractive habitat for any of them. But it is a corridor designed primarily for lynx.

'We're paying farmers to create these corridors so that more natural vegetation can link up areas of wild vegetation here on the hilltops. This one is fenced on both sides because there are livestock around that would otherwise graze it but if there are no livestock, we don't need to fence them,' says Curado. Fences up to two metres high don't deter gymnastic lynx. They simply leap over them. 'Using these corridors, any lynx reintroduced here, and other animals, can move from one area to another through plenty of cover. It's this fragmentation of the habitat remaining that contributed to lynx extinction here in the past.'

'So far we've created 56 ha of corridor with 13 farmers. They're 30 metres wide minimum, often twice that, and this one is two kilometres long. There's no olive harvesting within the corridor and most farmers get paid over 500 EUR a corridor each year to keep them like this. The money they receive is partly to compensate them for the loss of olive harvesting. The agreements run for eight years but we obviously want to get funding to extend them,' adds Curado. 'We also have more general management agreements with landowners covering a total of 18,000 ha across southeast Portugal; some of these are on land that reintroduced lynx could use. Lynx need a mixture of scrub and forest with pasture and clearings to survive and be able to catch rabbits.'

'We need to make sure farmers don't put out meat laced with pesticide to kill stray dogs or foxes because other animals might eat it. Lynx are probably less likely to but we don't want to take any chances,' comments Santos. 'Lynx usually breed in a cavity in an old tree base or between rocks, usually amongst dense vegetation, but there are few of these places left because we have more intensive farming here. We've been making barrel-shaped artificial dens of wood covered in cork to mimic hollow tree stumps and then mounting camera traps by them to see if they attract other mammals. We've put eight of them out on trial. We get foxes, badgers, mongoose, genets and others interested in them so we think they should attract lynx if they are reintroduced here,' he continues.

So another component of their agreements with landowners is to get these dens installed on their land and agree that scrub and other vegetation nearby shouldn't be cleared. Getting landowners on side is vital; but good community relations in general are vital too if lynx reintroductions are to succeed. It's an extremely important issue in Eduardo Santos' thinking.

'LPN works with landowners, managers and hunters to protect and create more habitat that's suitable for lynx but we also work with local people and school kids, telling them what we are doing and why species like the lynx are so important. It's a key priority for us,' he says. It's not easy to persuade farmers that they might see some benefit if lynx are returned to this part of Portugal. There is some small advantage that lynx will tend to keep other predators like foxes and mongoose under control but it's a marginal plus and most farmers aren't very bothered.

For the conservationists, though, rabbit numbers – top of the menu for lynx – is of huge consequence. So implementing measures to bolster their numbers is a vital part of the agreements LPN is negotiating too. These measures might include putting up electric fences around pastures that allow access for rabbits but prevent other wild and domestic grazers from cropping them; creating small water pools for rabbits to drink at; fertilising fields to improve the quality of pastures; putting out cereal and alfalfa grass for rabbit feed; digging underground shelters for them (they often can't dig in sun-parched hard soil); and putting fences around existing burrows to prevent damage to them. 'Between 2007 and 2012, the rabbit populations we monitored here either remained stable or, at best, doubled in numbers. But rabbit haemorrhagic disease [RHD] arrived in the 2012/3 winter and their numbers have dropped again by 70–90%, though they've not done so badly in olive plantations,' comments Santos. RHD is killing rabbits in Spain too. 'The virus has mutated and now we have a quite aggressive new strain that is doing much damage in rabbit populations. Consequently, the lynx populations will decrease in the 2013 census. We have to help rabbit populations recover,' comments Miguel Ángel Simón, director of the EU lynx programme in Iberia.

Domestic rabbits are routinely vaccinated against RHD and myxomatosis. And as part of the lynx conservation programme in the Doñana where wild rabbits have been captive bred for several years, they are immunised before release to avoid introducing diseased animals into the native rabbit populations. Research conducted over four years up to 2002 led by Dr Sonia Cabezas then at the Estación Biológica de Doñana, found that vaccination of wild rabbits was generally effective with an average of about 80% of them developing immunity to both diseases. But this average hid considerable variation – partly, it seems, depending on the body condition of individuals at the time of vaccination – and sometimes less than half of them developed immunity. 'Some of the variation was difficult to explain,' says Cabezas. 'We think some might have been due to variation in the effectiveness of the vaccine between different vaccine batches.' They recommended ensuring that each rabbit vaccinated was in good physical condition beforehand. Cabezas' research has also shown how important it is to get the habitat right as well as the physical condition of rabbits that are to be released. But vaccination doesn't confer permanent protection against these diseases nor does it fully protect the offspring of immunised adults. And it's costly if large numbers of rabbits have to be vaccinated. 'It seems like some immunity from both diseases is passed from mothers to kittens for a short period of time. The immunity to both diseases then seems to decline in the kittens when they are about five to nine weeks old,' comments Cabezas. So vaccines against these diseases that periodically kill vast numbers of rabbits – and may sometimes limit the recovery in the numbers of Iberian Lynx – are not a total answer but they are a significant help.

❖ ❖ ❖

So what are the next steps to increase the numbers of Iberian Lynx further and to widen their distribution? Expanding their population further in the Doñana will depend heavily on altering the habitat to the west and north of the national park where Stone Pine plantations (for pine nut production from their cones) occupy thousands of hectares of land. Much of this needs to be converted back to natural Mediterranean scrub and, where necessary, restocked with vaccinated rabbits if it is ever to support larger numbers of lynx than it does now. On the northern fringes of the national park, vast areas of land are irrigated by drawing water up from underground aquifers – some of it illegally – for intensive fruit growing. Strawberries are the dominant crop here and are mostly exported; other fruits include blueberries and raspberries. Spain is the biggest exporter of strawberries worldwide, with an industry worth an estimated 400 million EUR ($548 million). Vast expanses of plastic tunnels dominate the land and pesticide residues seep into the marshes downstream. Because they use large volumes of water, these developments are threatening the national park's internationally rated, wildlife-rich marshes by lowering the water table. UNESCO is so concerned that it is considering whether to remove World Heritage Site status from the Doñana, a step that would seriously impact on Andalucia's and Spain's prestige. The Spanish authorities are obliged to submit a thorough report to UNESCO in 2014 setting out the state of conservation in the Doñana and how they intend retaining the enormous wildlife value of this huge wetland.

In the Sierra Morena mountain range the three lynx populations (one original; two reintroduced) look set to expand further, supported by more reintroductions of captive-bred lynx from the breeding centres. If that continues, and rabbit numbers are not too badly reduced by disease, there's every reason to believe that lynx could spread across much of this huge, partly forested mountain range. And the recent reintroduction in Portugal could eventually result in a link-up with the Sierra Morena populations because the western end of these mountains reaches to the Portuguese border in a large tract of countryside thinly populated by people. 'We are looking at different locations to see which will best suit the Iberian Lynx,' said the Portuguese Secretary of State for Nature Conservation, Miguel Castro Neto, in October 2013. 'This is the first time that an Iberian Lynx born in captivity has been released in Portugal. It is a source of pride for Portugal and another pillar of the value of Portugal's natural resources and biodiversity and a recognition of the potential of our ecosystems.'

There are suggestions that reintroductions should take place further north in Spain too, an insurance policy based on predictions that southern Spain and Portugal will become hotter and more arid as climate warming takes hold. It's a view proposed by Miguel Bustos Araújo, a biogeographer at the National Museum of Natural Sciences in Madrid but it is not universally accepted. He and his fellow researchers argue that significant climate warming could render the existing locations for lynx uninhabitable for rabbits and that Iberian Lynx could become extinct if their populations were entirely located in the south. Reintroducing the animals further north where rabbits could more easily be sustained might be a sensible approach. Indeed, regional governments further north in Spain have, for some time, shown interest in the possibility of participating in the lynx reintroduction efforts. That interest has helped secure further EU funding until 2017 with a broader range of partners including the governments of Extremadura and Castilla-La Mancha regions to the north of Andalucía, Murcia to the east and Portugal. Its objectives? To bolster further the existing populations, to establish at least 70 territorial females in eastern Sierra Morena and 25 in Doñana; to prepare five new reintroduction areas, one each in Portugal, Castilla-La Mancha, Extremadura, Andalucía and Murcia, all of which are, of course, part of the historic range of the Iberian Lynx. While Extremadura's extensive oak-dotted pastures (*dehesas*), scrub and forested hills could provide excellent habitat, and there is much forest and scrub in Castilla-La Mancha too, some ecologists in Murcia argue that their forests might not be extensive enough or well enough protected to hold lynx.

The programme's undisputed success could result in the IUCN re-classifying the Iberian Lynx from Critically Endangered to Endangered, a move that many would consider academic and which could, possibly, convey an overly positive picture that much of the 'saving the Iberian Lynx' job is done. It most certainly isn't. Dr Urs Breitenmoser, a leading expert on lynx species at the University of Bern and Chair of the IUCN/SSC (Species Survival Commission) Cat Specialist Group believes that the issue needs serious consideration but only after a thorough scientific review of progress. 'We now have good monitoring in place and we will know when the population is in peril again. So I think it is right that we do a review even if lynx numbers fluctuate a little because rabbits occasionally get depleted by disease,' he comments. 'I think in the years to come we will need to find ways to do more releases of lynx but do them more cheaply as the species gains in numbers and distribution while its threat classification decreases.'

Without doubt, the continuing outbreaks of myxomatosis and the even more deadly RHD will have an impact on lynx recovery. Their numbers are likely to plateau, even fall a little, when disease decimates the rabbit population. But the recuperation and reintroduction of the attractive Iberian Lynx in Spain and Portugal has gathered substantial pace thanks to the commitment of governments, NGOs, hunters and farmers together with enormous public interest and concern both in Iberia and internationally. The last words are best left to Miguel Simón, director of the EU lynx programme in Iberia: 'The Iberian Lynx is a key species in the Mediterranean ecosystem. It is a top predator and if we preserve this species, we are preserving the whole ecosystem. It is our heritage, and we have to preserve it for future generations. We can't claim victory yet but now there is hope.'

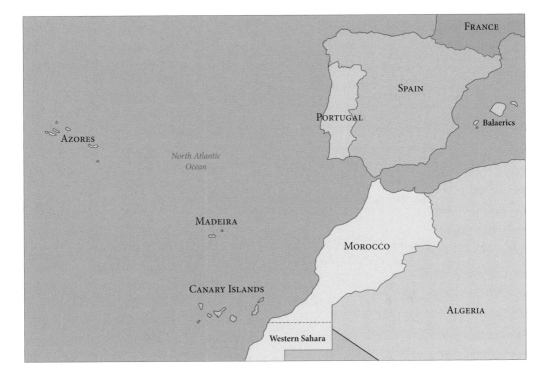

14

THE ENIGMA THAT'S NOT ALL AT SEA

ZINO'S PETREL

By the time they were rediscovered in the 1960s, these small, grey and white, ocean-going seabirds were almost certainly heading for extinction. Breeding in mountain burrows on the island of Madeira, rats and feral cats were killing virtually all of their chicks. With enormous conservation effort since then, including reducing predation, their breeding success has improved substantially; at least 80 pairs of Zino's Petrel are now known to come ashore each year to breed. There are almost certainly more pairs awaiting discovery in this often inaccessible terrain. One of the world's rarest birds, outside the breeding season they travel the great oceans – though how far they go no one is sure.

*I*t's approaching midnight. It's cold, dark as pitch and windy. Cloud swirls around us in eerie, damp sheets so it is impossible to see more than a couple of metres in any direction. And we are huddled behind a few boulders on a dangerously narrow path 1,800 metres up on a knife-edge mountain ridge, trying to eke out what little shelter there is. Sudden gusts of wind are blowing squalls of powdered soil that sting our faces. In the all-enveloping gloom we can barely make out the coal-black shape of the pock-marked cliffs behind us while the precipitous slopes down to the deeply gouged valleys way below are thankfully invisible in the cloud. Aside from the wind, all has been silent since we walked here on a narrow summit path an hour ago.

Then, quite suddenly, there's a cry. A ghostly, tremulous wail from somewhere amid the curls of cloud swirling around the pinnacles of the mountain peaks alongside us. And another wail, this one from a different direction. It sounds surreal, as if someone is trying to frighten us as we hunker down, already disorientated by the cloud and wind. 'That's it. That's their call. That's Zino's Petrel. The adults are flying in and locating their breeding burrows,' whispers João Nunes, an ornithologist and our guide for the night-time expedition. He is talking about one of the rarest birds in the world, one that breeds only here, high on the summit slopes of the mountains on Madeira, the popular tourist island about 600 km off the west coast of Morocco.

Said by the shepherds that graze their goats on these slopes to be the cries of their former colleagues who hadn't all survived the stomach-wrenching drops that characterise Madeira's ancient volcanic mountains, what we are hearing high in the mountains is actually a seabird of the vast Atlantic Ocean. The Portuguese name for Zino's Petrel, *freira*, means 'nun'; the inhabitants of Curral das Freiras (Nun's Valley) below claimed that the nocturnal wailings were the calls of the suffering souls of the nuns. The sisters had taken refuge in the valley from attacks on the island in the 16th century by French pirates.

Whatever superstitious tales have been created about their origin, each and every moonless spring night, come clear, star-sparkled skies or a dense veil of cloud, adult Zino's Petrels will fly from the sea surrounding this mountainous Atlantic island, gain nearly 2,000 metres in height and drop down near to their burrow. Then, they'll waddle awkwardly the last few metres to its entrance and relocate their solitary youngster to feed it on a sloppy, smelly mix of regurgitated fish and crustaceans. There might be 80 breeding pairs of Zino's Petrel, restricted to this 1,165 km² Portuguese island.

Have Zino's Petrels always been this rare? Almost certainly not, because fossilised bones that match today's Zino's have been found on several parts of Madeira and on the neighbouring island of Porto Santo to the northeast. Some were found in caves on lower ground suggesting that mountain-top breeding might be a more recent phenomenon. 'Why they now breed exclusively so high up we don't know,' says Nunes. 'Perhaps they moved up there to get away from human disturbance or from yellow-legged gulls which predate on young shearwaters and petrels breeding on low ground, or even perhaps from shepherd dogs.' One thing is certain. Madeira hasn't always been as it is today. Discovered in 1419 by the Portuguese explorer, João Gonçalves Zarco (whose statue graces Funchal), first spying it from Porto Santo – he named it Ilha da Madeira (Island of Wood) because of its dense cover of shrub-rich laurel forest. When Madeira was uninhabited, its seabirds such as the large brown and white Cory's Shearwater and delicate black Madeiran Storm Petrels would have nested in burrows on the forested slopes. The island's few hundred Manx Shearwaters – black and white seabirds similar in size to Zino's Petrel – do so today. Maybe some or all of the Zino's Petrels originally excavated their burrows on forested slopes too. No one knows!

Zino's Petrels are delicate, grey and white seabirds just over 30 cm in length with long, narrow wings; they are built for extended periods of gliding over the deep oceans where they spend the bulk of their lives. They breed nowhere else in the world but Madeira. It's a very precarious existence. The story of their discovery, their presumed extinction, and their rediscovery less than 50 years ago – coupled with their unusual name and amazing lifestyle – is extraordinary. But the story of Zino's Petrel is not just important for its own sake. The enormous efforts to conserve and enhance its small population in the face of a cornucopia of threats resonate worldwide with the threats faced by a whole host of island-breeding seabirds.

❖　❖　❖

By day, with the warm summer sun illuminating the very same slopes where the petrels were calling a couple of nights before, it's hard to believe that these small seabirds would fly up over steep valleys clothed in lush laurel forest and navigate their way, in darkness, amongst the sheer rock pinnacles and cliffs to nest on these incredibly steep slopes. But, tucked well inside arm-length burrows in the ochre-coloured soil between rocky ledges and surrounded by a scatter of broom and grasses, this is where young Zino's spend the first few months of their lives, totally isolated from the sea where the bulk of their future lives will be lived.

'They were first discovered in 1903 breeding in the mountains. Someone brought a few of the birds to Father Ernesto Schmitz, a priest on the island who was also a very keen naturalist,' says Dr Frank Zino, a general medical practitioner and ornithologist living in Madeira's capital, Funchal. 'But Schmitz wrongly identified them as Fea's Petrels, which, although their plumage is very similar, are bigger and heavier with larger bills. Fea's breed in small numbers on Bugio, one of the Desertas Islands about 25 km southeast of Madeira but not here.' To complicate matters a little further, the Bugio-breeding petrels are now named Desertas Petrels (of which there are probably a few hundred) and are recognised as a distinct species from Fea's Petrels (named after Italian zoologist Leonardo Fea), around 3,000 of which breed in the Cape Verde Islands.

Father Schmitz left the island five years later and memories of a petrel nesting high in Madeira's mountains faded. No one ever saw or heard them and they were presumed extinct. 'Then in 1940, a dead young petrel was picked up in the grounds of the Governor's Palace here in Funchal, presumably disorientated by the town's lights. My father [Alec Zino, a local ornithologist and businessman who died in 2004] got to see it and knew immediately that it wasn't a young Fea's Petrel because he was familiar with them on Bugio,' says Zino. 'Then another, identical dead youngster was found in Funchal in 1952 and my father became convinced that this was a new species and maybe the one that Schmitz discovered (but wrongly identified) in the mountains all those years back. He was also convinced that they weren't Fea's Petrels [Desertas Petrels] because these fledged youngsters were found in October. Fea's on Bugio don't fledge until December or later.' Alec Zino's conviction strengthened when Gregory Mathews, an Australian ornithologist and expert on petrels, published in 1934 a study of preserved Fea's Petrel skins and those of the birds found by Schmitz earlier that century. Mathews suggested that the two were sufficiently different to be subspecies.

Alec Zino had an almost lifelong interest in birds and natural history. In the mid 1960s with colleagues he made numerous visits to Madeira's high mountains at night to listen for any calls that might be petrels but heard nothing. But he wasn't the type to give up. Figuring that, if a man of Schmitz's experience could confuse the Madeiran Petrels with Fea's Petrel, then both might have similar calls. He played recordings of petrels from Bugio to shepherds on Madeira who grazed their sheep and goats high on the mountains. Only one shepherd, named Lucas, recognised the calls, and he knew where, at night, they could be heard. In April 1969, Lucas took Alec Zino to the high ridges where they heard the ghostly, night-time wailing. The petrels were still there. By mid June that year, after abseiling 100 metres above a 600 metre drop, they had found their breeding burrows with eggs.

Between then and the mid 1980s, Alec Zino and his son Frank carried out studies of the birds breeding in the mountains which culminated in a scientific paper in 1986 in which they suggested that this was a separate species from Fea's Petrel. The scientific names *Pterodroma madeira* for Zino's (named after Alec) and *Pterodroma feae* for Fea's became accepted by the international ornithological authorities. In Portuguese the two were known as the *freira* and the *gon-gon*, respectively. Alec Zino is generally referred to as the man who *re*discovered Zino's Petrel. But Schmitz – to whom the original discovery is attributed – wrongly identified the birds. So perhaps history needs a rewrite and Alec Zino referred to as its discoverer. What is it like, I asked Frank Zino as we sat outside his Funchal home one summer evening, to have a bird named after your family? 'It's pretty exciting,' he replied. 'I feel a great sense of responsibility but it's a fantastic honour too.'

So how many Zino's Petrels did Madeira have when they were rediscovered? In such hazardous and inaccessible terrain, with the adult birds coming in only after dark – and the nesting burrows on dangerously steep slopes – it was very difficult to know. The first systematic monitoring of the burrows, in 1986, found that only six of them were occupied. Over the years since, the number of occupied burrows in this original set discovered in 1969 has increased and other nesting areas have been found, some recently. Today there are six different areas of the mountain with breeding burrows and a total of up to 80 pairs breeding. There's convincing evidence, too, that its numbers are steadily, if slowly, increasing. That makes Zino's Petrel one of the rarest birds in the world, and certainly the rarest breeding bird in Europe. Classified by IUCN as Critically Endangered until 2004, it's now considered as Endangered, one small step in a positive direction. The upgrading is thanks to the enormous efforts made since its rediscovery by committed volunteers and staff from the Parque Natural da Madeira, which was established in 1982 and covers nearly two thirds of the island.

Zino's Petrel is protected under Portuguese law. The breeding sites have been designated a Special Protection Area (SPA) under the EU's Wild Birds Directive and lie within the Parque Natural. But it isn't this kind of formal designation that will allow this rare seabird to prosper; only practical protection will help do that. 'For many years, we've ringed all the young petrels in their burrows. And we've also been catching adult birds using mist nets at night,' says Frank Zino. 'But we are still catching some young adults that aren't sexually mature and have never been ringed.' Importantly, what this means is that there are young petrels being reared successfully somewhere else in these high mountains. Their breeding burrows remain undiscovered because there are so many precipitous slopes hereabouts, lots of them difficult and dangerous to access. So the count of 80 breeding pairs is an underestimate; somewhere else up here there are more.

❖   ❖   ❖

As birds that live and feed out on the open ocean (whatever the weather and however violent the sea), many petrels and closely related shearwaters are never seen, except by mariners and the most ardent bird watchers. So thoroughly adapted are they to a life away from land, you get the impression that they wouldn't bother to come ashore to breed if they could have found some other way! Worldwide, there are more than 90 species in the petrel and shearwater family, but there is confusion about exactly how many: several species are very rare and, as a result, rarely seen; some are difficult to differentiate from others visually; and many nest on very inaccessible and tiny, oceanic islands. Add to that the various disputes about which are distinct species and you have a subject area best left to the taxonomists. It is certainly not a subject for this book.

The name 'petrel' derives from the Latin name for the Christian saint, Peter, and refers to their habit of hovering just above the ocean waves with their feet barely touching the water, thus giving an appearance of walking on water as St Peter is said to have done. 'Shearwater' has a more prosaic derivation: their stiff winged, gliding flight low over the waves using remarkably little energy, tilting from side to side and seeming to 'shear' the water's surface.

When petrels do come to land to breed, it rapidly becomes obvious that they are exceedingly well equipped for a life on the ocean waves but hopelessly ill-equipped for getting around on land. Much worse than *ducks* out of water, they tend to land near their breeding sites… and then waddle and shuffle slowly to their egg or chick. Only a very few are able to walk a little more sedately. On the sea, though, they are expert swimmers; their webbed feet placed towards the rear of their bodies that make them so ungainly on land are powerful paddles in water.

While those petrels and shearwaters that breed colonially on open ground come and go by day, others that breed in burrows or crevices tend to be nocturnal, arriving at their nest sites in the dark and leaving again in the half-light of dawn (to minimise the chances of being picked off by predators, gulls especially). With their long, narrow wings they cannot simply give a few flaps and take off into the air. Cliff-ledge breeding species drop from their ledge and immediately gain control by opening their wings; ground-nesting (the majority) or burrow-nesting petrels try to run a metre or so down-slope to launch themselves airborne or they might be able to 'fall' off a very steep slope.

By day, those breeding in the open presumably find their nest site – just a scrape in the ground vegetation – by sight. But what about those, like Zino's, that come in off the sea to locate their burrows in complete darkness maybe several kilometres distant? It might be that they use an acute sense of smell to guide them to the correct burrow, though no one is at all sure. And while the open nesting species might be more vulnerable to predators than those nesting in burrows or in rock crevices, the birds have a final trick up their sleeves. Go too close to an incubating adult or a well grown nestling and you'll get a beak-full of foul-smelling regurgitated stomach oil sprayed at you for your trouble. Little wonder, then, that some of these birds used to be called 'stinker'.

Most petrels and shearwaters pair for life, though maybe a pair only meets up for each breeding season, the one finding the other on their way to the same nesting grounds or when they arrive. If pairs do separate and find new partners, it seems to be because of unsuccessful breeding; otherwise, these birds exhibit a lifetime of faithfulness. And a lifetime for a petrel or shearwater is a long life indeed. While some may live at least several decades, it is thought that a century is not impossible. No wonder we are encouraged to eat a diet rich in oily fish!

Long-lived birds such as these (most birds of prey adopt the same strategy) lay a single egg and might successfully rear a chick to independence every two or three years. That's more than is necessary to replace the adults and retain a stable population in terms of numbers because, once a bird reaches adulthood, it usually survives for many years thereafter. It is a strategy in complete contrast to that of most small land birds, typical garden birds for instance, or warblers. These are short-lived; two or three years at most. But they might lay several eggs and often successfully rear three or more youngsters each year, most of which later die.

Zino's start breeding in late March when the adults return at night to clean out their existing burrows or to excavate new ones. Some take over vacated rabbit burrows, which they then lengthen. Presumably the birds fly from the sea up one or more of the few deep valleys that penetrate as far as the high mountainsides. No one knows their route – or whether there are several routes – because they only come inland in darkness. Any moonlight deters them.

'Their burrows are tunnels four feet long, sometimes more, and always with a bend in them,' says Frank Zino. 'The birds dig them themselves with the claws on their feet wherever there's friable soil. Usually they're on slopes of about 45°. To get to them to ring the nestlings [by day when the adults are out at sea] we have to climb down on ropes. If we are catching adults in mist nets, you can always tell when you have a young, pre-breeding bird because their claws are sharp enough to scratch you. On breeding birds the claws are always blunt from digging!' The length of the burrow they dig or lengthen is related to the age of the pair that uses it, young birds making shorter tunnels which are extended in subsequent years. The adults, though, are 'burrow-faithful'; each pair returning to the same burrow year after year to breed.

In Zino's Petrels, a single, oval white egg is laid from mid May to mid June in a chamber lined with a bit of grass at the end of the burrow; there in the dark it is incubated for nearly seven weeks – until mid July or almost mid August – each parent alternating between sitting on it for several days and feeding at sea. Incubation periods are an endurance test; the sitting bird doesn't get fed. Only when its shift is relieved by its mate will it get the chance to feed again out at sea. If the egg fails to hatch, or is removed by predators from the burrow (rats and feral cats), the adults don't re-lay that season.

Both parents in turn feed the growing chick every two or three nights – only when there is no moonlight – on a 'soup' of partly digested fish, squid, crustaceans and stomach oil, a vile-sounding concoction but clearly a nourishing one. If moonlit nights intervene it might not get fed for several days. When feeding their youngster, the parents frequently go off fishing maybe a few hundred kilometres away. After rearing it for weeks, burrow-nesting species such as Zino's usually leave their fledged youngster to live off its fat reserves for several days before it makes its night-time bid to waddle out and flutter down to the sea, sometime around late September or early October. It's the same strategy that brings adults to their home burrow only on moonless nights and presumably evolved to give the youngster some protection against gulls that might otherwise make a tasty meal of them. It is their first flight and if successful, the young petrel will make it to the sea for the first time. All of the known nesting burrows face roughly northeast. On Madeira, that happens to be the direction of the predominant winds. Presumably, this has evolved to give an increased chance of lift – and survival – to young Zino's making their maiden flight; a clever piece of forward planning.

Petrels are among those seabirds rather unprepossessingly called 'tube noses'; their nostrils emerge through tubes on the top of their hooked upper beaks. They have a special gland between and above their eyes that allows them to drink seawater, essential for their maritime lifestyle. This gland filters salt out of the water and the concentrated salt solution is excreted in droplets at the base of their beak, allowing the tubes to direct it to the beak tip where it drops off.

Nearly all petrels are darkly coloured, often black above and lighter below (as is Zino's); some, though, are all dark or all light. The different species vary considerably in size, from a more delicate 26 cm long – the abundant Blue Petrel of the southern oceans for example – to an enormous 87 cm in the aptly named Giant Petrel, an albatross lookalike with a wingspan of over two metres. All of them feed by day or night on the water, and though a very few eat plankton and others tear pieces off dead whales with their sharp beaks, most catch small fish, crustaceans and squid, the smaller species sometimes plucking a morsel off the surface with their beaks as they use their wings to hover just above it. Larger species tend to dive underwater for fish. Most are colonial, maybe sometimes by force of circumstance because many breed on steep coastal slopes or tiny islands where space is at a premium. Some also tend to form large aggregations while far out at sea, especially if there is good feeding to be had in one particular area of water.

Excellent flyers, they often glide for long periods using ocean winds that propel them in huge loops from high above the ocean where the wind is fastest, down towards the sea surface and then up again into the next loop. It conserves their energy and the birds flap their wings very little. And, as they glide, swoop and shear the waves, it isn't always easy to differentiate some species. Zino's is very difficult – most claim impossible – to distinguish in flight from Fea's Petrel and from Desertas Petrel. Some petrels and shearwaters are known to fly very long distances. Many traverse vast areas of ocean and for some the limits of their maritime hunting zones are poorly known either during the breeding season or in winter. Short-tailed Shearwaters breed in Australia and New Zealand and then spend the northern summer in the North Atlantic or the North Pacific, thousands of kilometres away.

A few species are incredibly numerous – the all dark Sooty Shearwater found across most of the world's oceans is often considered the world's most abundant bird – while, at the other extreme, several petrels and shearwaters are considered to be at risk because they are seemingly so rare. Their rarity is often a result of breeding on small islands where their eggs and chicks are vulnerable to introduced predators such as rats. Twenty species are classified by IUCN as Vulnerable; another 11 (including Zino's) are considered Endangered.

❖ ❖ ❖

Many petrels declined historically because people took vast numbers of adults and eggs for food, the worst carnage often perpetrated by passing mariners short of food supplies and for whom some fresh meat and eggs was an experience not to be missed. Those human communities living on remote islands also exploited the huge seabird breeding resource they had readily available, though that availability was only for a short time each summer. Apart from meat and eggs, seabird fat was often used as fuel in lamps and their feathers in bed covers. Summer-harvested birds were often dried or pickled and eaten in winter when fresh food was often non-existent or scarce and fishing was difficult. It might sound appalling to our sensibilities and relative affluence that birds were harvested like crops, but these island populations often lived in perfect harmony with their wildlife. After all, a community cut off for most of the winter – every winter – is not going to survive for long if it was to overexploit one of the major food resources available to it. Some breeding seabird colonies are still harvested, though such harvests are mostly regulated today. On Tristan da Cunha for example – in the South Atlantic Ocean, over 2,000 km from the mainland – Great Shearwaters are still caught for eating. In New Zealand, maybe a quarter of a million young Sooty Shearwaters (often there called 'mutton birds') are harvested for oils, food and fats each year by the native Maori. They are dug out of their burrows, plucked and often preserved in salt. With their numbers well exceeding 20 million worldwide, a bit of regular harvesting is having no impact on their population.

'On most islands, introduced predators such as rats are the biggest threat to breeding seabirds,' comments Professor Mike Harris, Emeritus Research Fellow at the UK's Centre for Ecology and Hydrology, and an international expert on seabirds. 'But the threats vary from place to place. In the North Sea, for instance, over-fishing and climate change are more of a problem but I don't think human disturbance, apart from some very local instances, is generally more than a minor problem anywhere these days.' The once abundant Bermuda Petrel, or Cahow, breeding only on the island of Bermuda in the western Atlantic Ocean, formerly nested across much of the island. It used to be hunted for food but in recent years introduced cats, pigs and rats killed them and took their eggs. So the Cahow retreated to small offshore islands where they had to compete instead with more aggressive, and much larger, tropicbirds for nest sites. The petrels declined enormously. Conservation programmes to reduce predators, restore habitat and create artificial burrows that preclude entry by bigger birds are all helping to boost their population, now up to a few hundred adults. Worldwide, the mortality of albatrosses, Giant Petrels and some of the larger shearwaters caught accidentally by longline fisheries has attracted enormous publicity and continues to be a huge issue. Smaller petrels – like Zino's for instance – tend not to follow ships and are generally much less at risk.

With no one sure where on the oceans Zino's Petrels spend most of the year, with visits to their nest burrows only on dark nights, with their distinctly haunting calls and much else, you can be forgiven for thinking that Zino's Petrel is something of an enigma of a bird. But there are even more puzzling species. Take the seemingly very rare, small dark brown and white Beck's Petrel for instance. Seen only very occasionally from the 1920s onwards, not until 2007 was its identity confirmed and even now no one has ever found its nesting site. It might be the forested island of New Ireland north of New Guinea, or other islands nearby, but only Beck's Petrel really knows. And it hasn't yet given up its secret.

❖   ❖   ❖

In recent years, attempts have been made to try and find out where Zino's Petrel does spend its non-breeding months. Between 2007 and 2010, tiny data loggers weighing little over a gram have been attached for different lengths of time to the legs of adult Zino's caught at their Madeiran breeding sites. These record daylight intensity at frequent intervals, allowing calculations to be made – when the birds were recaptured and the loggers removed – of the birds' locations calculated from sunrise and sunset times at different latitudes across the ocean. The methods aren't very accurate but they do give an insight into the birds' travels. And, as many experts had thought, these are exceedingly well-travelled birds. Even in the breeding season, some flew as far north as the west of Ireland, halfway to the eastern US coast and south as far as the coast of The Gambia in West Africa. In the winter months it seems the Brazilian coast and West Africa as far south as the west coast of Namibia are all quite possible. These are distances of up to 10,000 km, maybe more. 'Some American birders have told me that they've seen them off the east coast of the US in winter, 5,000 km west. But I think it's almost impossible to tell Fea's and Zino's apart when they are in flight over the sea so I'm not convinced. They could be anywhere out in the Atlantic, or maybe even further away,' comments João Nunes.

Life has never been easy for Zino's Petrel. For centuries after the island's discovery, seabirds and their eggs – including, presumably, Zino's – were exploited for food. Along with fish and shellfish, they were an important source of protein. From early days, Black Rats got ashore from boats. They soon became established around dwellings but also in the countryside where ground-nesting seabirds and their eggs were an obvious source of summertime food. Some domesticated cats, imported by the early settlers and popular pets on Madeira ever since, frequently became feral. They too, make an all too easy meal of a seabird that moves around pretty clumsily on land. In the high mountains, intrepid sheep and goats have for centuries eroded the steep slopes into which the Zino's burrow and sometimes cause their burrows to collapse. And egg collectors – attracted by the bird's rarity – have also taken their toll in the past. 'All through the 1960s, 70s and 80s, the breeding success at the nesting sites we knew of was terribly low,' comments Frank Zino. 'Luckily, these petrels, like most other seabirds, are very long lived. Otherwise, the level of predation would have driven them to extinction by now I'm certain.' For instance, in 1986, when systematic monitoring of the (then few known) breeding ledges began, none of the young birds survived the summer and rats were strongly suspected as the killers. In 1991, ten adults were killed in one breeding area by feral cats.

The need to control these introduced predators was overwhelming. In 1986 the Freira Conservation Project (a joint initiative between the Funchal Museum of Natural History, the Parque Natural da Madeira and the local community) was set up in order to attract funding to begin regular monitoring of the birds and to tackle the predators. Since the start of the project, poison baits have been put out to kill rats, while feral cats are trapped and killed. The measures are positioned in a kind of cordon sanitaire around each colony to reduce the chances of either mammal making it to a Zino's burrow. Since the 1960s when no juveniles were being successfully reared, their breeding success has increased and few youngsters are now lost to the predators. While all rats seem to have been eradicated by poisoning them on the very much smaller Desertas and Selvagem islands, eradicating them on a huge mountainous island like Madeira is impossible: replacement rats appear from lower ground and docking ships are likely to reintroduce them. Also, Madeirans fed up with their domestic cats sometimes abandon them in the hills to get rid of them. So baiting and trapping around the Zino's breeding sites continues to be an absolutely essential part of the plan to bolster their population and the petrel has certainly begun to prosper as a result.

All of the mountain area in which Zino's Petrel breeds has been purchased by Madeira's regional government to ensure its protection. Shepherds are now banned from grazing goats and sheep on the highest land and a large area has been fenced, with grids on the few access roads, to keep them out. The shepherds were compensated for the small reduction in grazing area. As a result, there has been a massive recovery in the mountain vegetation on these topmost slopes. Erosion has reduced too. The hope is that Zino's might extend their breeding areas as their population slowly increases in number.

Overfishing around Madeira – which is steadily depleting some fish species in the sea areas elsewhere – doesn't seem to be a problem for these birds. The Madeiran fishing industry is thriving. And, according to Sociedade Portuguesa para o Estudo das Aves (SPEA), the Portuguese bird protection society in Madeira, almost all the many species of seabird breeding here are increasing in number. There is, it seems, plenty of fish to go round.

❖ ❖ ❖

The future for Zino's Petrel was looking rosier than ever until August 2010 when disaster struck. A vegetation fire, seemingly started deliberately, badly damaged the whole nesting area. Vegetation cover was lost and many of their burrows collapsed as the now bare soil on the slopes eroded. A few days later, 53 nests were visited to assess the damage. Just 13 juveniles had survived and the surveyors found 25 dead juveniles and three dead adults that must have been in the burrows feeding their chicks when the fire struck. They also found some burrows empty of eggs and some eggs that had been deserted. Approximately 60% of the burrows had been partially or completely destroyed and another 20% had the entrance blocked by soil and rocks. Before the end of the breeding season, all but one of the surviving juveniles managed to fledge and, as far as anyone knew, get away to sea. The others had either died of starvation – their parents maybe deterred from returning to their now barren mountain slopes with no vegetation cover – or they had been taken by predators because not all of the fire-damaged traps could be re-set in the cordon sanitaire in time. Just 20% of the nesting burrows remained in good condition, a very depressing prospect after years of successfully increasing their breeding numbers.

Visiting the mountain-top breeding area three days after the fire, Frank Zino was obviously shocked by the amount of damage and destruction but remained cautiously positive about the future. 'The total destruction of the habitat is alarming, but after some very light rain, there are a few blades of grass. Certainly the bracken is starting to come through the ashes and there is sprouting from the charred remains of gorse. These may help to keep the soil together, though it's not ideal,' he recorded after his visit. 'It will be interesting to see how many of the seeds in the soil have survived the intense heat, but we will have to wait until next spring to find out. We have to hope for light rains to compact the soil and start some basic vegetation developing,' he added.

Parque Natural staff reacted very quickly to halt further erosion and renovated around 100 natural burrows. They also built about 60 artificial ones to replace those destroyed. Such artificial burrows have been used successfully by Desertas Petrels on Bugio Island. They are basically aluminium tubes ending in a nesting chamber inserted into the slopes to simulate a burrow. The entrance has a small horizontal platform for the adult birds to alight on. Anti-erosion blankets made of biodegradable coconut fibre (which allows plants to grow through) were pegged down in the burnt nesting areas to prevent soil erosion by wind, to help maintain soil moisture and protect the surface from any storm impact. Seeds of native plants were sown and cat traps and rat poison boxes put in place to return the previously existing protection ring that surrounded all the known nesting ledges. All this hard and often dangerous work on steep slopes with eroding rock and soil slowly paid dividends. During the following 2011 breeding season, the nests had an initial occupancy rate of around 60% although this gradually fell and by the end of the breeding season 16 juveniles had left their nests and made it out to sea. It was a decent result and gave the people involved hope that this setback in Zino's fortunes would be a very temporary one.

Satisfyingly, their nesting habitat had soon recovered fully, burgeoning again with flowering plants, grasses and shrubs by the 2012 breeding season, which unfortunately turned out to be less productive. Just eight juveniles were fledged and many nesting burrows were unoccupied. Eight juveniles are, of course, infinitely better than zero, which it often was in the early days of Zino's conservation here, but it was not good news. The reluctance to use their traditional slopes to breed, even though they had revegetated, is impossible to explain but it might be because the adult birds could still detect the smell or changed texture of the burnt soils. In all probability these birds have an acute sense of smell, acute enough to distinguish their own nesting burrow from all others in complete darkness. A very faint odour of burnt vegetation – not detectable by people – could have put a veritable spanner in the works. With petrels living often for several decades, an occasional poor breeding season is of little or no consequence. But it is very unsettling for the conservationists involved all the same.

Good news, though, came very soon. In the 2013 breeding season, 16 chicks were reared successfully, and another 16 in 2014 so the colony is back to where it was in terms of breeding productivity the year before the fires. All the good work has paid dividends. And it would be good if the other locations that Zino's breed in on these high mountains could be identified. 'This mountain area and the steep slopes the petrels burrow into are very difficult to search,' comments Nadia Coelho of the Serviço do Parque Natural da Madeira. 'But we will keep searching because there must be other breeders somewhere here. We know that other birds are being raised.' So the population of Zino's is almost certainly a little larger than anyone dared imagine.

For a bird nesting in burrows – whether dug themselves, purloined from rabbits and extended, or provided for them – near the very highest peaks on this isolated island, and seemingly nowhere else, it is exceedingly difficult to boost its population substantially unless the birds are able to adapt to take up breeding residence lower down these precipitous slopes. That would require yet more investment of time and money providing rat and cat deterrents and getting shepherds to agree to larger areas of land being excluded from grazing livestock. By no means impossible, but not easy either. With a seabird like Zino's Petrel, ranging over a huge ocean area for much of its life and only coming on land to breed – and then in the most inaccessible terrain – there are practical limits on what can be done to boost its numbers.

While techniques such as captive breeding to try and boost their numbers is out of the question for a bird that requires vast areas of sea for hunting, the existing strategy of controlling predators, trying to ensure that there are no significant changes to its breeding areas caused by fires or disturbance, and providing artificial nest burrows if there is a shortage of natural nesting sites will continue. It is proving to be effective. For many years Zino's Petrels on the high peaks of Madeira must have struggled to raise any juveniles because of rat and feral cat predation. Today, that predation has been reduced substantially and their breeding record has improved enormously. The birds have recovered, too, from the fires that devastated their breeding slopes more recently. And there are other Zino's Petrels breeding elsewhere in these rugged mountains, keeping their secret to themselves, for now at least. These mysterious seabirds may never be abundant, and there might well be setbacks ahead as their numbers slowly increase. But their small population is certainly on the road to recovery. Alec Zino would surely have been proud.

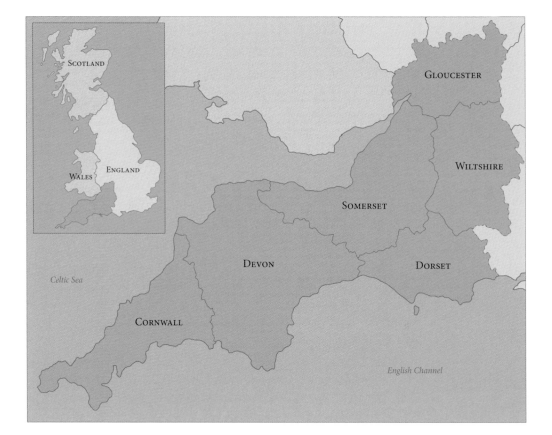

15

NO MORE SINGING THE BLUES

LARGE BLUE BUTTERFLY

Understanding the ecological needs and life cycle of an animal is an important prerequisite before any attempt is made to reintroduce it into the wild; even when its habitat might appear to be perfectly suitable, it not always is. Probably no animal reintroduction in the world illustrates this better than that of the gorgeous Large Blue Butterfly. To say that it has a complex lifecycle is a gross understatement; until the amazing intricacies of its lifestyle were unravelled, it proved impossible to reinstate it at the British sites where it had become extinct. The detective work completed, today Large Blues flutter once again on the flower-rich slopes in southwest England where they had been absent for decades.

On a warm summer's day, standing on the steep, flower-filled slopes of Collard Hill, it is easy to be mesmerised by the view. A canvas of fields and hedgerows cover the wide open Somerset flatlands below, spreading south towards the little market town of Somerton – long ago the capital of Wessex – a little way beyond the sluggishly meandering River Cary. As I gaze and squint in the bright sunshine, Caroline Kelly from the UK-based charity Butterfly Conservation, my guide on this visit, is crouched nearby on the sloping grassland examining the pink-purple flowers of aromatic thyme plants with a sharply pointed pencil. It is protracted and exacting work. After all, individual thyme flowers are barely a few millimetres across and what she is looking for is smaller still. This isn't the first thyme plant that Caroline has examined as we walk across these slopes replete with yellow rockroses and straw-coloured rosettes of Carline Thistle. She searches another few thyme flowers. 'I think there's one here,' she suddenly says. 'Can you see it, just between the tiny petals? There; it's very small, off-white, about a millimetre in diameter.'

I have to admit it wasn't easy to see at first; a minute sphere inside the flower head of a tiny, perfectly formed and vibrantly coloured flower. But there it was all right, tucked inside the delicate petals, a little bit of potential life with a huge story attached to it. This little life-form was testament to the success of an incredibly long and convoluted detective story that would have tried the abilities of Scotland Yard's finest. Not only that, but this tiny egg would not be here if it wasn't for the enormous persistence of a whole set of conservationists, amateur butterfly enthusiasts and organisations who have been working collaboratively and incredibly assiduously over the last 30 years. And continue to do so today. The Large Blue Butterfly – its eggs laid in thyme flowers – is back in Britain after becoming extinct here in 1979, and these populations in the southwest of England are thriving to such an extent that they are considered the best in Europe. Despite its name and although it is indeed the largest of Britain's blue butterflies, the adult really is quite a small chap. With a wingspan of up to 5 cm, its upper wing surfaces a vibrant blue and the undersides having a silvery sheen, its most distinctive markings are the black spots and border visible when it opens its wings. In its characteristic fluttery flight, these merge into an inky blue, a gorgeous sight on a summer's day.

Walking across the steep, sunbathed grasslands of Collard Hill – owned by The National Trust – Caroline watches for an adult Large Blue ahead of us. It is a while before we see one, flying away from a thyme plant and off into the distance. 'It's getting pretty warm here today. And when it gets too hot for the adults they usually seek out some shade low down in the vegetation and sit it out. This afternoon, I doubt there'll be any to be spotted. They'll all be cooling themselves,' she says. There are other butterflies here: stunning black and white Marbled Whites scurry past in profusion while little orange and brown Small Heaths settling down on blue scabious flowers are just two.

It was in 1857 that a German entomologist, Professor P.C. Zeller, first spotted the central role that thyme flowers play in the life of the Large Blue. 'I saw them sit down on the stems of thyme and, after sipping from a few flowers, bend their abdomens between the flower stalks, on which they deposited a pale green egg, sometimes not without some apparent pains. I gathered a score or so of twigs, each with a single egg,' he wrote at the time.

❖ ❖ ❖

The Large Blue occurs from Western Europe east to southern Siberia, Armenia, Mongolia, Japan and China. Its presence in the UK was first described in 1795 in an illustrated book by the naturalist and illustrator William Lewin, although it had probably been discovered before that. Between the late 18th century, and maybe up until about 1840, there were an estimated 90 colonies in the south of England, though the exact number is rather imprecise. The colonies probably comprised anything from a few tens to a few hundred adults; the largest probably contained a few thousand adults in their 'best' years. But, in general, the colonies were isolated from each other. These butterflies also didn't travel far – perhaps only a kilometre or two at most – not the ideal strategy if your habitat is declining.

Ironically, less than a century after the butterfly was discovered in the UK, it started to die out. Colonies in Northamptonshire disappeared around 1860; South Devon in 1906 and Somerset in the late 1950s. 'New' sites for the butterfly were found in 1891 on the north coast of Devon and Cornwall but the news soon got around and hundreds of collectors swooped on the area, finding other sites along this coast where Large Blues were equally abundant. By the 1920s these were in decline too, though mainly because of changes in the habitat rather than the depredations of collectors. In the 1940s more large colonies, some holding up to perhaps 10,000 adults, were found further along the Devon and Cornwall coasts but they, too, started to decline in the 1950s and Large Blues here fluttered their last in 1973. By 1950, they were only present on 25 British sites (perhaps a few tens of thousands of adults altogether), which rapidly declined to just two colonies totalling about 300 or so butterflies by 1972. They disappeared from the Cotswolds between 1960 and 1964; all the sites on the north coast of Devon and Cornwall were empty by1973 and the very last British site, on Dartmoor, was vacated in 1979. Large Blues were extinct in Britain. Much the same was happening in parts of Western Europe too. They became extinct in the Netherlands and only one colony now exists in Belgium. Their populations have been reduced to less than ten colonies in most northern European countries while in much of Mediterranean Europe (especially Spain, southern France and northern Italy) and in all Eastern European countries, habitat destruction and changes in land management are reducing their numbers overall.

Some of their English sites had been ploughed up to grow crops or had been planted with conifers, destroying the habitat these insects relied on. But much of its grassland habitat appeared the same as it always had; the red ants still occurred, whose presence were a known requirement for the Large Blue (though their precise role wasn't understood), and thyme, known to be the plant on which the butterfly laid its eggs and on which the caterpillars fed, still flowered joyously. No one understood why these butterflies had become extinct.

Could it, for instance, have been due to over-collecting? Certainly butterfly collecting had taken its toll. It had been a Victorian obsession to take samples of as many species as possible and pin them in display cabinets, a practice continued into recent decades. Because most insects are small and the majority cannot be identified without the examination of minute morphological characters, entomologists today often make and maintain insect collections. And without many well kept insect collections, our knowledge of insects would be extremely poor. Large collections are conserved in museums and universities where they are maintained and studied by specialists. Many amateur entomologists and collectors keep collections too, but the majority follow the Code of Guidance issued by the Royal Entomological Society. With today's photographic technology producing high definition images, there is very much less need to obtain specimens, kill them and keep them for study. In the mid 19th century there were over 3,000 butterfly collectors in Britain. Today, there might be just a few hundred ardent collectors remaining. Many British butterflies are now protected by law (including the Large Blue) so catching and collecting them is illegal. Nevertheless, there are still a few fanatics who seem to have a compulsive need for possession way beyond normal behaviour, determined to collect even rare species, often flouting the law to do so.

No one knows how many Large Blues were ever taken. According to Michael Salmon in his book, *The Aurelian Legacy: British Butterflies and their Collectors* (University of California Press, 2000), when the butterfly collection of Baron J. Bouck, a Fellow of the Entomological Society of London (to which he was elected in 1921) came up for auction in 1939, it was found that he had amassed over 900 Large Blues – he probably threw away far more. A colony in Northamptonshire was almost certainly destroyed by greedy dealers and collectors. A documented raid by butterfly collectors in 1896 at some of the Cornwall colonies netted

2,000–3,000 adults, some individual collectors taking 500 or so. It was greed on an epic scale. Maybe all this collecting helped drive the species to extinction in parts of north Cornwall and Gloucestershire, but in other parts of the Large Blue's range some sites were less well known and collection was probably non-existent. Even after collecting was banned, the butterfly continued to disappear inexorably. And no one knew why.

Many early collectors also wanted to breed butterflies – not difficult with some of the common species whose caterpillars chomped to their hearts content on commonly available plants. But at home, however such enthusiasts nurtured the cut thyme stems with the Large Blue eggs, even if the eggs hatched into minute larvae (their caterpillars), those larvae never seemed to live for more than maybe three weeks. Certainly, no butterfly collectors ever reared an adult Large Blue; the mystery of its life cycle saw to that. And this butterfly was not going to give up its secrets that easily.

❖ ❖ ❖

Enter Jeremy Thomas, then a young PhD student and now Professor of Ecology at the University of Oxford. When the butterfly was reduced to just two colonies in 1972, Thomas, who was based at the forerunner of today's Centre for Ecology & Hydrology (CEH) in Dorset, was asked by the then Nature Conservancy if he would interrupt his research on the ecology and conservation of Black and Brown Hairstreak butterflies to study the Large Blue. As Thomas recalls, there were then few entomologists who could even attempt to unravel the mystery of the Large Blue's decline. He takes up the story:

'Between May and September for the next five years I lived on Dartmoor with Britain's last Large Blue butterflies. I took a scatter-gun approach, studying every aspect of their life cycle, their behaviour, how many eggs they laid, egg survival and how many caterpillars were in each thyme plant because there was something about their ecology we didn't understand, and that gap in our knowledge meant we couldn't conserve them. It was like a detective story, slowly eliminating all the possibilities from the enquiry until only the solution remained.'

'The Large Blue butterfly has a peculiar life cycle. It lays its eggs on thyme flower buds, and when the larvae hatch they feed on the flowers for two weeks and then fall to the ground. What follows is the strangest part. Red ants carry the larvae into their nests where they live for the next ten months feeding on ant grubs, until they pupate and emerge as adults. We had known since 1914 that the Large Blue spent part of its life in red ant nests. But after months of laborious work, locating ant nests by leaving trails of cake crumbs [he used sweet Battenberg cake!] across Dartmoor, I discovered that the Large Blue's larvae only survived in the nests of one ant species – *Myrmica sabuleti* – and that species was declining too. But why?'

'As has since been found with other declining species, changes in farming were responsible. We discovered that alterations in grazing, coupled with myxomatosis in rabbits, left grassland too tall and shaded for the heat-loving ants to survive. And with them went the Large Blue. All this knowledge came just too late to save the last British Large Blues. Just when we knew both the cause of its decline and how to reverse it, it was gone. For me it was a huge disappointment: after years of hard work I felt I had failed. But what we learned, of course, paved the way for its successful later reintroduction.'

Thomas' detective work produced further detail of the Large Blue's life cycle, even more fantastic than anyone would dare believe. After hatching in its thyme flower (further south in Europe, the eggs are often laid in similarly coloured marjoram flowers but marjoram usually flowers too late for British large blues), the tiny caterpillar feeds on the flower and sheds its skin twice as it grows larger until it is in its third stage, the third instar. The first three larval instars feed on the thyme flowers but the fourth drops to the ground and thereafter depends on the attentions of the particular red ant it parasitises, *Myrmica sabuleti*. The little caterpillar tricks the ants into taking it into their underground nest by secreting a seductive fluid that they feed on and even 'singing' to the ants so that they believe it is a queen ant grub. The ants stroke the caterpillar with their antennae, making it produce more of the attractive fluid; the ants continue to do this until the caterpillar raises half its body into the air. That's a signal. When it happens, an ant picks the caterpillar up with its jaws and takes it into its nest. In the comfort of the nest, the parasitic caterpillar devours ant larvae all winter, growing and eventually pupating and hibernating. Through its time in the ant nest, the caterpillar might devour 500 or so ant grubs. Often, the ant colony will bring in too many Large Blue caterpillars or the ant colony will be too small to supply enough grubs for the butterfly caterpillar. When this happens, the caterpillars usually eat all the ant eggs and larvae, eliminating the colony. With no more to feed on, the caterpillars starve to death.

The *M. sabuleti* ant workers are 4–5 mm long and their tiny nests are made in soil, under or inside some rotten wood or under stones and in moss. Large Blue larvae can develop in the nests of other red ants; five different species foraged underneath thyme plants at the Dartmoor site Jeremy Thomas worked on. All of them would adopt Large Blue caterpillars, the numbers adopted depending on how abundant each species' workers were. But the butterfly larvae survival rates differed with each ant species. Survival was over five times greater in colonies of *M. sabuleti* than with any other red ant but for this a high density of *M. sabuleti* was needed with thyme flowering within two metres of their underground nest entrance. And the *M. sabuleti* ants needed to adopt at least two thirds of the caterpillars available at the site for a Large Blue population to survive long term. So plenty of *M. sabuleti* ants had to be present or Large Blues were in trouble.

To make itself less obvious to the ants, and thereby less likely to be rejected by them, a Large Blue caterpillar accommodated in the nest assumes the ants' scent and mimics their sounds. Once it pupates and becomes a chrysalis, it will rub its head to make a scraping sound similar to that made by the ants. Failure to adopt any of these measures puts the caterpillar at risk of being attacked and eaten by the ants because they might then recognise it as an imposter and not the queen ant they had been fooled into accepting.

'It had always been in my mind from the outset that the Large Blue caterpillars might be chemical mimics of ants but I had no proof,' comments Thomas. 'It is, after all, a very dangerous lifestyle for the butterfly to have evolved unless there is some really close "protection" from the ants such as by mimicry. But it wasn't until the 1990s that researchers working with me were able to confirm this and identify the chemicals. And it wasn't until 2008–2009 that we found that the larvae and pupae were also acoustical mimics of the sounds produced by adult queen sabuleti ants.'

When the adult butterfly is ready to emerge from its pupa (or chrysalis), usually sometime from mid June to late July, the emerging adult either crawls out of the ant burrow or the ants carry it back outside and leave it on the ground. There they usually encircle it and ward off any predators that attempt to attack it as its wings unfold and harden. When the butterfly is ready to fly, the ants retreat back into their nest, their extraordinary job done for another year. Warmed up, and with its wings dried off, the adult Large Blue flutters off to fulfil its aim in its short life – maybe a week or two – to mate and then find a thyme plant in flower on which to lay its eggs (if it's a female).

❖ ❖ ❖

Crucially, Thomas had discovered that the Large Blue was only able to trick successfully one species of red ant, *Myrmica sabuleti*. If it entered the nests of other ant species, the caterpillar was more likely to be rejected, attacked and killed. Or, at best, very few Large Blues would be nurtured to become adults, not enough to keep the butterfly colony going. He had also found that this particular ant required warm ground, which could only be created if the vegetation was kept short and well-grazed. A near-imperceptible difference of just a centimetre in grass length could change the ground temperature by two or three degrees causing the ant — and the butterfly with it — to perish. A widespread decline in sheep and cattle grazing, together with myxomatosis, which decimated wild rabbits after the 1950s, caused a lot of traditionally managed, flower-rich grassland to grow too tall and cool for the ant, thereby interrupting the complex lifecycle of the butterfly. Although the vegetation didn't look much different, it was taller and, with less sun penetration, the ground underneath where the ants lived was cooler.

With its requirement for extremely warm conditions, *M. sabuleti* is abundant only in south-facing, short-grazed turf, typically less than two or three centimetres tall; if grazing is removed so that the height of the sward gets above even four centimetres, these ants decline dramatically and other ant species become more abundant. Thomas discovered that when the vegetation height changed almost imperceptibly from one to two centimetres, the temperatures in the ants' brood chambers near the soil surface dropped by two or three degrees Celsius.

It means that the vegetation where the ant and Large Blues are to thrive has to be grazed most of the year – by cattle, sheep or ponies – but not from around May to late July (the precise times depending on the year), so that the thyme plants can flower fully. It's not easy to get it just right; warmth, rainfall – and thereby growing conditions – can alter drastically from one year to the next. Allow grazing too late in the spring and you can find much of the young growth of thyme chomped back, clearly not a desirable outcome. 'When working out the management prescriptions,' says David Simcox, Project Manager for the Large Blue Reintroduction Programme (and a long time colleague of Jeremy Thomas), 'you must acknowledge the reality that farmers are trying to earn a living. Sometimes they would like to take their animals off sites a little bit earlier than we would like and on to richer pasture. All site management is about compromise and trying to meet many aims. If you also take into account the vagaries of the weather and rabbit populations, it can get very complicated. You can decide the correct stocking level of cattle on a site only for the rabbit population to crash; then you need more cattle to do more grazing. The converse is also true. Not all farmers have spare animals or spare grass to be able to react that quickly.' In places where scrub has taken over and on rough coastal grasslands, grazing by hardy ponies or cattle is best, whereas most inland grasslands can be grazed by either sheep or cattle. If rabbits occur on the site, their grazing also has to be factored in. And some patches of scrub, perhaps gorse (around the roots of which the ants often have their nests) or clumps of bramble and blackthorn, need to be retained to provide shelter for the adult butterflies in bad weather.

So the size of a Large Blue colony in Britain is correlated with the number of *M. sabuleti* ant nests present, which in turn is correlated with the amount of short turf. This contrasts with warmer climates in southern Europe where the Large Blue has less specialised requirements and breeds in taller turf. There, grazing can be lighter or even absent for a few years provided the rank vegetation is cut occasionally to reopen the habitat and prevent it getting overgrown permanently by scrub or trees. The largest known former Large Blue colonies in England covered 10–20 ha of habitat where there were probably a few thousand thyme plants and maybe one *M. sabuleti* nest every 1–2 m². From his research, Jeremy Thomas believes that a safe population of 400–1,000 adult butterflies could be supported on just 1 ha under ideal conditions, but that populations of less than 400 might not always survive.

'Thomas's painstaking research was a watershed moment for conservation because it showed the importance of managing habitats after a mistaken focus on letting nature take its course during the 1970s,' comments Dr Martin Warren, Chief Executive of Butterfly Conservation. 'The Adonis Blue, the Silver-spotted Skipper and the Heath Fritillary have all been saved from near extinction using ideas from Thomas's scientific research.' Jeremy Thomas showed clearly that collecting wasn't the primary cause of the demise of the Large Blue in the UK, rather that it was the management of their grassland habitat – and the impact subtle changes in that management had on the abundance of one species of red ant. And who would have ever realised that such a subtle change could cause an animal's extinction?

❖   ❖   ❖

As of 1996, the IUCN categorises the Large Blue as Near Threatened globally, just one step away from being of Least Concern. At first sight it might seem rather optimistic for a butterfly whose fortunes have declined drastically in several countries. But a regional classification for Europe published in 2010 – the *European Red List of Butterflies* – compiled by a team of over 50 experts Europe-wide and coordinated by Butterfly Conservation Europe (BCE) and IUCN, places it in the Endangered category; in Europe it has declined in flower-rich grasslands, one of its main habitats, by more than 90% over the last two decades.

'I think I agree to that Near Threatened assessment worldwide because the species is widespread and not rare in Siberia, China, Mongolia and Japan,' comments Chris van Swaay of Dutch Butterfly Conservation and an expert on the species. There are no reports of a decline there and it is likely that the situation in Siberia is not negative. It looks like the assessor considered this large enough to counter the bad situation in Europe. It might not be more abundant but it is widespread over a huge area in Asia, so altogether the population might be large. Also in Europe there are big differences as the species is abundant in a few localities – in

Germany and the UK for example – while it is very widespread in low densities in the Alps. Every time I am in the Alps around the tree line I encounter them, but rarely more than a few per day,' he adds.

The Large Blue is one of just 29 butterflies (out of 451 species in the EU) listed on the Annex to the EU's Habitats Directive which means that Member States have legal obligations to protect and enhance its populations. In some parts of Europe such as the UK, Belgium and Denmark, it only occurs in protected areas such as nature reserves, but its susceptibility to small changes in managing its habitat can jeopardise its status even there. It is, after all, a notoriously pernickity creature with a highly complex life cycle that doesn't always fit perfectly with what land management might be needed to protect other vulnerable species (of plants or animals) on the very same piece of land.

So how does its status in Europe – where it has been more extensively studied than elsewhere – compare with that of other European butterflies?

According to BCE, geographical Europe has 482 species. A third of them are found nowhere else in the world. Overall, about 9% of European butterflies are Threatened in Europe (less than, for example, the figure for birds and mammals) and a further 10% are Near Threatened. The figures, though, represent minimum estimates as trends are poorly known in many countries including some of the large Eastern European countries. The bad news is that about a third of the species are currently declining while 4% are increasing and more than half of the species are stable. For the remaining 10%, the current information is too limited to be sure. Among the most endangered species are the Danube Clouded Yellow, now thought to be confined to a few sites in Romania, and the Violet Copper, a beautiful wetland species that has undergone drastic declines in many countries.

The current main threat to European butterflies is the destruction of their habitat or its break-up into scattered remnants. Over half of Europe's butterflies rely on traditional grazing to maintain their flower-rich, grassland habitats, habitats that are being squeezed out from both directions. On one hand, in Western Europe farmland is generally being more intensively used and large numbers of once traditionally managed hay meadows and pastures have been ploughed – and wetlands drained – and converted to intensive crop growing. In contrast, the abandonment of farmland and its natural conversion to scrub and woodland is happening on a substantial scale in parts of Eastern Europe. Considerable areas of former farmland – some of them meadow – have been abandoned in Eastern Europe as the often more intensive collective farming of communist days has disappeared and more people have been keen to leave the land. There has also been some abandonment of meadows and alpine pastures in mountain regions. Climate warming is affecting the distribution of several species too and may have an increasing impact into the future. Overall, butterfly populations have moved northward by about 75 km in the last 20 years as overall temperatures have risen. They are likely to move yet further.

So butterflies that inhabit grassland, like the Large Blue, are in a poorer position than many other butterfly species. BCE has collated information on the abundance of 17 grassland species Europe-wide and found a staggering 70% decline in their abundance in the two decades since

1990. Martin Warren, one of the compilers of the *European Red List of Butterflies* comments: 'The rapid decline of so many species is extremely worrying. They point to a major loss of wildlife and wild habitats across Europe. Far more effort is needed to support the traditional farming systems on which many species depend and protect key areas from development.' With EU Common Agricultural Policy funds being pared back and some more environmentally friendly farming supports likely to be hit hardest, it is unlikely that the situation will improve in the short term at least.

The state of the UK's butterflies isn't rosy either. Butterfly Conservation published its most recent assessment in 2011, providing ten-year trends for the 59 species that breed regularly in the UK. Since 1995, an estimated 10,000 members of the public have participated in their organised recording scheme and have produced over six million sightings of butterflies UK-wide. Results indicate that nearly three quarters of UK butterfly species have declined in abundance over the decade to 2010 and that the distributions of over half of them declined too. The biggest single fall was for the High Brown Fritillary, showing a near 70% drop in abundance over the decade. A large orange and black beauty often inhabiting woodland clearings where bracken is dominant, its fortunes are fading rapidly and it now survives in few places.

But why are many of Britain's butterflies declining? As with European butterflies generally, habitat loss – more intensive farming and, sometimes, abandoning a former use such as annual meadow cutting – and habitat fragmentation which isolates small butterfly populations – are the main reasons. Highly variable summer weather may also be a contributor, ironically counteracting the mainly beneficial effects (for warmth-loving butterflies) of climate warming.

But there were positive outcomes too. Thirty-one species out of the 59 showed some evidence of increase in either their distribution or their abundance. A minority of species, mostly those common in a range of habitats, extended those ranges substantially, spreading northwards in response to climate warming. In addition, there are promising signs that the long-term declines of some threatened butterflies have been slowed or reversed by conservation initiatives such as more appropriate land management by farmers paid for by some kind of agri-environment scheme and by the protection of key populations at conservation sites such as nature reserves. Clouded Yellows, for instance, increased in abundance by a staggering 235% while their distribution stayed the same! It is a migratory species coming to Britain in vast numbers in some years; when it does, it finds that clovers – one of its caterpillar's main foodplants – are abundant on much of our farmland, most of them cultivated varieties. But the Clouded Yellow is far from fussy; hence its success. The other butterfly ringing up a huge increase is the one and only Large Blue, with a recorded increase in abundance of 271% and an expansion in its range. A success indeed. The best sites now contain the greatest densities of Large Blue butterflies to be found worldwide.

❖ ❖ ❖

Back in the early 1980s and armed with the enormously detailed knowledge gained by Jeremy Thomas in his pioneering research on the Large Blue's life cycle, it was time to attempt a reintroduction to a suitable British site. He takes up the story again:

'As their old home on the edge of Dartmoor was being grazed to encourage the ants, David Simcox and I set out to find a donor population, easier said than done. We needed to find butterflies elsewhere in Europe that emerged at the same dates as the thyme buds in southwest England. Yet in other areas with similar climates – such as northern France and the Netherlands – the Large Blue was also extinct. Several unsuccessful attempts later, we finally found a population on the Swedish island of Öland and brought back 250 caterpillars which David reared in the lab until their final larval stage. These we released every evening for ten days, making mad dashes from CEH [then the Institute of Terrestrial Ecology] at Furzebrook in Dorset to the release site on Dartmoor.'

'Twenty-five years on, Large Blues live in around 30 colonies in southwest England. Two of the largest sites support 4,000–5,000 adults – populations not seen in this country since the 1950s. The project has been a huge success. But the successful reintroduction of the Large Blue butterfly is about much more than a single species. Its greatest legacy is that it shows that conservationists can reverse the decline of a globally threatened insect species once they understand the factors driving it. It may seem obvious now in an era of evidence-based policy-making, but 25 years ago this was new, and hugely influential. The project taught us that insect conservation must be based on ecological science, and it has become a paradigm for other efforts to conserve insects in temperate climates.'

'The other key ingredient in the project's success is the hard work and cooperation of many individuals in many organisations. Even without the time and land these organisations and individuals donate, this one project to save a single species is costly, and finding that funding is a constant battle. But in creating a flagship for wildlife it represents a net gain to conservation, and through it we have learned how to conserve many other species as well as helping to predict the impacts of climate change. On a personal level, I get a thrill every time I see the Large Blue butterfly, and I will never tire of seeing it.'

Caterpillars from Öland (removed with the permission of the Swedish Nature Conservancy) were released at three UK sites between 1983 and 1992 while a fourth release to a site in Gloucestershire failed, possibly because of the significant climate difference between there and southern Sweden. There were, of course, huge risks in reintroducing Large Blues from such a distant population. 'We didn't really know if it was going to work at all since, in Sweden, the adults fly about a month later than they do here,' comments David Simcox. 'So I brought eggs back, reared the early instar larvae on thyme and later Jeremy put them down on sites on the edge of Dartmoor. We weren't sure if the lifecycle would go through in 48 weeks to be in synchrony with the thyme flowering or in 52 weeks after the thyme had finished flowering. As it happened, it came through in 48 weeks which was exactly what we were hoping for. It was a success!'

There is also the issue that the Swedish population is genetically slightly different from the extinct UK population. And that's not surprising considering that the two populations were totally isolated from each other. 'But,' says Simcox, 'the two populations are ecologically and behaviourally similar. And we wanted to obtain the butterflies from a northerly donor population which relied on thyme for the caterpillars just as the UK population always had, and not a population from southern Europe that uses marjoram not thyme.' It was a case of Hobson's Choice; either Large Blues were to fly again in England…or they were not. The answer was obvious.

After these early successes, between 1992 and 2004 the Large Blue was reintroduced successfully to four different sites in Somerset's Polden Hills (including Collard Hill), all from caterpillars taken from other Somerset sites established with Swedish caterpillars. Since then, it has colonised naturally from these to another 22 sites, all within just a few kilometres of each other. Because Large Blues don't fly great distances, it has achieved this natural colonisation using sites as 'stepping stones' and by taking 14 years to reach the furthest away site. The largest UK sites might now support 1,000–5,000 Large Blues per hectare, more than any other known population worldwide. Six other sites in Somerset have the potential to support them; in other words their land management is right and they have good populations of thyme and of the requisite red ant. Reintroductions to at least one of these looks likely to be necessary (they are probably too far from existing sites for natural recolonisation) but natural spread could do the rest over time.

These days, Large Blues can even be spotted from the train: near Castle Cary in Somerset, some of its largest populations fly on railway embankments which are managed by Network Rail to encourage the butterfly. There are two populations that have already been established in the Cotswolds in Gloucestershire and another two sites ready for reintroductions. These are all sites where they were known to occur prior to their extinction in the UK. It's a distance of about 100 km in a direct line to their existing colonies in Somerset, far further than a Large Blue will fly. The locations of the Gloucestershire sites, all on sun-warmed, south-facing slopes, will remain a closely guarded secret until the populations are successfully established. From these releases, it is hoped the butterfly will spread naturally to other nearby meadows, potentially doubling the estimated UK population of 20,000 adults.

But how does David Simcox, the programme's project manager, do the tricky job of rearing caterpillars removed as eggs from a site in Somerset and release them successfully in Gloucestershire?

'The first step is to check that the donor population has enough eggs; that means doing a lot of sample counts of eggs on thyme across the site. It's a slow job,' he says, replete with understatement. 'Really, we're then collecting up excess eggs on a plant because we know that if more than two or three caterpillars get taken into an ant nest, they won't make it to adults. Three caterpillars in a nest and it's about a 1% chance of an adult ever getting out, simply because the ants can't feed them'.

'So we pick off thyme stems with eggs in their flower heads and mount them in a damp oasis block covered in foil so that no water can touch the thyme flowers. The eggs hatch and the caterpillar burrows into the flower. The first instar [its first stage before skin moult] stays hidden but the second is visible on the flower. I try to make sure they're not too close together physically because they're cannibalistic, the smaller ones eating the larger ones! The third instar I take off the flowers and put each one in a small individual plastic box with its flower. I've got hundreds of boxes to look at daily to see when they shed their next skin (and are then about 7 mm long) because that's when we have to get them to the receiving site within two to three hours. That usually occurs between 3 p.m. and 6 p.m. (precision is a feature of this process!) because its timing, believe it or not, coincides with the peak foraging time of the sabuleti ant.'

'We put them on the ground at the receiving site where we know there are strong colonies of the ants; we dot them at about four metre intervals because we don't want any one ant colony picking up too many caterpillars. And if ants don't pick them up within 48 hours they don't survive,' he adds.

David Simcox has devoted his working life almost entirely to the recovery of the Large Blue. Jeremy Thomas spent years of painstaking and systematic study to winkle out the intimate details of this glorious butterfly's life cycle, without which there would have been no hope of ever having it returned to Britain. The continuing Large Blue reintroduction programme is still heavily underpinned by science at Oxford University and CEH and implemented by a collaborative partnership between Butterfly Conservation, the Gloucestershire Wildlife Trust, J&F Clark Trust, The National Trust, Natural England, Network Rail, Oxford University, Somerset Wildlife Trust, South Somerset District Council and private landowners. Farmers play a key and often unsung role in this success story; without their control over grazing, there would be no Large Blues. A veritable array of other professional biologists and committed amateur enthusiasts have devoted an enormous amount of time and effort to manage the protected sites and diligently record the numbers of butterflies at the now numerous locations where the Large Blue prospers and where it is being reintroduced. That large partnership is vital to the success of the whole project because they all have key roles to play; it also illustrates the huge commitment displayed by a range of organisations to nurture this insect back.

The Large Blue is most certainly the smallest physical example in this book of a species that has been saved. But it is without doubt one of the most visually attractive, and its recovery is one of the most amazing stories that can be told.

16

THE BIRD THAT DIDNT FOLLOW THE DODO

MAURITIUS KESTREL

Few animals have got as close to extinction as the Mauritius Kestrel. By the mid 1970s there were just four wild birds left on the island of Mauritius in the Indian Ocean. Many Mauritian species had already gone extinct, including that most famous of birds, the Dodo. Almost all of the forest that originally clothed Mauritius, and was once inhabited by maybe 4,000 kestrels, had been felled. Introduced predators such as rats and mongooses had taken their toll; so, too, had pesticides like DDT. From the late 1970s, a concerted effort by Carl Jones and a team of biologists – using a range of measures including captive breeding, protecting nest sites from predators and providing nest-boxes – started to reverse the kestrel's downward trend. By 2014 their numbers had risen to at least 400.

As a young boy in his home town of Carmarthen in Wales, Professor Carl Jones – fascinated with animals – bred kestrels in his back yard. He could never have guessed that some of that early experience would later help him to successfully rescue one of the world's rarest birds that was just a whisker away from extinction. By chance it was for another species of kestrel, the Mauritius Kestrel, that Jones would lead a last ditch conservation effort, a bird somewhat smaller and browner than its European cousin and confined to Mauritius, the Indian Ocean island nation off the coast of Madagascar. The auguries were not good; this was, after all, the island where the Dodo had been discovered and annihilated within 70 years of its first being formally recorded. But the recovery of the Mauritius Kestrel – from just four remaining wild birds – is entirely positive. It is one of the most remarkable stories of conservation in the world. 'I had always known what I wanted to do for as long as I can remember. I wanted to work with wildlife, to visit remote areas and to contribute to the conservation of the most endangered species. But dreaming is not enough and I realised that I needed some higher qualifications,' he said when he was nominated for the 2012 Indianapolis Prize, the world's leading award for animal conservation.

When the first Portuguese explorers came ashore on Mauritius in 1507, this 2,000 km², subtropical island would have been very different. It was uninhabited and most of it was covered in dense, evergreen forest, a high proportion of its species found nowhere else in the world and it had no mammals other than bats. Changing 'ownership' to the Dutch, then the French, the British took control of Mauritius in 1810 during the Napoleonic Wars and it remained under British rule until its independence in 1968. Prior to its discovery, Mauritius might have held as many as 4,000 kestrels. 'In good habitat today we have a pair about every square kilometre plus floating birds so I accept the likelihood of a population of around that size. Pristine Mauritius had high densities of lizards, their main food, so I have no problem accepting a figure of 1,000–1,500 pairs and a total of 3,000–4,500 birds on the island pre human colonisation,' says Jones.

But as the kestrel's forest habitat disappeared and what remained became invaded with non-native, rampant shrubs, its ability to spot and hunt prey as it had always done – under the canopy of the forest trees – became more and more restricted. At the same time, animals introduced to the island, such as mongooses, Crab-eating Macaques, Black Rats and feral cats, were killing many of the adult kestrels and eating their eggs. Human persecution might have played some, albeit smaller, role in their downfall too. Locally the kestrel is known as *mangeur de poules* (chicken-eater) because of its believed, but unlikely, depredations on domestic poultry. It has led to unnecessary persecution in the past and may be part of the reason for its disappearance from some of its former range.

The most severe decline, though, was in the 1950s and 1960s when DDT and other similar pesticides were used widely as an insecticide for the control of malaria-carrying mosquitoes and agricultural pests. Absorbed by the birds' tissues from the prey they caught, the insecticide caused eggshell thinning and breakage, thereby reducing the kestrel's breeding performance, as it had for birds such as Brown Pelicans and Bald Eagles in the US and Peregrines in Europe around the same time. By the late 1950s, only 20–25 birds could be found, all in the Black River Gorges in the south of the island where more forest remained and where pesticides had not been used. By 1970 the population was thought to number between six and ten pairs; by 1974 it was down to a mere four birds, including a single breeding female. The future survival of this species looked highly unlikely.

A few years later, its fortunes were to change for the better. With the help of Gerald Durrell (1925–1995), the founder of the Durrell Wildlife Conservation Trust on Jersey, Carl Jones who was then working for BirdLife International (and later became the Scientific Director of the Mauritian Wildlife Foundation, MWF) found support from the government of Mauritius and the US-based Peregrine Fund to begin a major conservation programme. Intensive conservation efforts began. These included protecting breeding pairs against predators, incubator rearing of rescued eggs to produce more chicks, captive breeding of a few pairs and the release of young birds back into the wild, and the provision of nestboxes.

By 1985, kestrels were still restricted to an area of no more than 50 km^2 in the southwest of the island, an area of precipitous cliffs and steep ravines, and within that mainly to the best sections of native forest. But they had started to increase, albeit slowly. By 1991 there were at least 30 wild nesting pairs and a population of 170 birds in four forested but separate areas of the island. Three years later, some 346 young kestrels had been released back into the wild in three different mountainous areas of the island and the total population at the end of the 1990s was thought to be 600–800 birds. With the benefit of hindsight that figure is now thought to have been over-optimistic and realistically the population numbered about 500.

The success of the project resulted in an IUCN upgrade of the Mauritius Kestrel from Critically Endangered to Endangered and, more recently, to Vulnerable, an enormous change in its official status over a comparatively short time period. But why still Vulnerable? Because the population is restricted, as it always has been, to just one island where it could still suffer a sudden decline because of some unexpected environmental change or disease for example.

The kestrels are to be found mostly in the remaining forests of the island, especially in the Black River Gorges National Park, where most nest in natural sites on cliffs and in tree cavities rather than in nest-boxes. Today, apart from routine monitoring and the provision of nest-boxes, nothing else seems to be necessary to assist the species' survival. It is doing well for the first time in hundreds of years.

❖ ❖ ❖

Falcons are fast-flying, streamlined birds of prey usually with fairly long pointed wings and narrow tails. Many of them are masterly in the air, snatching smaller birds or large insects in flight. Others catch their prey on the ground by hovering above them and then dropping suddenly or by swooping down from a perch; rodents, ground-living insects, snakes and lizards are the main prey of a few. Characterised by remarkable eyesight for spotting and catching their prey, they are to be found in a huge range of habitats from remote tundra to city centres. The Peregrine is almost certainly the best known, found throughout much of the world and renowned for its steep dives through the air – known as a stoop – reaching speeds approaching 200 km per hour as it closes in on an unsuspecting pigeon whose death is instant.

Ranging in length from a tiny 15 cm (the dark blue and cream Collared Falconet of southern Asia) to 60 cm (the blotchy dark grey and white Gyrfalcon of the northern hemisphere), female falcons are almost always larger than males, in some species very noticeably so. They don't construct any kind of nest; most breed in tree cavities or on cliff ledges; in urban environments, some, like the Peregrine, have taken to nesting on high building ledges or bridge spans. A few nest in the abandoned nests of other birds; the attractive Red-footed Falcon of Eastern Europe for instance, nests colonially in the abandoned nests of rooks high in trees.

There are 61 species of falcon worldwide and they are divided into two groups: caracaras and forest falcons; and falcons, kestrels and falconets. Caracaras are, to some extent, the odd ones out. They are buzzard-sized, relatively long-legged birds often inhabiting arid places and they feed on the ground by catching large insects and small animals though they will also take carrion and even fruit. One or two species of caracara have rather odd food choices; the Black Caracara of South America catches ticks that it picks off the back of tapirs to add to its diet.

Of the 14 kestrels, many of them are predominantly coloured in various shades of brown. Some have a wide distribution; the Common Kestrel occurs across Europe, North Africa and the very west of Asia while the American Kestrel is found throughout the bulk of North and South America. Others are very much more restricted, like the Mauritius Kestrel, or the Banded Kestrel of Madagascar, albeit a far larger island. Many kestrels exhibit typical hunting behaviour of hovering at a height of around 10 or 20 metres over open country and swooping down on prey on the ground, usually small mammals, lizards or large insects. They can fly in stationary air, even indoors in barns and, while hovering, they face towards any slight headwind. But not all of them hover; the russet-coloured Fox Kestrel of central Africa prefers to fly down from a perch to catch its prey; the Seychelles Kestrel is a swooper, spotting something and diving down to grab it; while the Mauritius Kestrel hunts by means of short, swift flights through forests picking off geckos and other prey and sometimes chasing prey on the ground.

With relatively short, rounded wings compared to most falcons, the Mauritius Kestrel is better adapted for hunting, rather sparrowhawk-like, under the canopy of the forest. This flight capability makes it very skilled at plucking small prey from tree trunks and branches. Reaching a maximum length of 30 cm, it's smaller than the Common Kestrel but larger than the American Kestrel. Studies comparing different falcons suggest that the Mauritius species originally came from eastern Africa via Madagascar, eventually reaching Mauritius around 1.7 million years ago where it evolved to become the bird we see today.

The staple of the Mauritius Kestrel's diet is the bright green *Phelsuma* geckos that live in trees – usually on high branches – or on exposed rock outcrops; they make up over 80% of their diet while other prey includes lizards, other species of gecko and small snakes. They'll also take adult and young birds including some introduced to the island such as Red-whiskered Bulbul, Waxbill, Spice Finch and young Barred Ground Doves; most of these seem to be taken on the edges of forests or in more open habitat rather than within forests themselves. Large insects including cockroaches, locusts, cicadas and dragonflies, as well as a few small mammals such as shrews and rats, make up the rest. They search for prey from a perch, then make short, fast dashes chasing their quarry once it is spotted, the bird flying, hopping and running among branches in pursuit. Geckos try to evade capture by zigzagging and moving to the other side of a branch but kestrels are highly manoeuvrable and can fly in a tight circle of less than a metre diameter. When pursuing small birds to kill, an attack becomes a tail-chase and most birds can out-distance a pursuing kestrel. Consequently, the majority are caught by surprise attacks and brief chases. Sometimes kestrels will hover in the air and capture prey in short aerial chases like a hawk or by diving down onto it on the ground, while active flying insects such as dragonflies are caught after a brief sally from a perch. Research has found that an adult male in good quality forest needs to hunt for an estimated three hours per 14 hour day to provide for his own needs; in non-native habitat it takes more like five hours to get enough.

Other Indian Ocean islands also have endemic kestrel species, that is, species that are unique to that one place. The Seychelles Kestrel had declined to very small numbers but has recovered to a stable population of at least several hundred breeding pairs. It has the advantage that it breeds on at least four of the many islands that constitute the Seychelles. Two other endemic species are confined to the much larger island of Madagascar – the Banded and the Madagascan Kestrels – both of which occur there in large numbers. Another, the Réunion Island Kestrel, found 200 km from Mauritius, became extinct during the 1600s. They were considered a pest because they were thought to kill poultry (though that seems unlikely because they were no bigger than a Common Kestrel) but hunting – then using fairly primitive weaponry – is unlikely to have been able to kill them off. So the reason for their demise is something of a mystery because, at that early date, introduced predators were not present in any numbers and even rats probably would not have presented much of a problem for the birds.

Like most other falcon species, the Mauritius Kestrel does not build a nest. Instead, it nests in natural cavities in trees and on cliff ledges. It has also adapted to nesting in artificial nest-boxes fixed to trees as have some other species of falcon around the world. Nest-boxes were put up to allow kestrels to breed in a wider range of habitats and areas where they would not have nested otherwise because of a lack of natural nesting cavities. These nest-boxes have allowed the Mauritius Kestrel to successfully breed in young secondary forests where breeding would otherwise be unlikely.

A female Mauritius Kestrel typically produces two to five eggs in November or December which she incubates for 30 days. After hatching, both parents feed the young and in less than 40 days they will begin to take their first flights. The parent birds are strongly territorial, defending their nest very ably against intruders but, interestingly, their breeding territories appear to have 'ceilings' so that kestrels may overfly others' territories unchallenged. For the next year, the young will stay in or near their parents' home range as they learn to hunt and survive on their own. About 70% of all young birds of prey die before they reach adulthood; young, inexperienced birds make easier targets for predators and, as they learn to hunt, they may become injured or killed if they fly into trees or other objects. Some may not gain the hunting skills they need in time, and they will starve.

Although historically they have been forest dwellers, with the massive changes to Mauritius's environment, especially the clearance of most of its forest, the kestrels have become more tolerant of degraded forest and open areas. In this respect they are somewhat typical of many other falcons, several of which have adapted to changing circumstances. Peregrines, for instance, have adapted to urban living by using high rise building ledges as surrogate cliff breeding sites and preying mainly on city pigeons that make an easy meal.

❖　❖　❖

> Mauritius is a fascinating, world-in-one-island slice of paradise. Its very name conjures up images of tropical luxury and stupendous extravagance. While in many destinations famed for cobalt-blue seas, white sandy beaches and luxury hotels, you may eventually find yourself wishing for something to do besides sunbathing and swimming, it's often hard to know what to do next in Mauritius. The island is loaded with historic sights, cultural diversity, geographic variation and almost limitless activities to distract you from the daily grind of beach and pool.

That's a typical extract (this one from the Lonely Planet website) extolling the attractiveness of Mauritius for a luxury holiday. But few readers of holiday brochures would ever imagine that Mauritius is also the site of terrible devastation.

When it was first discovered, it was uninhabited and almost totally covered in forest; wet forest in a large tract of the centre of the island surrounded by drier evergreen forest, and a much smaller area of open, dry, palm-rich but less dense woodland along part of the west coast. There were smaller areas of wetland and coastal mangrove. The forests were especially dense and their very high tree density appears to have been an adaptation to withstanding cyclones, which are fairly commonplace in this part of the world. Mauritius then had no land mammals; instead it had reptiles, birds and land crabs that were probably abundant in number. It also had four species of forest-dwelling skink (a type of lizard), the largest of which probably preyed on other smaller lizards and on hatchling tortoises. There were no larger predators, so many birds evolved to become flightless – the Dodo was the size of a goose and the Red Hen (a rail related to moorhens and coots) the size of a domestic chicken. They had no need to be able to fly; there was nothing to get away from. Their wings shrivelled.

Starting soon after colonisation, forest felling began. In 1753, Mauritius had 164,000 ha of native forest; by 1804 it was down to 127,000 ha and less than 50 years later no more than 28,000 ha remained. But it didn't stop there; by 1980 only 2,388 ha of native forest survived. That's a miniscule 1.5% of the original area. Forest clearance for farming and timber accounted for much of it but cyclones, too, cleared large sections as it was opened up. The human population of Mauritius, which rose from under 19,000 in 1767 to 1,296,000 by 2013, continues to put pressure upon remaining areas of native vegetation. In place of forest there are extensive areas given over to crops and plantations of non-native trees. Introduced shrubs are often invasive, changing the nature of the island vegetation even more. And Mauritius has 19 species of naturalised non-native birds and a further 13 introduced mammal species, several of them predatory and wreaking havoc on the island's native animals. Introduced rats and other predators devour the eggs and chicks of a range of birds – including the kestrel. The kestrel's decline was once thought to be due mainly to predation, in large part by introduced Crab-eating Macaques. But research has found that this is an over-simplification and although these monkeys are a problem preying upon the contents of accessible nests, they can't get on to sheer cliff faces where many of the kestrels nest in cavities.

Today, thousands of hectares of Mauritius are under tea, sugar cane, pine and eucalyptus plantations and most of the island's once rich wildlife has suffered enormously; there have been drastic declines in the populations of its bird endemics including the Echo Parakeet, Pink Pigeon, the little Mauritius Fody – and the Mauritius Kestrel. One of the most alarming features of Mauritius's remaining forests is their rapid and seemingly irreversible degeneration into exotic scrub and thickets. The native plants, which have little competitive ability, are increasingly being outcompeted and displaced by vigorous introduced species. Trampling and browsing by introduced deer is another factor altering the forest character. This affects the kestrel, because hunting beneath any forest canopy that's now full of scrub becomes increasingly difficult. It is also likely to result in further declines of other rare endemic birds.

Several introduced shrub species are involved in this degeneration; two of the most important are a species of privet and guava. On mountain slopes the privet forms dense stands and in upland areas the guava has become a dominant plant. They not only change the plant composition of the forest but also radically alter its structure into a dense scrub layer. Furthermore, introduced fruit-eating birds such as Common Mynahs and Red-whiskered

Bulbuls spread the seeds of these exotic, invasive shrubs in their droppings. They are highly mobile birds and the seeds are dispersed widely, a double whammy for the native Mauritius vegetation. Research has found that seeds passing through a bulbul's gut germinate much more effectively than those that don't get eaten.

With this huge amount of habitat change and the introduction of predators previously unknown on Mauritius, it isn't surprising that many native Mauritian species have become extinct in the last few hundred years: the once abundant Rougette or Lesser Flying Fox; the Mauritius Night Heron in the late 17th century; the Mascarene Teal, a small duck hunted until it was killed off; the large Raven Parrot; the Mauritius Domed and the High-backed Tortoise are just some of the animals that have gone forever. And not forgetting the Dodo of course. It isn't just the very unusual or rare species that have declined or been lost; coupled with the degradation of native plants, the numbers of common insects, geckos and small birds – all prey items of the kestrel – have declined too.

Since 1987, the MWF has been managing the Ile aux Aigrettes nature reserve. This little island just off the coast of Mauritius is a glorious showcase of what Mauritius perhaps looked like before European settlers arrived. As a sanctuary for species that exist nowhere else in the world, it is the perfect place to raise awareness of their beauty and importance. And in spite of all the degradation, there are still very many species unique to Mauritius, which together with a series of neighbouring islands form the isolated 'biodiversity hotspot' of the Indian Ocean, a region that urgently needs greater protection. 'What Mauritius needs now,' says Vikash Tatayah, MWF Conservation Director, 'is a halt to the invasion of exotic species. We have a large number of plants and animals that are causing great havoc so we need an effective quarantine policy to stop more invasive species entering the country. It's one of our major battles here if not the top one.'

But this is just the start. The MWF estimates that, at the very least, 6,000 ha of forest are needed to support the island's endemic wildlife. The highest one third of the mountains have mostly retained their forest, which is rich in indigenous biodiversity but is also being invaded. More forest is needed lower down too. This would involve reforesting land in the foothills rendered unprofitable by the fall in global sugar prices. 'We need to see if we can reverse the trend by reclaiming these marginal areas. So instead of the agriculture encroaching, we want the forest to reclaim the land,' says Tatayah. The MWF has been lobbying the Mauritius government to produce a policy for the restoration of marginal land, and it has become one of the highest recommendations in the government's recent National Forestry Policy Action Plan. But it is still uncertain whether there is the political will for it to happen. The Black River Gorges National Park in the southwest of Mauritius was designated in 1994 and protects over 6,000 ha of forest; it is home to a substantial population of kestrels and several other rare species confined to the island. There are other government-protected areas on Mauritius including the more recently designated Bras D'Eau National Park in the northeast but this area doesn't have kestrels.

Today this tropical island retains its regularly sun-soaked holiday beaches but, over the few centuries since human occupation began, Mauritius has changed beyond recognition.

Numerous species have gone extinct, the inevitable consequence of so much habitat destruction, hunting and the arrival of a cornucopia of introduced animals the native species on the island had never been accustomed to.

❖ ❖ ❖

The discovery and subsequent rapid extinction of the Dodo on Mauritius is an object lesson in how vulnerable a species can be. Especially if it is flightless, unaccustomed to predators (humans included) and rather ponderous in its movements. The story of the Dodo – immortalised in Lewis Carroll's *Alice's Adventures in Wonderland* (1865) and in such commonly used phrases as 'dead as a dodo' – is a dubious claim to fame, today exploited by Mauritius's tourism brochures.

The curiously named Dodo was a metre tall pigeon, probably brownish grey, and named perhaps after its pigeon-like call or from a mispronunciation of Portuguese or Dutch words such as *dodoor* (meaning 'sluggard') but more probably from *dodaars* (meaning either 'fat-arse' or 'knot-arse', referring to the knot of feathers on its hind end!). Whichever, neither is very complimentary. Contemporary drawings suggest that Dodos were plump, somewhat ungainly and covered in plenty of meat. But current thinking is that their ungainliness and obesity were exaggerated. They seem to have fed off a mix of fruits, nuts and land crabs and they lived mainly in drier woodland. More importantly, they couldn't fly and they nested on the ground, a rather fatal combination if there are hungry people about. Before humans started encroaching, there were probably no predators capable of killing one.

First mentioned by a Dutchman, Vice-Admiral Wybrand van Warwijck who visited the island in 1598, various accounts from the time give mixed reports about Dodo meat, some describing it as tasty, others as nasty and tough. Tasty or not, there are scattered reports of mass killings of Dodos for provisioning of ships for long voyages and, like many animals that evolved in isolation from significant predators, the Dodo was entirely fearless of humans. Combined with their inability to fly, it made them easy prey for sailors who clubbed them to death. Archaeological investigations, though, have found scant evidence of excessive hunting of the birds, overturning the long-standing notion that the Dodo was hunted to extinction for food. It was probably one of several factors that put paid to it.

In the early years of the 17th century, the small numbers of settlers on Mauritius introduced dogs, pigs, cats, rats, and Crab-eating Macaques which would have plundered Dodo nests and competed with the birds for limited food resources. Pigs, in particular, have a formidable reputation for seeking out and eating eggs and hatchlings of ground birds. At the same time, people started felling the island's forests where the Dodos nested and fed. And occasional flash floods from tropical downpours might have been responsible for washing away some nests. The impact of introduced animals on the Dodo population, especially the pigs and macaques, is currently considered more severe than the impact of hunting for food. Rats were perhaps less of a threat since Dodos would have been used to dealing with local land crabs and could see off a rat.

If we can't be certain about the causes of their extinction, some controversy surrounds the date of their extinction too. The last widely accepted record of a Dodo sighting is the

1662 report by shipwrecked mariner Volkert Evertsz of the Dutch ship *Arnhem* who described birds caught on a small islet off Mauritius. There's also a description from around 1680 by Benjamin Harry, chief mate on the *Berkley Castle*. And a sighting was reported in the hunting records of Isaac Johannes Lamotius in 1688. Anthony Cheke, who with Julian Hume wrote the authoritative *Lost Land of the Dodo* (Yale University Press, 2008) points out that some mentions of the name Dodo after 1662 actually refer to the island's Red Rail (another large land bird that went extinct) to which the name seems to have been transferred. Cheke believes the actual Dodo was extinct by or around 1662. Whatever, it must have been rare for some time before that and it's unlikely that any survived past the last decades of the 17th century, just 100 years after it was discovered.

Since then, many scientists have doubted that the Dodo had ever existed; it seemed altogether too strange a creature, and some believed it a myth or an invention of perspectives altered by many months at sea, rather like the myth of the mermaid (see Chapter 6). For a long time the bird was forgotten. Not though by Lewis Carroll. The Dodo in his stories is supposedly a caricature of the author whose real name was Charles Dodgson. A popular but unsubstantiated belief is that Dodgson chose it because of his stammer, and thus would accidentally introduce himself as 'Do-do-Dodgson'. With the popularity of the book, the Dodo became a well-known and easily recognisable icon of extinction. Today, the Dodo is certainly the most famous but it is, unfortunately, far from being the only animal to go extinct on Mauritius. There are many others. By the 1970s, adding one more to this depressing list looked very much to be the fate of the Mauritius Kestrel as well. Thankfully, it was not to be.

❖ ❖ ❖

With just four surviving wild Mauritius Kestrels by 1974 – and extinction looming – some rapid work was needed to try and improve their breeding performance and secure their tiny population. The Durrell Wildlife Conservation Trust and BirdLife International, with support from the Mauritius government and US-based Peregrine Fund, pioneered the work. Egg manipulation, a fairly new idea in the late 1970s, was the first step. First laid clutches of eggs were removed from nests and incubated artificially in an aviary built for the purpose by the Mauritius government so that the parents laid a second clutch which they then reared themselves. In this way, the numbers of young kestrels increased much more quickly. 'Mauritius Kestrels will lay up to four successive egg clutches in a season if they need to but the third and fourth clutches have very low viability so we never removed more than the first clutch,' comments Jones. It proved highly successful; in 1995 Carl Jones and colleagues concluded that 95% of female kestrels re-laid within a fortnight. Production of young kestrels increased substantially.

Most of the young kestrels hatched in incubators in the breeding centre were hand-reared and then released when they were sufficiently mature; a few of them were retained for captive breeding. The released birds were then used to supplement the initial tiny population surviving in the southwest of the island while others were released into other forested areas where kestrels had disappeared entirely to try and re-establish new populations. Some wild pairs, too, were supplied with mice or day-old (chicken) chicks to supplement their diet in order to increase the number of eggs they laid.

Where natural tree cavity or cliff cavity nest sites were in short supply, nest-boxes were provided; in parts of the island without cliff cavities and few tree cavities, almost all the kestrels used boxes. Natural nesting cavities were often improved by removing rocks from the cavity floor, replacing or providing a suitable surface for them to nest on, and providing suitable perches in front of the cavity in order to encourage their use. Other cavities accessible to predators were deliberately blocked to prevent kestrels from trying to use them. At the same time, introduced predators such as the Small Indian Mongoose and feral cats that prey on fledglings were trapped in the vicinity of some of the nests or prevented from getting near by putting up fences.

Captive breeding began in 1973 and between 1978 and 1992, 190 fertile eggs were laid by captive birds in the aviary where the birds were held; 129 of these hatched, producing 103 chicks that were reared, mostly by hand, and 84 young kestrels were released into the wild as the end product. From the three pairs of kestrels sent as a safeguard in 1986 to the World Centre for Birds of Prey run by the Peregrine Fund in Idaho, US, 36 young had been reared; of these, 32 were returned to Mauritius and 25 of these also released into the wild. Research published by Jones and colleagues showed that a total of 333 kestrels were released in the ten years up to the end of the 1993/4 breeding season; one third of these had been bred in captivity while the rest were reared from eggs harvested from the wild. About 257 of them survived to independence and more than half of them survived their first winter. The programme had been a notable success.

Juvenile kestrels are known to be particularly vulnerable to predators, especially for their first two weeks after their release because they spend a lot of time on the ground. Consequently, cats and mongooses were trapped around the release sites. By the 1993/4 season, an estimated 56–68 pairs – from both reintroduced birds and from wild birds – had established territories in the wild, creating a post-breeding population of 222–286 birds. Their prospects looked good. DDT and its sister pesticides had been banned, kestrels were not hunted, and predators could be controlled at those nest sites considered to be the most vulnerable.

Populations of animals derived from so few founders should, at least theoretically, have some problems. Undoubtedly, today's large population of Mauritius Kestrels, descended as it is from just four founder birds, is extremely limited in genetic diversity – what geneticists call a bottleneck – an issue explored in other chapters in relation to species such as the European Bison (Chapter 5). 'The problem is that we don't have a non-inbred population to compare with in order to try and work out what impact it might have. When you look at the Mauritius Kestrel and compare it with other small falcons their rate of egg fertility is 75% which is a little on the low side since we would expect it to be above 80%, but that's not much of a difference,' comments Jones. 'One comparison that we can make is by looking at egg size before the bottleneck [by looking at eggs in museum collections] and after. Those laid before it had an average weight of 18.3 g while those laid more recently averaged 16.8 g. So there are some inbreeding impacts but quite subtle and of course we don't know how egg size affects the fitness of the resulting birds anyway,' he adds.

Research published in 2008 by Steven Ewing of Glasgow University (and now at the UK's RSPB) and co-workers concluded that the rates of in-breeding and loss of genetic variation in one well monitored population on the island were extreme and among the highest yet documented in a wild vertebrate population. They also concluded that this genetic deterioration could affect their long-term viability but that the introduction of birds from another population on the island might help diversify it a little more. 'There isn't any mixing between the different groups we've re-established on the island, and there is no good evidence that there is any genetic difference between the different populations anyway,' comments Carl Jones. 'We have a western [in the Black River Gorges area] and an eastern population [centred on the Bambous Mountains] although the western one is split into two with a small, isolated southern group. So in practice we have three subpopulations. There's conflicting advice about whether we should purposely mix the populations but in 2015 we are intending to extend the subpopulation in the south by moving birds into it from the eastern population.'

Nevertheless, and in spite of the genetic bottleneck, the kestrels have shown a remarkable ability to adapt to different habitats on the island since their original forest habitat has largely disappeared. Previously found only in the forests where they fed almost wholly on geckos, they have more recently adapted to other habitats. Not only that but they have become much more flexible in their choice of prey and hunting behaviour too. And that augurs well for their future survival. The Mauritius Kestrel certainly isn't alone among falcons in showing adaptability; it is reminiscent of some of its fellow falcons in other parts of the world where many Peregrines, for instance, have adopted city life, where Common Kestrels have become regular hunters along the verges of motorways and Lesser Kestrels have taken to nesting under the roofs of buildings. Jones and his team encouraged this versatility with the Mauritius Kestrel; they had purposely released birds in a variety of habitats, many of them alien to its traditional hunting and breeding grounds. In lowland savanna – about as different from their traditional forests as it was possible to get – birds showed great versatility; they perched on fence posts and pounced on insects, and they chased and caught small birds, shrews, lizards and geckos other than those they preyed on in the forest. Research established that kestrels hunting in agricultural areas and in degraded habitats catch fewer geckos and more agamid lizards, shrews and birds instead. Many of the released kestrels in the east of Mauritius, attracted by established pairs, have moved into areas of degraded and fragmented forest to breed. And, even more surprisingly, kestrels released on the forested island of Ile aux Aigrettes flew back to the mainland and hunted in suburban gardens. A couple even set up shop in a village!

Research published in 2014 by Dr Samantha Cartwright, a research ecologist at the UK's University of Reading, shows that in new habitats such as sugarcane fields, the kestrels have adopted a 'live fast and die young' strategy. Cartwright and her colleagues used over 20 years of detailed data gathered on some of these birds. 'Kestrels born in agricultural areas have more offspring earlier in life and are more likely to die earlier but ultimately produce the same number of offspring through their life as they would have done had they originated in their traditional forested areas. Where you are born seemingly matters for how you live your life as an adult,' said Cartwright. What all this strongly indicates is that the Mauritius Kestrel most certainly has a future. Not only that but, based on the amount of habitat available, Jones and colleagues have predicted that their rise will continue through natural recruitment to give an eventual population of perhaps 500–600 birds.

Due to its outstanding success, the release programme ended after the 1993/4 breeding season, though the population has been regularly monitored over the years since to check on its progress. By 1997, the island was home to 400–500 birds and although there were estimates that their numbers had increased even further – some were guessing nearly 1,000 birds – these ideas now seem over-optimistic. In the 2012/3 breeding season, MWF found that of 88 nesting pairs, 52% were using nest-boxes, 37% used cliff cavities and just 10% were using tree cavities. Of these 88 pairs, nearly half successfully fledged youngsters (a total of 89 young kestrels). With the Bambous population at about 208 birds and the numbers in the Black River Gorges at 154, the total population of Mauritius Kestrels in 2012/13 stood at 362. That's an apparent reduction from the peak count of maybe 500 (the Black River Gorges population has declined in recent years) but the restoration of this exceedingly rare bird is a huge success story considering that at its low point only four birds existed.

Conservationists on Mauritius have no illusions of a job complete. It will probably require more captive rearing of harvested first clutches from wild pairs to release further juvenile kestrels in new areas on the island, together with continuing predator control and the provision of long-lasting nest-boxes wherever there are insufficient natural nesting cavities. More resilient PVC nest-boxes have so far not proved as popular with kestrels as wooden boxes, though they have been readily accepted by equally rare Echo Parakeets.

The Mauritius Kestrel will never be anywhere near as abundant as it was when the island still retained its forest cover 400 years ago. But it has not gone the way of so many other species once common on this Indian Ocean island. The story of the Dodo, symptomatic of the enormous destruction of the natural habitat of this island, is a classic example of how rapidly a wild species can slide into oblivion. The Mauritius Kestrel, too, came within a whisker of extinction. We might very easily not have had it with us today – there were no back-up populations in zoos – but for the prescient thinking and urgent action that was taken to rescue it 40 or so years ago.

17

ENDPIECE

The previous chapters have described a wide range of animals whose declines have been halted and reversed. Some, like the Humpback Whale, have recovered naturally when the cause of its demise – commercial whaling – ceased. Others, such as the Arabian Oryx and the European Bison, had become extinct in the wild and were recovered by breeding captive animals, releasing them into suitable habitat within their original ranges and protecting their small but growing populations. Many others such as the Iberian Lynx and the Whooping Crane had been reduced to very small numbers. A combination of action to secure more productive breeding for those that remained in their natural habitat, together with some captive breeding and releases to slowly increase their numbers, has proved successful. For several, such as Zino's Petrel and the Florida Manatee, captive breeding is not an option and their recovery has been predicated on reducing or eliminating the threats they formerly faced and satisfying their life support needs in the form of more or improved habitat.

So when do we assume that a species is recovered? Do recovery plans state a population size to be aimed at or a combination of population size and distribution? Should we be aiming to re-establish the numbers that were present before their decline? Or what? The answer is pretty mixed. Some plans have very clear objectives. The Florida Manatee Recovery Plan, for example, requires an 'average annual rate of adult survival of 90% or greater and an average annual percentage of adult female manatees accompanied by first or second year calves in winter of at least 40%'. For the Iberian Lynx the goal is 'to conserve and recover populations in order to ensure their viability in the long term'.

So should recovery goals be more standardised? Alana Westwood at the Department of Biology, Dalhousie University in Halifax, Nova Scotia thinks they should. With co-workers, she examined conservation legislation published in the US, New Zealand, the EU, Australia and Bolivia and found that none had any that defined recovery. What she has proposed is a system based on established medical principles; the proposed framework has five stages: diagnosis, treatment, stabilisation, rehabilitation and recovered. What constitutes a recovered state for a particular species needs to be defined during diagnosis. 'It might be suitable to aim for a historic population of one species, whereas this is not possible for a species whose original habitat has undergone massive land conversion. What we advocate is that whatever's decided, it must be quantifiable and determined by the best available science,' says Westwood. 'So it won't be the same for every species. Species at risk need to be monitored throughout the recovery process until they are finally assessed as reaching a recovered state. As with any patient, we need to follow up: measure, monitor and quantify their recovery until we are sure they are safe.'

Unlike the detailed IUCN listing of threatened species worldwide, there is no comprehensive database of recovered species. To identify them, one must trawl through the Red List to identify those whose populations are increasing and, maybe, moving from a more threatened category to a less threatened one. The animals whose stories have been told in previous chapters are just a small selection of many whose declining fortunes are being reversed; this chapter summarise some others.

The American Alligator, inhabiting swamps, streams, rivers and lakes in the southeast US had been hunted for its skin for centuries. Drainage and pollution of its habitat also decimated many; by the 1960s its survival was in doubt. Improved protection, wetland conservation and the licensing of commercial alligator farms using captive bred animals producing thousands of hides each year has removed the pressure on wild populations. By 2013, there were an estimated five million alligators back in the southeast US.

On much of the US coast, in the Caribbean, in Central America and along the west coast of South America, the Brown Pelican is today a common sight. In the late 19th and early 20th centuries, though, these and other pelican species were hunted for their feathers which were used to adorn women's clothing, particularly hats. And in the early decades of the 20th century fishermen killed them by the thousand too. The hat feather trade was stopped but in the 1960s and 1970s DDT and related pesticides were causing pelican eggshells to thin and break during incubation. It had the same impact on its cousin, the larger American White Pelican as it did for birds of prey such as Peregrines in the US and Europe. Brown Pelicans disappeared or became rare. These persistent pesticides were banned in the 1970s and pelican numbers soon started to increase. Combined with reintroductions in parts of their range, a more tolerant attitude from fishermen and legal protection, they recovered well. By 2010, the world population was estimated to be about 650,000.

The US's national bird, the Bald Eagle was another victim of the scourge of DDT as well as pollution of rivers and lakes where it fished and shooting. Only 400 pairs were left across this vast continent by the 1960s out of maybe a half million originally. By 2014 there are around 70,000 Bald Eagles on the North American continent, nearly half of them in Alaska.

Steller's Sea Lion, cousin to some of the most popular zoo and aquarium mammals in the world, and one of the most intelligent is another. Found along the west coast of the northern US, around Alaska and along the eastern Russian and Chinese coasts south to Japan, they were hunted for their meat and skins or killed because they took fish. Culling was discontinued in the early 1970s and most populations were protected legally. Nevertheless, they underwent a dramatic population decline of about 70% between the late 1970s and 1990 due to a variety of causes. Today, though, the subspecies inhabiting seas along the North American coast south to California has increased at an average rate of more than 3% per year; their population was estimated at about 65,000 in 2011. The other subspecies – inhabiting seas around Alaska and eastern Russia – has also started a slow increase across most of its range; by 2011, there were an estimated 78,000 of them. There are still less of them than previously but Steller's Sea Lion is recovering well. IUCN classified it as Endangered as recently as 1996; by 2012 it had been upgraded two categories to Near Threatened.

Some animals have been reduced to much more precarious numbers before their fortunes have been reversed. Keeping parrots in captivity, especially the most colourful ones, has long stimulated a massive and lucrative international trade in these intelligent birds and, while much of it today is prohibited, the illegal market is still rife. Lear's Macaw, vibrant metallic blue in colour with a patch of yellow on its face, is a large, impressive parrot. Lear's remained elusive in the wild until 1978 when a population was located in northeast Brazil. In 1983, this only known population was estimated at just 60 birds and, with collecting still a huge cash temptation, its prospects looked bleak. Intensive conservation efforts since then have seen its numbers gradually rise and by 2011 the population was over 1,000. These conservation initiatives included improved habitat protection; schemes to plant large numbers of Licuri Palms, the nuts of which are the macaw's preferred food; a compensation scheme for farmers whose crops are sometimes pillaged by Lear's; and plans to evaluate new sites for the release of captive-bred birds. The threat of capture for the bird trade appears to have receded and the bird is fully protected under Brazilian law. Infiltration of trading networks and improved surveillance at breeding sites has resulted in the arrest of poachers, smugglers and collectors.

The rescue of another kind of parrot – the vivid, emerald green Echo Parakeet – is one of the more remarkable success stories. By the early 1980s, it had dwindled from probably several thousand to ten birds on Mauritius (its only location). It had not bred successfully since the early 1970s because of forest destruction, nest predation, disturbance by humans, feral pigs and deer, and competition with more plentiful birds including the introduced Rose-ringed Parakeet. It seemed doomed to extinction. Research and conservation efforts led by Carl Jones (alongside work on the Mauritius Kestrel – Chapter 16), including captive breeding, resulted in a stabilised situation by the late 1980s, with more young birds hatching. By the mid 1990s, at least 50 were present; double that by 2000. To improve their breeding success nestboxes were provided, fencing was erected to stop predator access at nest sites, habitat was improved, introduced nest competitors such as rats and Common Mynahs reduced, and eggs and young from failing nests were incubated and raised by foster parents. By 2012 there were nearly 600 parakeets and more habitat is available for further expansion. IUCN upgraded the species from Critically Endangered to Endangered as a result. Other seriously declining Mauritian species have been recovered too: the Mauritius Fody, a small olive-coloured forest bird with a red head; the Pink Pigeon; the Round Island Skink, a lizard extinct on Mauritius but present on one of its tiny offshore islands, to name a few.

Many islands around the world, long isolated from the mainland, evolved their own particular array of species; a good number of them became endemics. Almost without exception, whenever humans arrived in such places, they set about felling forests, growing crops and introducing non-native animals and plants. Some of these spread rapidly and introduced mammals such as rats, cats, rabbits, goats and many others have wreaked ecological havoc on many islands worldwide. It is the impact of all this change that conservation biologists are trying to address in recovering those native species that survived such onslaughts.

The Seychelles Magpie Robin, black with a white wing patch, inhabits woodlands, plantations and gardens where it forages in leaf litter for invertebrates. Historically, they are thought to have lived on eight of the Seychelles' islands. Predictably, habitat destruction and introduced predators (domestic cats and rats) greatly reduced its numbers and by 1970 they were on the verge of extinction with only 16 remaining, all on Frégate Island. In 1990 BirdLife International began conservation efforts; birds were transferred to several other islands over the following 18 years and most are now breeding. Feral cat eradication, habitat creation, supplementary feeding, nest protection, restrictions on pesticide use, rat removal and other measures have all helped. By 2012, the total population was about 250 birds; IUCN revised the Seychelles Magpie Robin status from Critically Endangered to Endangered.

The Rodrigues Fruit Bat or Flying Fox, a large bat that's endemic to the island of Rodrigues in the Indian Ocean, remains classified as Critically Endangered even though its numbers have been restored from around 70 in the 1970s to maybe 15,000 today. A successful captive breeding programme was pioneered by the Durrell Wildlife Conservation Trust in the 1970s and breeding populations of this bat are held at numerous zoos. On Rodrigues, efforts have concentrated on restoring their natural habitat and raising awareness of them among local people. It formerly inhabited other islands in the vicinity but no longer; cyclones have a dev-astating impact on them – and are now the major threat – while deforestation has contributed, especially where mature fruit trees and important roost trees were felled.

Many islands also have endemic reptiles. One of those is the Antiguan Racer, a harmless, lizard-eating snake found only on tiny Great Bird Island off the coast of Antigua in the Caribbean. It was once common on the main island of Antigua but, from the 15th century on, forests were felled to grow sugar cane, rats colonised and preyed on anything they could (including racer eggs) while mongooses introduced to kill the rats took birds, frogs and racers instead. Great Bird Island was mongoose-free but not rat-free; in 1995 there were just 50 racers there. Conservation work led by Dr Jenny Daltry, then with the Durrell Wildlife Conservation Trust and now with FFI, included poisoning rats. The racers started to increase. They have also been reintroduced to other small islands in the group and the total population by 2014 is over 1,000. It is still classified as Critically Endangered because it is susceptible to predators if they reinvade (rats did so on Great Bird Island in 2001 but were killed off), to hurricanes causing storm flooding and because the population has low genetic diversity.

On the Galapagos island of Espanola, forty years of re-introducing a subspecies of the famed Galapagos Tortoises has paid dividends. Their numbers have increased from just 15 in the 1960s to more than 1,000 by 2014. There is now a stable breeding population. Much of the success is down to eradicating goats that devoured most of the vegetation the turtles relied upon.

Animals that have a very much wider distribution than a single island can also suffer enormous declines and then recover, sometimes in one part of their range, then in another.

The Red Kite, a stunning bird of prey, is one. Inhabiting most of Europe east into Turkey, they were common scavengers in the Middle Ages across the UK, in cities and in the countryside. But city tolerance changed as refuse and waste food stopped being dumped. They became aves non grata! Always detested in the countryside because they took farmyard poultry and young rabbits, they were frequently killed. The last Red Kite over London was seen in 1859. By 1870 they were extinct in England; in Scotland they hung on until 1900. Only in the wildest, least populated parts of central Wales did a few pairs survive; here their numbers were down to six breeding pairs in the 1960s. Their breeding success was poor until an adult female from Germany wandered west and seemingly introduced some new genes into their depleted population. With active nest protection to stop the depredations of egg collectors, with the help of many farmers with kites on their land and a reinvigorated tiny population, their breeding success started to improve and numbers slowly increased.

By 2004, Wales had 375 pairs of red kites and by 2011 there were over 1,000. From 1989 on, Swedish birds were released at a site in northern Scotland and a mix of Swedish and Welsh birds (to diversify their genetic mix) in southern England. By 2011, the English Red Kite population was over 800 pairs and spreading; reintroductions in other parts of the UK have followed. A sighting of the first Red Kite in London for 150 years was reported in 2006 and, by 2014, there were maybe 2,000 breeding pairs in the UK plus many birds as yet too young to breed. Experts think the UK could eventually support up to 10,000 pairs. However, despite the promising recovery in one part of its European range, the Red Kite is listed as Near Threatened globally because it is experiencing a moderately rapid population decline elsewhere. That's due mostly to poisoning from baits put out to kill crows, foxes and other deemed pests and to changes in land-use across most of southern Europe as pasture is converted to more intensive crop growing. A steady reduction in refuse tipping as well as competition with Black Kites might be other factors. Red Kites had also declined in much of northern Europe but most of those declines seem to have halted, maybe even reversed. According to BirdLife International, this mixed bag of changes in the fortunes of Red Kites nevertheless produces a European population of up to 25,000 breeding pairs.

❖ ❖ ❖

In planning a programme of actions to attempt to reverse a declining population of animals – or to reintroduce one back to part of its previous range if it has become extinct in the wild – a whole range of issues need to be taken into account from the start. One of these is, perhaps, the most obvious: the cause, or causes, of the decline must be absent or, at the very least, reduced sufficiently to provide a real prospect that the species is able to recover. One of the best examples is the Humpback Whale. Once it had been given protection from being hunted by whalers over 50 years ago, its numbers started to increase. They face other threats but their scale is unlikely to jeopardise the recovery of this giant of the world's oceans.

For many other recovering animals, the factors that caused their decline are not as readily obliterated or, even if they appear to have been removed, they might return. This happened to the reintroduced Arabian Oryx in the Omani section of the Arabian Desert; their numbers increased initially, only for hunters to start capturing them to sell to collectors. Others were shot and a successful reintroduction failed because the original threats to their survival returned. Several other recovering species need constant vigilance to deal with resurgent threats; in the case of Black Rhino killed for their horn this involves advanced surveillance and armed protection, while for breeding Zino's Petrel it involves ensuring that rats and feral cats can't access their mountain breeding burrows.

Often, there are several factors responsible for causing steep declines in a species. The Piping Plover, a sparrow-sized wading bird, was never hunted or much exploited and never encountered any direct conflict with the human race. While in the 19th and early 20th century, it was sometimes killed for its feathers to decorate ladies' hats, legislation stopped that trade and the plovers recovered well. The major, almost terminal, decline of the species was due to increased urban development close to the coastal sandy beaches and lakesides they inhabit, to shoreline stabilisation works, habitat loss and increased human disturbance, plus disturbance from dogs and cats. No one noticed that the little Piping Plover was being squeezed out of its habitats. Improved protection at their breeding sites, seasonal restrictions and public education to limit disturbance and the control of coastal and inland shore and lakeside development, have all helped to reverse a downward slide in their population. By 2006 the Piping Plover population numbered over 8,000 breeding birds, a gain of over 70% since 1991.

Not all recoveries have been as successful. The Californian Condor, an all-black vulture with a wingspan of nearly three metres, declined through the 20th century due mainly to persecution and accidental ingestion of fragments from lead bullets and shot left in carcasses. Many condors died from lead poisoning; a situation having parallels with the vultures of the Indian subcontinent dying from eating diclofenac-contaminated carcasses they ate (Chapter 10). In 1987 the Californian Condor became extinct in the wild when the last of the six wild individuals was captured to join a captive breeding recovery programme. The programme increased their number to well over 200 by 2003 and releases began. Breeding in the wild resumed and, by 2012, the total population stood at 173 individuals in captivity and 213 in the wild, primarily in California, although there had been some releases elsewhere. But none of its populations are yet considered self-sustaining.

Since 2008, California has banned lead shot in cartridges within the condor's range but not for all prey and not all hunters are complying. In Arizona and California lead substitute bullets are being made available too. Nevertheless, it isn't much benefitting the condors. Terra Kelly of the University of California, Davis and colleagues published research in 2014 showing that as condors mature they become less reliant on (lead-free) managed food provisions and more reliant on carcasses of animals killed by hunters. As a result, they found no significant difference between the pre- and post-2008 concentration of lead in condor blood. The condor's future – and the future of other carcass-scavenging animals – now depends on new proposals to phase out lead bullets and shot in California by July 2019. This expands the 2008 ban on lead hunting ammunition in California condor habitat and covers shooting of all wildlife including game mammals, game birds, non-game birds and non-game mammals such as coyotes. Might the regulations be diluted? Only time will tell.

What is happening with the California Condor illustrates the folly of reintroducing a species to its former location when the cause of its decline has not been eliminated. The factory-scale captive breeding and reintroduction scheme for Houbara (Chapter 7) in North Africa, the Middle East and Western Asia has been established seemingly with little regard for ensuring that the birds released have suitable habitat available and without reducing one of the major causes of its decline – falconry – in the first place. Only in relatively small, protected areas is there an attempt to improve their often overgrazed desert habitats. Nevertheless, because such huge numbers are being released, some are surviving, their numbers are increasing and IUCN seem content.

❖   ❖   ❖

Understanding the ecological needs of a species is perhaps an obvious prerequisite to stand a chance of successfully recovering their populations or being successful with a reintroduction. What habitats do they require? Is there a sufficient extent of that habitat? What are their feeding requirements? Can they be met? Do we understand their life cycle needs? Without any doubt, the most thorough such assessment was that done for the Large Blue butterfly in England; a classic piece of detailed ecological, almost forensic, investigation that proved essential before this insect could be returned to its former grassland sites. And it has proved highly successful.

The Siberian Tiger requires an enormous area of forest so it has been vital to ensure that forest management allows for vast expanses to remain while also accommodating commercial timber extraction in certain areas. But it has also been equally necessary to control the hunting of tiger prey – animals such as deer – to make sure the tigers have enough to hunt.

For an animal as specific in its food requirements as the Iberian Lynx – virtually only predating on rabbits – if that food supply is itself subject to wild fluctuations, it presents its own challenges. There is no point in constantly holding back reintroductions of lynx into other parts of Spain or Portugal because the cycles of disease that sweep through their rabbit populations are not easy to predict or quantify. But releasing lynx when rabbit numbers are obviously low is not sensible either.

Another animal whose survival is bound up with a very particular choice of prey is the Black-footed Ferret in the US and its favourite prey, little burrowing, rodent-like, prairie dogs. Not only do prairie dogs constitute up to 90% of the ferret's diet, the ferrets often take over prairie dog burrows to raise their young. The ferrets went into terminal decline because their rodent prey was being poisoned on a huge scale as a virtual war against them was fought by cattle ranchers who detested their soil burrowing lifestyle and because of disease. Traditional grassland prairies were also converted on a huge scale to crop growing monocultures, reducing both prairie dogs and the ferrets that preyed on them. The Black-footed Ferret was declared extinct in 1979.

Until, that is, Lucille Hogg's dog Shep brought a dead one back to her door in Meeteetse, Wyoming, in 1981. Suddenly, that declaration of extinction seemed a little premature. And after searching cattle ranches locally, a small residual population was discovered. But it was not to last; by 1987 they, too, had died out and the Black-footed Ferret was extinct in the wild. A number of captive breeding programmes spearheaded by the US Federal Fish and

Wildlife Service were set up and since 1991, ferrets have been reintroduced in eight western US states and Mexico, though its populations are considered to be self-sustaining in just three. Prairie dogs have been reduced substantially in numbers too. But in national parks and reserves they are protected and many have adapted to life away from the prairie in more urban environments. Black-footed Ferrets are seemingly finding enough of them to hunt. By 2013, there were about 1,200; still rare, and they can inhabit only a tiny fraction of the land area they once hunted over, but these polecat-lookalikes are making a comeback.

❖ ❖ ❖

Long gone are the days when protected areas such as national parks or reserves were designated because of their wildlife value and any people who happened to live within their boundaries simply moved out compulsorily. Working with local communities to integrate their lives within protected areas so that the people and their economies are supported – while the wildlife to be protected gets local support – is now de rigueur. Reintroducing an animal back to a location where it formerly occurred, and where local communities might have played a key role in its extinction, or implementing measures to substantially boost an existing population, must take full account of the wishes and needs of local communities. Without their support, such a scheme is unlikely to succeed. The forested mountains in central Africa where Mountain Gorillas have their stronghold, mostly protected as national parks, is a good example of how this can be achieved, often under very difficult circumstances of intermittent armed unrest and war. Many local communities have been encouraged to help conserve gorillas because the protection of the animals provides opportunities for employment as rangers, tour guides, in service roles and much else, improving the economic viability of their communities and providing the wherewithal to provide improved education and health facilities.

For some species, though, getting the support of local communities – or a particularly strident part of a local community – seems virtually impossible to achieve. The sleepy little village of Arbas east of Lourdes in the French Pyrenees doesn't look the sort of place to have violent riots. But in 2006 it did – and all because of Brown Bears. The French government's plan to bolster the tiny population of 25 bears in these forested mountains included releasing three bears translocated from Slovenia where there's a strong population. 'Gendarmerie intelligence warned us that there might be a few protestors, mostly farmers worried about their sheep being attacked. But 250 turned up, smashing anything they could find outside the mairie [town hall], trying to break in, spraying paint and throwing bottles of blood. Eighty gendarmes tried to keep order,' recalls François Arcangeli, the softly spoken and charming former Mayor of Arbas and President of Pays de l'Ours-Adet, an organisation promoting bear conservation.

Of the five introduced in 2006 (three near Arbas and two elsewhere), one gave birth to two cubs. But two of them, both females, subsequently died. One fell from a cliff in a rare freak accident. The other was killed by a car on a road outside Lourdes, much to the delight of many local farmers and the sorrow of conservationists. Here much of the problem lies with shepherds; over the past two centuries, many sheep and goat herders have gradually abandoned the traditional practice of using dogs to guard their flocks, which, at the same time, have grown larger in number. As bears reclaim parts of their historic range, they may attack and eat livestock. But a compensation scheme is available; so, too, is cash to employ shepherds (over 80 have been employed); for trained Pyrenean mountain dogs to stay with the sheep; and electric fencing to contain flocks at night. But farmers claim their livelihood is under threat even when statistics show that far more sheep die because of bad weather, falls on steep slopes and dog attacks. According to the latest data on compensation, bears take around 200 sheep a year in the Pyrenees out of 60,000 sheep in total. Slowly, opposition is declining according to Arcangeli, now Conseiller Régional in the Midi-Pyrénées regional government where he represents the Green Party. 'They are less and less opposed. The measures to protect sheep flocks are being put in place gradually and bear kills are stable or even decreasing. The opposition is a minority,' he says.

The French Authorities have not yet tried to reintroduce any more bears and the isolated population in the Pyrenees is struggling to survive. Further reintroductions are probably their only hope of survival but they will probably not go ahead until the concerns, however irrational, of local farmers are largely overcome. Brown Bears are not threatened worldwide; they remain abundant with over 200,000 individuals and are categorised by IUCN as of Least Concern. However, once native to much of Asia, North Africa, the Middle East, Europe and North America, its global range has shrunk and the Brown Bear is threatened with numerous local extinctions, of which the population in the French Pyrenees is just one.

❖　❖　❖

It is also necessary to consider in what way the reintroduction of a species is going to impact habitats and other species. Perhaps the best example is the reintroduction in the mid 1990s of the Grey Wolf in the Yellowstone National Park. Once abundant across North America, it had been hunted to extinction everywhere except in Alaska and Canada, with some populations surviving in parts of the northern US States bordering Canada. By the 1920s they had been eradicated in Yellowstone; with their main predator gone, Elk increased enormously and because of their heavy browsing the vegetation started to change. Aspens, willows and cottonwoods were disappearing rapidly, so Elk killing was introduced and continued for decades. The loss of wolves allowed Coyotes to flourish, too, and that in turn caused the numbers of Pronghorn (antelope-like mammals) they preyed on to burgeon.

By 2012, 17 years after the first releases, Yellowstone has ten packs totalling about 90 Grey Wolves. They again control Elk and Coyotes; this has allowed woodland vegetation and trees to recover around stream sides and that provides improved habitat for birds, beavers and other species including fish. With Coyote numbers down, there are more foxes which possibly means that plant-eating rodent numbers are reduced, thereby allowing a more verdant plant cover overall. Wolf kills also provide food for other scavenging birds and mammals. In the US State of Wisconsin, too, they appear to have brought environmental benefits. 'Plant communities where there are wolves have significantly higher species richness than plant communities outside wolf pack territories,' says Ramana Callan, Assistant Professor at the Ranger School at Wanakena, New York, who has studied their impact. 'It's either due to local reductions in White-tailed Deer grazing density or to changes in the foraging behaviour of the deer. They can no longer stay in one area for extended periods of time and must be more vigilant and mobile. The wolves are likely to reduce beaver and Coyote populations but many species – migrant birds for example – might benefit from the increased diversity and structure of shrubs with deer numbers reduced,' she adds.

Very small animals can have pretty dramatic impacts too. One is Australia's Burrowing Betong, or Boodie, a small rat-like marsupial. Before white settlers arrived, it was common across all of Australia except Queensland. The colonists killed them, considering them a destructive pest. As ranches spread over the grasslands, livestock grazing reduced vegetation cover, shrinking their habitat. Introduced foxes and cats killed them while rabbits possibly competed with them for food. Gradually, their populations on the mainland disappeared and the Boodie survived as only three remnant populations on small offshore islands. Listed by IUCN in 1994 as Endangered, by 2008, thanks to successful conservation efforts both by government agencies and the private sector, they were upgraded to Near Threatened. Their populations and range are still increasing and they've been reintroduced to another five localities on islands and the mainland. In total there are about 7,000 Boodies, though some populations fluctuate enormously in response to rainfall and drought. But reintroductions to yet more locations are difficult; foxes and feral cats have to be eradicated first. The Boodie will never be commonplace again. Research in recent years has shown that these little marsupials served a very important function in the Australian grassland ecosystem. As they foraged, they mixed organic matter into the soil, spreading fungi and seeds, and aerating it. This mixing increased water absorption into the soil, provided opportunities for seeds to germinate and plants to grow, and reduced combustible material under trees, decreasing the likelihood of fire, thereby helping to maintain the balance of trees, shrubs and grasses. Their loss contributed to the widespread soil deterioration across parts of the continent exacerbated by introducing cattle to the land. So returning them to at least some restricted areas of the Australian mainland will benefit biodiversity in general, not just the Boodie.

It's a very different picture for the European Beaver. Most of its populations had been exterminated by the 16th century; by the 20th century, only eight European populations remained. So most of Europe's rivers have not had a beaver for over 400 years. Originally, there might have been 60 million of them. They were hunted to near extinction for their pelts which were used to make gloves, hats and other clothing; for meat and for castoreum, a secretion of their scent gland believed (wrongly) to have medicinal value. Beavers are vegetarian, so they don't kill fish. But they do block small streams and create river pools; and they nibble the bark off alders, aspens and willows. Nevertheless, by 2014 with reintroductions and natural range expansion over many years, beavers have returned to 23 of the 29 European countries where they formerly occurred. Have they caused problems? Seemingly not. In the Netherlands, the first reintroductions were made in 1988 to the Biesbosch National Park, a maze of waterways, river channels and creeks in the floodplain of the Rivers Rhine and Meuse in the south of the country. By 2013, there were at least 250 beavers resident in the national park breeding in about 90 lodges. They have done little damage to pasture and pose no threat to livestock though they can cause small-scale farm crop damage. The relatively few young trees they kill by eating the bark in winter often regrow from the stump and economically valuable trees are rarely de-barked anyway.

Anglers are often divided on the benefits and disbenefits of having beavers re-established on rivers. But a study published in 2012 by biologists from the University of Southampton, UK, based on a large range of expert and fishery manager experience, together with an extensive research review concluded that, overall, beavers should have a positive impact on wild salmon populations. The study's findings indicate that beaver damage to fisheries, primarily due to dams impeding fish movements and reducing the availability of suitable spawning habitat, can be off-set by the benefits of increased habitat diversity and the resulting abundance and productivity of fish, including salmon. In Norway, where there is a valuable salmon sport fishing industry and where beavers are widespread, fisheries authorities consider that there is no significant impact. Based on their Biesbosch experience, the Dutch plan to reintroduce them to other rivers and predict that they will eventually have a population of maybe 8,000 countrywide.

Beavers were exterminated in England by the 12th century and by the 16th century in Scotland. Contained populations have now been licenced in several places in the UK and a reintroduction trial in Argyll, Scotland, is due for completion in 2015, after which the Scottish government will take a decision on whether to allow reintroductions more widely. At the same time, though, illegally released or escaped beavers have established themselves on Scotland's River Tay where there is now a thriving population of over 150. Beavers can travel large distances and it is quite probable that they will spread naturally to other Scottish rivers via lochs that inter-connect them, licenced or not. In 2006, there were estimated to be at least 639,000 beavers across Europe. Soon, their numbers might approach one million.

❖ ❖ ❖

The IUCN, in their *Guidelines for Reintroductions and Other Conservation Translocations* (2013) suggest that a reintroduced population of a species should be as genetically diverse as possible. The perceived wisdom is that a population with more genetic diversity between its individuals is more adaptable to a changing environment and more likely to have survivors if some new disease strikes. Also, reproduction between closely related individuals can lead to reduced vigour, reproductive output and lower survival. To be practical, though, a reintroduction has to make use of what's available, often very few individuals and all of them related to each other. So their genetic diversity is very limited to begin with.

This is a consideration for the European Bison (Chapter 5). All of today's wild-living bison originate from just seven founders of the Białowieża population in Poland. But conservationists concerned with the future of Europe's largest living land animal have wisely ensured that the bison bred from these original animals are spread widely across several countries in herds that are often separated by hundreds of kilometres. That at least minimises the chances of disease spread that could otherwise destroy much of their regained population.

With the Iberian Lynx (Chapter 13), research has found that its population has historically been genetically restricted and its enormous decline over the last century or so has been due largely to human actions such as hunting and trapping. Whether a more genetically diverse population of lynx would have adapted better to the changing land uses and habitats around them – and thereby survived in greater numbers – no one will ever know.

For the reintroduced Arabian Oryx (Chapter 2) the situation was a little better. The animals had been bred in captivity from the last few captured in the Saudi desert augmented with others donated by the Saudi and Kuwaiti royal families who had been breeding them for some years in their outdoor collections. They had been captured originally in very different parts of the vast Saudi desert, a land area at least the size of France and Spain combined, and were likely more distantly related.

Reintroduction of the Large Blue butterfly necessitated a larger genetic 'risk'. There were none left in the UK from which a population could have been bred. The Swedish population that was chosen for the reintroduction was clearly genetically different from the extinct UK population; the populations had been isolated from each other and had habituated to different climate regimes at the very least. But the decision was taken to use Swedish Large Blue eggs because the UK and Swedish populations are ecologically and behaviourally similar. And it was important that the butterflies were from a northerly donor population which relied on thyme for their caterpillars just as the UK population always had, and not a population from southern Europe that used marjoram for rearing them.

There is a debate amongst conservation scientists about the use of such 'genetic substitutes'. Most would argue against replacing an extinct species with a similar but different species; many would baulk at replacement with a different subspecies of the same species. But is this all too precious given the circumstances we have in which some species are being lost forever and all too frequently? Professor Carl Jones has a more controversial view. He is an advocate of using analogue species as replacements for extinct ones. He often cites the Peregrine conservation programme, whereby the extirpated eastern US subspecies was replaced by a hybrid of related subspecies but became almost identical to the original birds as a result of selection pressures imparted by the habitat. Jones has also concluded that every Indian Ocean island once had its own endemic flightless rail – a ground bird related to moorhens – and believes that the Guam Rail is a viable substitute that could be used for reintroduction to those islands where their own rail species has been driven to extinction. Other biologists have gone further. Anthony Cheke, who with Julian Hume wrote *Lost Land of the Dodo. An Ecological History of the Mascarene Islands* (A&C Black, 2008), argues that the much smaller Nicobar Pigeon from islands in Southeast Asia should be introduced to Mauritius to replace the long extinct Dodo. It is the Dodo's nearest living relative.

And even extinction is not necessarily what it used to be! Some experts are mulling over the possibility of 'recreating' extinct species; taking some DNA from a museum-held specimen of a species extinct in the wild and reviving it. So we might end up with, for instance, a genetically engineered Dodo in Mauritius. Whether such resurrected species would be precisely the same as the originals is in doubt. Even more dubious is whether anyone should spend time on such flights of fancy, and should instead expend some energy trying to prevent even more existing species sliding that way.

❖ ❖ ❖

So what might the success stories of the future be? The animals starting to recover now from a very low ebb but which, invariably thanks to enormous efforts on the part of governments, NGOs and committed individuals, are likely to be the recovered species of the next few decades? The biggest gains are likely to be in Europe and North America, maybe China too.

Different experts have different suggestions. Most, though, emphasise several reptiles whose fortunes are increasing; species such as the Tuatara, a large, primitive lizard once abundant in New Zealand but now confined to a few small islands. Or, amongst amphibians – many of which have suffered catastrophic declines worldwide – the tiny Mallorcan Midwife Toad, thought to be extinct until 1980, but for which a conservation programme is proving successful. Amongst birds, the ultra rare Madagascan Pochard, once believed extinct, could become a success; its numbers down to a handful at just one lake where captive breeding and other measures are bolstering the population. The Short-tailed Albatross, still confined to very few islands in the Pacific and with a breeding population a fraction of its original size, could also see its fortunes improved. Such charismatic seabirds are at last receiving more protection – and more attention – internationally while fishery kills are being reduced, albeit slowly. Mammals might include the 30 cm tall Pygmy Hog of which maybe 200 at best survive in Assam. If reintroduction programmes, public education and support, plus better habitat protection all work, they might have a future. Of the primates, the Cao Vit Gibbon, believed until 2002 to be extinct, but with well over 100 individuals at one site on the China/Vietnam border, is receiving considerable attention; with habitat restoration, support from local people and help from both governments, their future looks at least a little brighter.

There will be others, too, that will be brought back from the brink. Keep an eye out for news of the striking white plumaged and red-faced Asian Crested Ibis in China. Maybe also the few remaining Persian Fallow Deer in Iran and its reintroduced population in Israel. Watch for the spread of the Californian Condor and the panther in Florida. And expect to see beavers spread along many more of Europe's rivers and Grey Wolves re-conquer some of the lands they haven't roamed for far too many centuries.

APPENDIX

THE IUCN RED LIST CLASSIFICATION

The International Union for the Conservation of Nature (IUCN) is the world's main authority on the conservation status of species and the IUCN Red List of Threatened Species is the world's most comprehensive inventory of the global conservation status of plants and animals. The Red List is based on precise criteria to evaluate the extinction risk of thousands of species and subspecies. These criteria are relevant to all species and all regions of the world. Its aims, according to IUCN, are to provide scientifically based information on the status of species and subspecies at a global level, to draw attention to the magnitude and importance of threatened wildlife, to influence national and international policy and decision-making, and to provide information to guide actions to conserve biological diversity.

The assessments to categorise each species are made by accredited assessors including BirdLife International, the Institute of Zoology (the research division of the Zoological Society of London), the World Conservation Monitoring Centre, and many Specialist Groups within the IUCN Species Survival Commission. The IUCN aims to have the category of every species re-evaluated every five years if possible, or at least every ten years. This is done in a peer reviewed manner through IUCN Species Survival Commission Specialist Groups whose Red List Authorities are responsible for a species, group of species or specific geographic area, or in the case of BirdLife International, an entire class: birds.

The lists are intended to be an easily and widely understood system for classifying species at high risk of global extinction. They aim to provide an explicit, objective framework for the classification of the broadest range of species according to their extinction risk. Extensive consultation and testing in the development of the system strongly suggests that it is robust across most species. However, it should be noted that although the system places species into the threatened categories with a high degree of consistency, the criteria do not take into account the life histories of every species. Hence, in certain individual cases, the risk of extinction may be under- or over-estimated.

Threatened species, those facing a higher risk of global extinction are categorised as: Critically Endangered, Endangered and Vulnerable. But the Red List also includes information on plants and animals that are categorised as Extinct or Extinct in the Wild; and on plants and animals that are either close to meeting the threatened thresholds or that would be threatened were it not for an ongoing conservation programme (Near Threatened).

This is what IUCN itself says of its own system (IUCN, 2014):

> The IUCN Red list is an invaluable conservation resource, a health check for our planet
> – a Barometer of Life.
>
> The IUCN Red List is the world's most comprehensive information source on the global conservation status of animal, fungi and plant species and their links to livelihoods. Far

more than a list of species and their status, the IUCN Red List is a powerful tool to inform and catalyse action for biodiversity conservation and policy change, critical to protecting the natural resources we need to survive. It provides information on population size and trends, geographic range and habitat needs of species.

Many species groups including mammals, amphibians, birds, reef building corals and conifers have been comprehensively assessed. However, there is much more to be done and increased investment is needed urgently to build The IUCN Red List into a more complete 'Barometer of Life'. To do this we need to increase the number of species assessed from the current count of 71,576 to at least 160,000 by 2020, improving the taxonomic coverage and thus providing a stronger base to enable better conservation and policy decisions.

The IUCN categories (simplified from their published descriptions) are:

EXTINCT

A species is Extinct when there is no reasonable doubt that the last individual has died. A species is presumed Extinct when exhaustive surveys in known and/or expected habitat, at appropriate times and throughout its historic range have failed to find it.

EXTINCT IN THE WILD

A species is extinct in the wild when it is known only to survive in captivity or as a naturalised population (or populations) well outside its past range. It is presumed extinct in the wild when exhaustive surveys in known and/or expected habitat, at appropriate times throughout its historic range have failed to record an individual.

CRITICALLY ENDANGERED

A species is critically endangered when it is considered to be facing an extremely high risk of extinction in the wild.

ENDANGERED

A species is endangered when it is considered to be facing a very high risk of extinction in the wild.

VULNERABLE

A species is vulnerable when it is considered to be facing a high risk of extinction in the wild.

NEAR THREATENED

A species is near threatened when it has been evaluated against the criteria but does not qualify for critically endangered, endangered or vulnerable now, but is close to qualifying for, or is likely to qualify for, a threatened category in the near future.

LEAST CONCERN

A species is of least concern when it has been evaluated against the criteria and does not qualify for critically endangered, endangered, vulnerable or near threatened. Widespread and abundant species are included in this category.

The definitions of the criteria used by IUCN to determine which category a species fits into are lengthy and complex. They are not reproduced here in full but can be read at: *www.**iucn**.org/about/.../* ***species**/...**iucn**.../**iucn**_red_list_categories_**criteria**/*

The criteria take into account detailed information on the size of a species' population; its geographic range and distribution; the degree of fragmentation of populations; rates of decline; its population structure; an assessment of extinction risk; changes in its habitat; known exploitation and other factors affecting it, and more.